LAGOON ENGINE

YUKIRU SUGISAKI

VOLUME 2

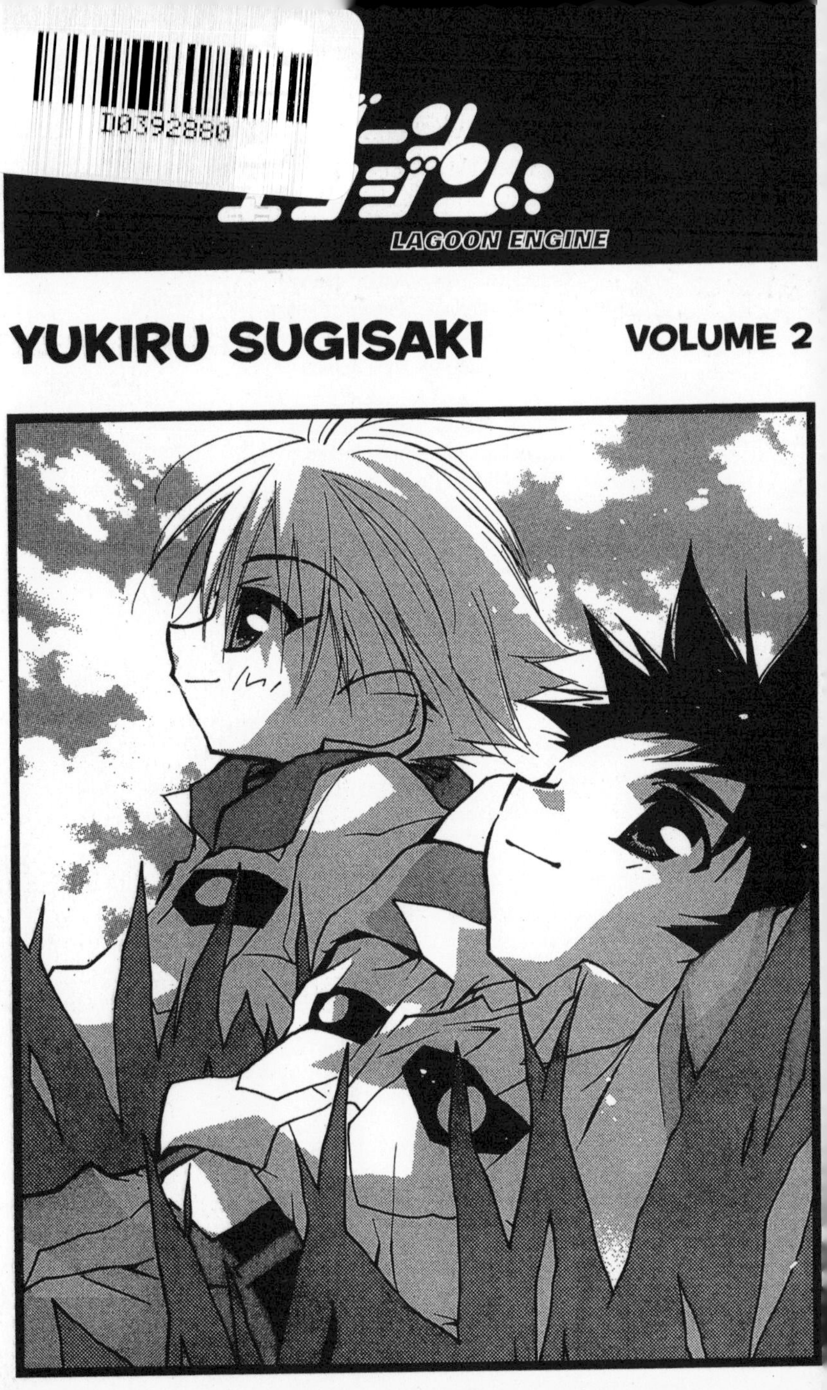

Lagoon Engine Vol. 2
Created by Yukiru Sugisaki

Translation - Alethea Nibley & Athena Nibley
Associate Editor - Peter Ahlstrom
Retouch and Lettering - Abelardo Bigting
Production Design - Eric Pineda
Cover Design - Anna Kernbaum

Editor - Paul Morrissey
Digital Imaging Manager - Chris Buford
Pre-Press Manager - Antonio DePietro
Production Managers - Jennifer Miller and Mutsumi Miyazaki
Art Director - Matt Alford
Managing Editor - Jill Freshney
VP of Production - Ron Klamert
Editor-in-Chief - Mike Kiley
President and C.O.O. - John Parker
Publisher and C.E.O. - Stuart Levy

A  TOKYOPOP® Manga

TOKYOPOP Inc.
5900 Wilshire Blvd. Suite 2000
Los Angeles, CA 90036

E-mail: info@TOKYOPOP.com
Come visit us online at www.TOKYOPOP.com

ISBN: 1-59532-603-0

First TOKYOPOP printing: May 2005

10 9 8 7 6 5 4 3 2 1

Printed in the USA

LAGOON ENGINE

VOLUME 2

BY
YUKIRU SUGISAKI

HAMBURG // LONDON // LOS ANGELES // TOKYO

Summary & Character Introduction

Yen and Jin are *Gakushi*, working to exorcize spirits known as *Maga*. Their family, the Ragun family, is the main Gakushi family. Though they're still in elementary school, their father trains them every day to help with the family business by giving them exorcism assignments on the side!

等軍焔 YEN RAGUN

A sixth grader, the eldest son in the Ragun family. He gets excellent grades, takes things seriously, and has a strong sense of responsibility. When fighting Maga, he is in charge of spreading barriers and analyzing the enemy.

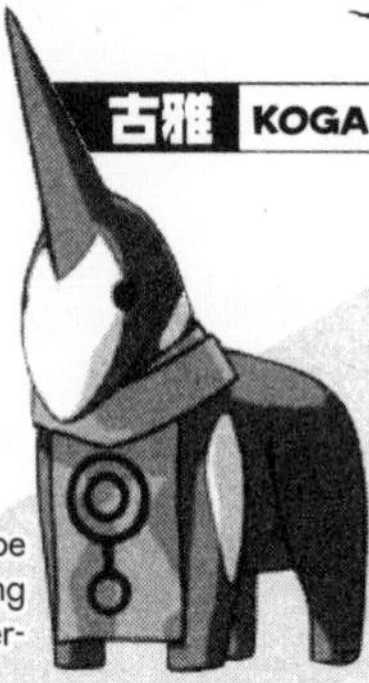

古雅 KOGA

Yen's Maga. A perception-type Maga who excels at gathering data, analyzing, and remembering.

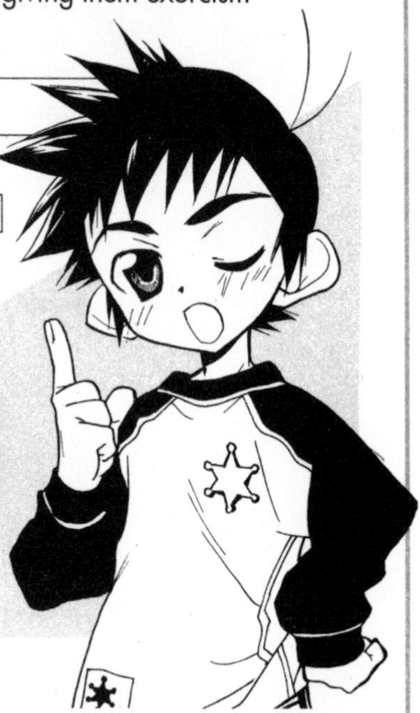

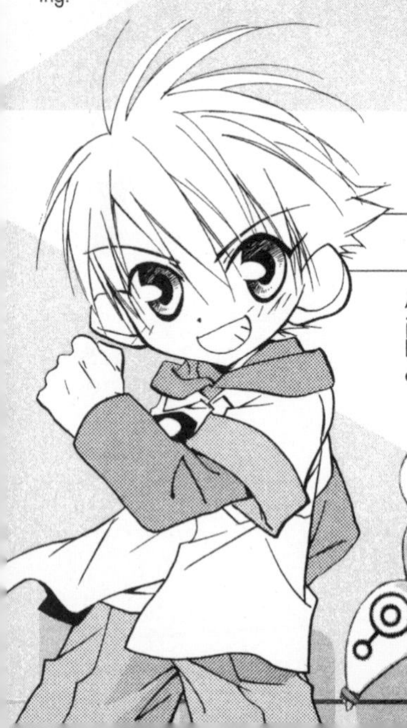

JIN RAGUN 等軍陣

A fifth grader, the second son in the Ragun family. He's just a little conceited, with a short fuse, but he relies heavily on others. When fighting Maga, he's in charge of attacking.

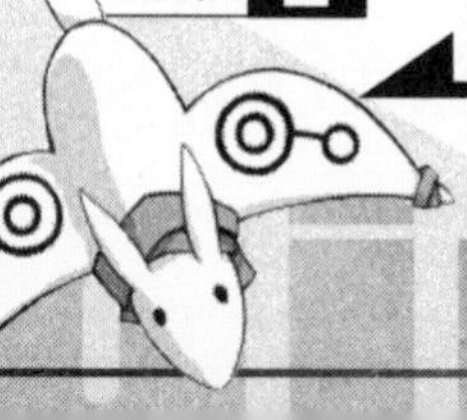

SORA 宙

Jin's Maga. An attack-type Maga with strong offensive power.

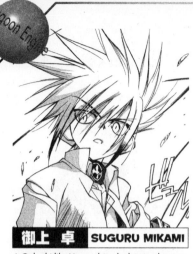

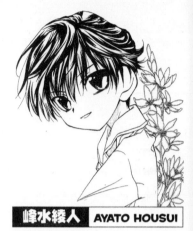

峰水綾人 AYATO HOUSUI

A sixth grader and Yen and Jin's cousin, he is staying at the Ragun household. He's a kind honor student who understands Yen and Jin.

御上 卓 SUGURU MIKAMI

A Gakushi like Yen and Jin, he has just become the head of the Mikami branch of the Ragun family. When he's called *branch,* he snaps.

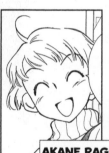

等軍秀明 HIDEAKI RAGUN

The current head of the Ragun family, Yen and Jin's father. He warmly watches over his as-yet-inexperienced sons.

Yen and Jin's mother, a popular novelist. She has a flighty personality, but she has plenty of love for her children.

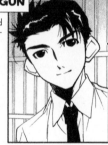

AKANE RAGUN 等軍紅音

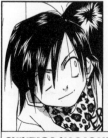

もりばやし恵礼 EREI MORIBAYASHI

Yen and Jin's childhood friend, she's in the same grade as Jin. She's energetic and competitive, and quick to fall in love? She and Jin quarrel often.

Akane's editor. A single 28-year-old who likes to cross-dress, he's currently looking for a significant other (?).

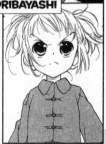

SHINTARO NAGASAKU 永作慎太郎

CONTENTS

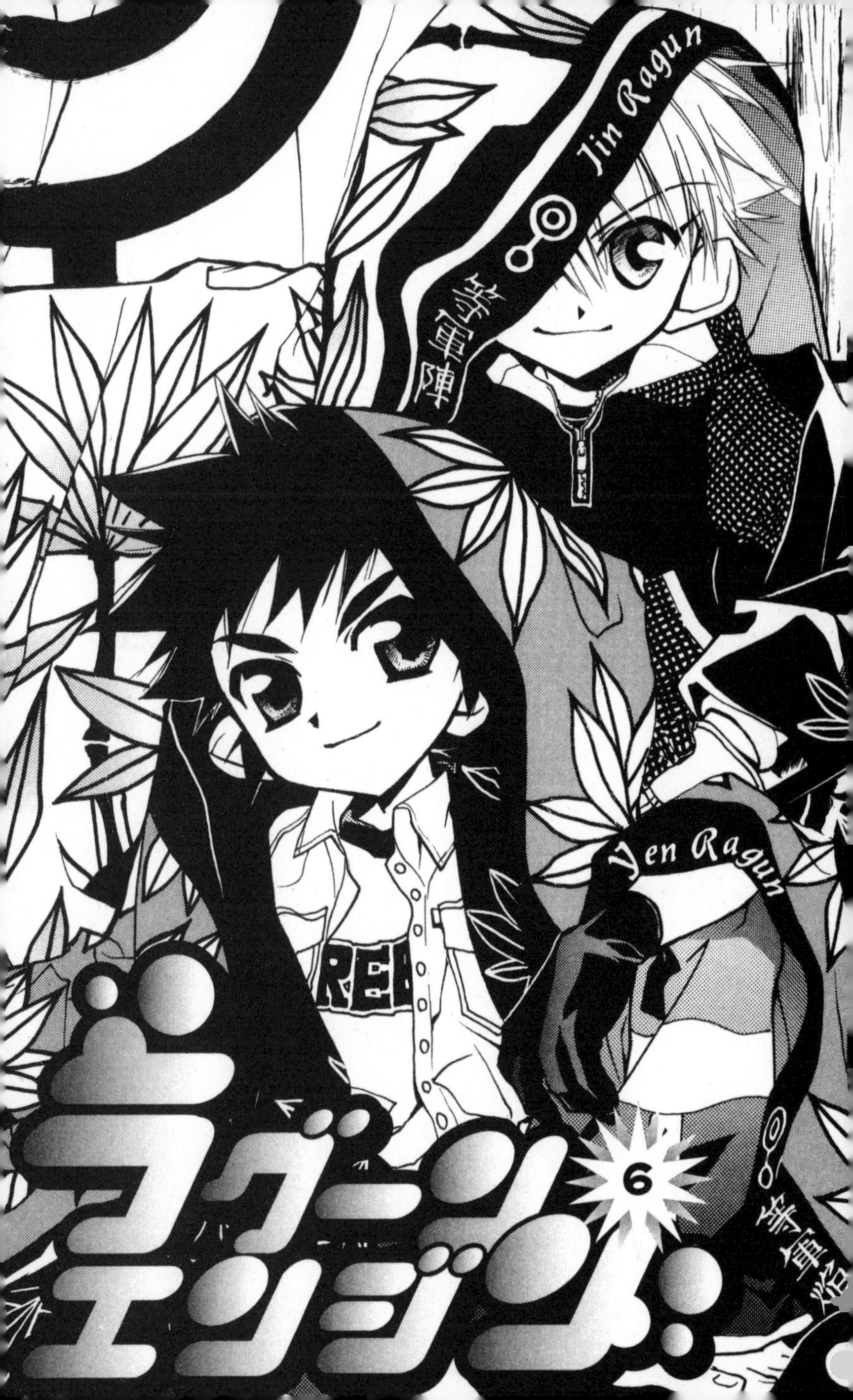
Jin Ragun
Yen Ragun
ラグーンエンジン
6

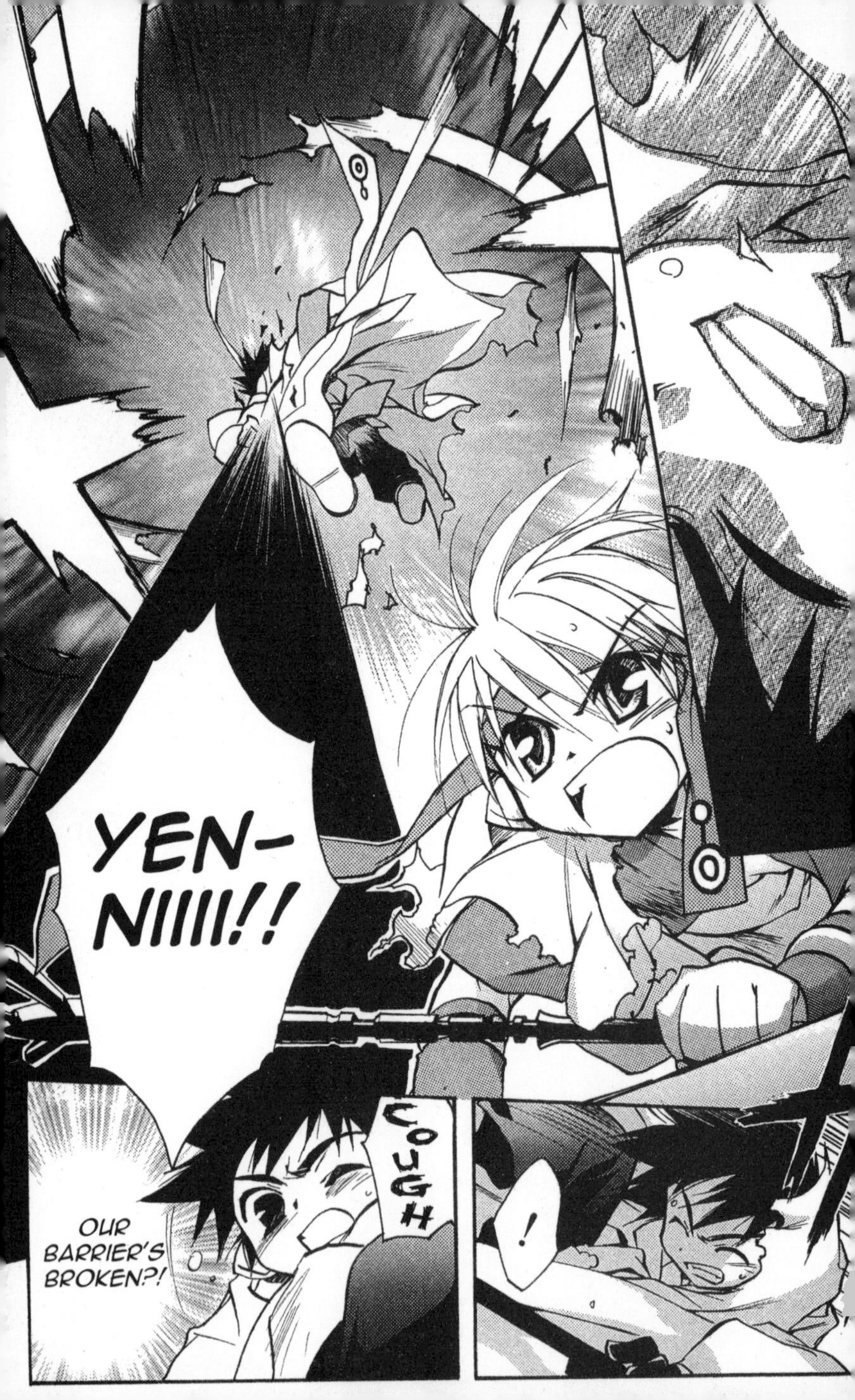
YEN-NIIII!!
!
COUGH
OUR BARRIER'S BROKEN?!

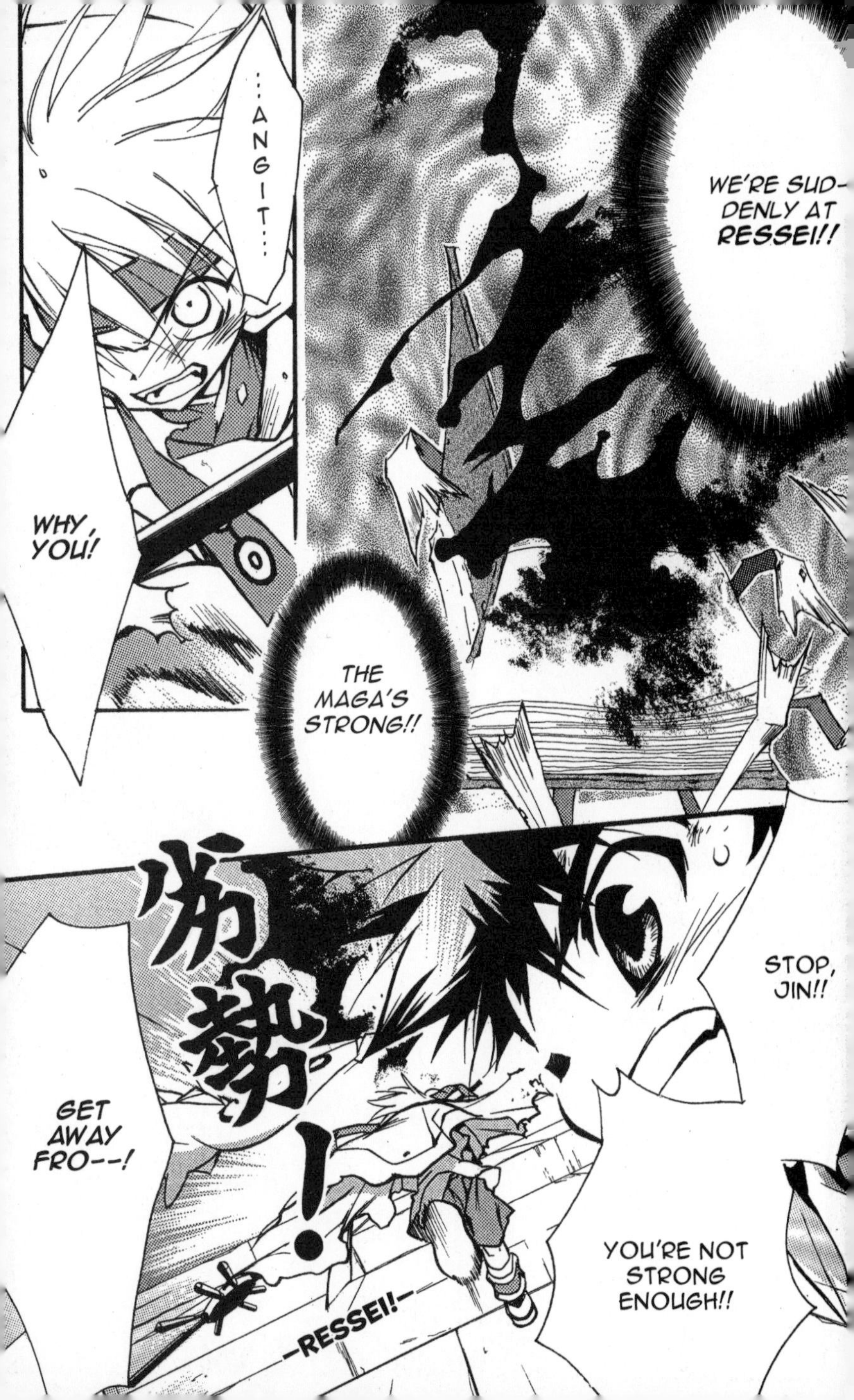
WE'RE SUD-DENLY AT RESSEI!!
THE MAGA'S STRONG!!
...ANGIT...
WHY, YOU!
STOP, JIN!!
YOU'RE NOT STRONG ENOUGH!!
GET AWAY FRO--!
烈勢!
-RESSEI!-

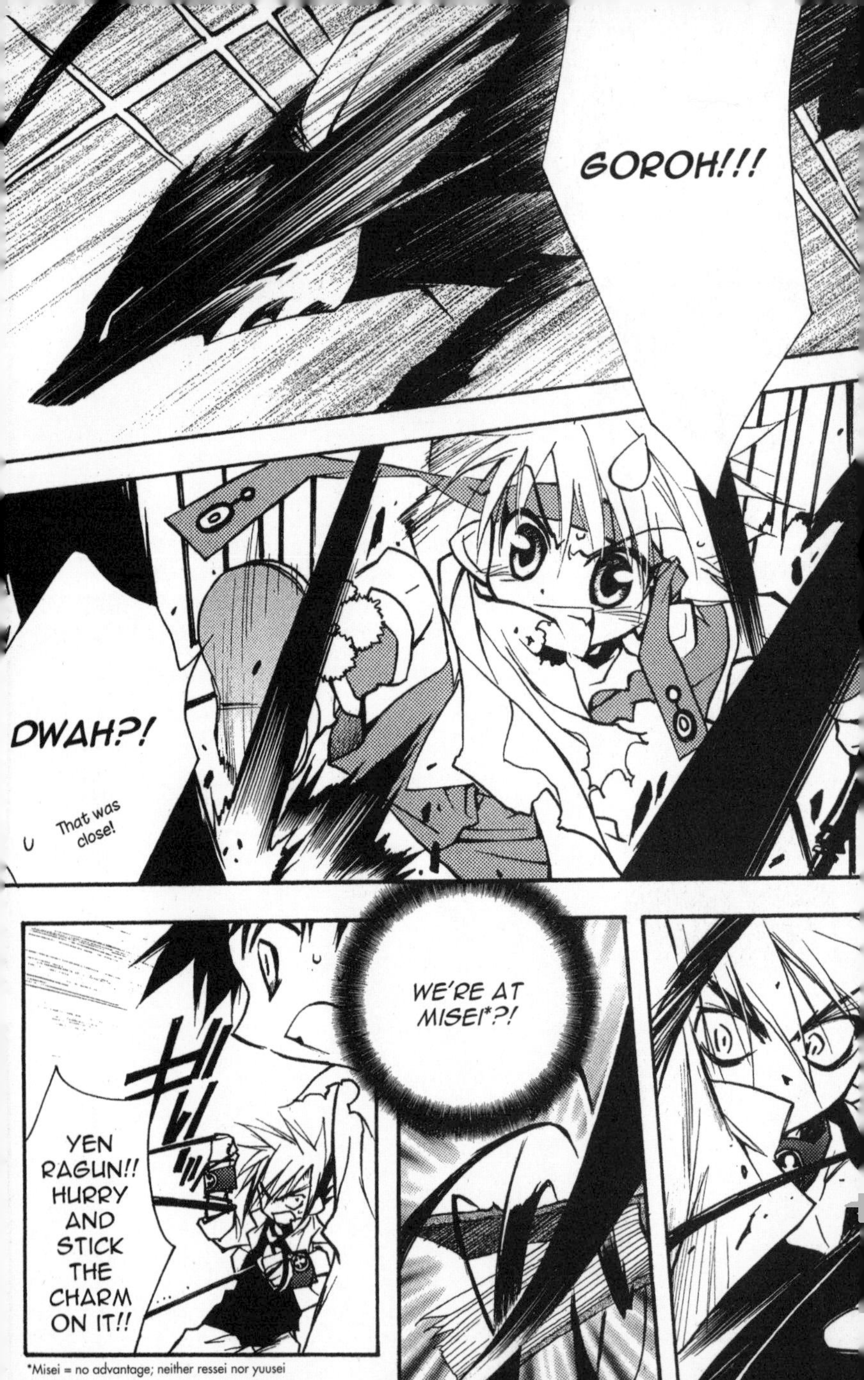
GOROH!!!
DWAH?!
That was close!
WE'RE AT MISEI*?!
YEN RAGUN!! HURRY AND STICK THE CHARM ON IT!!

*Misei = no advantage; neither ressei nor yuusei

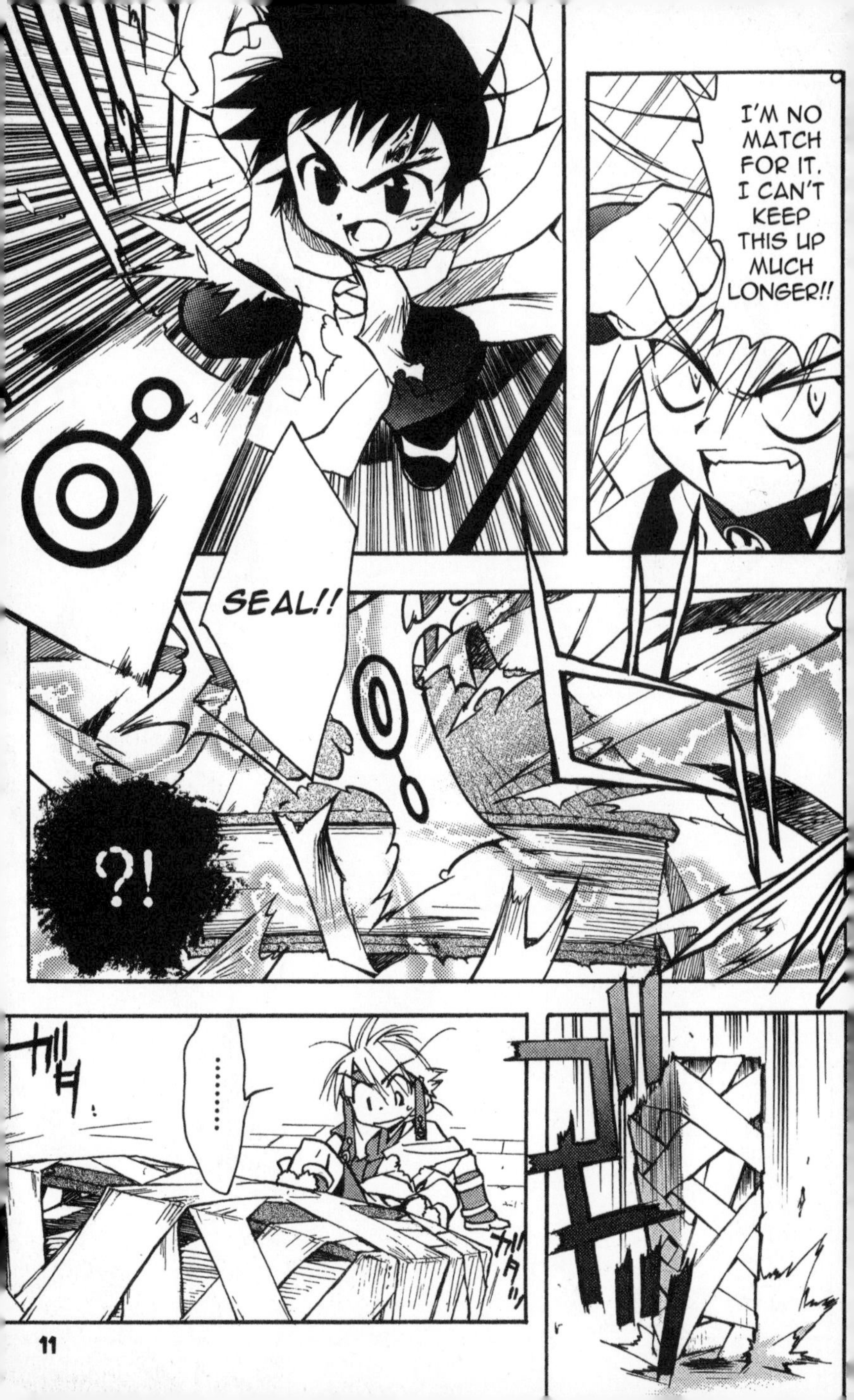
I'M NO MATCH FOR IT. I CAN'T KEEP THIS UP MUCH LONGER!!
SEAL!!
?!
......

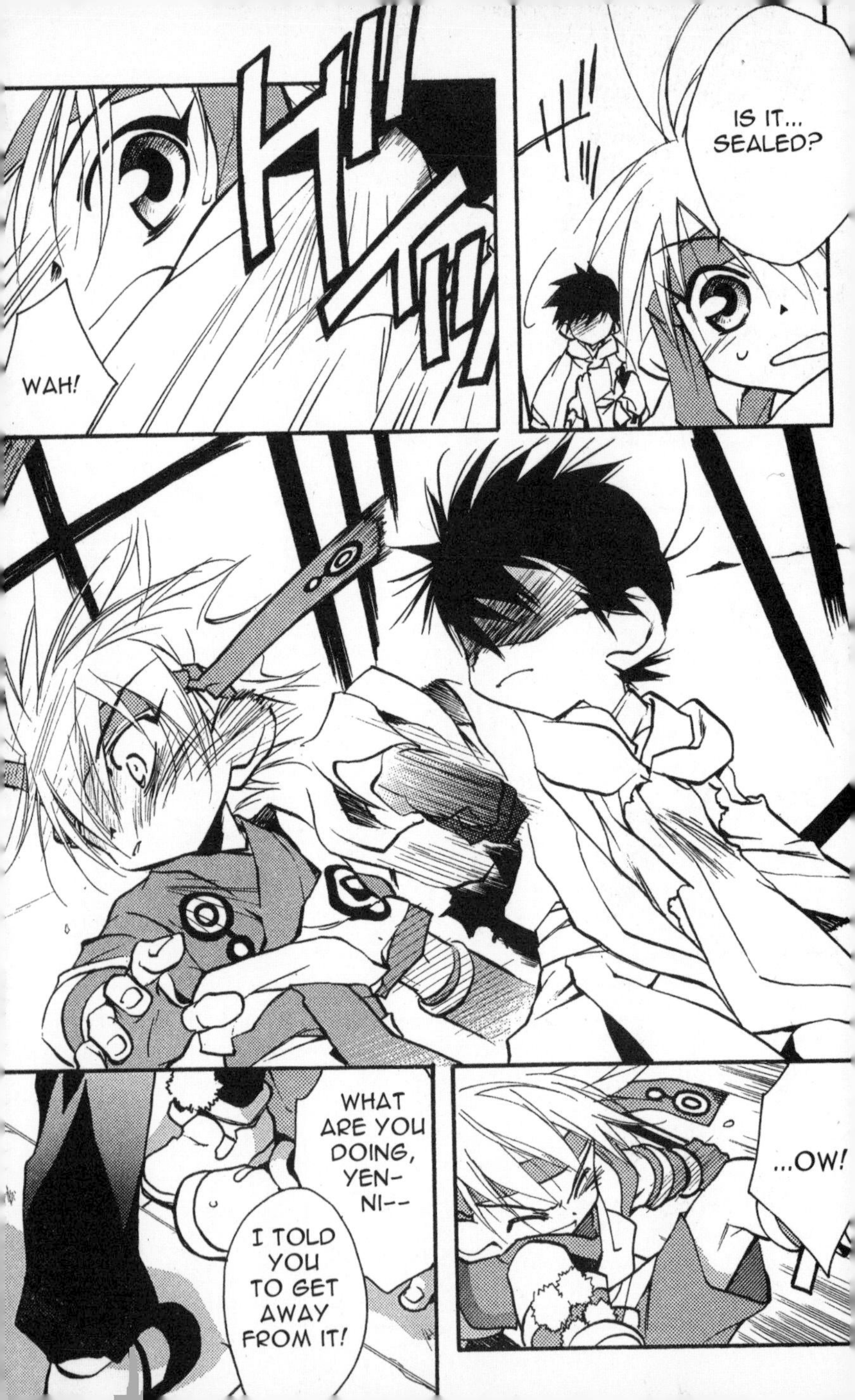
IS IT... SEALED?
WAH!
...OW!
WHAT ARE YOU DOING, YEN-NI--
I TOLD YOU TO GET AWAY FROM IT!

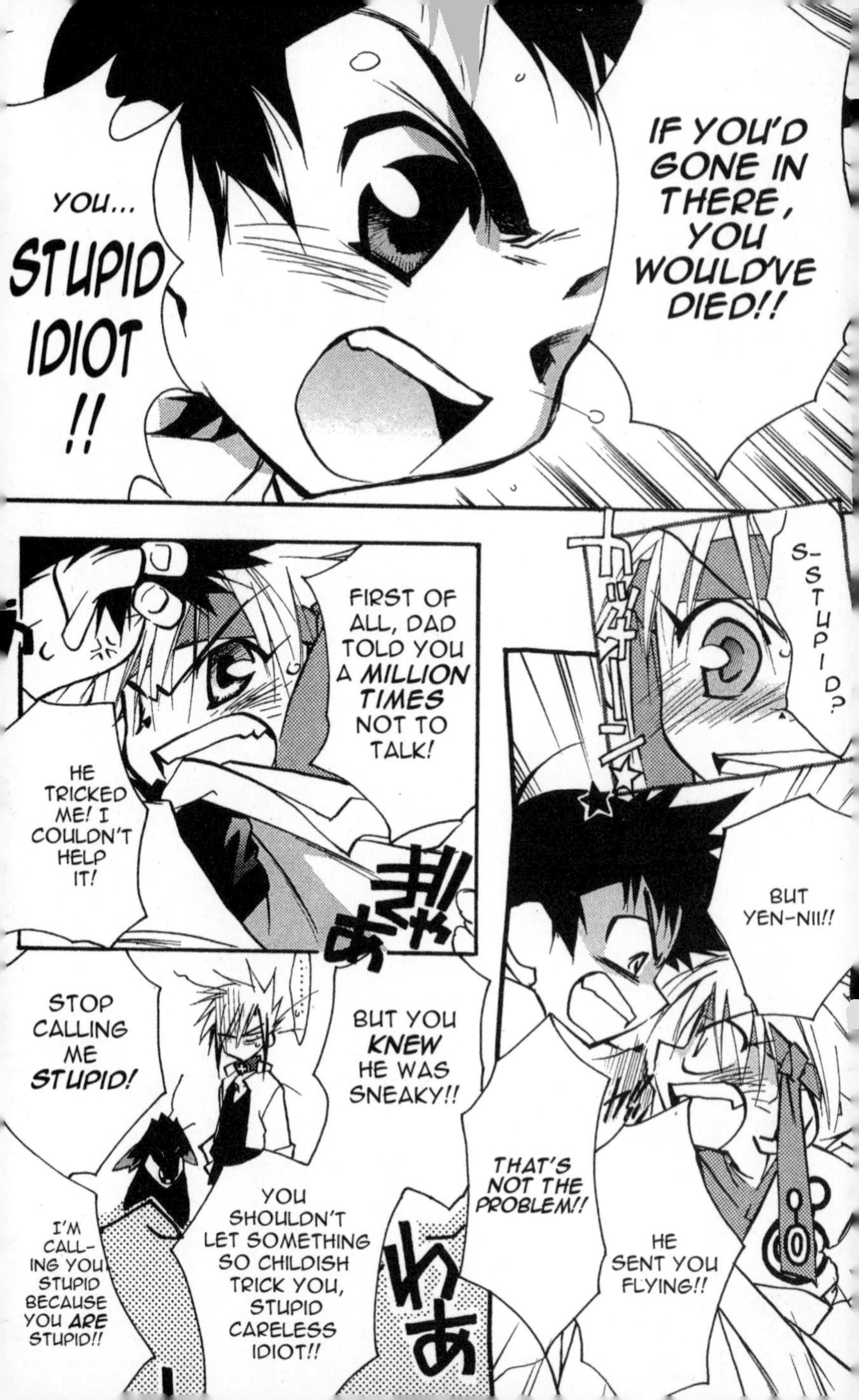
IF YOU'D GONE IN THERE, YOU WOULD'VE DIED!!
YOU... STUPID IDIOT!!
S-STUPID?
FIRST OF ALL, DAD TOLD YOU A *MILLION TIMES* NOT TO TALK!
HE TRICKED ME! I COULDN'T HELP IT!
BUT YEN-NII!!
THAT'S NOT THE PROBLEM!!
HE SENT YOU FLYING!!
BUT YOU *KNEW* HE WAS SNEAKY!!
STOP CALLING ME *STUPID!*
YOU SHOULDN'T LET SOMETHING SO CHILDISH TRICK YOU, STUPID CARELESS IDIOT!!
わあ
I'M CALLING YOU STUPID BECAUSE YOU *ARE* STUPID!!

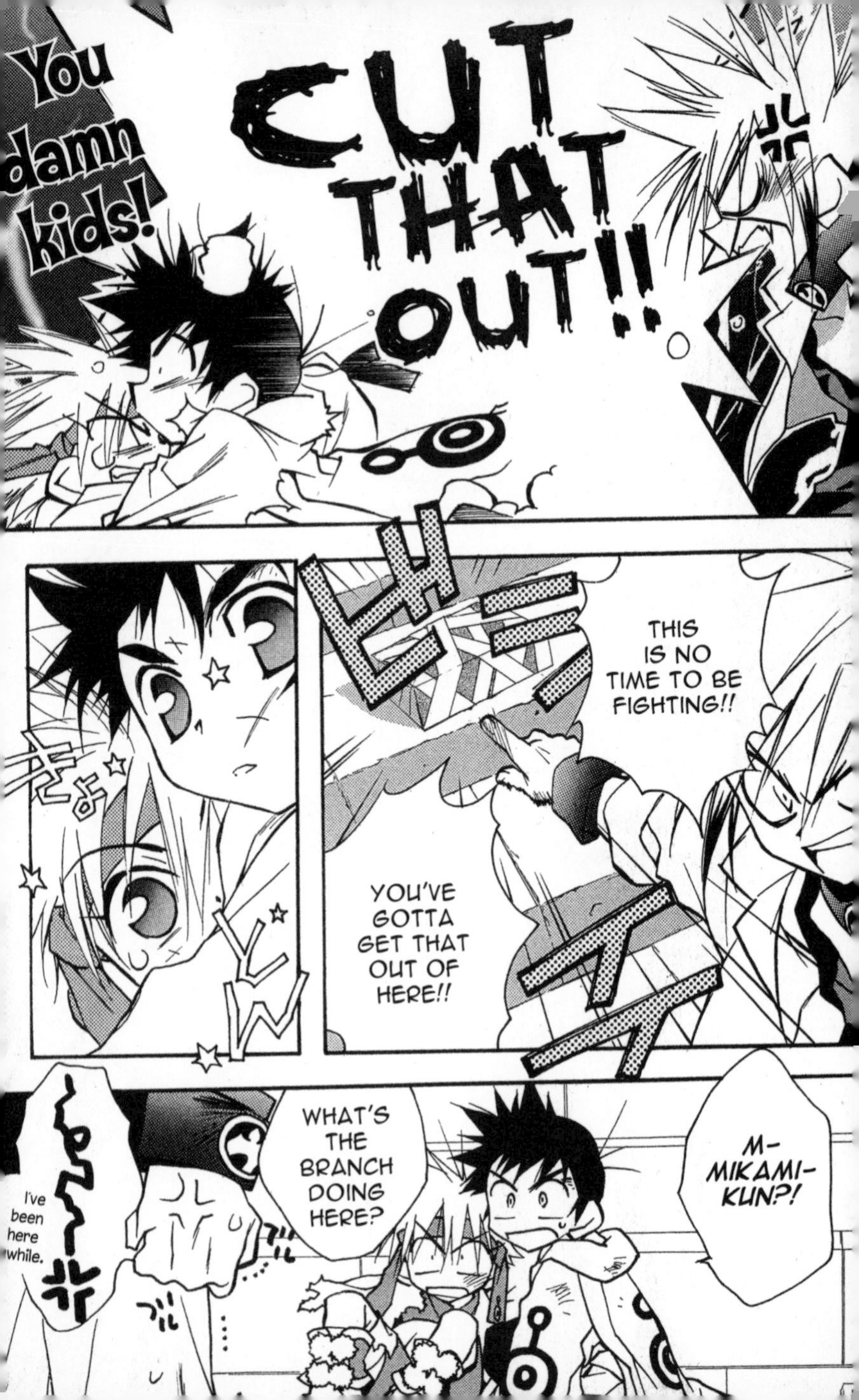
CUT THAT OUT!!
You damn kids!
THIS IS NO TIME TO BE FIGHTING!!
YOU'VE GOTTA GET THAT OUT OF HERE!!
M-MIKAMI-KUN?!
WHAT'S THE BRANCH DOING HERE?
I've been here while.

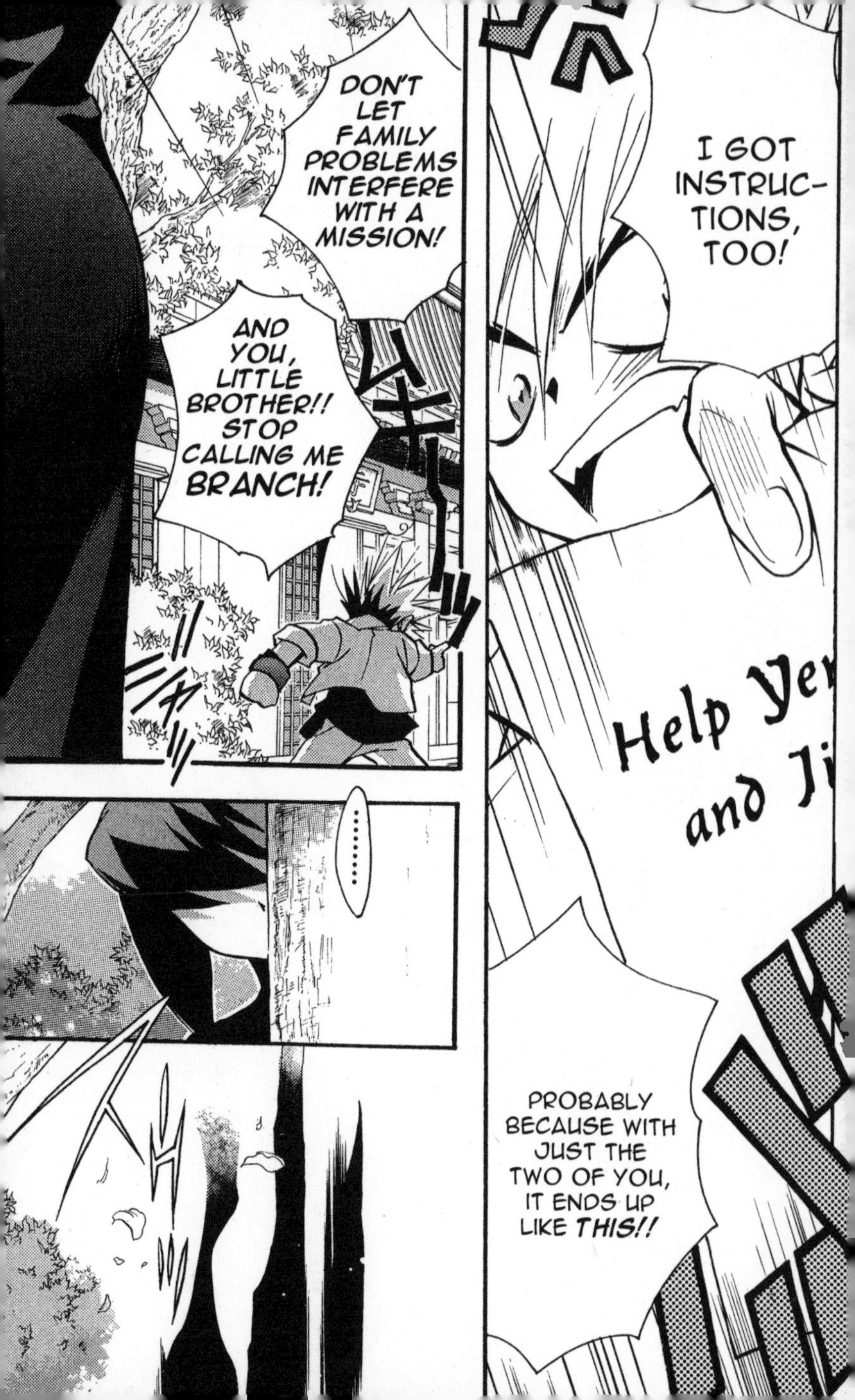
I GOT INSTRUC-TIONS, TOO!
PROBABLY BECAUSE WITH JUST THE TWO OF YOU, IT ENDS UP LIKE *THIS!!*
DON'T LET FAMILY PROBLEMS INTERFERE WITH A MISSION!
AND YOU, LITTLE BROTHER!! STOP CALLING ME **BRANCH!**
....

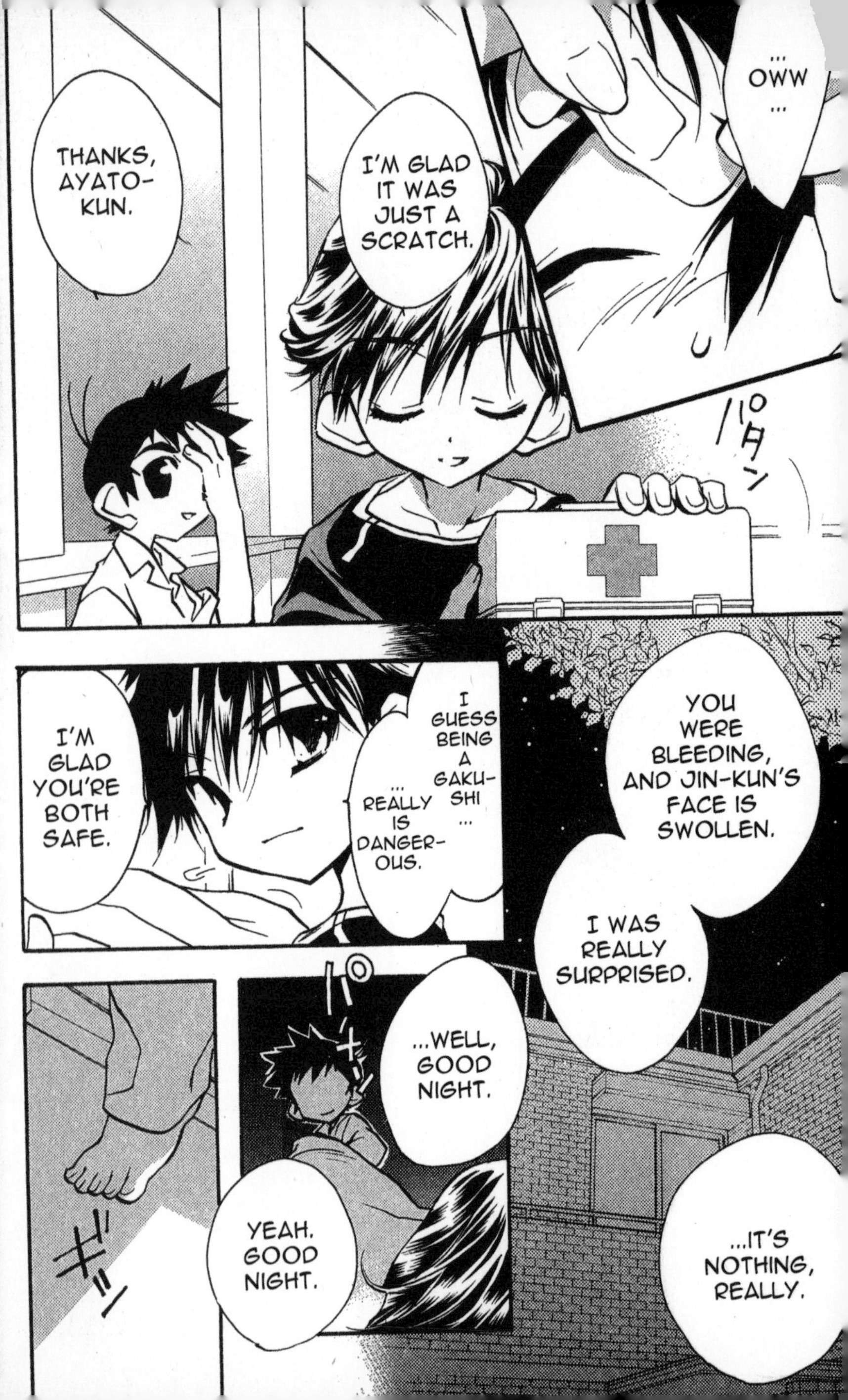
...OWW...
パタン
I'M GLAD IT WAS JUST A SCRATCH.
THANKS, AYATO-KUN.
YOU WERE BLEEDING, AND JIN-KUN'S FACE IS SWOLLEN.
I WAS REALLY SURPRISED.
...IT'S NOTHING, REALLY.
I GUESS BEING A GAKU-SHI ...
... REALLY IS DANGER-OUS.
I'M GLAD YOU'RE BOTH SAFE.
...WELL, GOOD NIGHT.
YEAH. GOOD NIGHT.

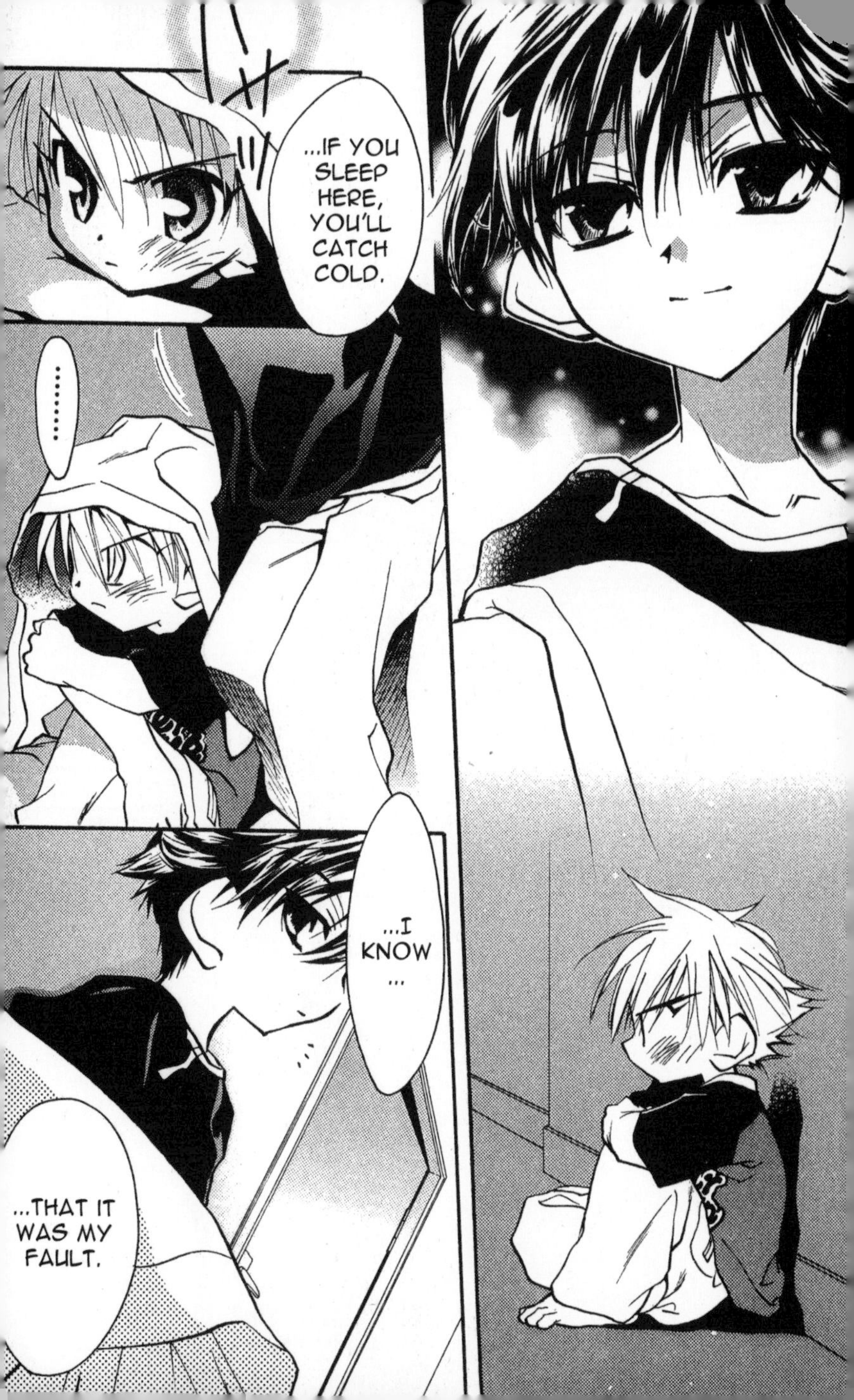
...IF YOU SLEEP HERE, YOU'LL CATCH COLD.
......
...I KNOW ...
...THAT IT WAS MY FAULT.

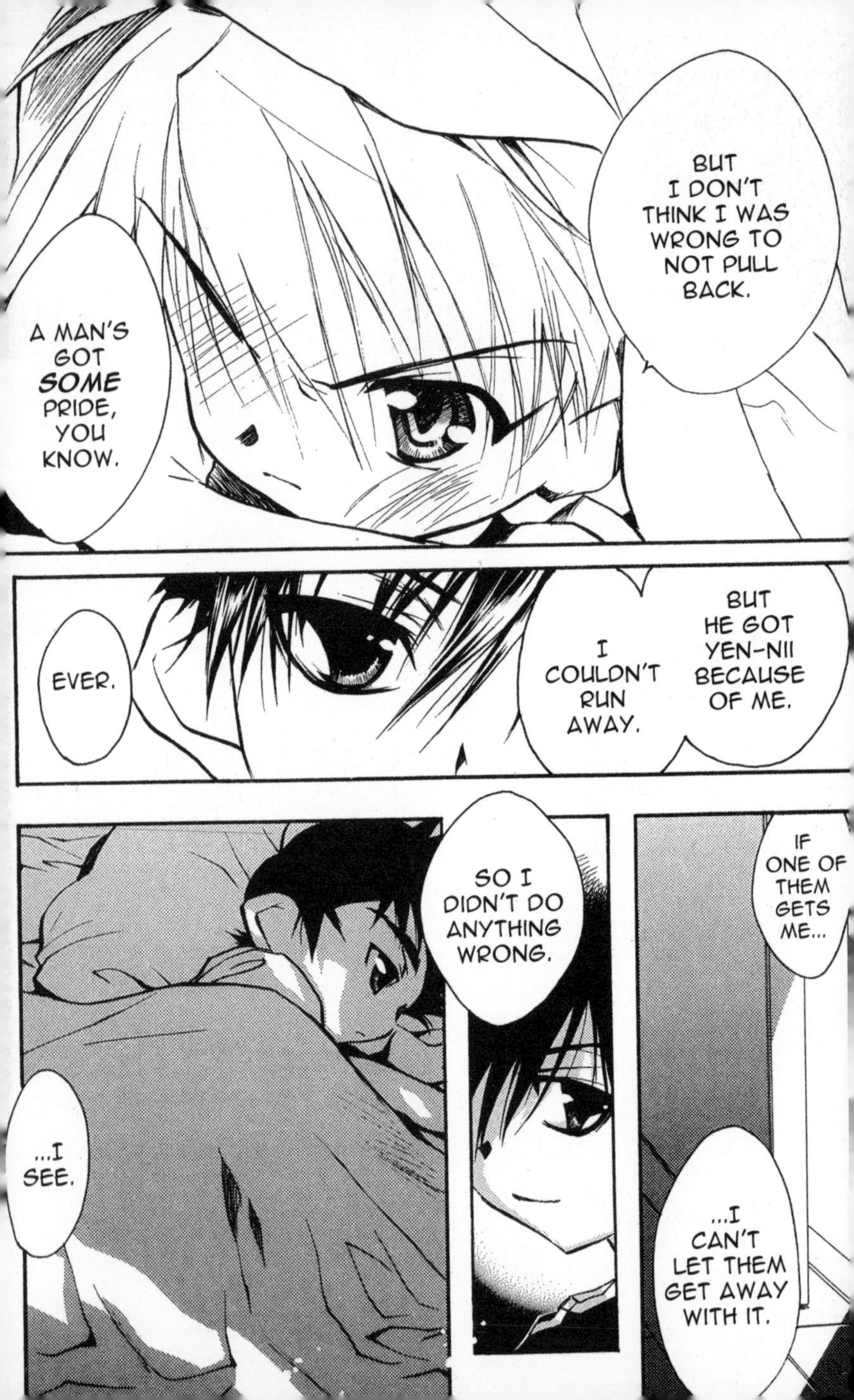
BUT I DON'T THINK I WAS WRONG TO NOT PULL BACK.
A MAN'S GOT *SOME* PRIDE, YOU KNOW.
BUT HE GOT YEN-NII BECAUSE OF ME.
I COULDN'T RUN AWAY.
EVER.
IF ONE OF THEM GETS ME...
...I CAN'T LET THEM GET AWAY WITH IT.
SO I DIDN'T DO ANYTHING WRONG.
...I SEE.

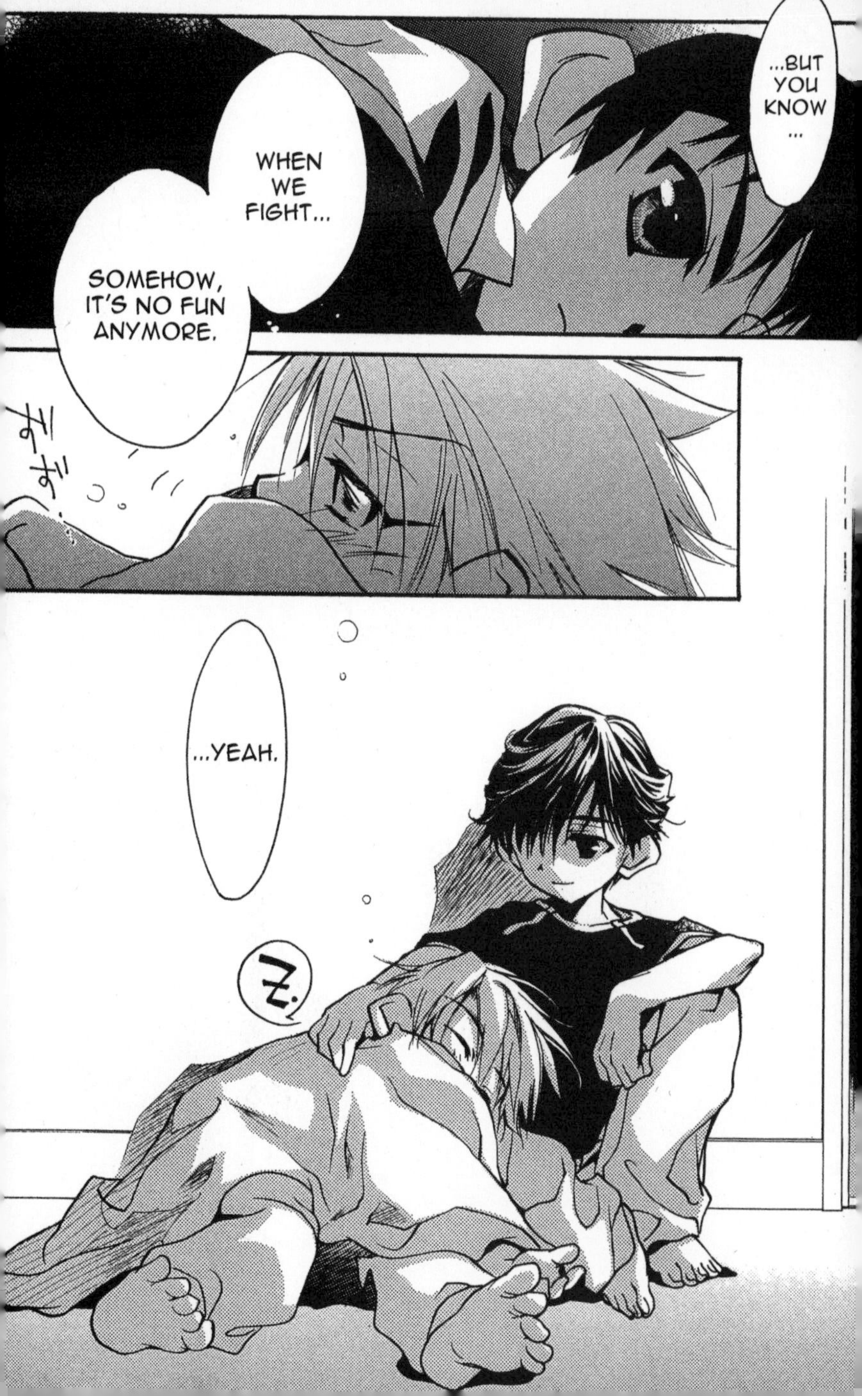
...BUT YOU KNOW ...
WHEN WE FIGHT...
SOMEHOW, IT'S NO FUN ANYMORE.
...YEAH.
Z.

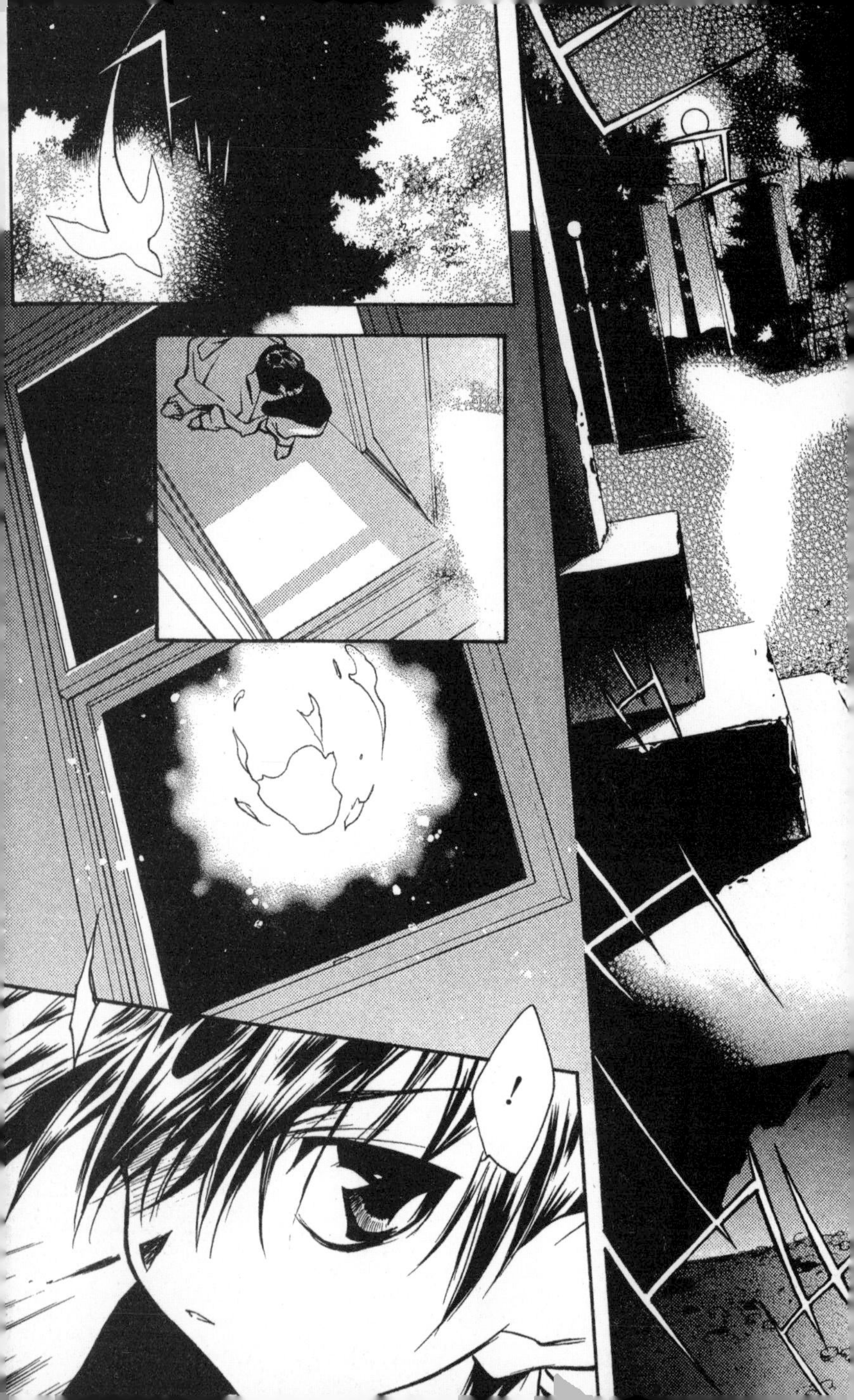
!

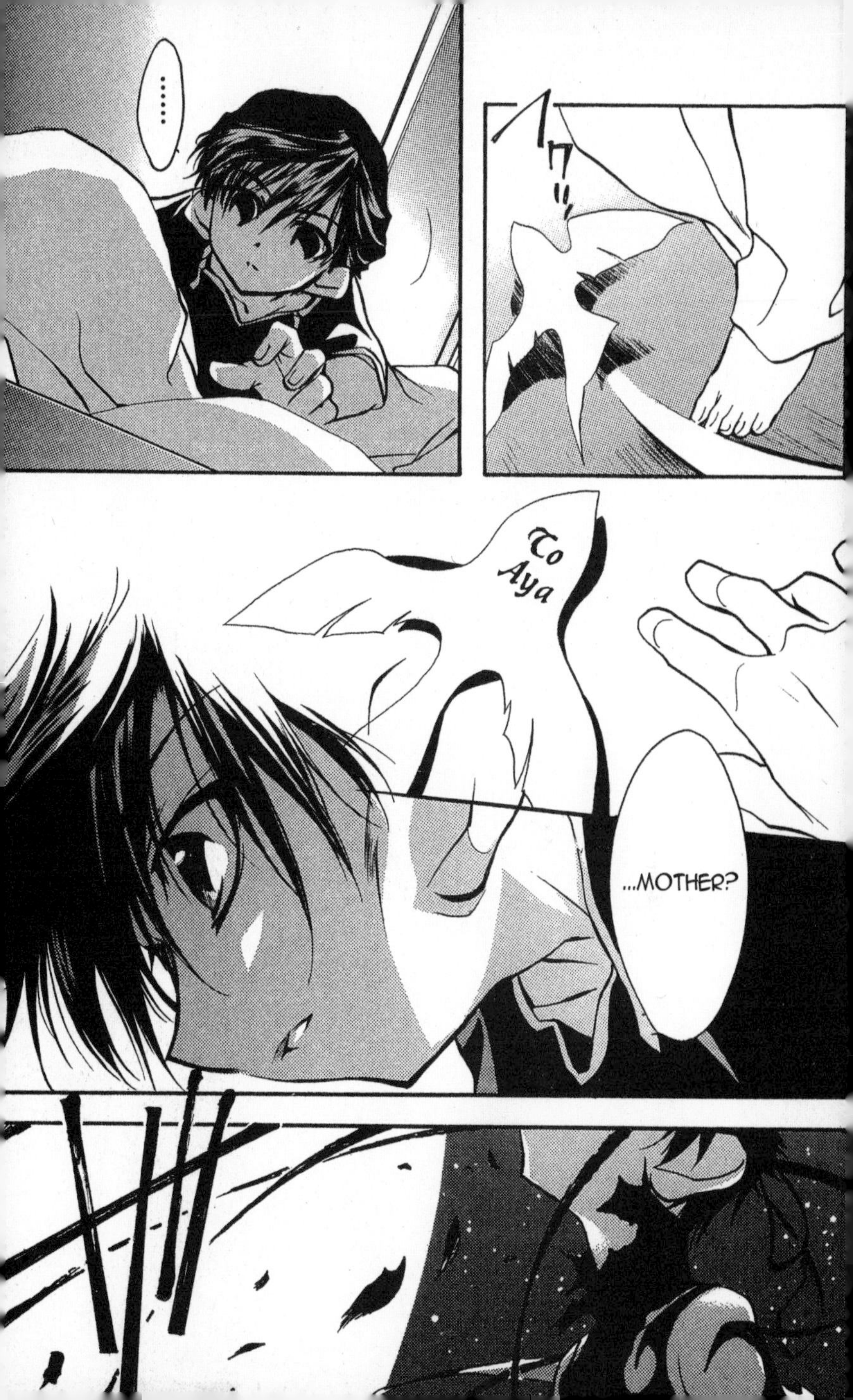
......
To Aya
...MOTHER?

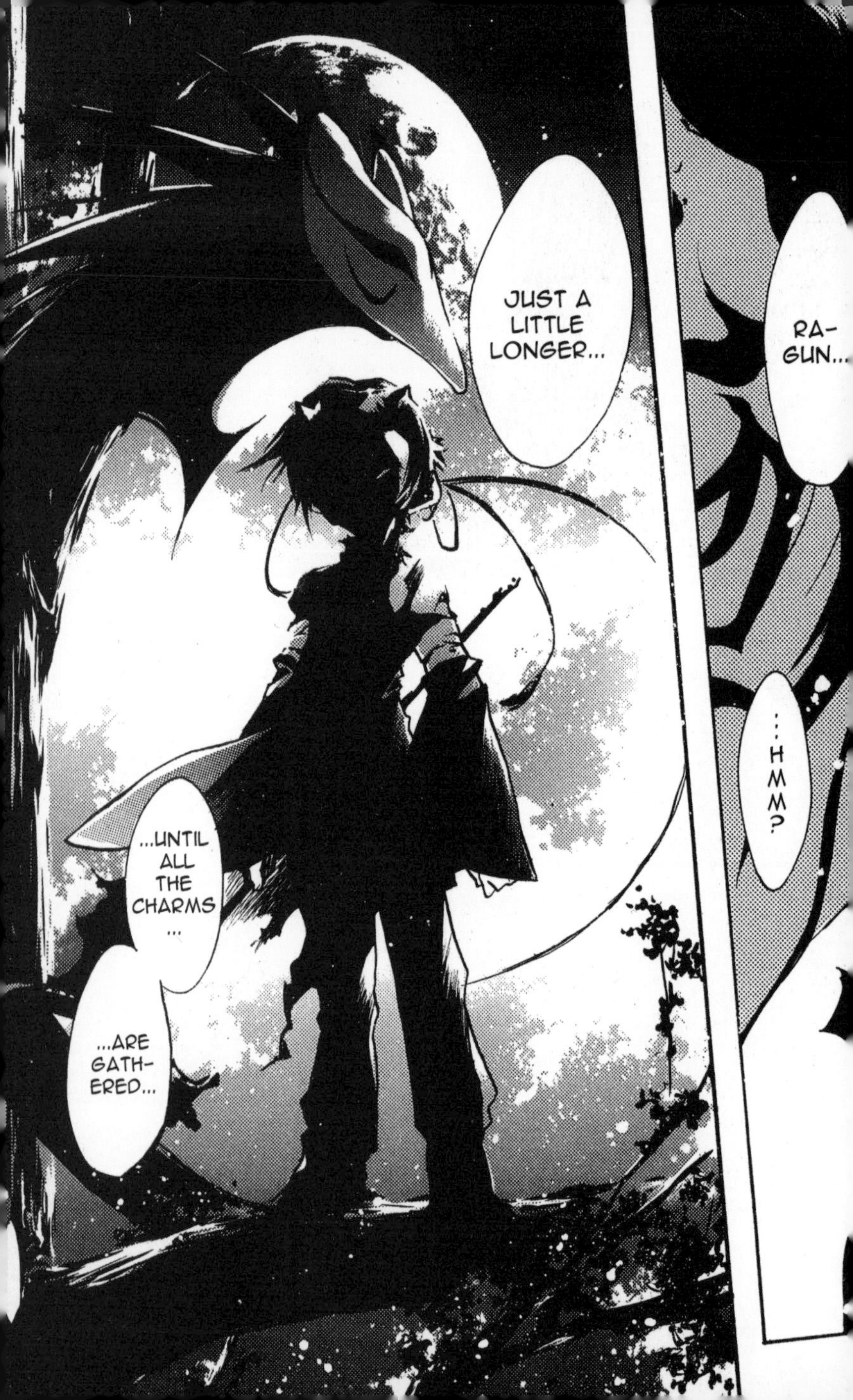
RA-GUN...
...HMM?
JUST A LITTLE LONGER...
...UNTIL ALL THE CHARMS...
...ARE GATHERED...

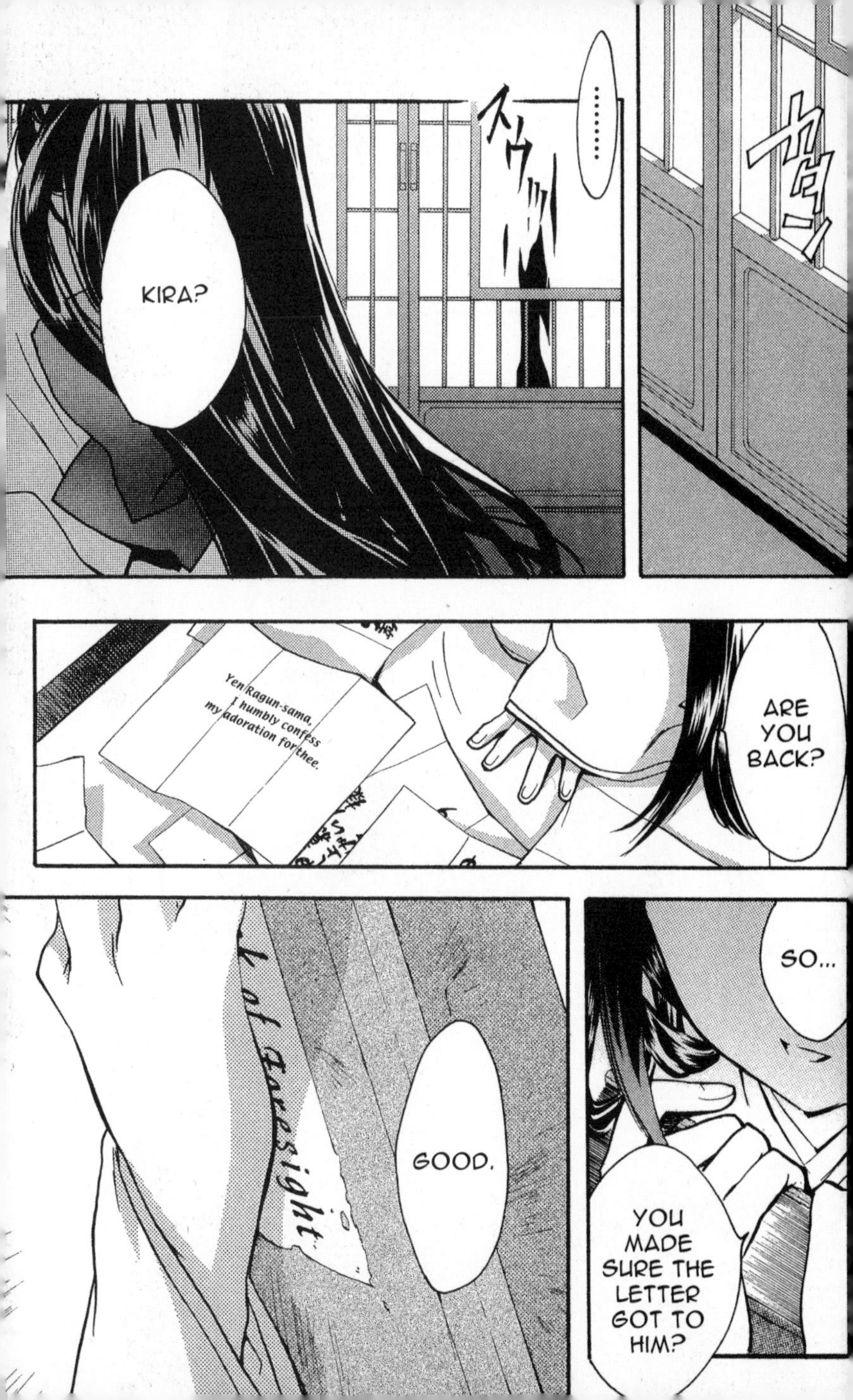
カタン
......
スウッ
KIRA?
ARE YOU BACK?
Yen Ragun-sama, I humbly confess my adoration for thee.
SO...
YOU MADE SURE THE LETTER GOT TO HIM?
GOOD.

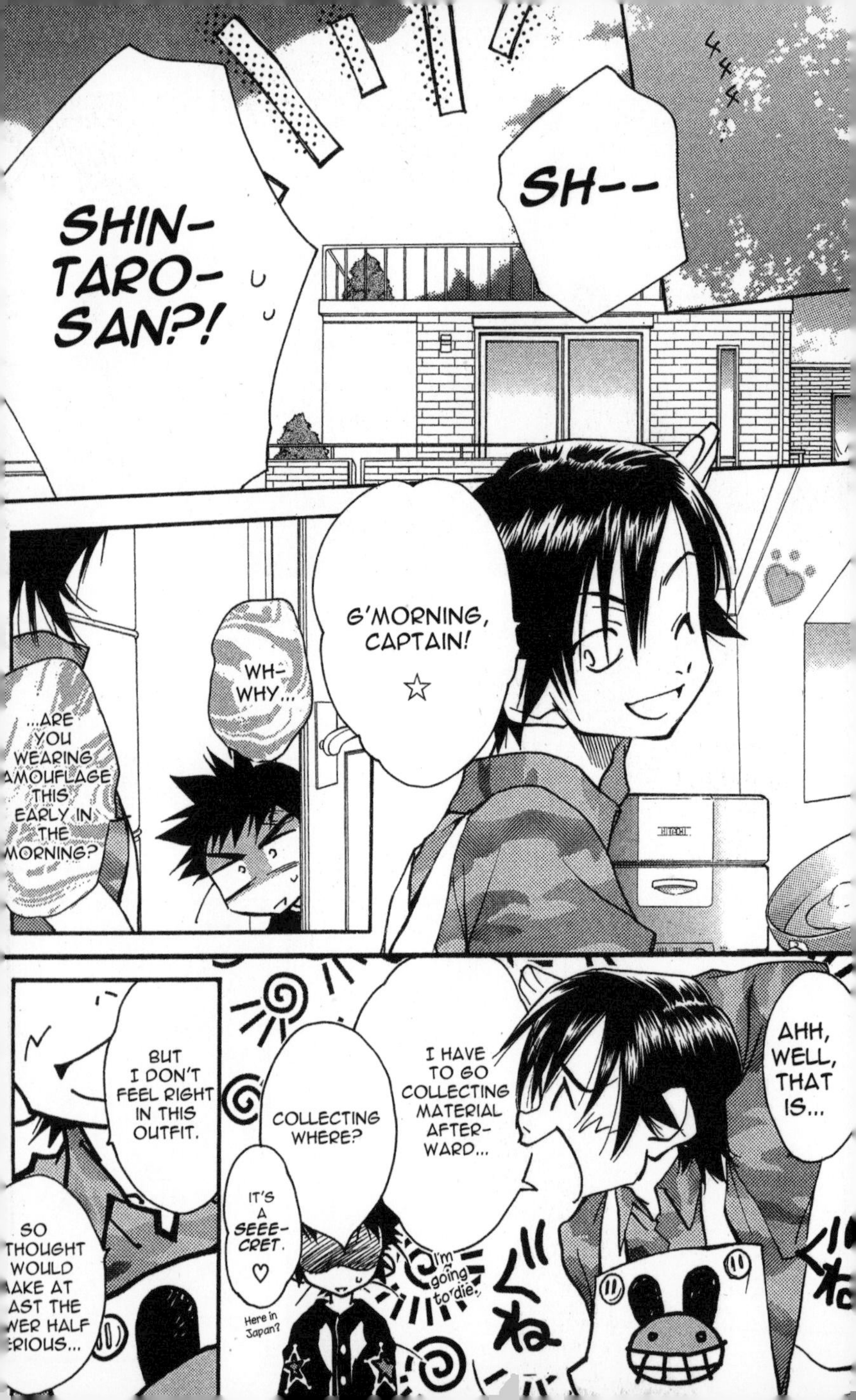
SH--
SHIN-TARO-SAN?!
G'MORNING, CAPTAIN! ☆
WH-WHY...
...ARE YOU WEARING AMOUFLAGE THIS EARLY IN THE MORNING?
AHH, WELL, THAT IS...
I HAVE TO GO COLLECTING MATERIAL AFTER-WARD...
COLLECTING WHERE?
IT'S A SEEE-CRET. ♡
Here in Japan?
I'm going to die
BUT I DON'T FEEL RIGHT IN THIS OUTFIT.
SO THOUGHT WOULD AKE AT AST THE WER HALF ERIOUS...

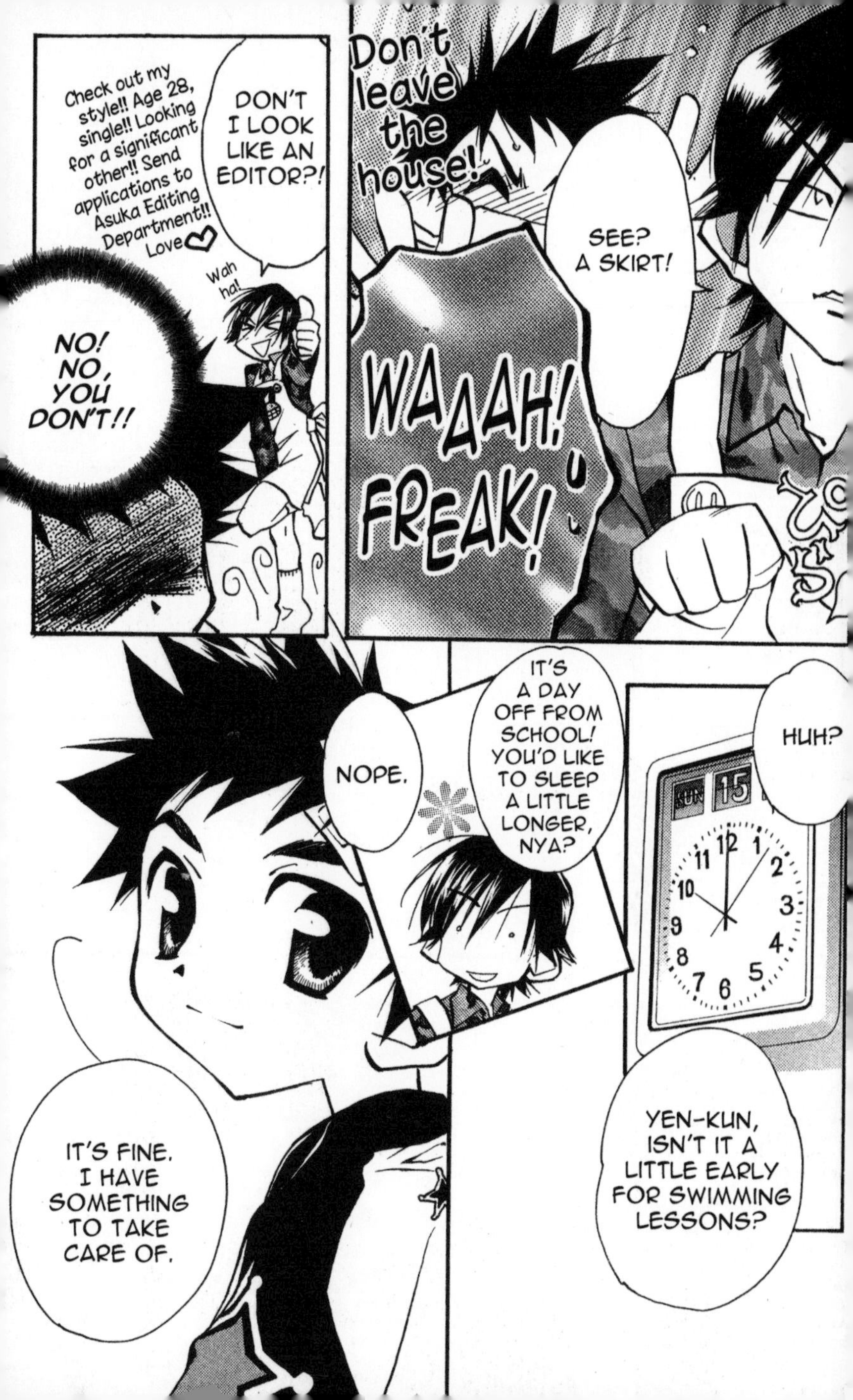
SEE? A SKIRT!
Don't leave the house!
WAAAH! FREAK!
DON'T I LOOK LIKE AN EDITOR?!
Check out my style!! Age 28, single!! Looking for a significant other!! Send applications to Asuka Editing Department!! Love
Wah ha!
NO! NO, YOU DON'T!!
HUH?
YEN-KUN, ISN'T IT A LITTLE EARLY FOR SWIMMING LESSONS?
IT'S A DAY OFF FROM SCHOOL! YOU'D LIKE TO SLEEP A LITTLE LONGER, NYA?
NOPE.
IT'S FINE. I HAVE SOMETHING TO TAKE CARE OF.

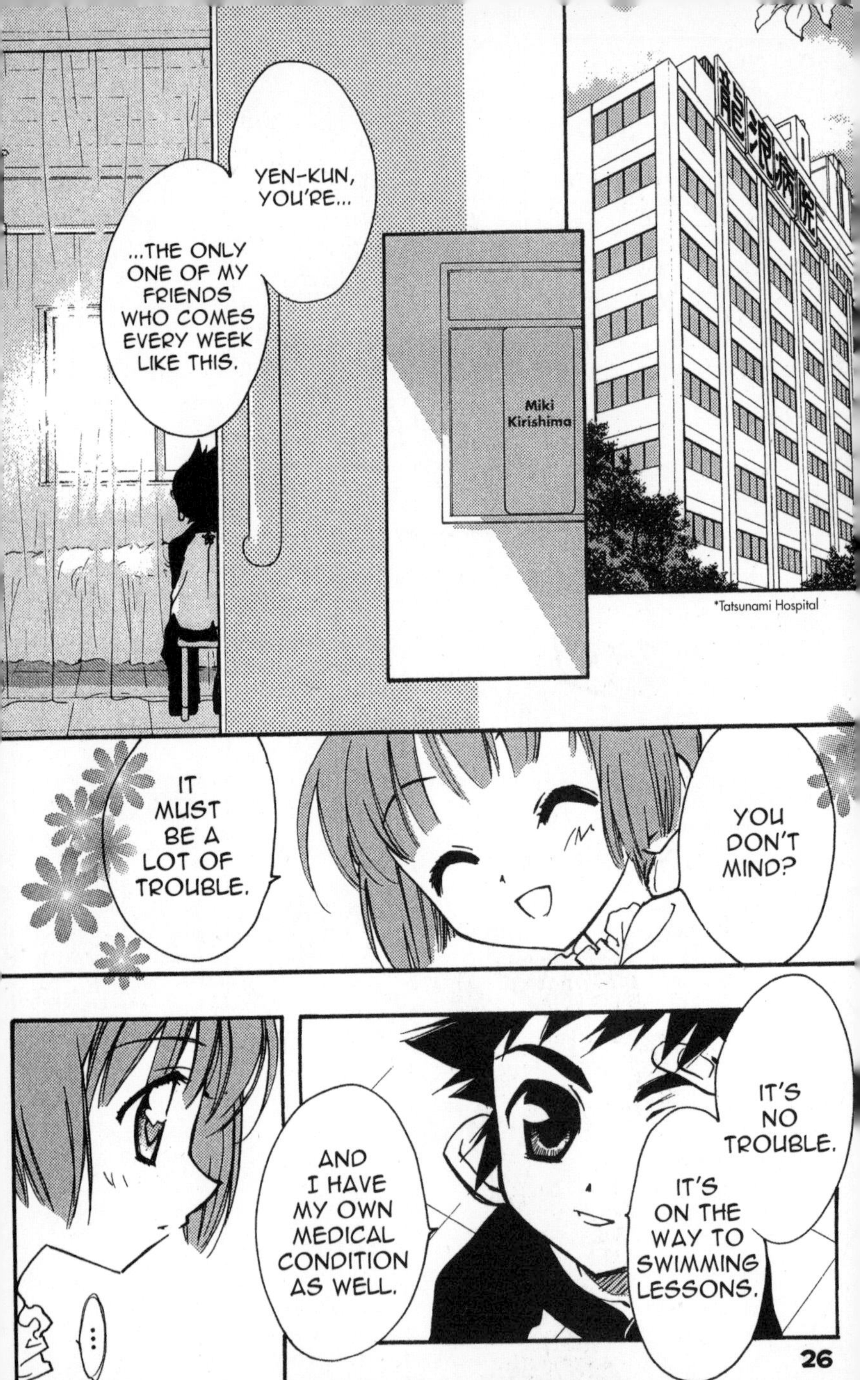
*Tatsunami Hospital
Miki Kirishima
YEN-KUN, YOU'RE...
...THE ONLY ONE OF MY FRIENDS WHO COMES EVERY WEEK LIKE THIS.
YOU DON'T MIND?
IT MUST BE A LOT OF TROUBLE.
IT'S NO TROUBLE.
IT'S ON THE WAY TO SWIMMING LESSONS.
AND I HAVE MY OWN MEDICAL CONDITION AS WELL.
...

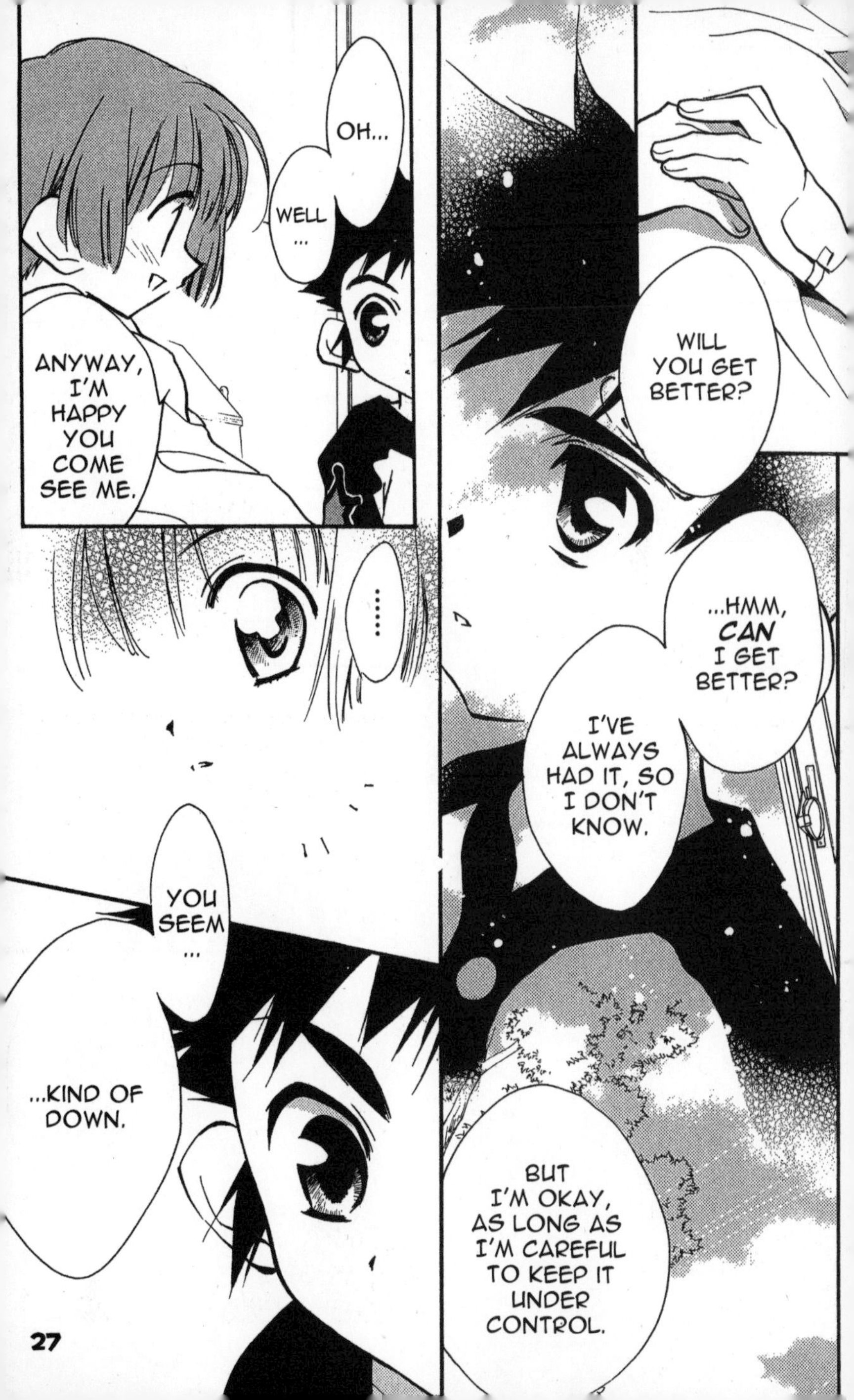
WILL YOU GET BETTER?
...HMM, CAN I GET BETTER?
I'VE ALWAYS HAD IT, SO I DON'T KNOW.
BUT I'M OKAY, AS LONG AS I'M CAREFUL TO KEEP IT UNDER CONTROL.
OH...
WELL ...
ANYWAY, I'M HAPPY YOU COME SEE ME.
......
YOU SEEM ...
...KIND OF DOWN.

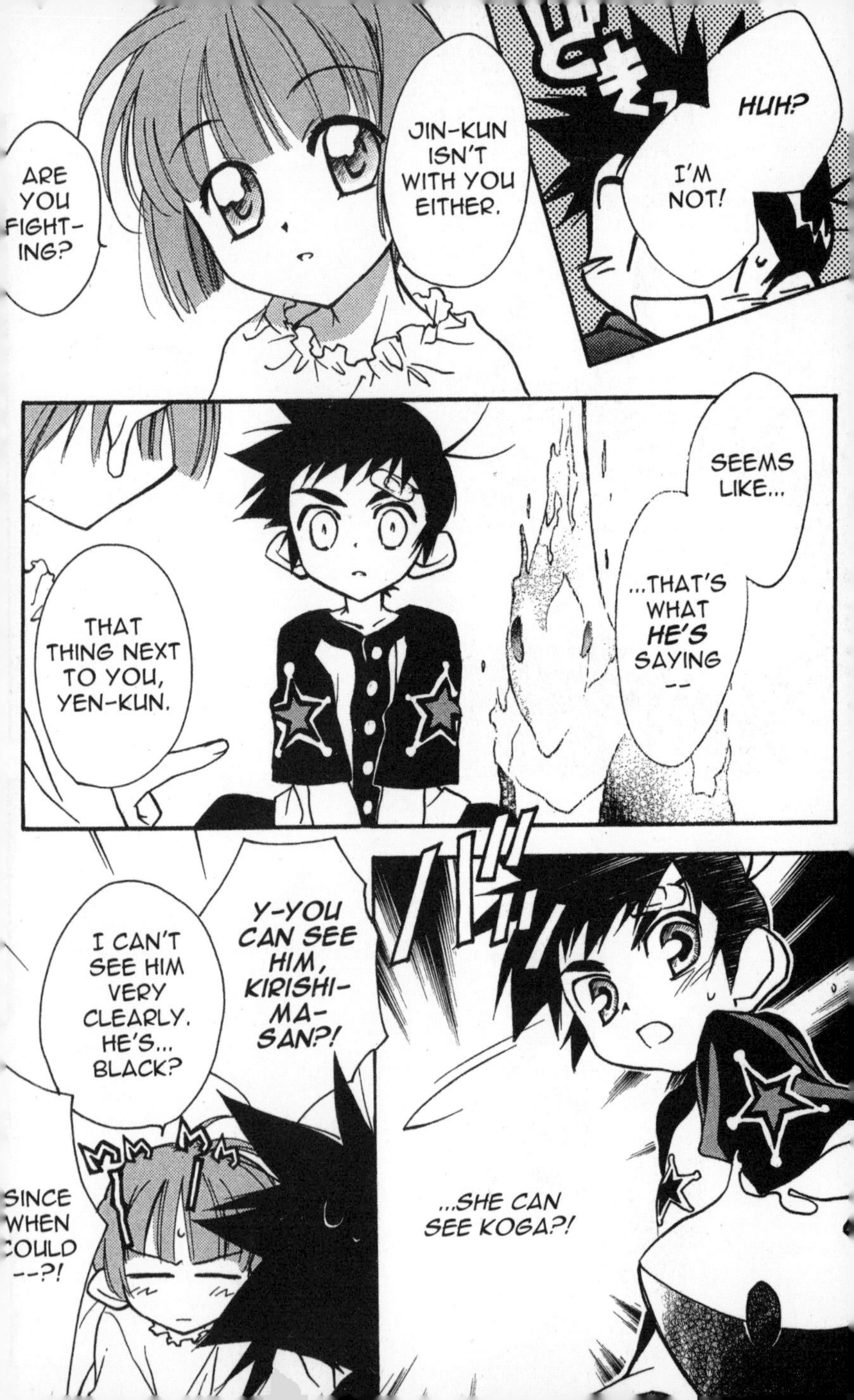
JIN-KUN ISN'T WITH YOU EITHER.
ARE YOU FIGHTING?
HUH?
I'M NOT!
SEEMS LIKE...
...THAT'S WHAT *HE'S* SAYING --
THAT THING NEXT TO YOU, YEN-KUN.
Y-YOU CAN SEE HIM, KIRISHIMA-SAN?!
I CAN'T SEE HIM VERY CLEARLY. HE'S... BLACK?
SINCE WHEN COULD --?!
...SHE CAN SEE KOGA?!

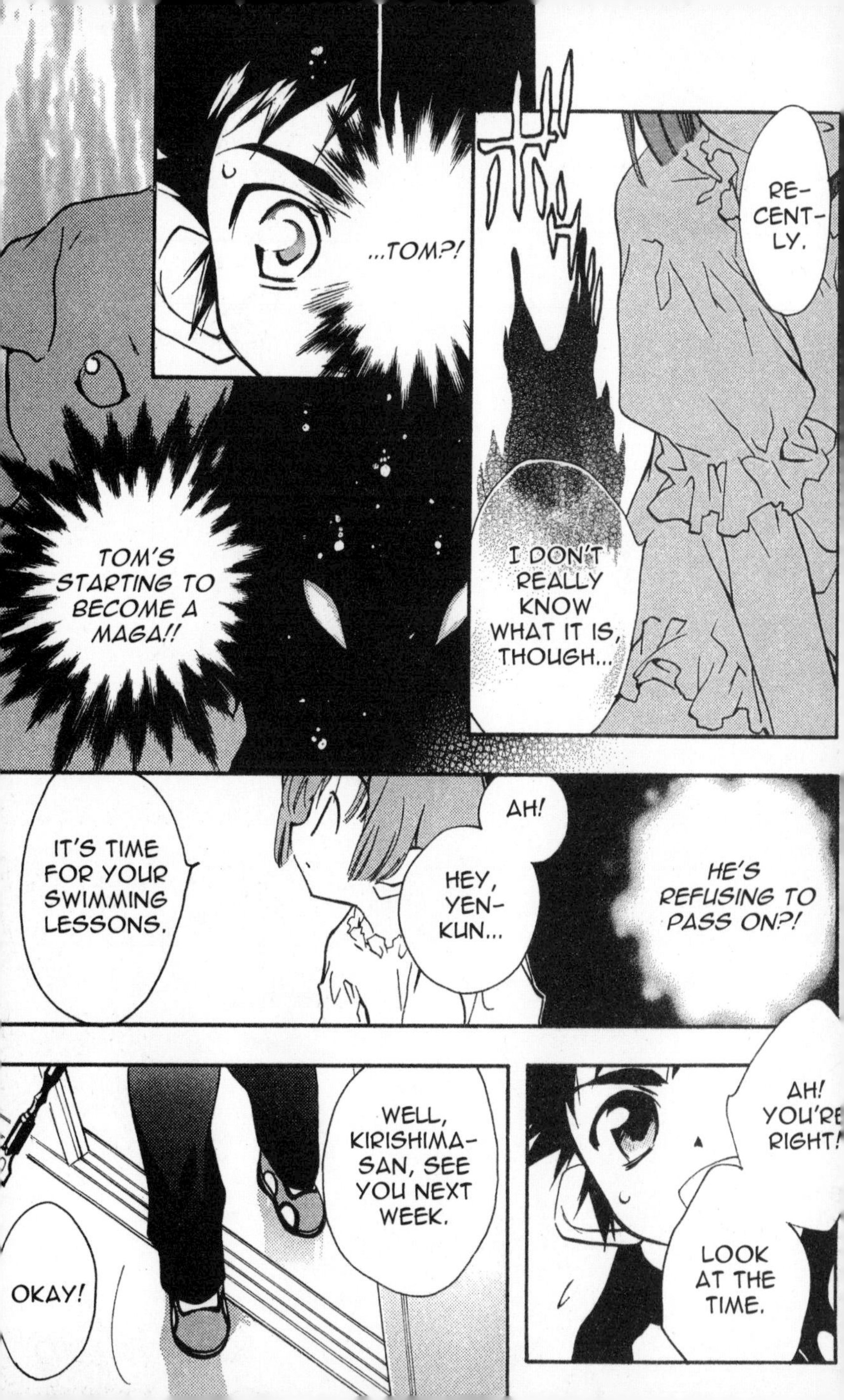
RE-CENT-LY.
I DON'T REALLY KNOW WHAT IT IS, THOUGH...
...TOM?!
TOM'S STARTING TO BECOME A MAGA!!
HE'S REFUSING TO PASS ON?!
AH!
HEY, YEN-KUN...
IT'S TIME FOR YOUR SWIMMING LESSONS.
AH! YOU'RE RIGHT!
LOOK AT THE TIME.
WELL, KIRISHIMA-SAN, SEE YOU NEXT WEEK.
OKAY!

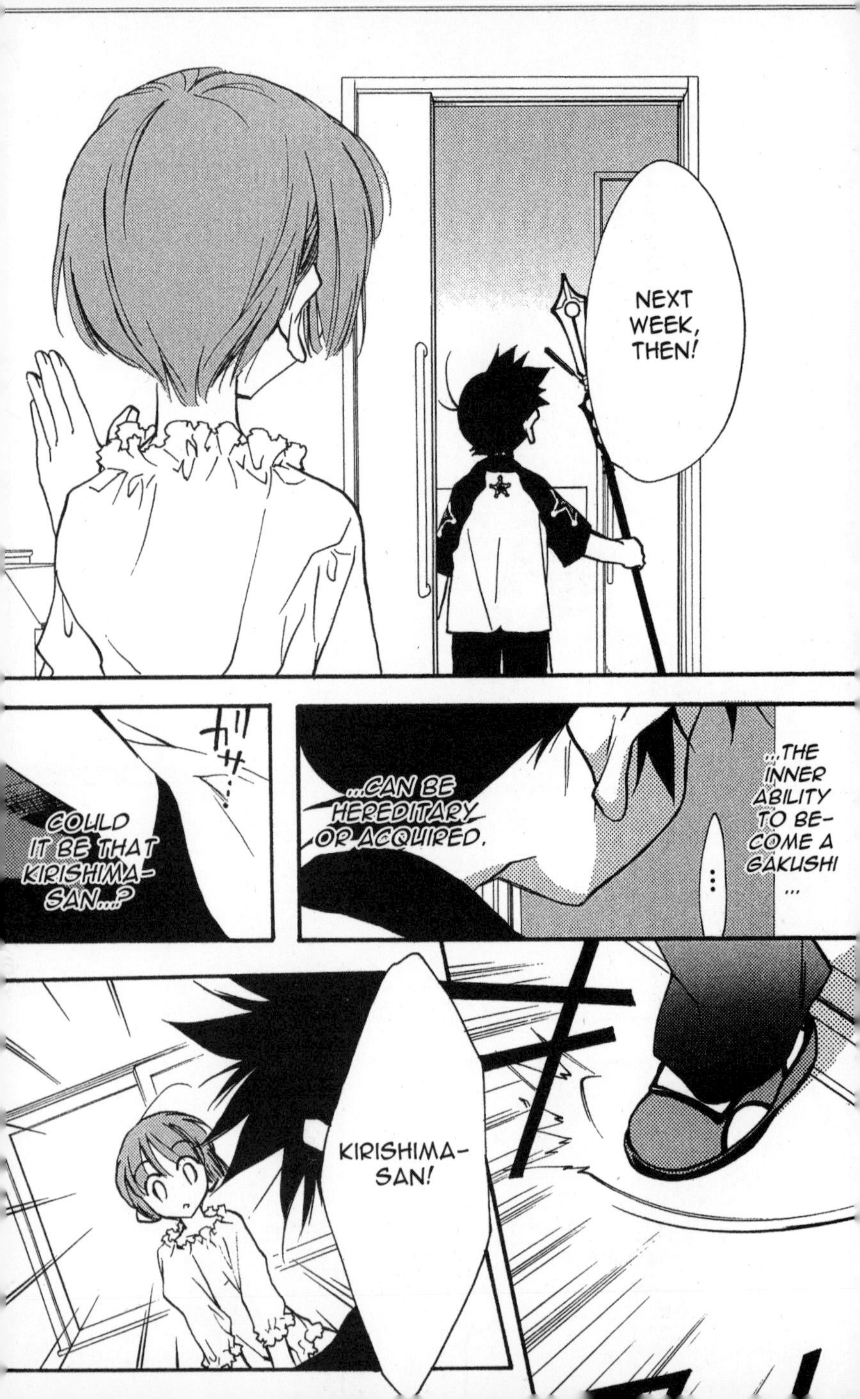
NEXT WEEK, THEN!
...THE INNER ABILITY TO BE-COME A GAKUSHI ...
...
...CAN BE HEREDITARY OR ACQUIRED.
COULD IT BE THAT KIRISHIMA-SAN...?
KIRISHIMA-SAN!

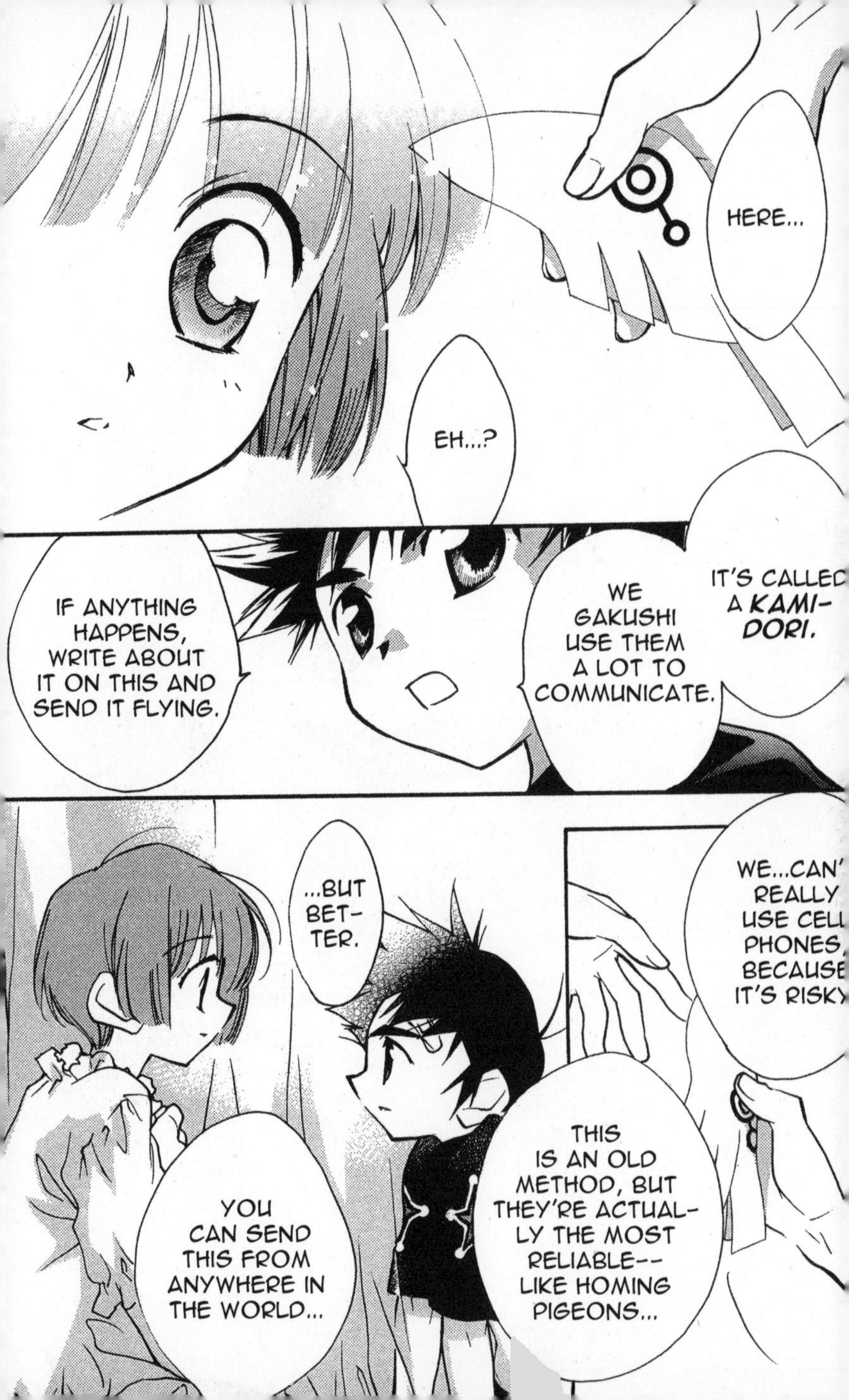

HERE...
EH...?
IT'S CALLED A *KAMI-DORI.*
WE GAKUSHI USE THEM A LOT TO COMMUNICATE.
IF ANYTHING HAPPENS, WRITE ABOUT IT ON THIS AND SEND IT FLYING.
WE...CAN' REALLY USE CELL PHONES, BECAUSE IT'S RISKY
THIS IS AN OLD METHOD, BUT THEY'RE ACTUAL-LY THE MOST RELIABLE--LIKE HOMING PIGEONS...
...BUT BET-TER.
YOU CAN SEND THIS FROM ANYWHERE IN THE WORLD...

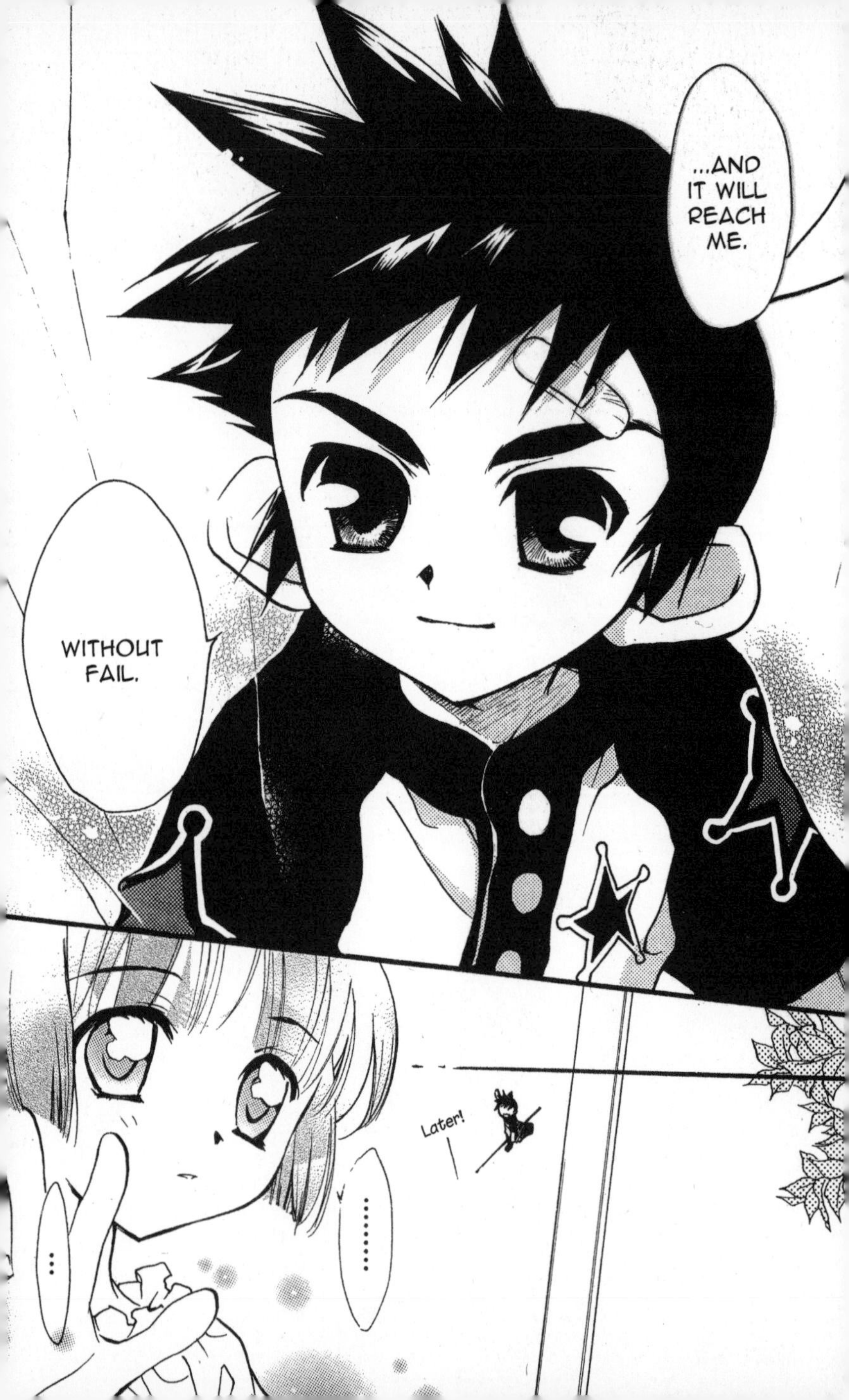
...AND IT WILL REACH ME.
WITHOUT FAIL.
Later!
....
...

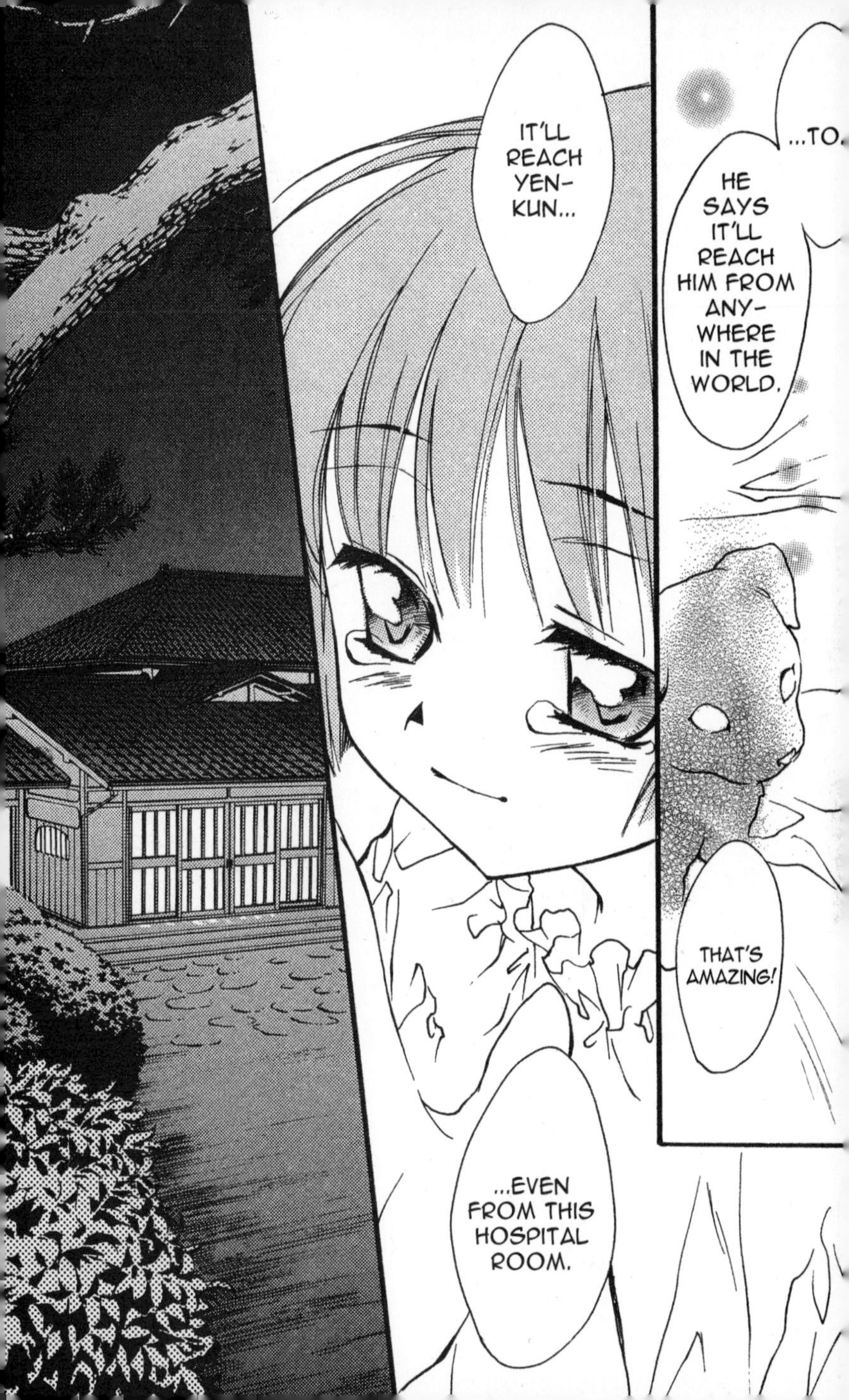
...TO.
HE SAYS IT'LL REACH HIM FROM ANY-WHERE IN THE WORLD.
THAT'S AMAZING!
IT'LL REACH YEN-KUN...
...EVEN FROM THIS HOSPITAL ROOM.

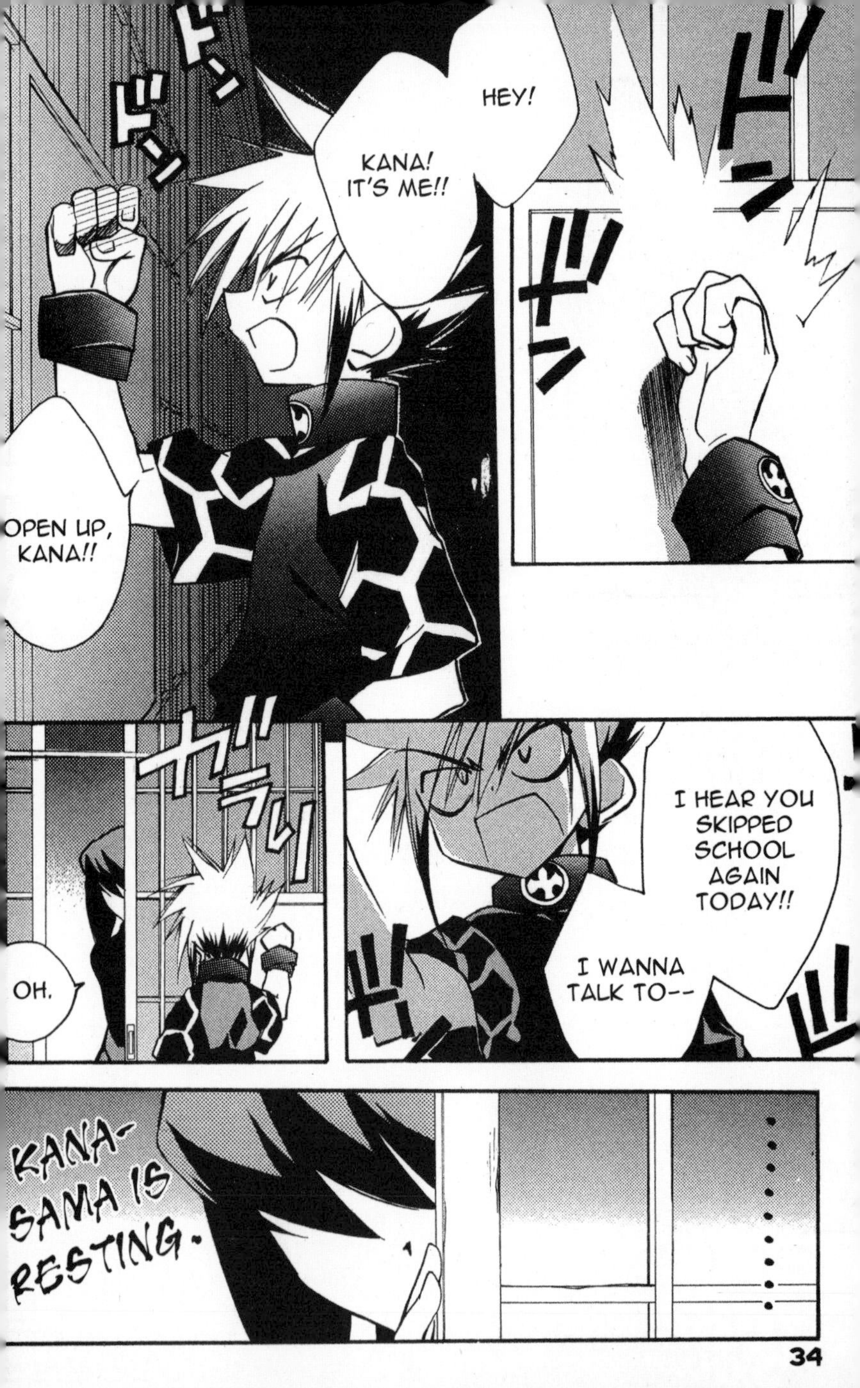
HEY!
KANA! IT'S ME!!
OPEN UP, KANA!!
I HEAR YOU SKIPPED SCHOOL AGAIN TODAY!!
I WANNA TALK TO--
OH.
......
KANA-SAMA IS RESTING.

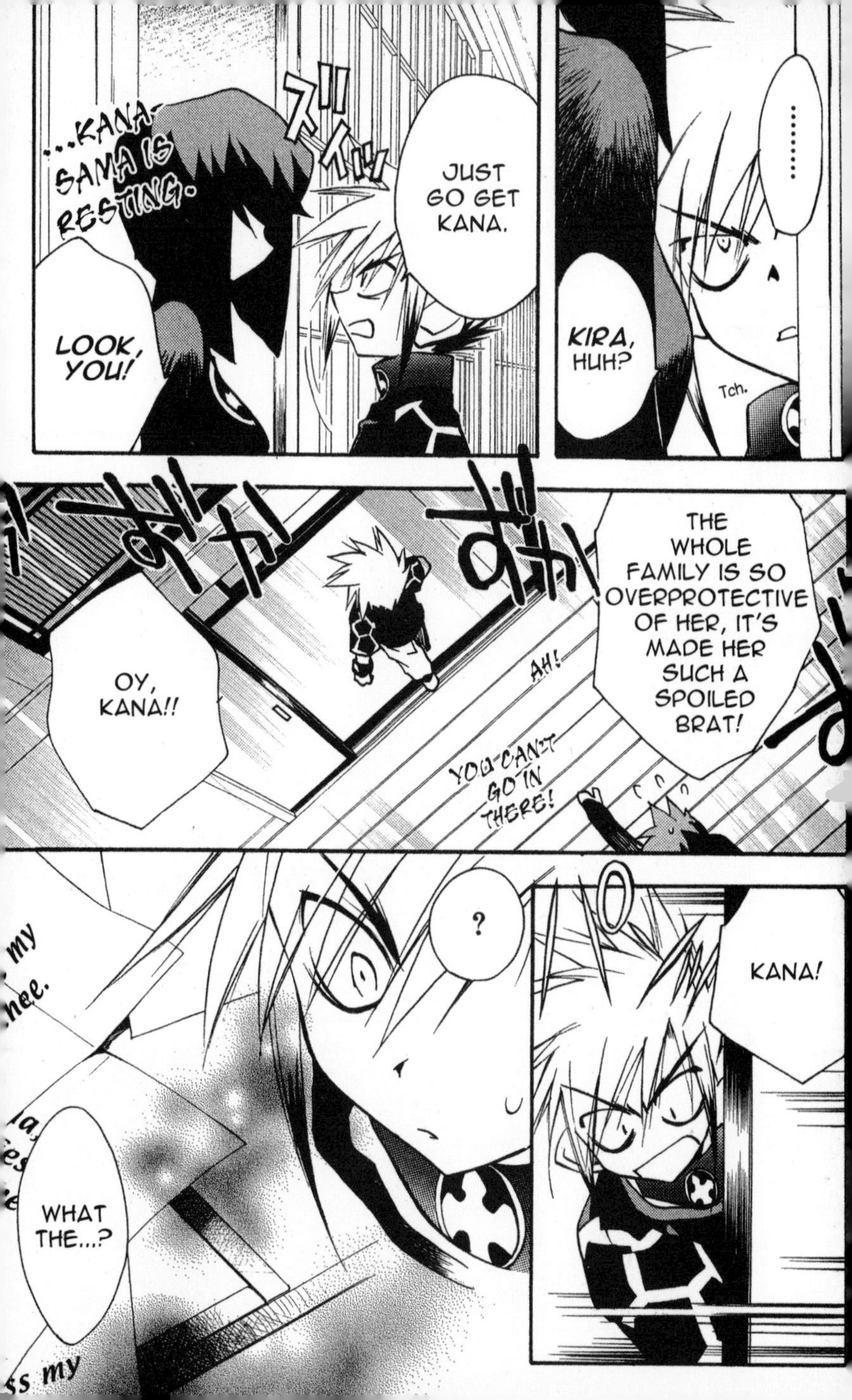
......
KIRA, HUH?
Tch.
JUST GO GET KANA.
...KANA-SAMA IS RESTING.
LOOK, YOU!
THE WHOLE FAMILY IS SO OVERPROTECTIVE OF HER, IT'S MADE HER SUCH A SPOILED BRAT!
AH!
OY, KANA!!
YOU CAN'T GO IN THERE!
KANA!
?
WHAT THE...?

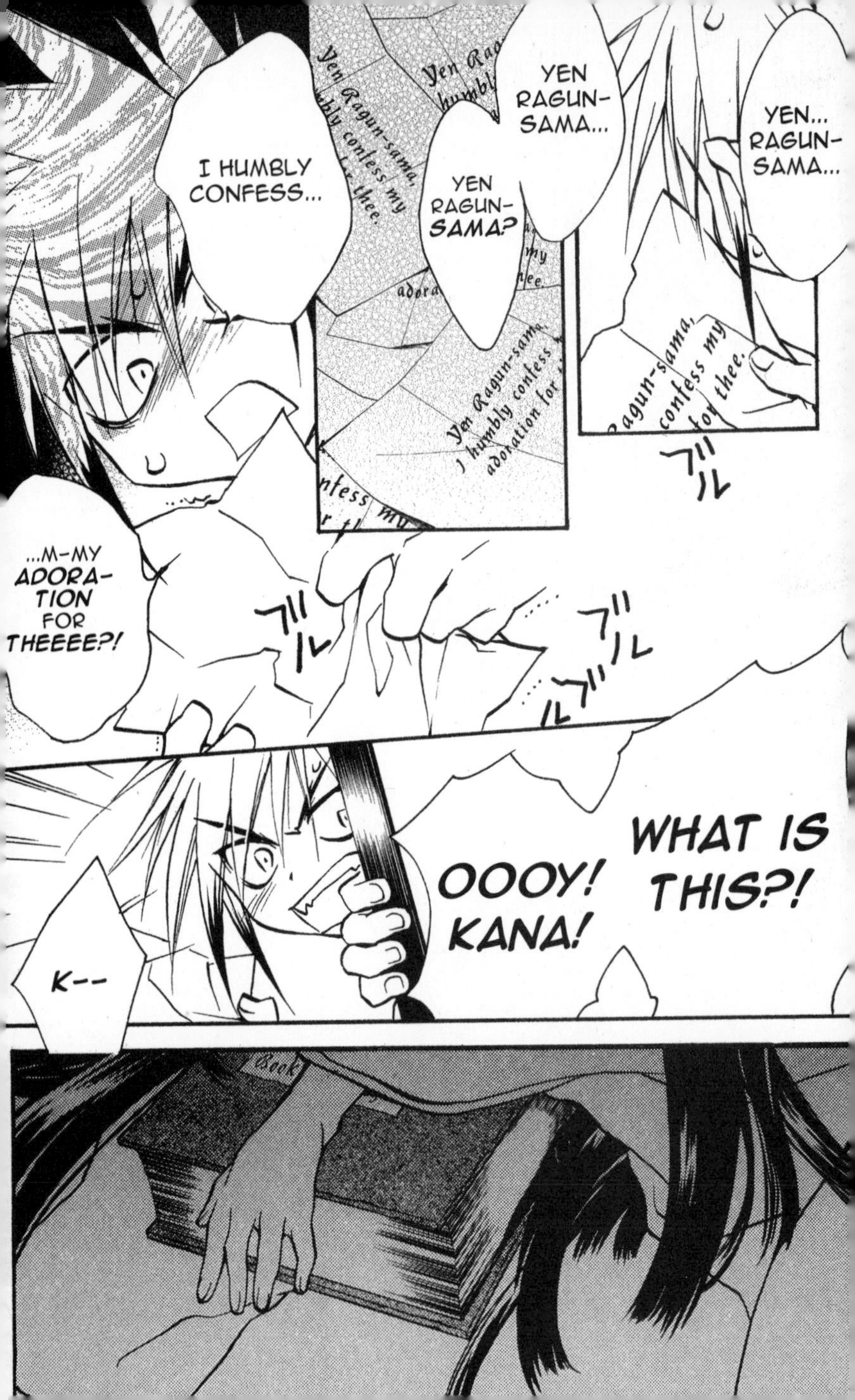

YEN... RAGUN-SAMA...
Ragun-sama, confess my for thee.
YEN RAGUN-SAMA...
YEN RAGUN-SAMA?
Yen Ragun-sama, I humbly confess my adoration for thee.
Yen Ragun-sama, I humbly confess adoration for
I HUMBLY CONFESS...
...M-MY ADORATION FOR THEEEE?!
ブル
ブル
ブル
ブル
WHAT IS THIS?!
OOOY! KANA!
K--
Book

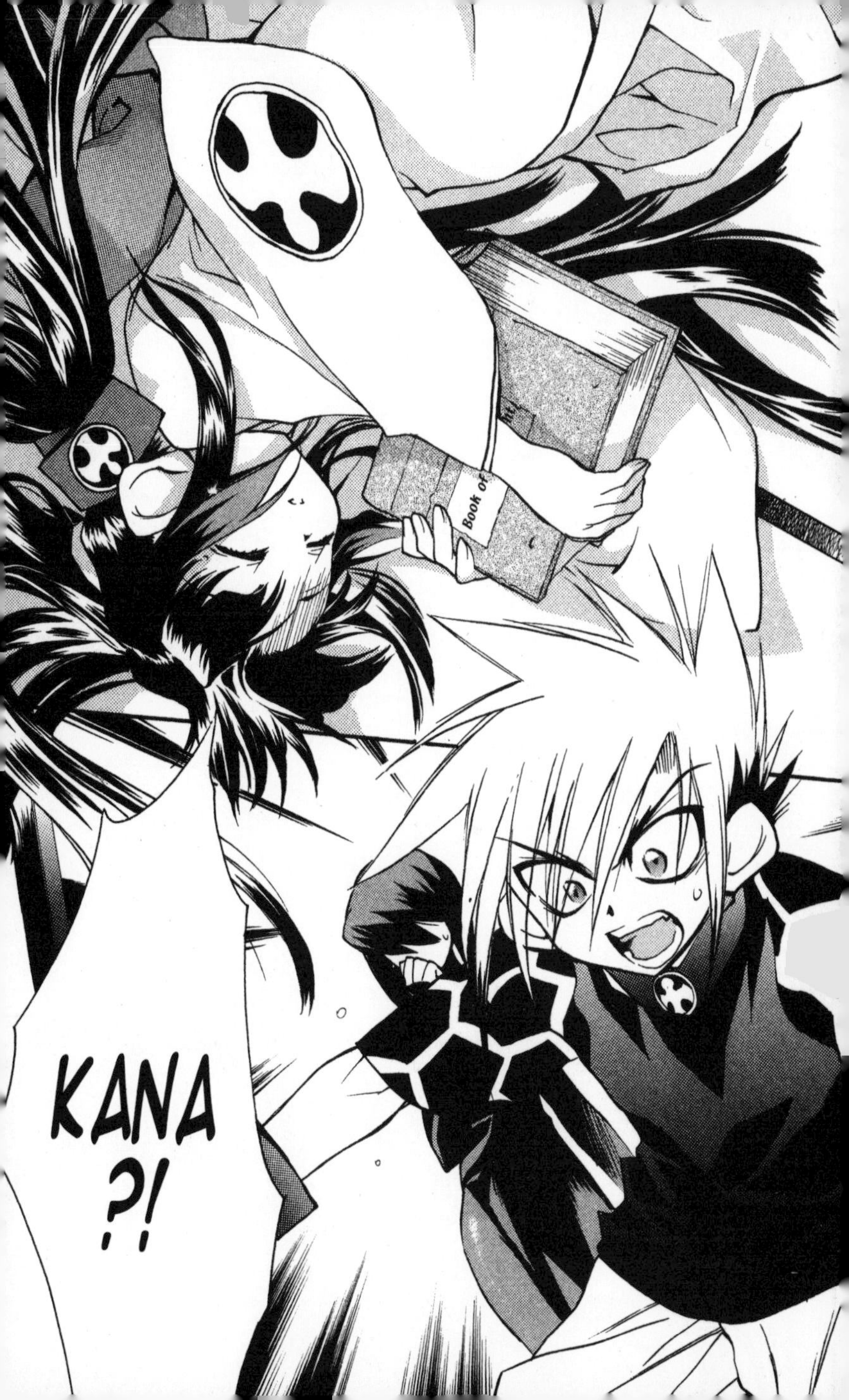
Book of
KANA ?!

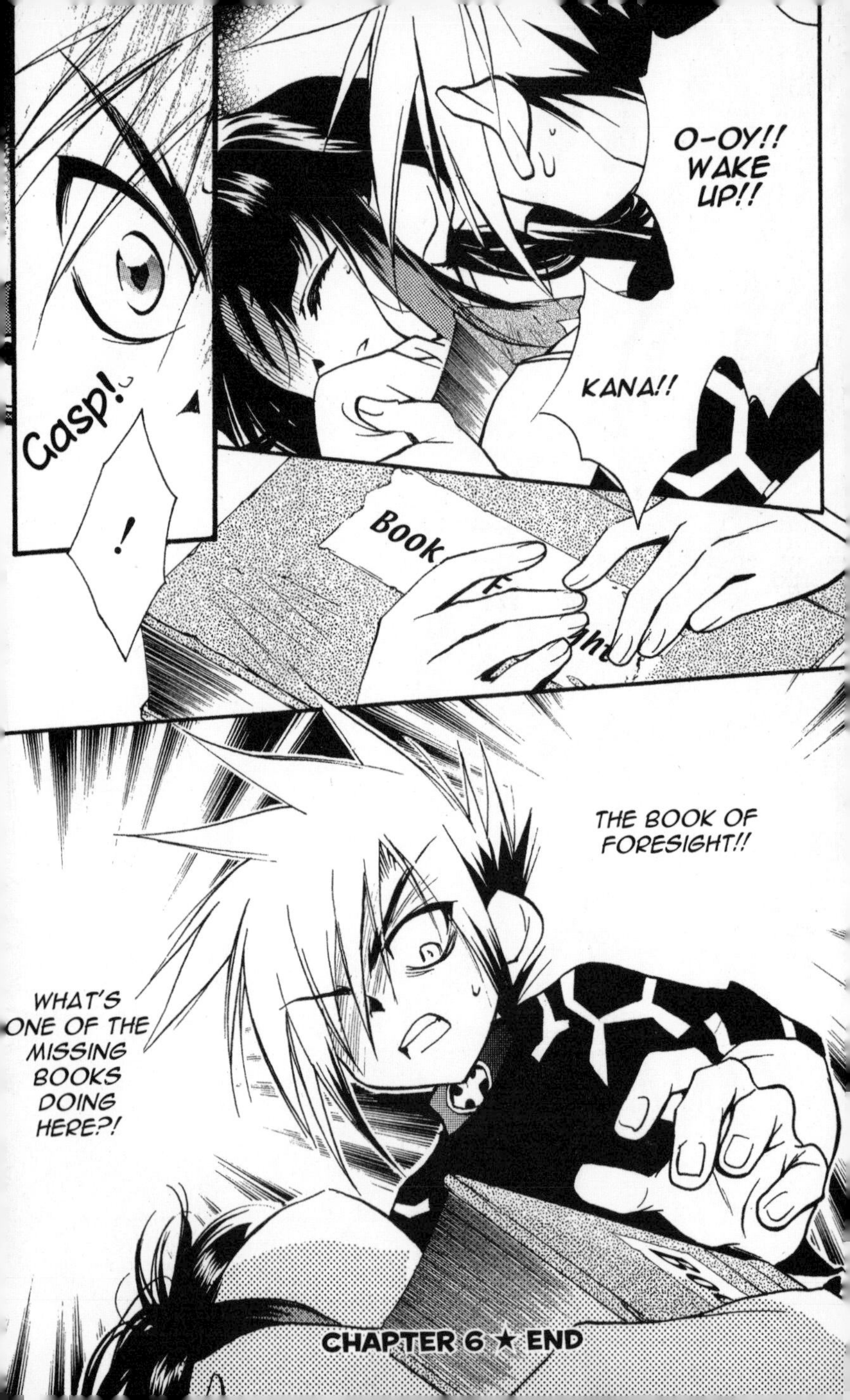
O-OY!! WAKE UP!!
KANA!!
Gasp!
!
Book
THE BOOK OF FORESIGHT!!
WHAT'S ONE OF THE MISSING BOOKS DOING HERE?!
CHAPTER 6 ★ END

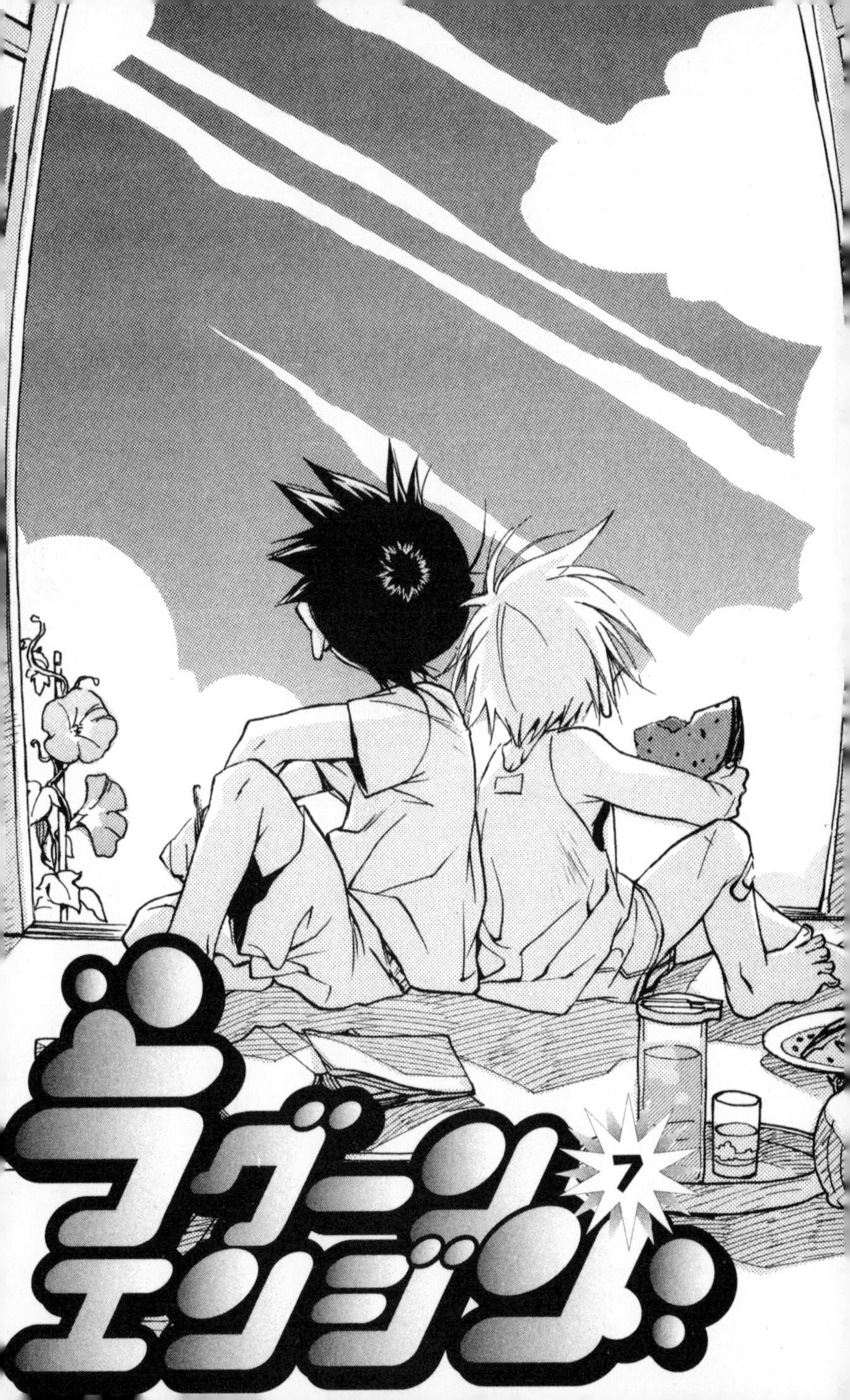
ラグーンエンジン
7

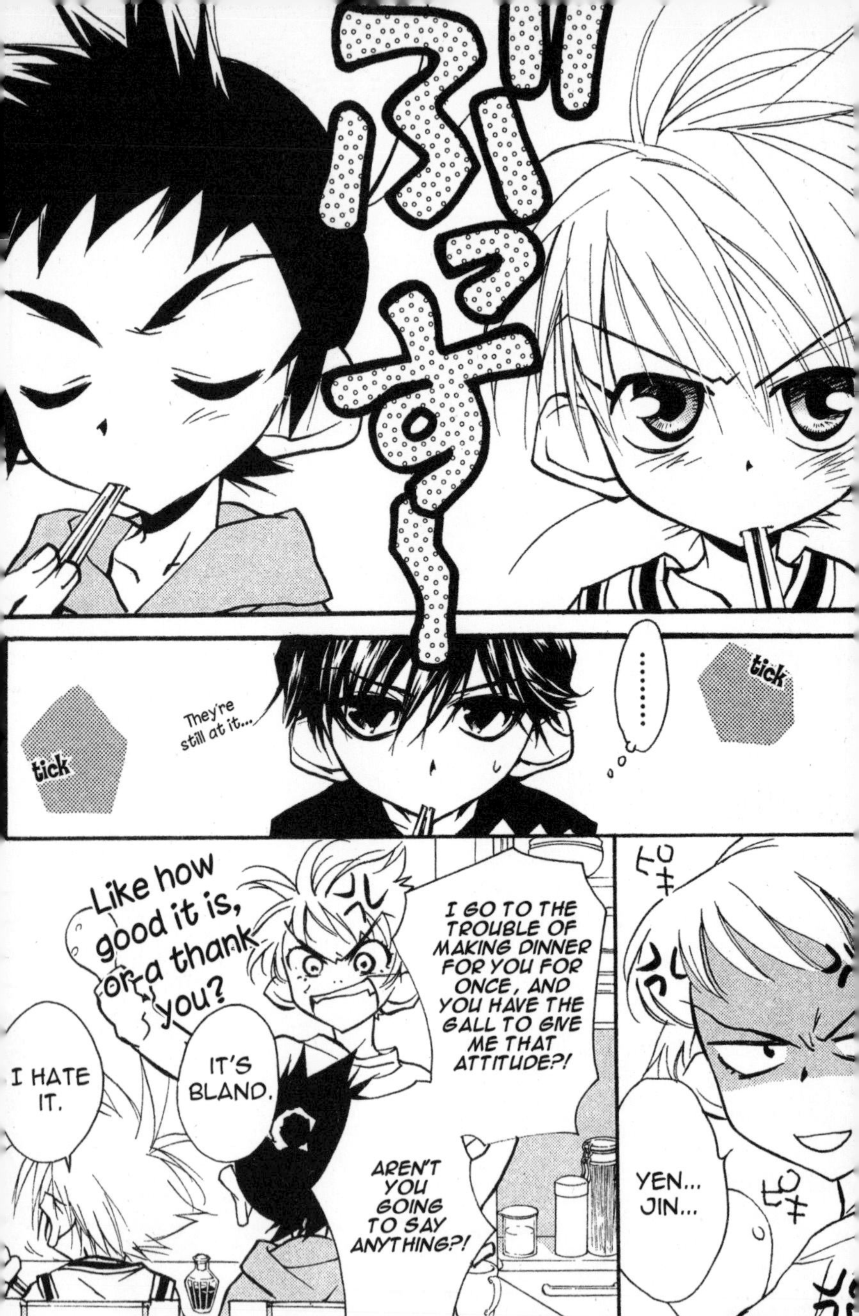
tick
......
They're still at it...
tick
YEN... JIN...
I GO TO THE TROUBLE OF MAKING DINNER FOR YOU FOR ONCE, AND YOU HAVE THE GALL TO GIVE ME THAT ATTITUDE?!
Like how good it is, or a thank you?
AREN'T YOU GOING TO SAY ANYTHING?!
IT'S BLAND.
I HATE IT.

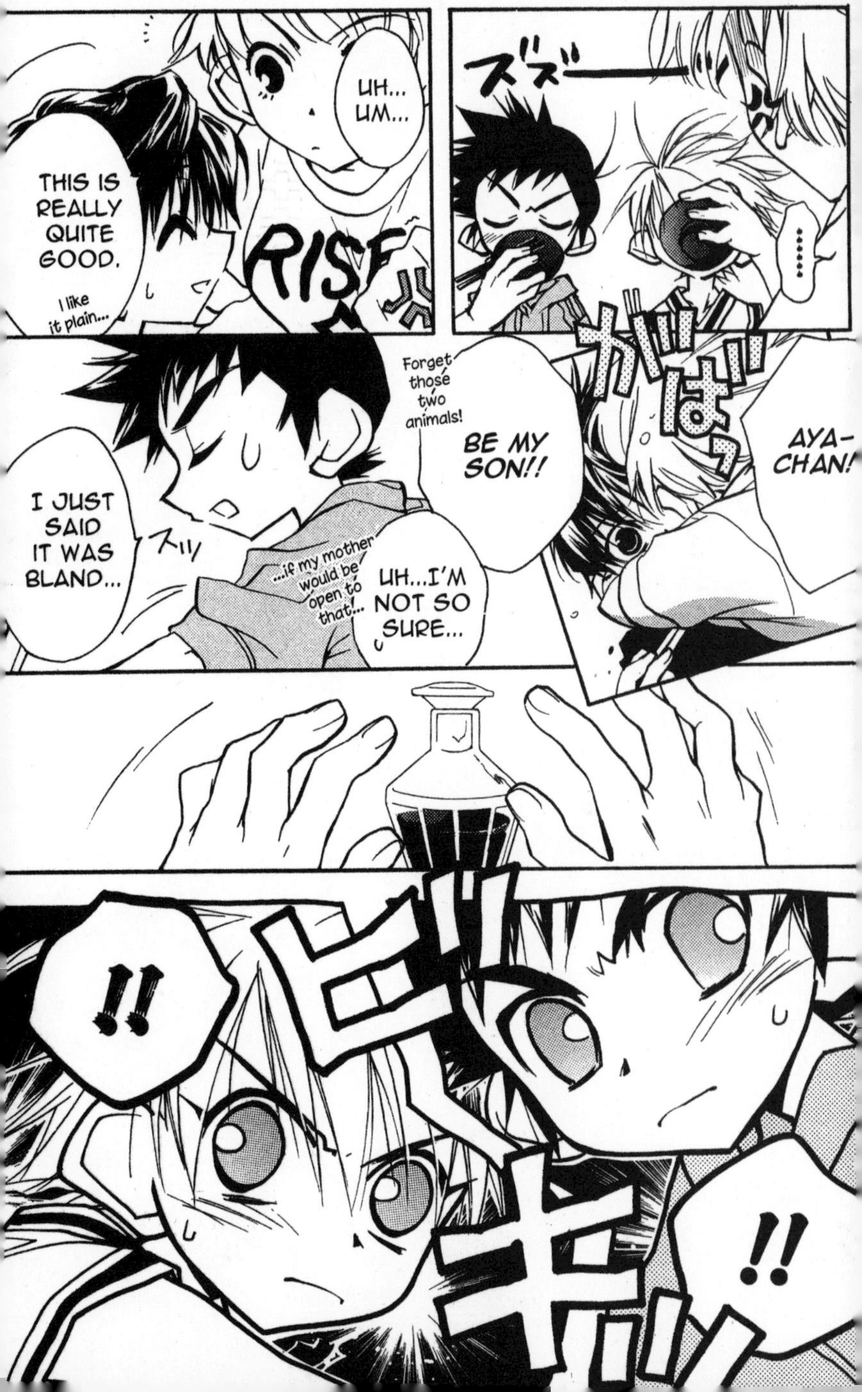
ズズー
......
UH... UM...
THIS IS REALLY QUITE GOOD.
I like it plain...
AYA-CHAN!
がばっ
BE MY SON!!
Forget those two animals!
UH...I'M NOT SO SURE...
...if my mother would be open to that!...
スッ
I JUST SAID IT WAS BLAND...
!!
ビキッ
!!

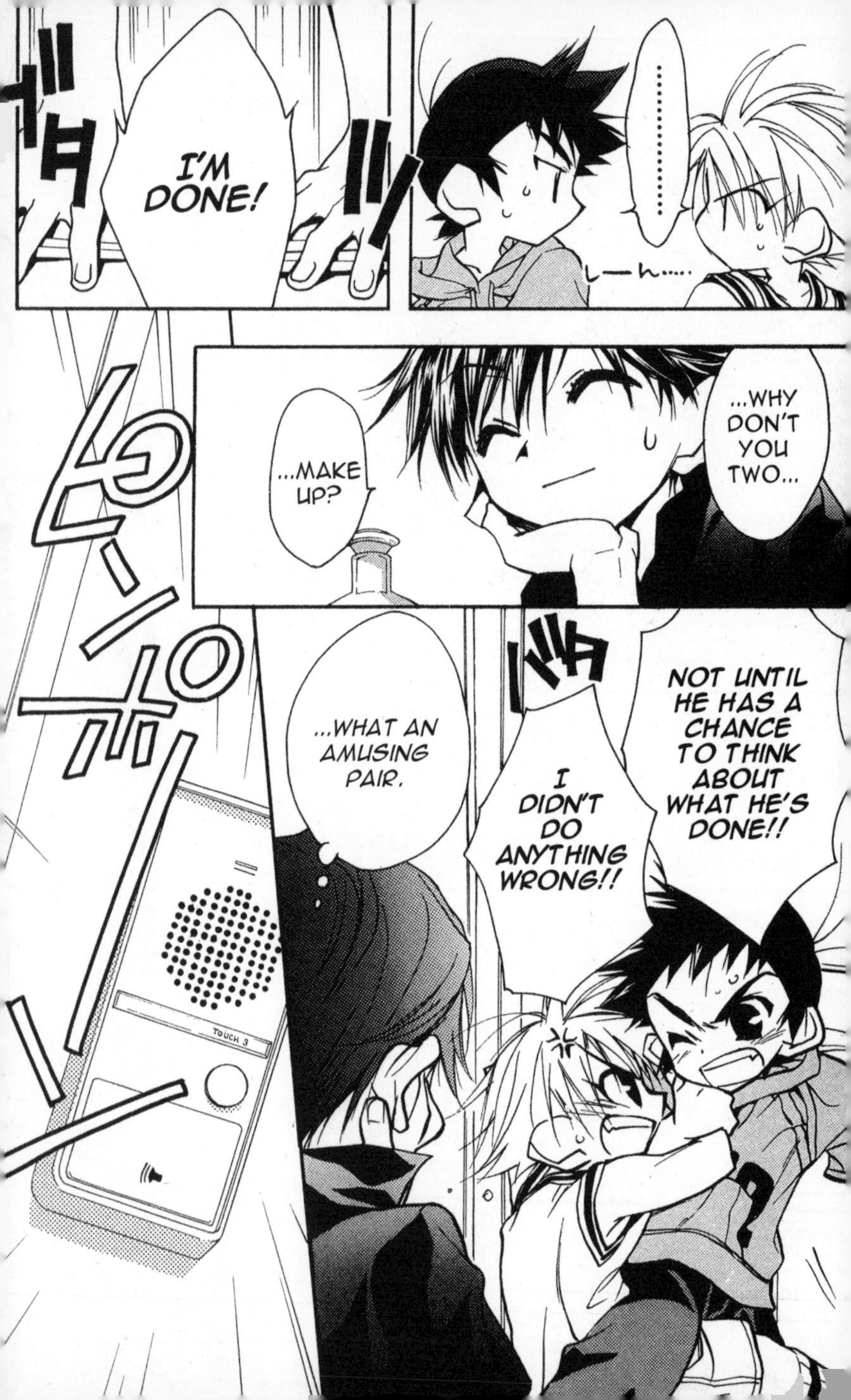
......
I'M DONE!
...WHY DON'T YOU TWO...
...MAKE UP?
NOT UNTIL HE HAS A CHANCE TO THINK ABOUT WHAT HE'S DONE!!
I DIDN'T DO ANYTHING WRONG!!
...WHAT AN AMUSING PAIR.
TOUCH 3

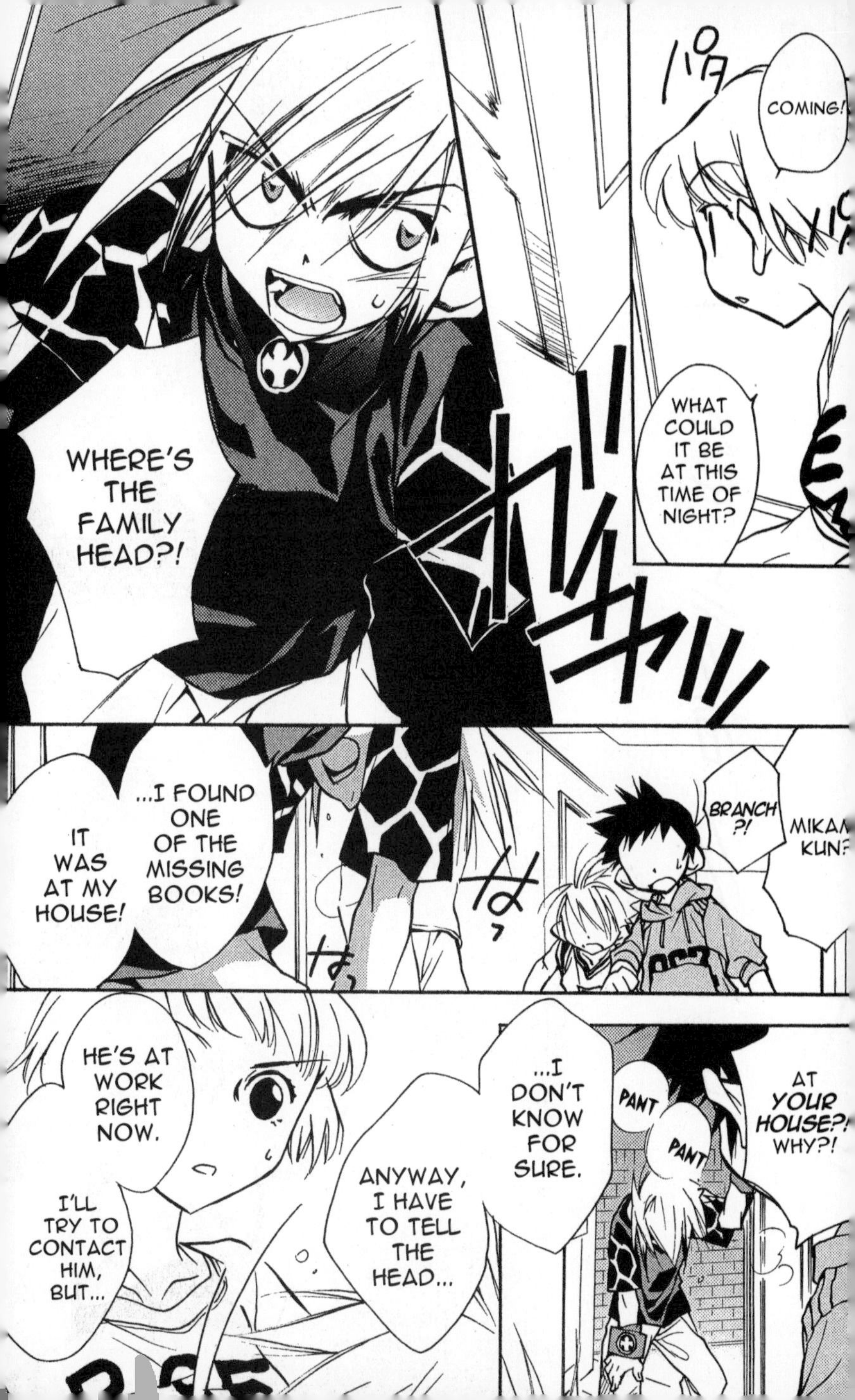
COMING!
WHAT COULD IT BE AT THIS TIME OF NIGHT?
WHERE'S THE FAMILY HEAD?!
MIKAM KUN?
BRANCH?!
...I FOUND ONE OF THE MISSING BOOKS!
IT WAS AT MY HOUSE!
AT YOUR HOUSE?! WHY?!
PANT
PANT
...I DON'T KNOW FOR SURE.
ANYWAY, I HAVE TO TELL THE HEAD...
HE'S AT WORK RIGHT NOW.
I'LL TRY TO CONTACT HIM, BUT...

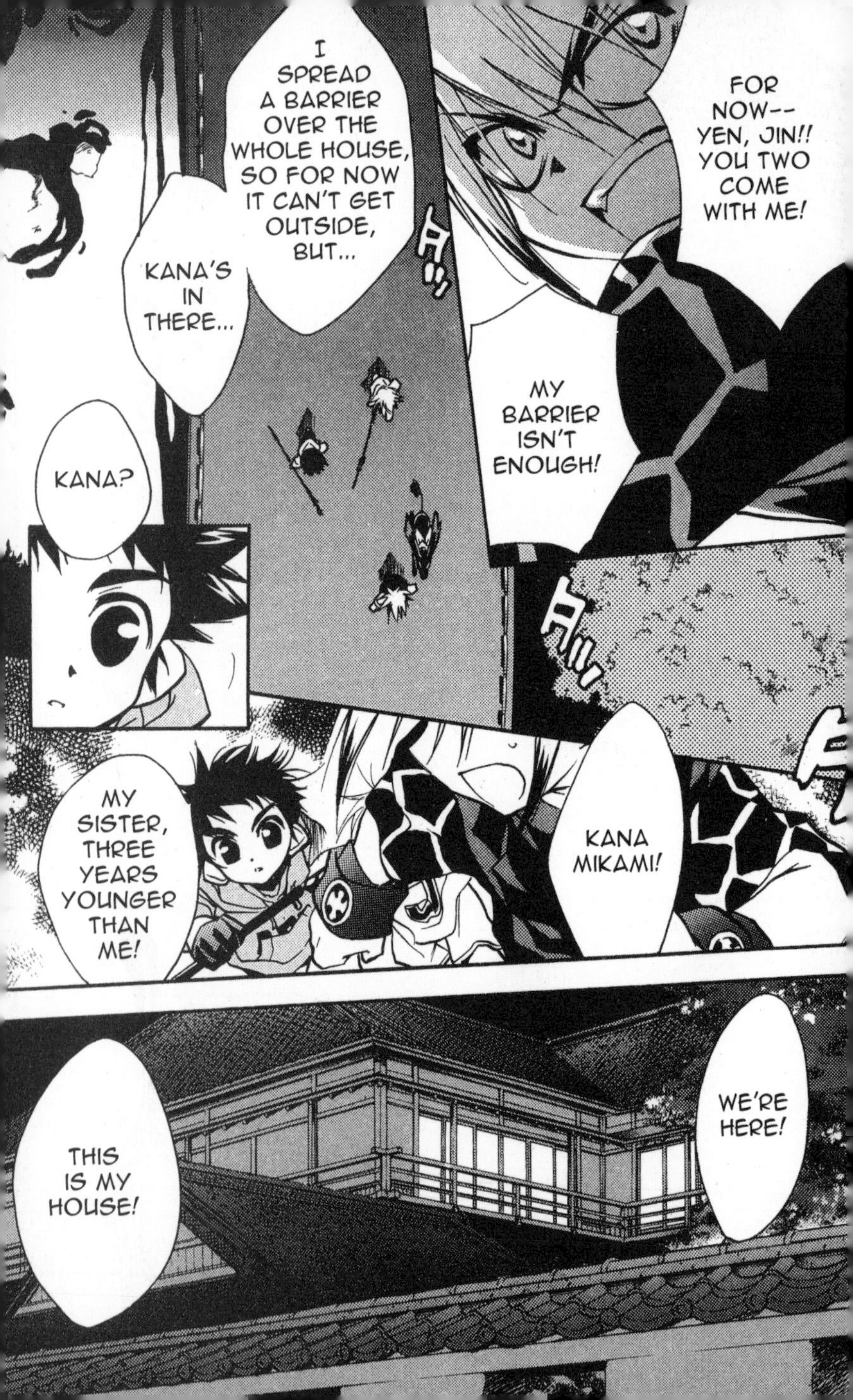
FOR NOW-- YEN, JIN!! YOU TWO COME WITH ME!
MY BARRIER ISN'T ENOUGH!
I SPREAD A BARRIER OVER THE WHOLE HOUSE, SO FOR NOW IT CAN'T GET OUTSIDE, BUT...
KANA'S IN THERE...
KANA?
KANA MIKAMI!
MY SISTER, THREE YEARS YOUNGER THAN ME!
WE'RE HERE!
THIS IS MY HOUSE!

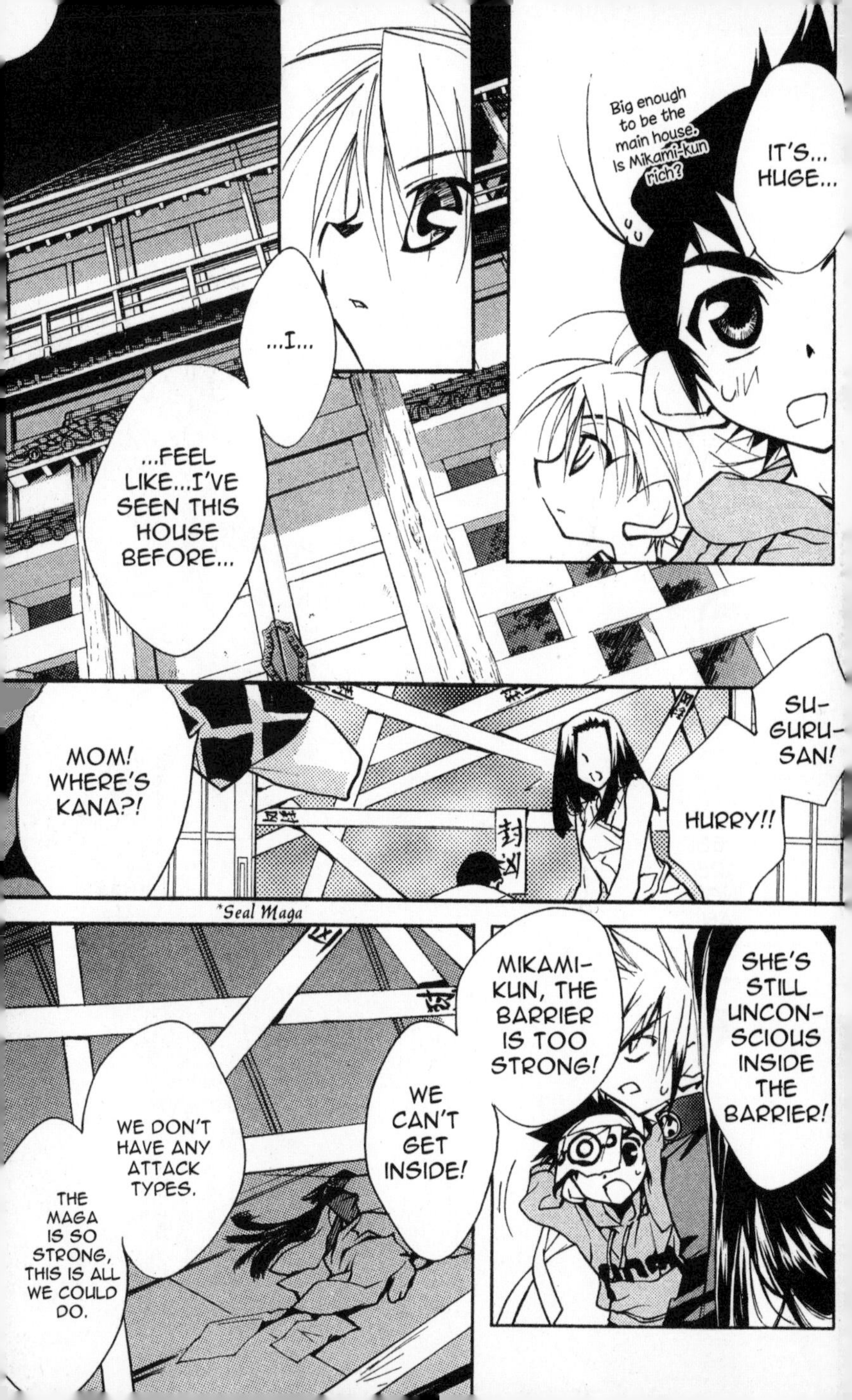
IT'S... HUGE...
Big enough to be the main house. Is Mikami-kun rich?
...I...
...FEEL LIKE...I'VE SEEN THIS HOUSE BEFORE...
SU-GURU-SAN!
HURRY!!
MOM! WHERE'S KANA?!
*Seal Maga
SHE'S STILL UNCONSCIOUS INSIDE THE BARRIER!
MIKAMI-KUN, THE BARRIER IS TOO STRONG!
WE CAN'T GET INSIDE!
WE DON'T HAVE ANY ATTACK TYPES.
THE MAGA IS SO STRONG, THIS IS ALL WE COULD DO.

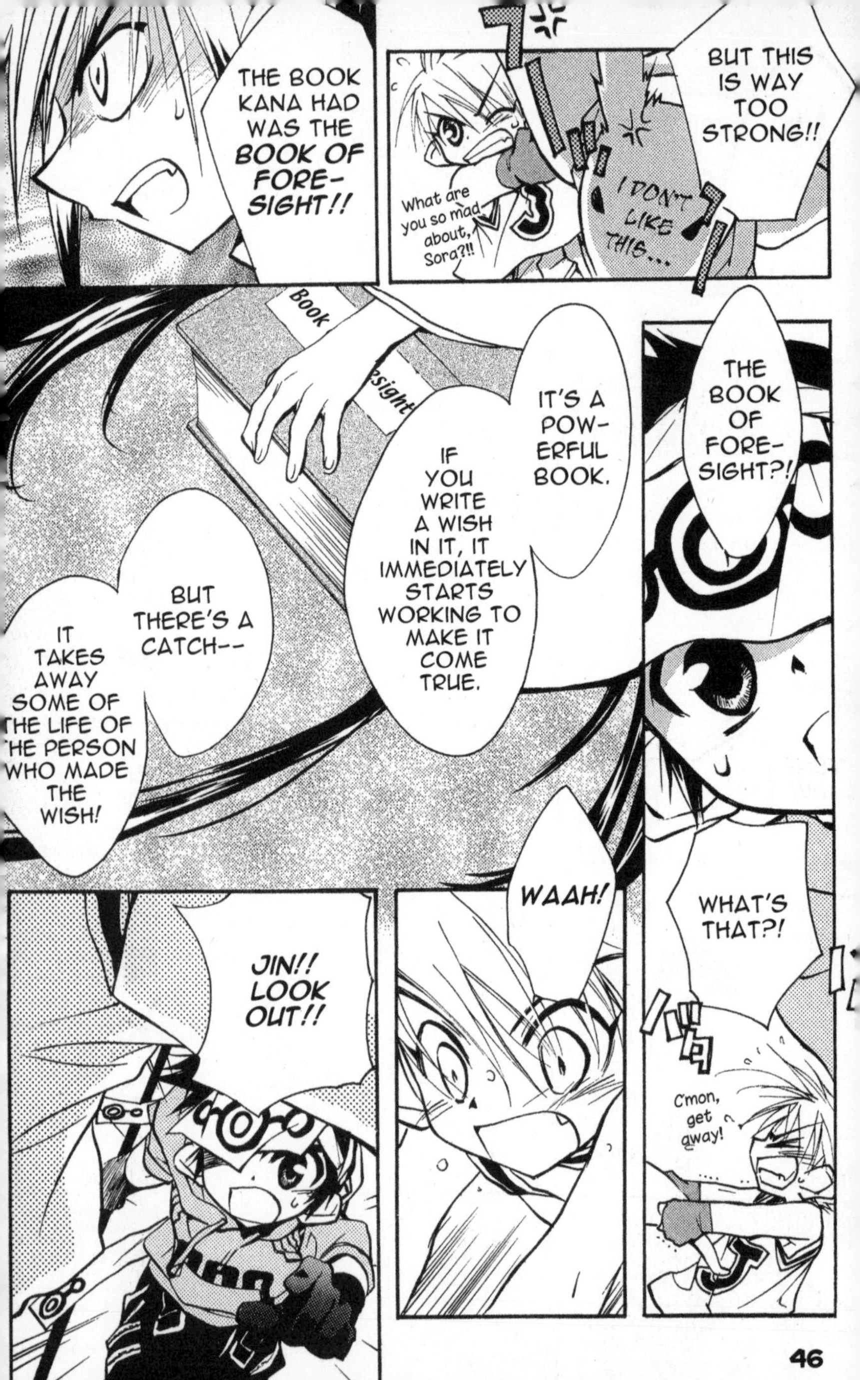
BUT THIS IS WAY TOO STRONG!!
I DON'T LIKE THIS...
What are you so mad about, Sora?!!
THE BOOK KANA HAD WAS THE BOOK OF FORE-SIGHT!!
THE BOOK OF FORE-SIGHT?!
Book
IT'S A POW-ERFUL BOOK.
IF YOU WRITE A WISH IN IT, IT IMMEDIATELY STARTS WORKING TO MAKE IT COME TRUE.
BUT THERE'S A CATCH--
IT TAKES AWAY SOME OF THE LIFE OF THE PERSON WHO MADE THE WISH!
WHAT'S THAT?!
C'mon, get away!
WAAH!
JIN!! LOOK OUT!!

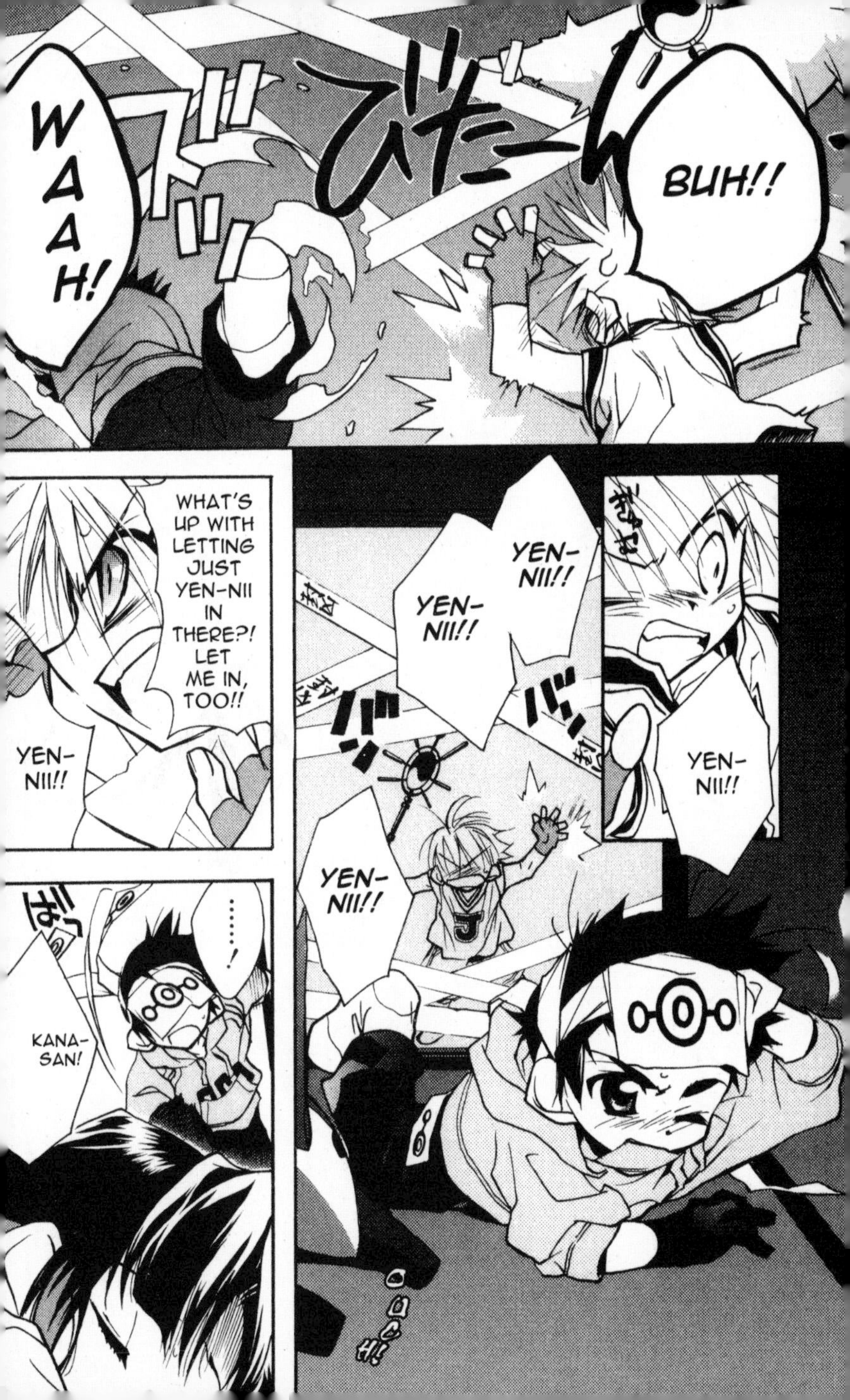

BUH!!
WAAH!
YEN-NII!!
YEN-NII!!
YEN-NII!!
YEN-NII!!
WHAT'S UP WITH LETTING JUST YEN-NII IN THERE?! LET ME IN, TOO!!
YEN-NII!!
......!
KANA-SAN!

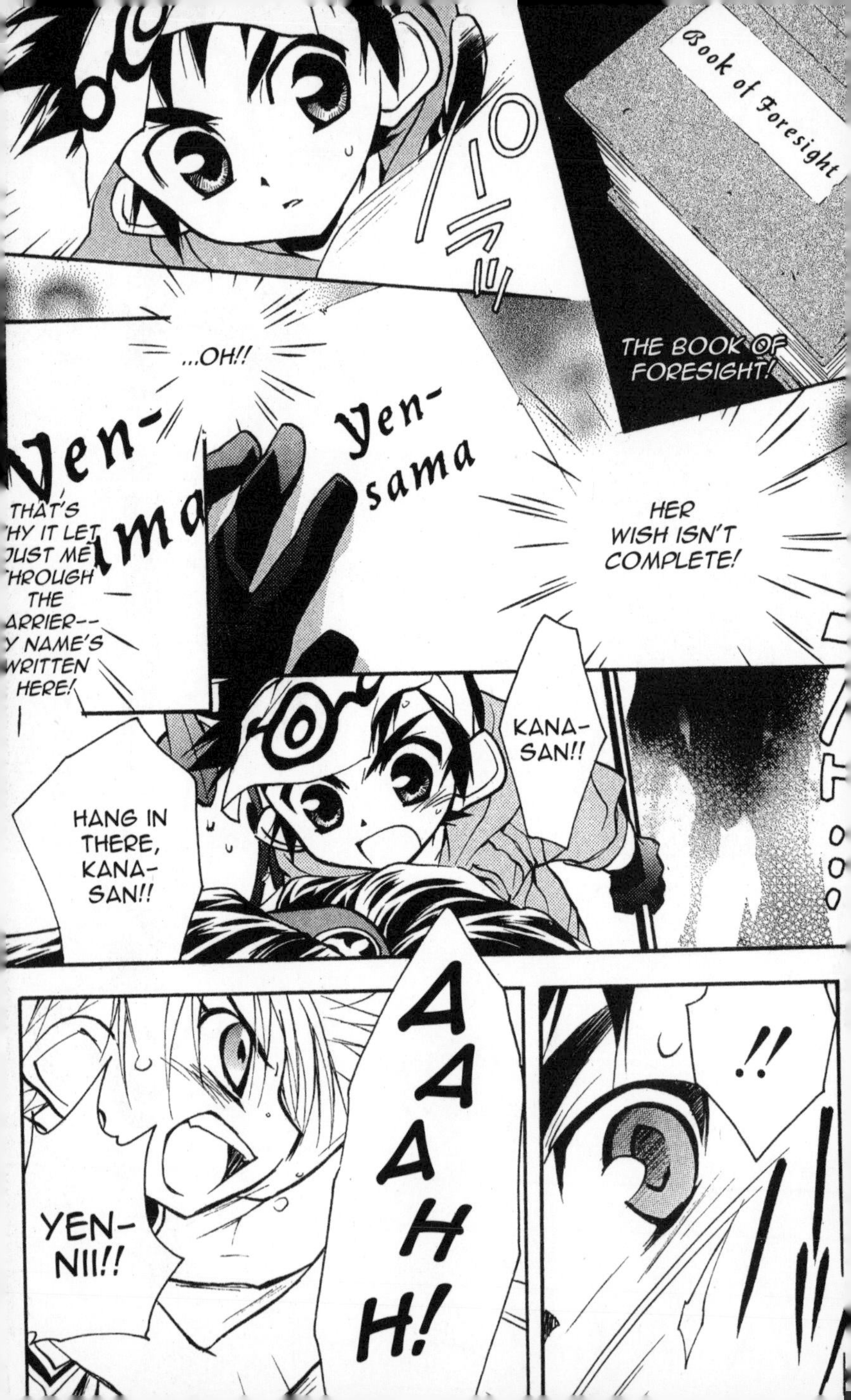
Book of Foresight
THE BOOK OF FORESIGHT!
HER WISH ISN'T COMPLETE!
...OH!!
Yen- sama
Yen- ima
THAT'S HY IT LET JUST ME HROUGH THE ARRIER-- Y NAME'S WRITTEN HERE!
KANA-SAN!!
HANG IN THERE, KANA-SAN!!
!!
AAAHH!
YEN-NII!!

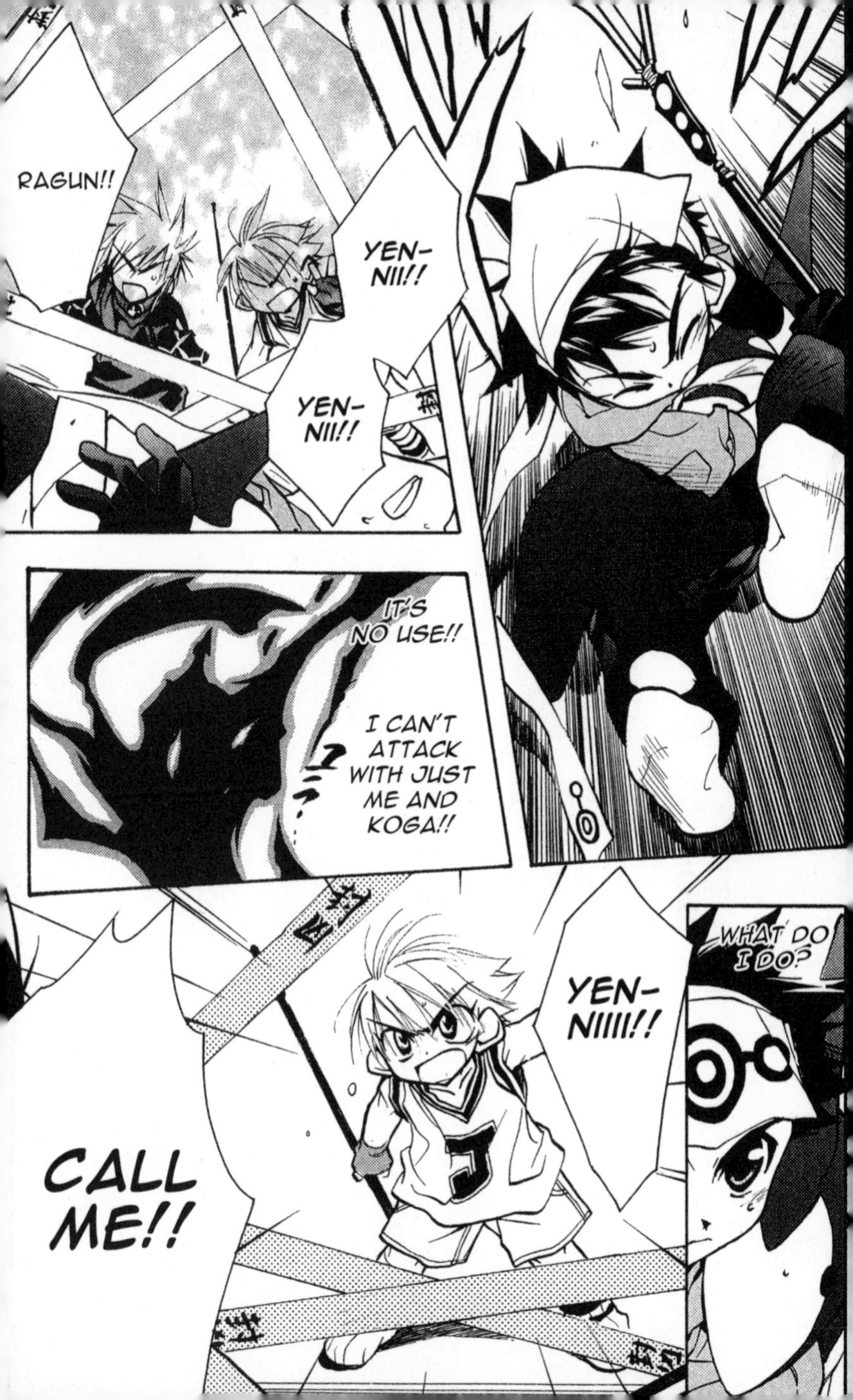
YEN-NII!!
YEN-NII!!
RAGUN!!
IT'S NO USE!!
I CAN'T ATTACK WITH JUST ME AND KOGA!!
WHAT DO I DO?
YEN-NIIII!!
CALL ME!!

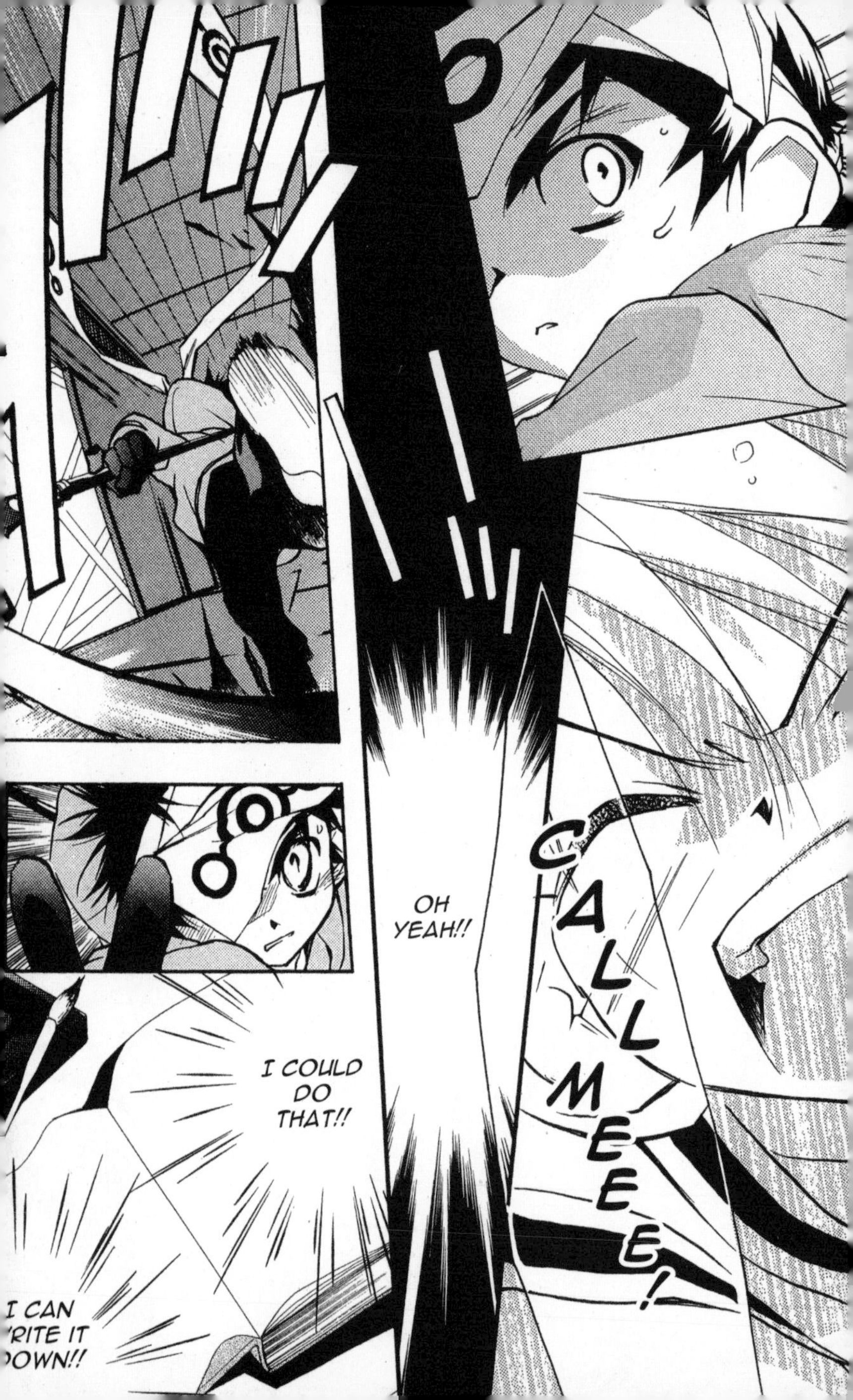
CALL MEEEE!
OH YEAH!!
I COULD DO THAT!!
I CAN RITE IT OWN!!

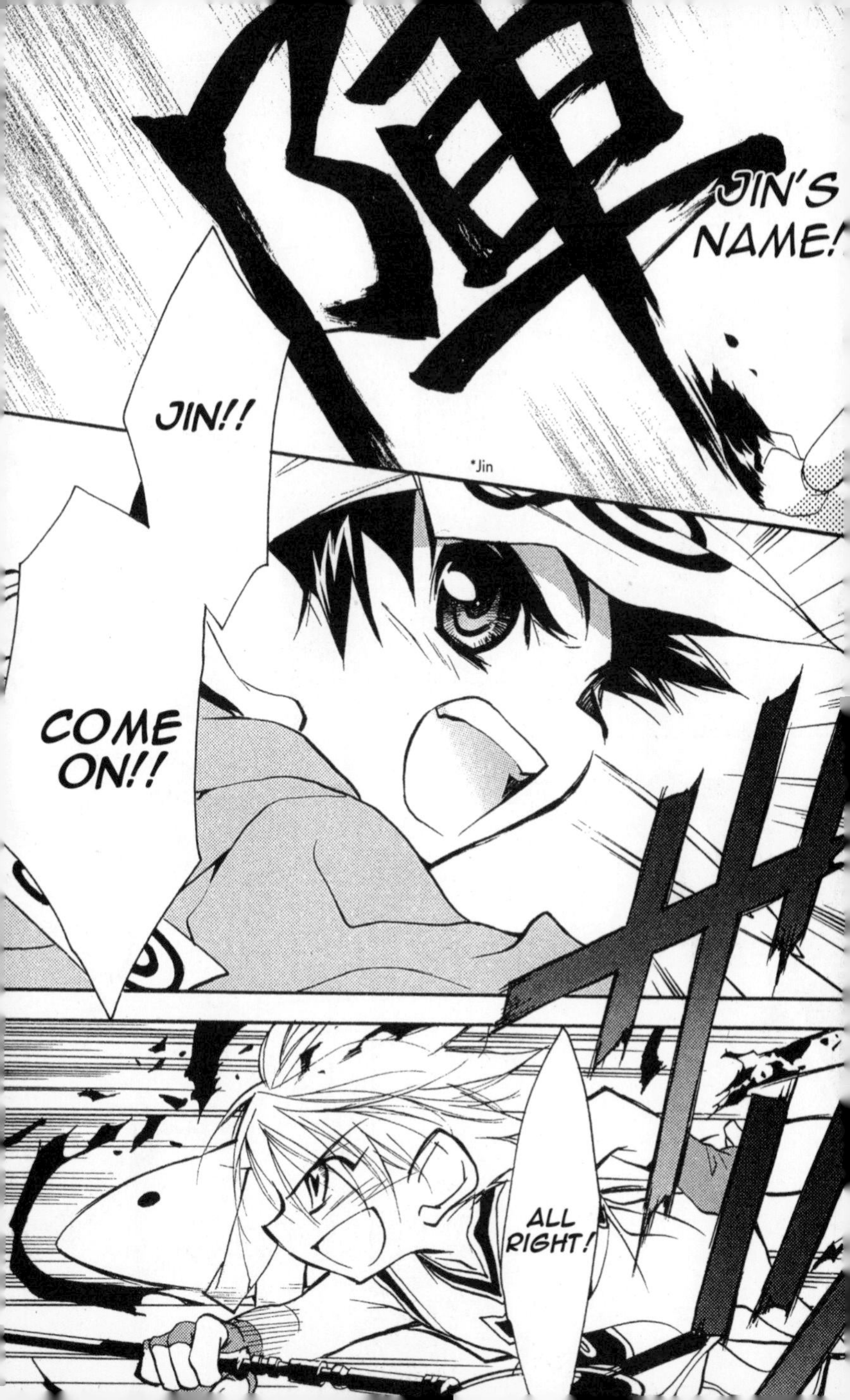
JIN'S NAME!
*Jin
JIN!!
COME ON!!
ALL RIGHT!

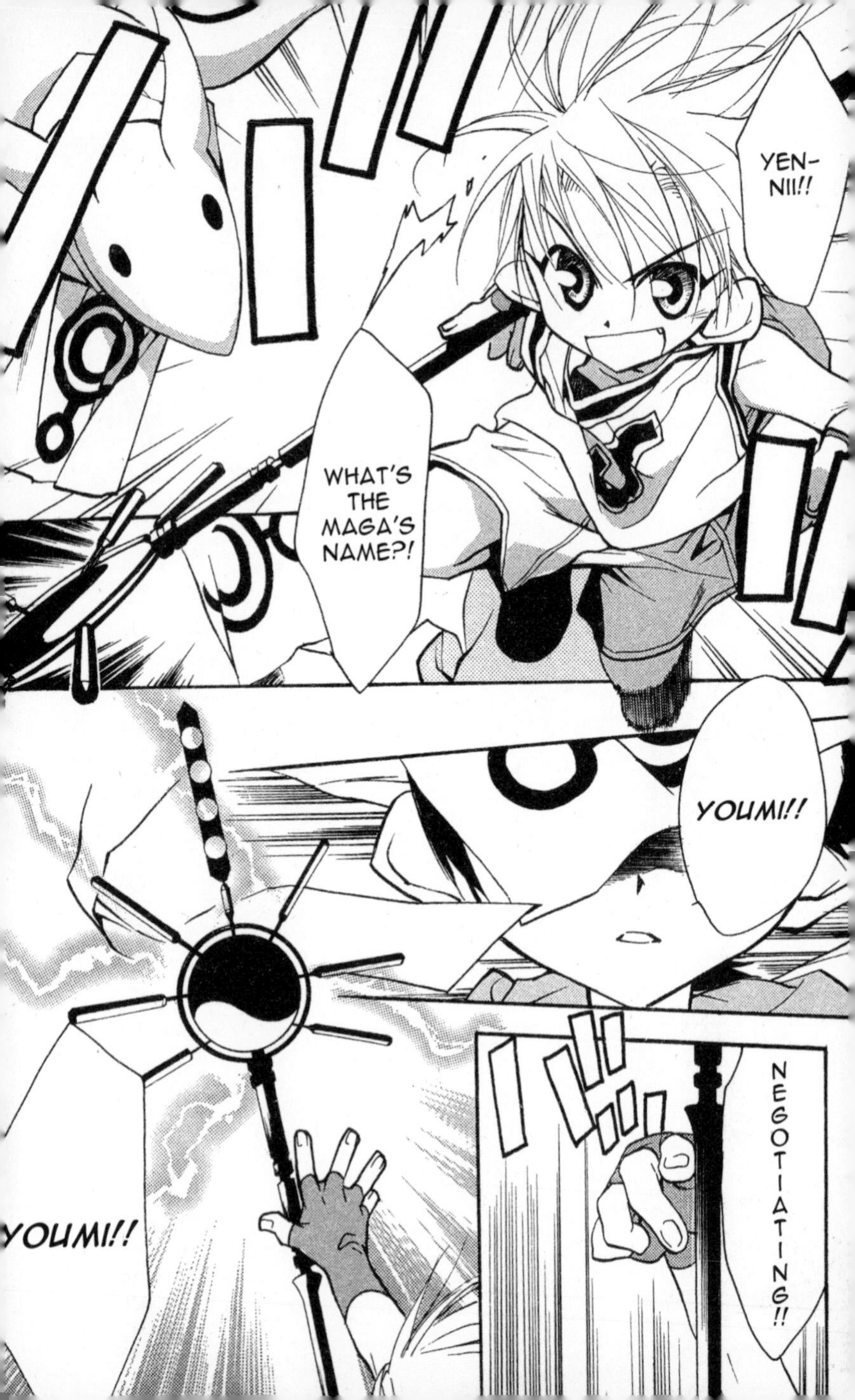
YEN-NII!!
WHAT'S THE MAGA'S NAME?!
YOUMI!!
NEGOTIATING!!
YOUMI!!

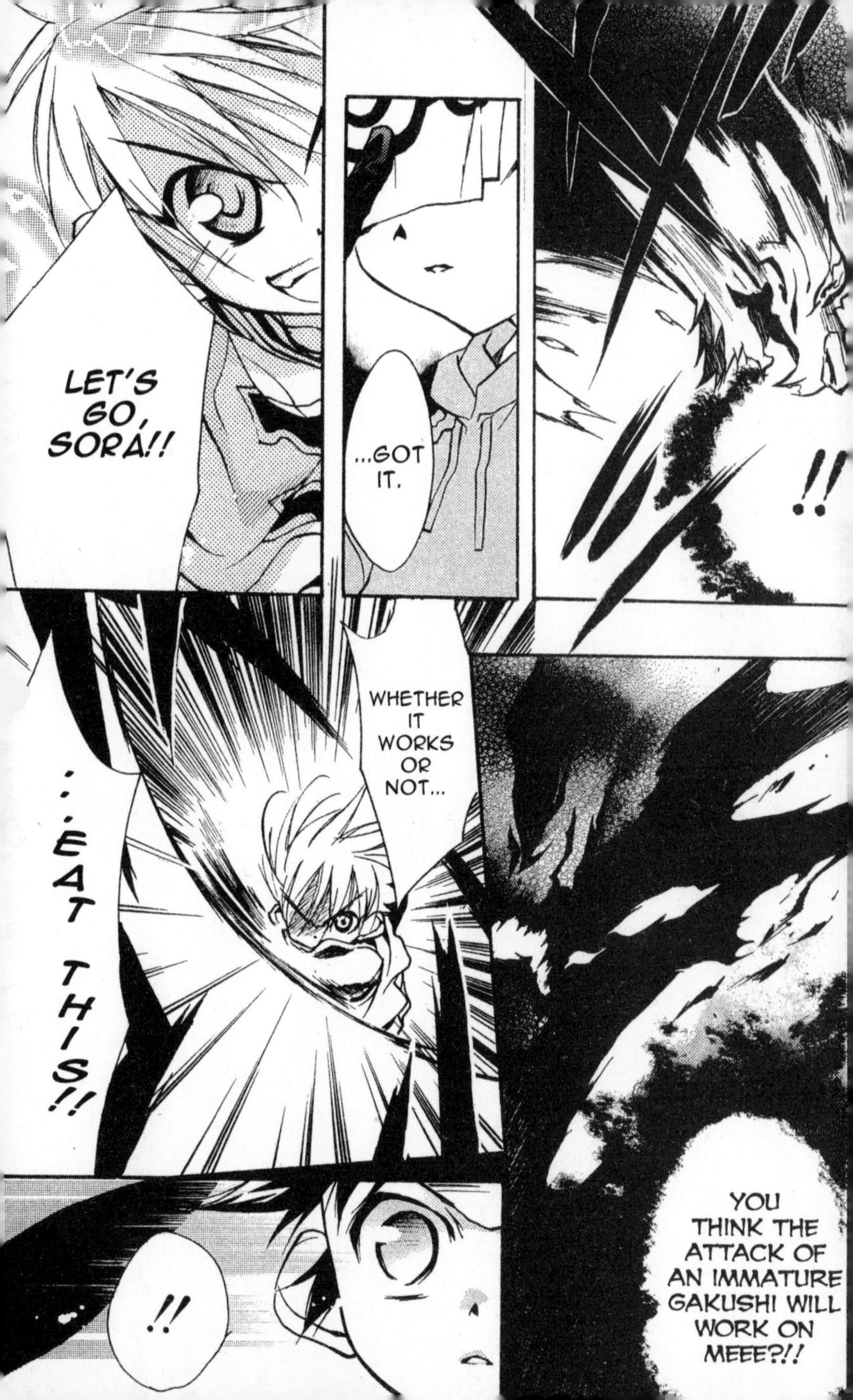
!!
...GOT IT.
LET'S GO, SORA!!
YOU THINK THE ATTACK OF AN IMMATURE GAKUSHI WILL WORK ON MEEE?!!
WHETHER IT WORKS OR NOT...
...EAT THIS!!
!!

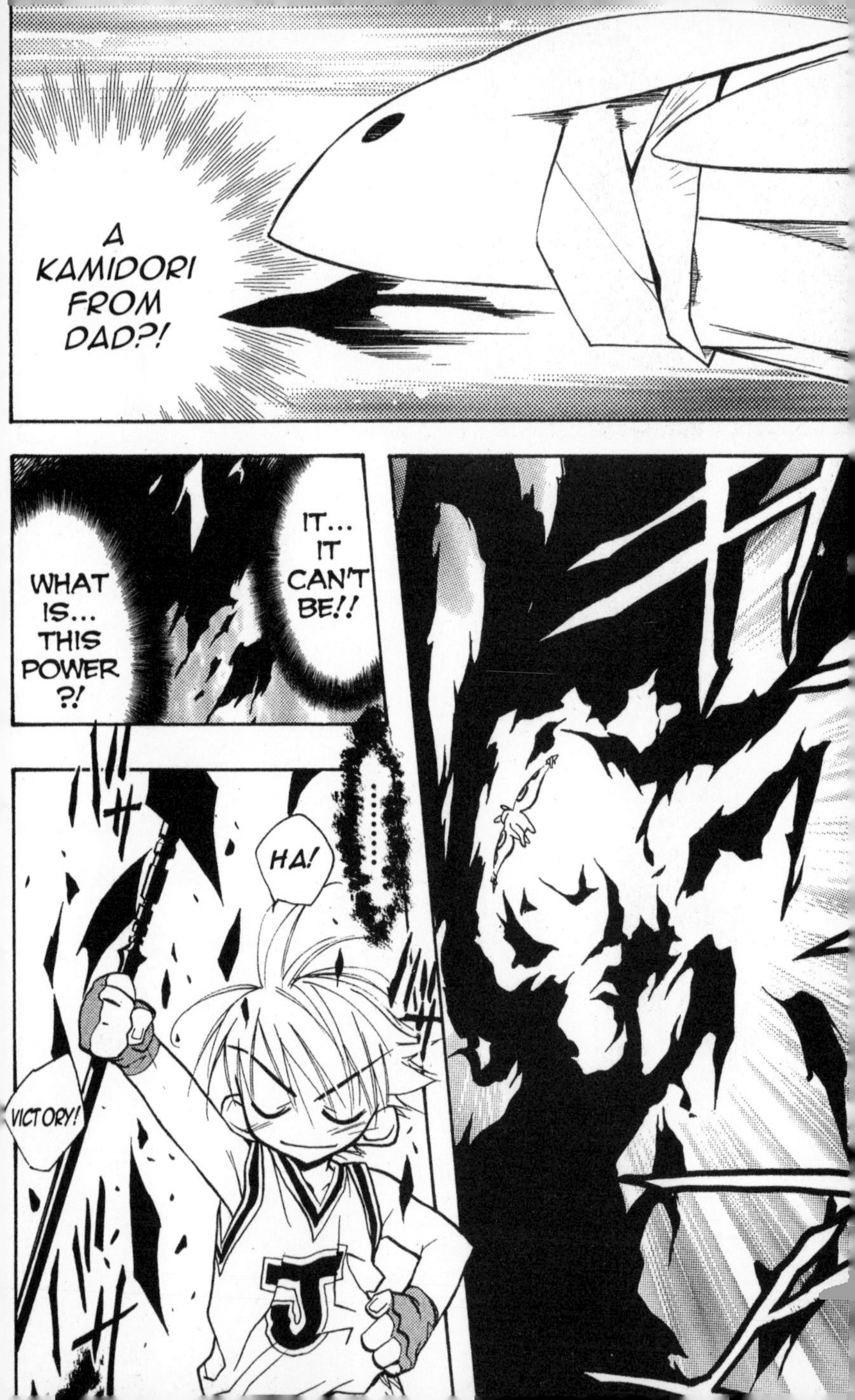
A KAMIDORI FROM DAD?!
IT... IT CAN'T BE!!
WHAT IS... THIS POWER?!
......
HA!
VICTORY!

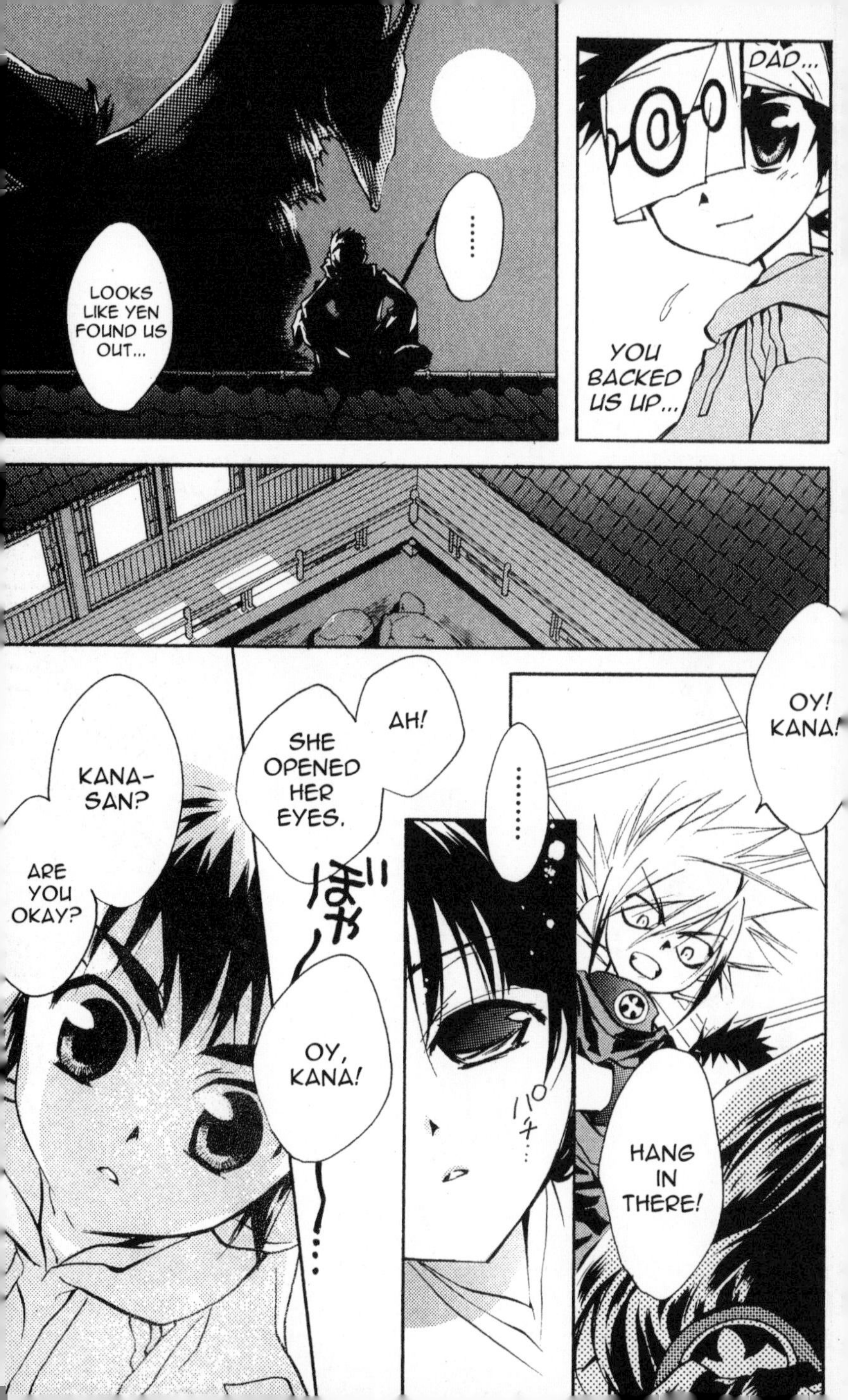
DAD...
YOU BACKED US UP...
......
LOOKS LIKE YEN FOUND US OUT...
OY! KANA!
....
ハッ...
HANG IN THERE!
AH!
SHE OPENED HER EYES.
ぼや〜
OY, KANA!
...
KANA-SAN?
ARE YOU OKAY?

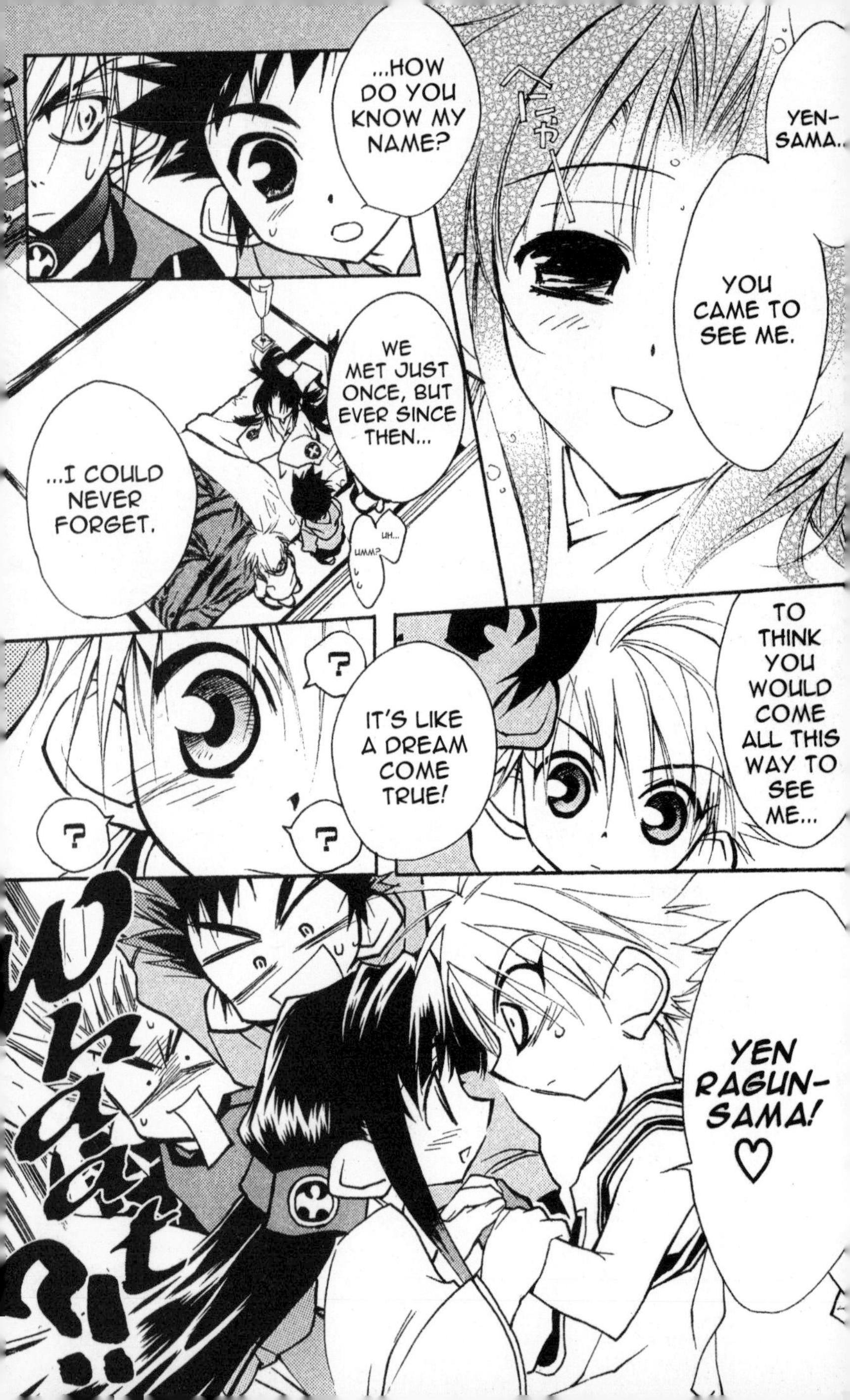
YEN-SAMA..
YOU CAME TO SEE ME.
...HOW DO YOU KNOW MY NAME?
WE MET JUST ONCE, BUT EVER SINCE THEN...
...I COULD NEVER FORGET.
UH... UMM?
TO THINK YOU WOULD COME ALL THIS WAY TO SEE ME...
IT'S LIKE A DREAM COME TRUE!
?
?
?
YEN RAGUN-SAMA! ♡

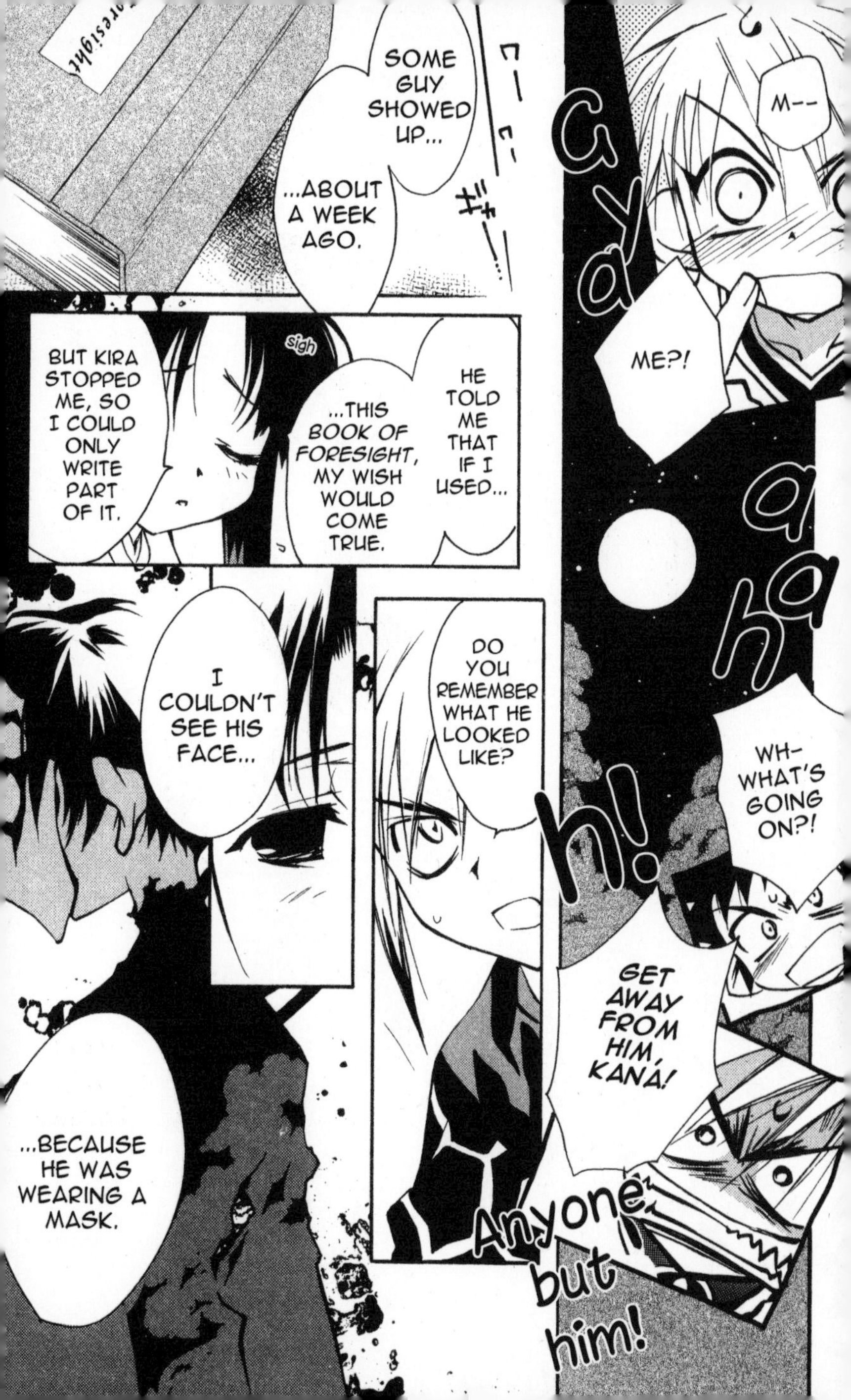
M--
ME?!
Gyaaahh!
WH-WHAT'S GOING ON?!
GET AWAY FROM HIM, KANA!
Anyone but him!
Foresight
SOME GUY SHOWED UP...
...ABOUT A WEEK AGO.
HE TOLD ME THAT IF I USED...
...THIS BOOK OF FORESIGHT, MY WISH WOULD COME TRUE.
sigh
BUT KIRA STOPPED ME, SO I COULD ONLY WRITE PART OF IT.
DO YOU REMEMBER WHAT HE LOOKED LIKE?
I COULDN'T SEE HIS FACE...
...BECAUSE HE WAS WEARING A MASK.

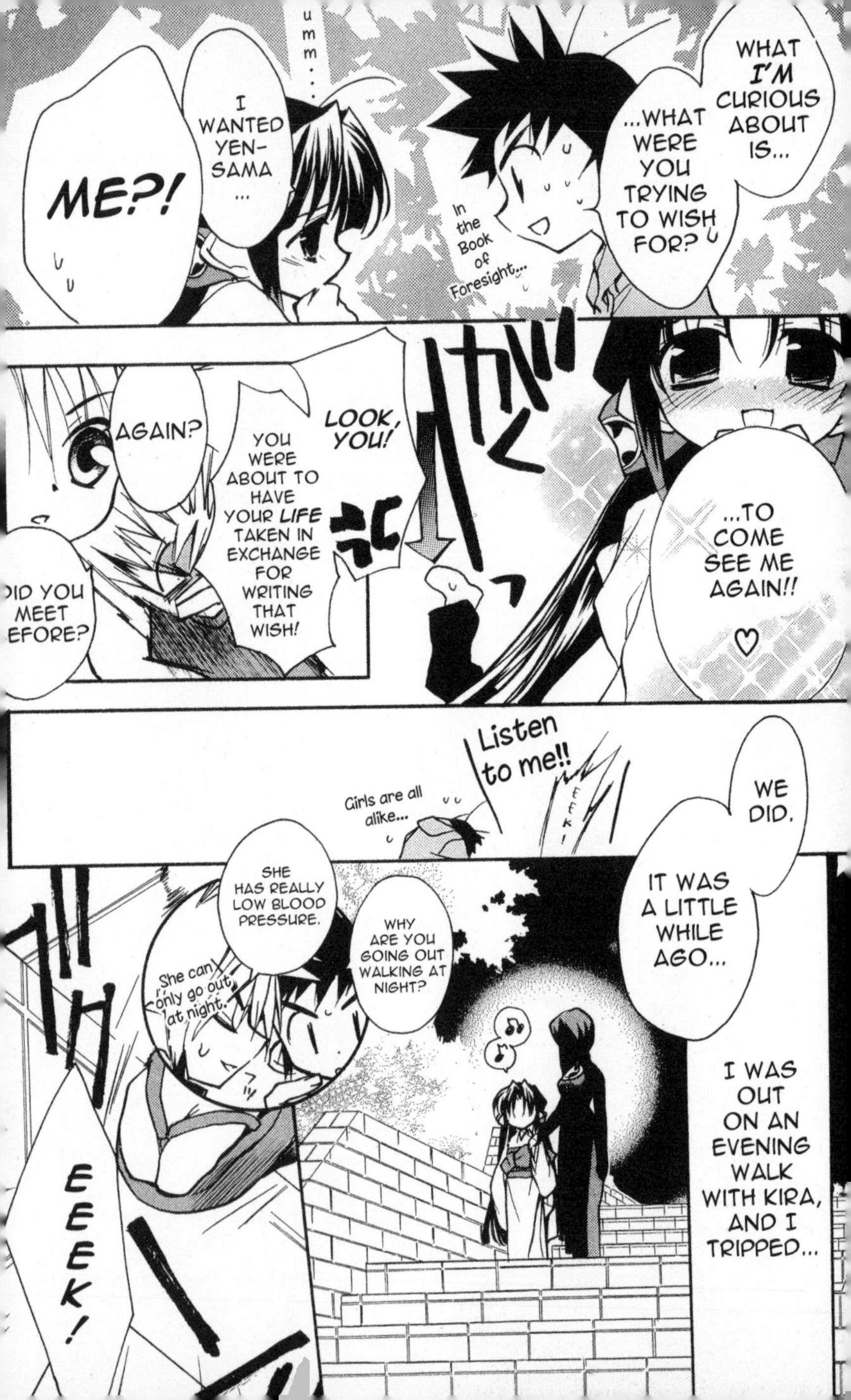
WHAT I'M CURIOUS ABOUT IS...
...WHAT WERE YOU TRYING TO WISH FOR?
In the Book of Foresight...
umm...
I WANTED YEN-SAMA...
ME?!
...TO COME SEE ME AGAIN!! ♡
LOOK, YOU!
YOU WERE ABOUT TO HAVE YOUR LIFE TAKEN IN EXCHANGE FOR WRITING THAT WISH!
AGAIN?
ID YOU MEET EFORE?
WE DID.
Listen to me!!
EEEK!
Girls are all alike...
IT WAS A LITTLE WHILE AGO...
I WAS OUT ON AN EVENING WALK WITH KIRA, AND I TRIPPED...
WHY ARE YOU GOING OUT WALKING AT NIGHT?
SHE HAS REALLY LOW BLOOD PRESSURE.
She can only go out at night.
EEEEK!

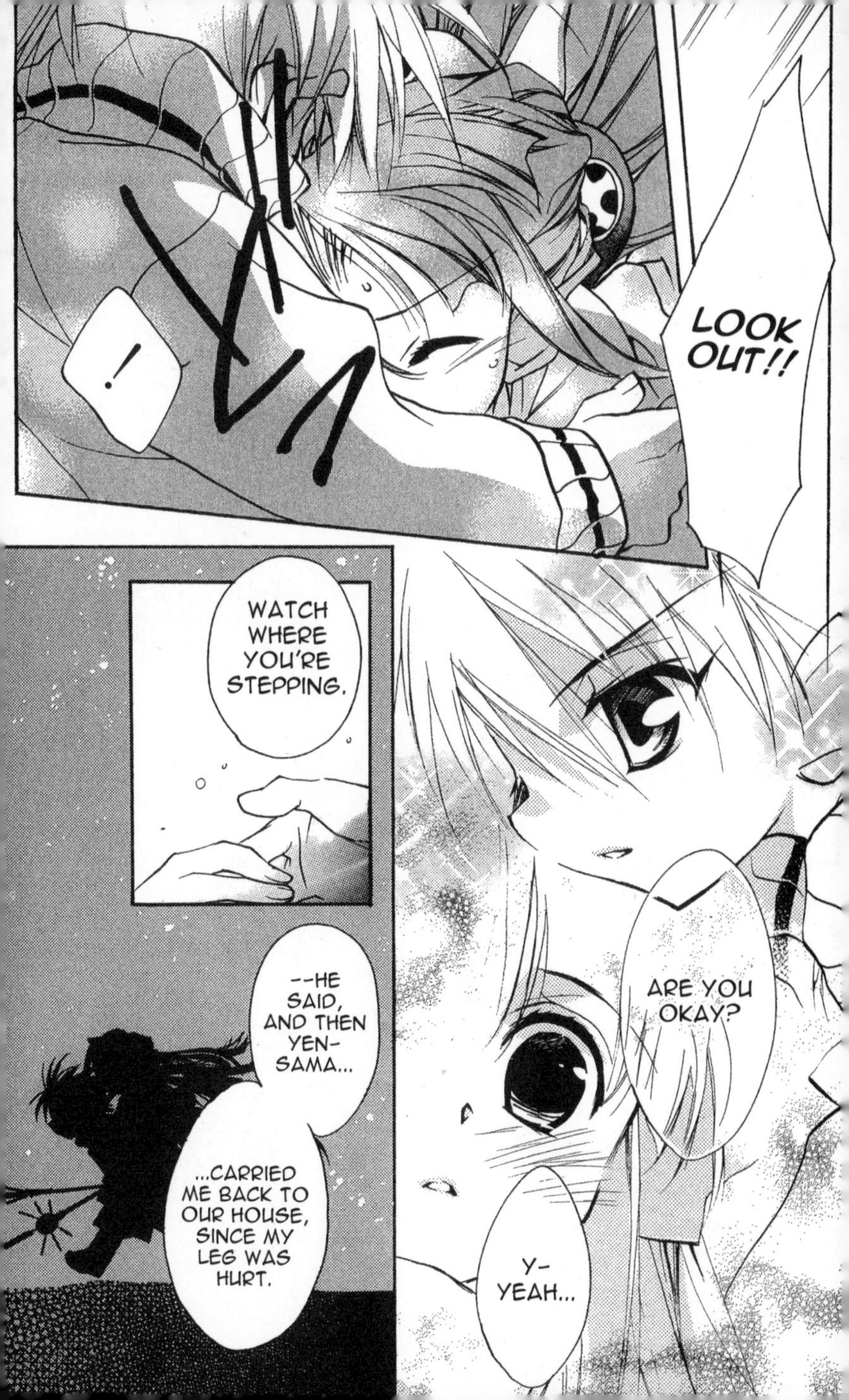
LOOK OUT!!
!
ARE YOU OKAY?
Y-YEAH...
WATCH WHERE YOU'RE STEPPING.
--HE SAID, AND THEN YEN-SAMA...
...CARRIED ME BACK TO OUR HOUSE, SINCE MY LEG WAS HURT.

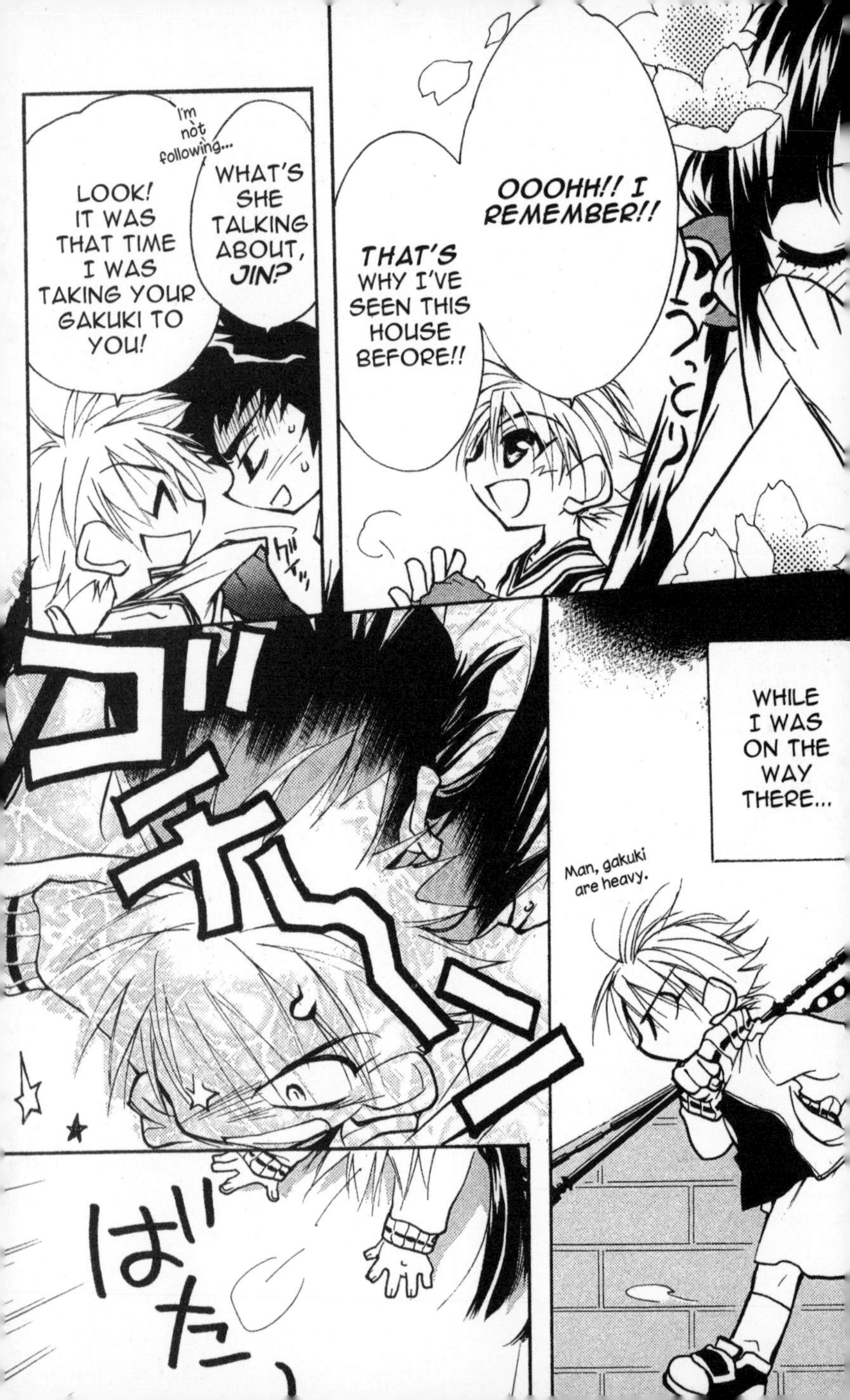
OOOHH!! I REMEMBER!!
THAT'S WHY I'VE SEEN THIS HOUSE BEFORE!!
I'm not following...
WHAT'S SHE TALKING ABOUT, JIN?
LOOK! IT WAS THAT TIME I WAS TAKING YOUR GAKUKI TO YOU!
WHILE I WAS ON THE WAY THERE...
Man, gakuki are heavy.
ゴキーン
ばたー

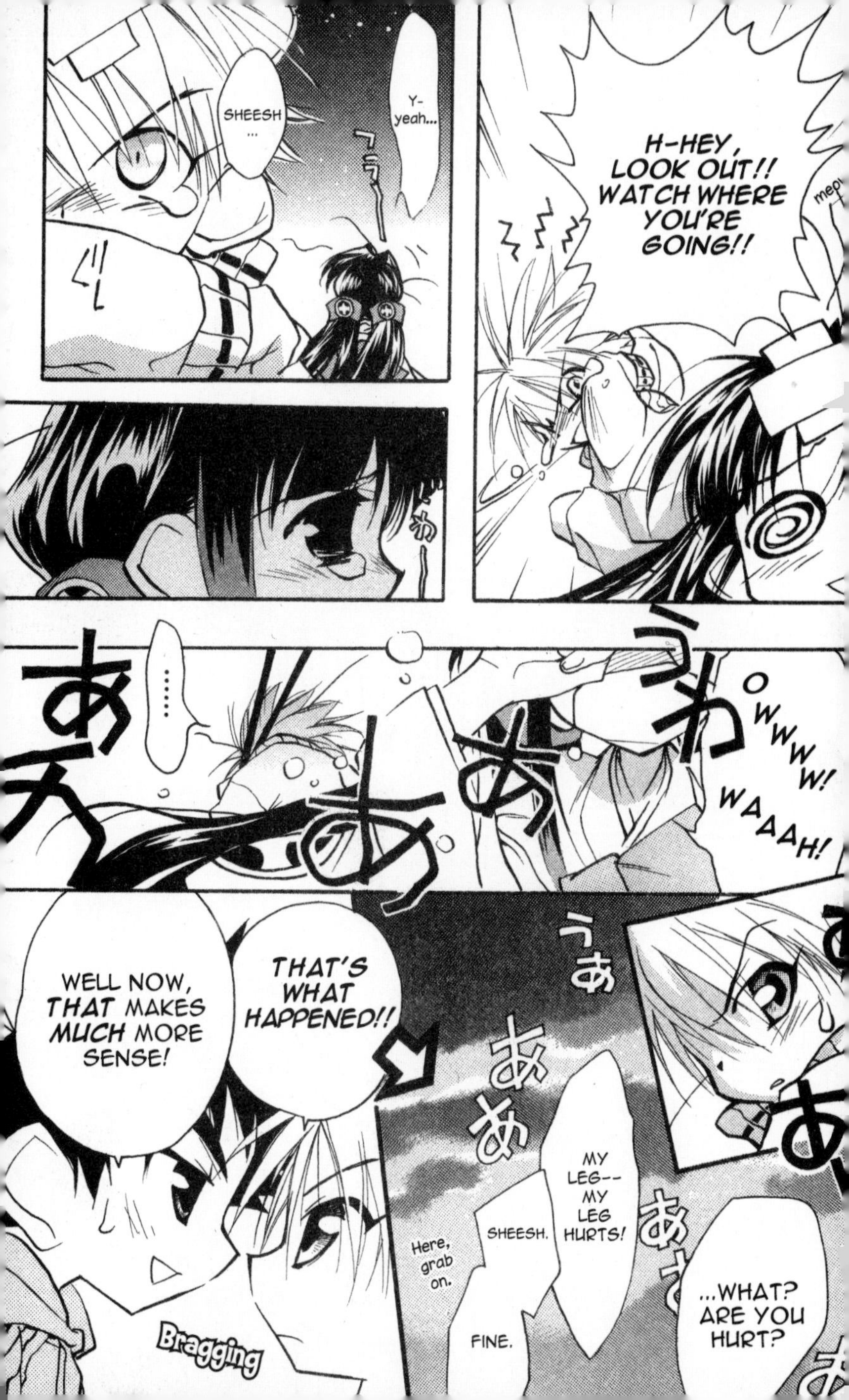
H-HEY, LOOK OUT!! WATCH WHERE YOU'RE GOING!!
Y- yeah...
SHEESH ...
OWWWW! WAAAH!
......
...WHAT? ARE YOU HURT?
MY LEG-- MY LEG HURTS!
SHEESH.
Here, grab on.
FINE.
THAT'S WHAT HAPPENED!!
WELL NOW, THAT MAKES MUCH MORE SENSE!
Bragging

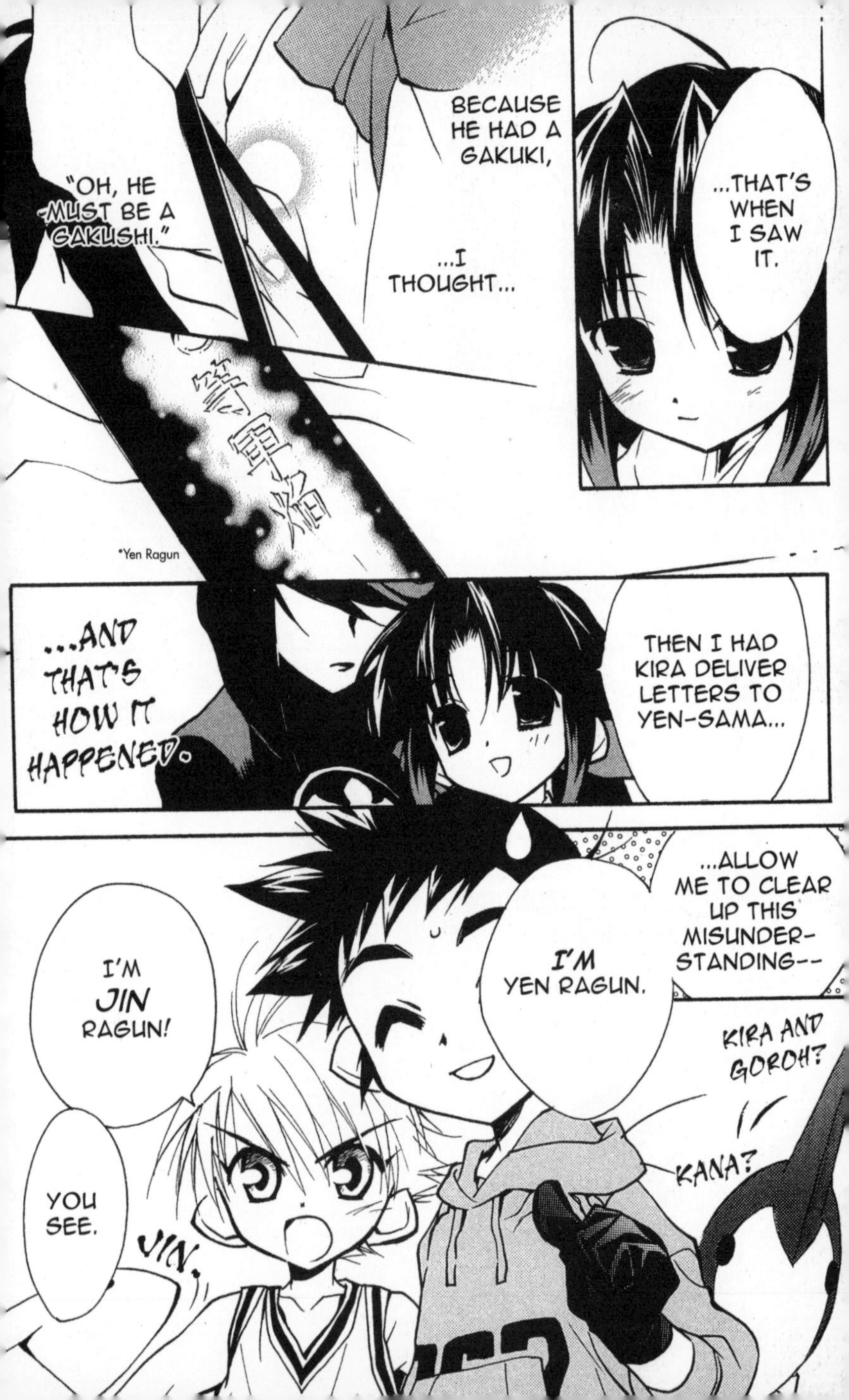
...THAT'S WHEN I SAW IT.
BECAUSE HE HAD A GAKUKI,
...I THOUGHT...
"OH, HE MUST BE A GAKUSHI."
*Yen Ragun
THEN I HAD KIRA DELIVER LETTERS TO YEN-SAMA...
...AND THAT'S HOW IT HAPPENED.
...ALLOW ME TO CLEAR UP THIS MISUNDER-STANDING--
KIRA AND GOROH?
I'M YEN RAGUN.
KANA?
I'M JIN RAGUN!
YOU SEE.
JIN.

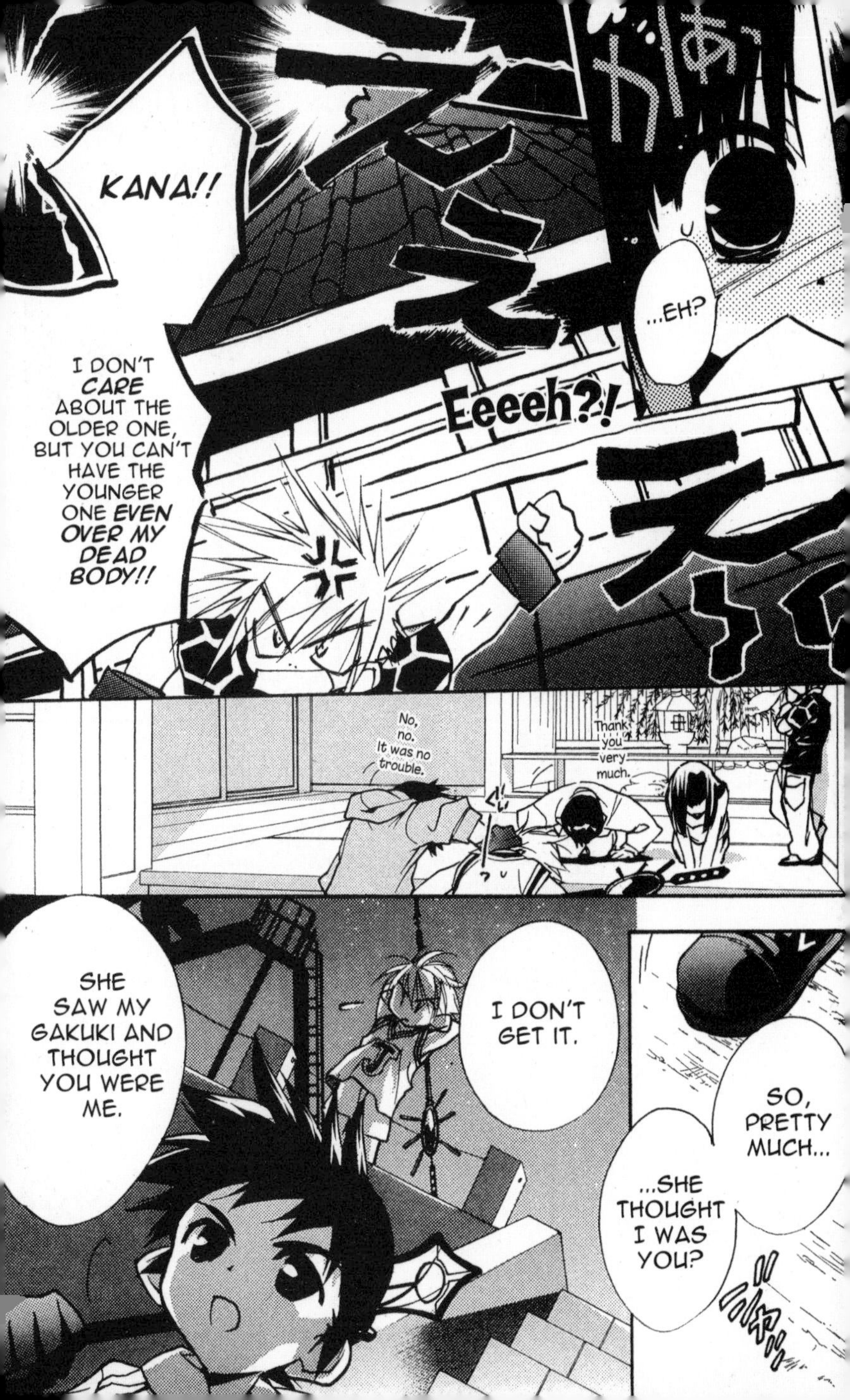
...EH?
Eeeeh?!
KANA!!
I DON'T CARE ABOUT THE OLDER ONE, BUT YOU CAN'T HAVE THE YOUNGER ONE EVEN OVER MY DEAD BODY!!
Thank you very much.
No, no. It was no trouble.
SO, PRETTY MUCH...
...SHE THOUGHT I WAS YOU?
I DON'T GET IT.
SHE SAW MY GAKUKI AND THOUGHT YOU WERE ME.

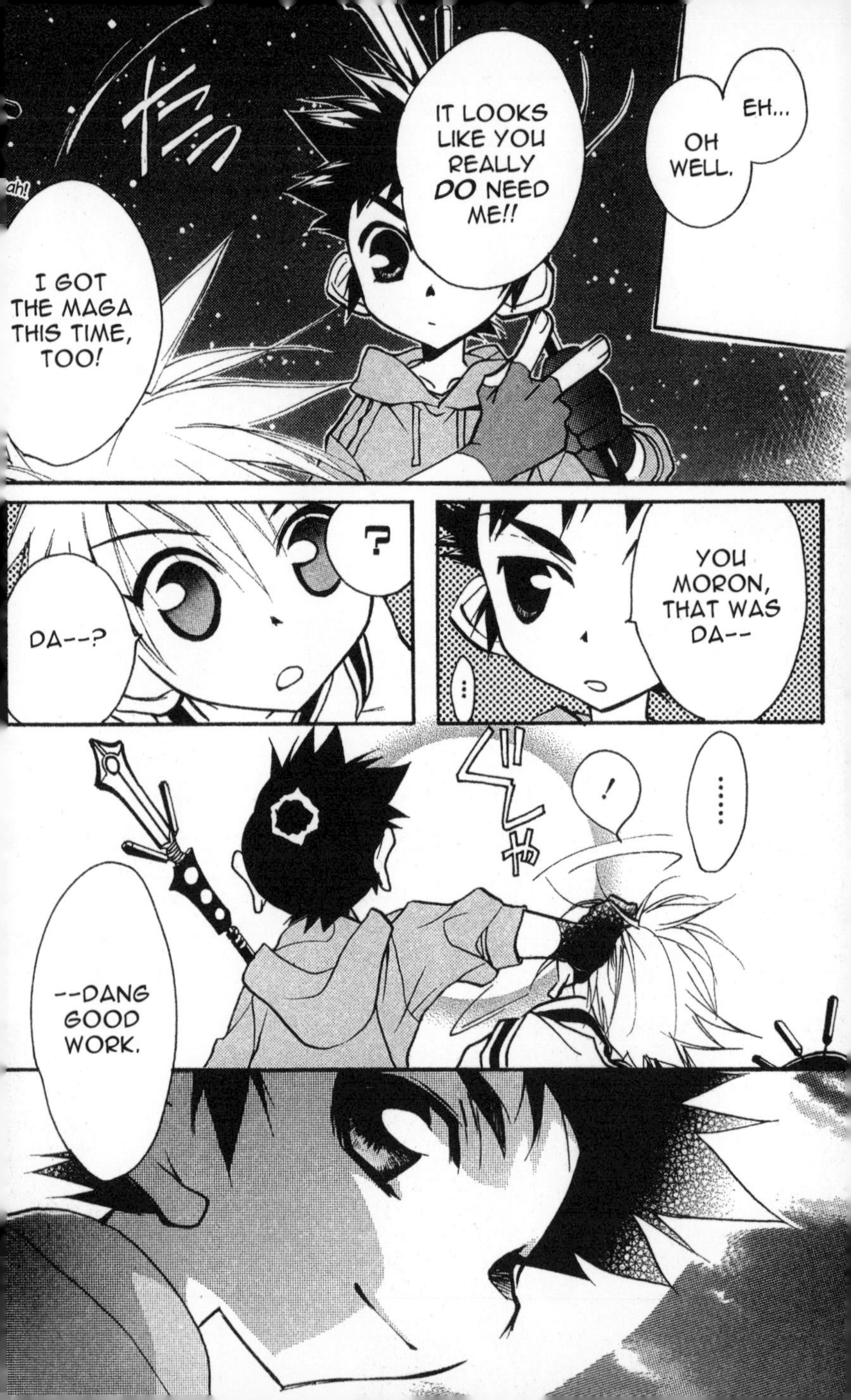
EH... OH WELL.
IT LOOKS LIKE YOU REALLY DO NEED ME!!
ah!
I GOT THE MAGA THIS TIME, TOO!
YOU MORON, THAT WAS DA--
...
?
DA--?
......
!
--DANG GOOD WORK.

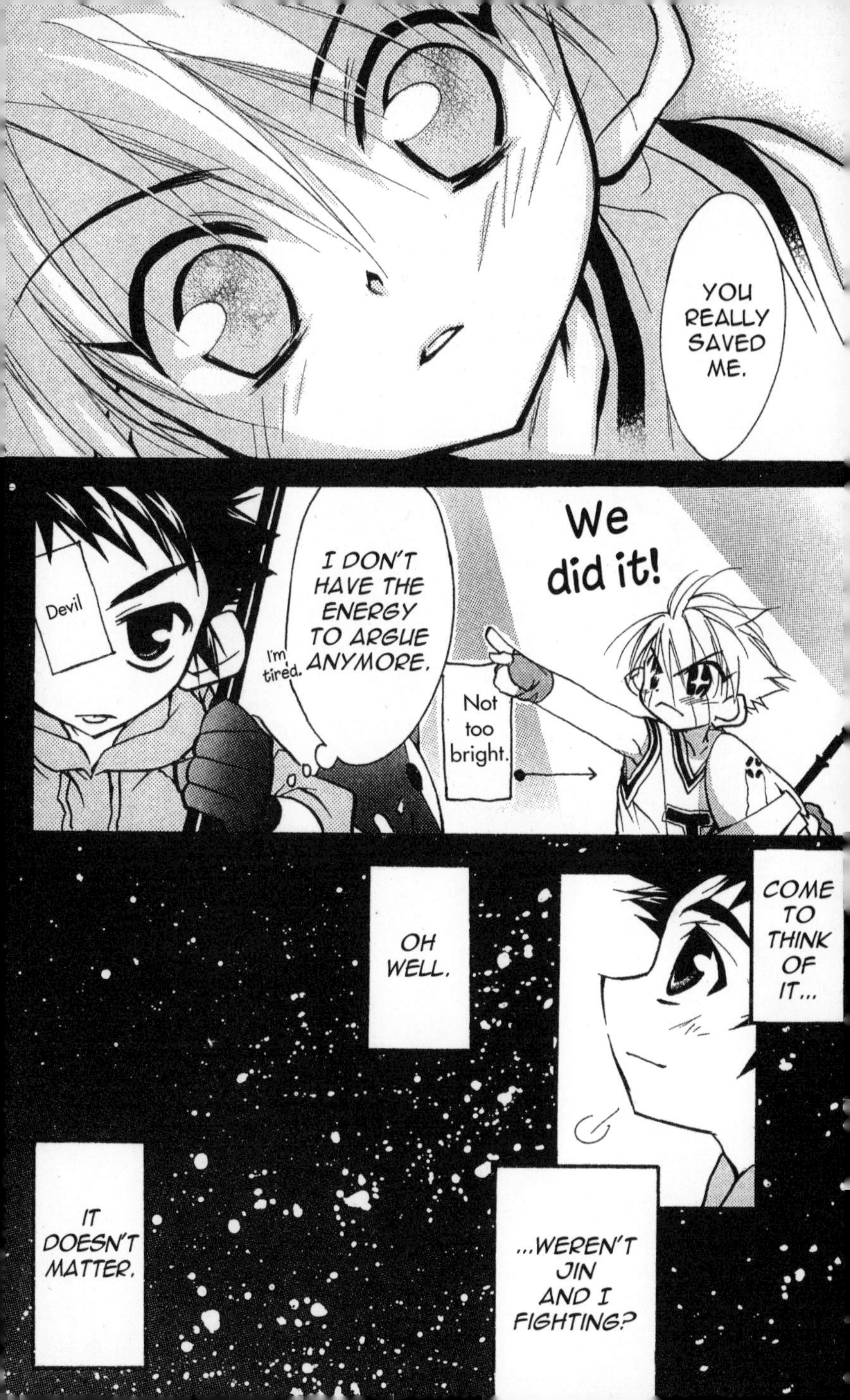
YOU REALLY SAVED ME.
We did it!
Not too bright.
I DON'T HAVE THE ENERGY TO ARGUE ANYMORE.
I'm tired.
Devil
COME TO THINK OF IT...
...WEREN'T JIN AND I FIGHTING?
OH WELL.
IT DOESN'T MATTER.

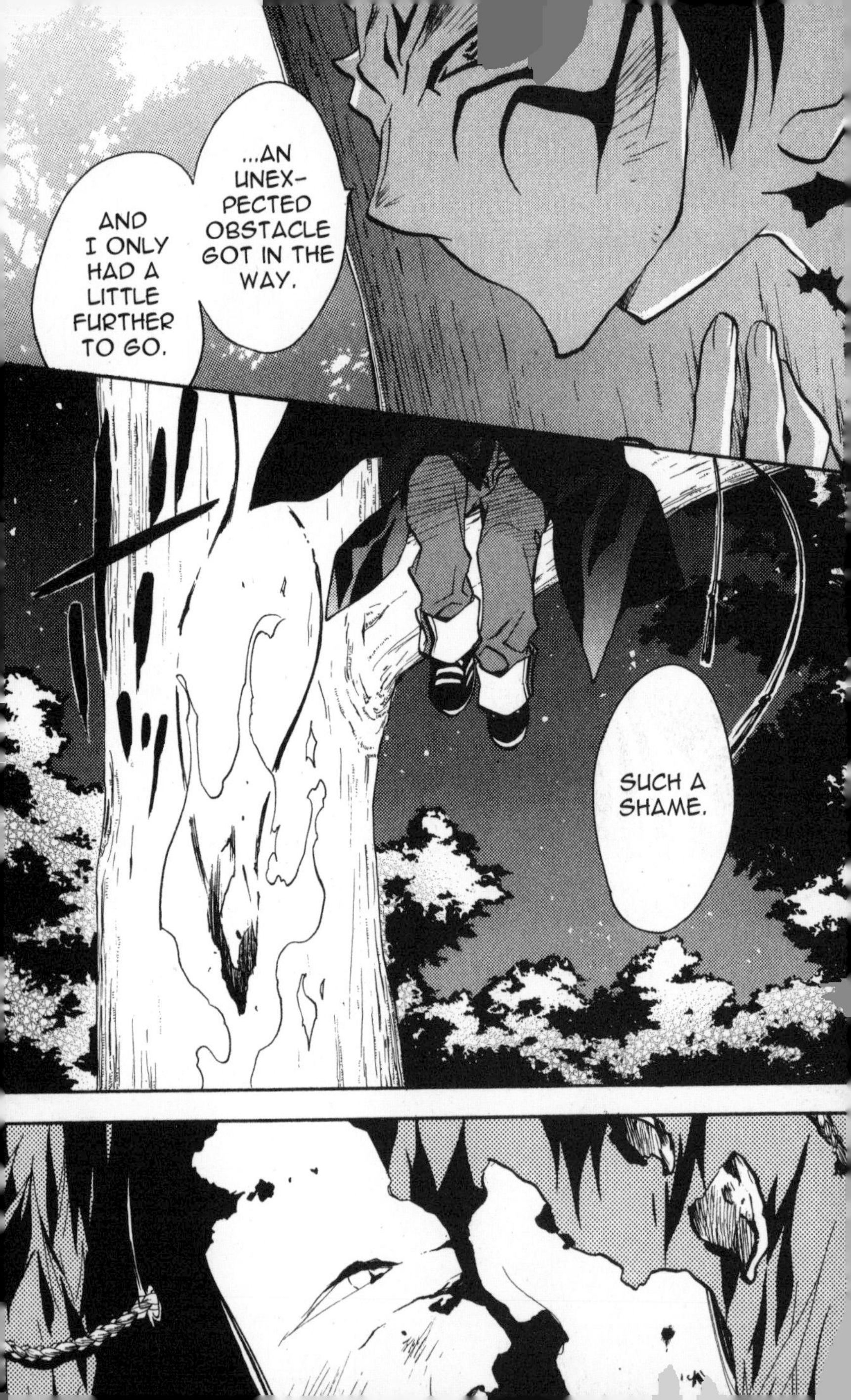
...AN UNEX-PECTED OBSTACLE GOT IN THE WAY.
AND I ONLY HAD A LITTLE FURTHER TO GO.
SUCH A SHAME.

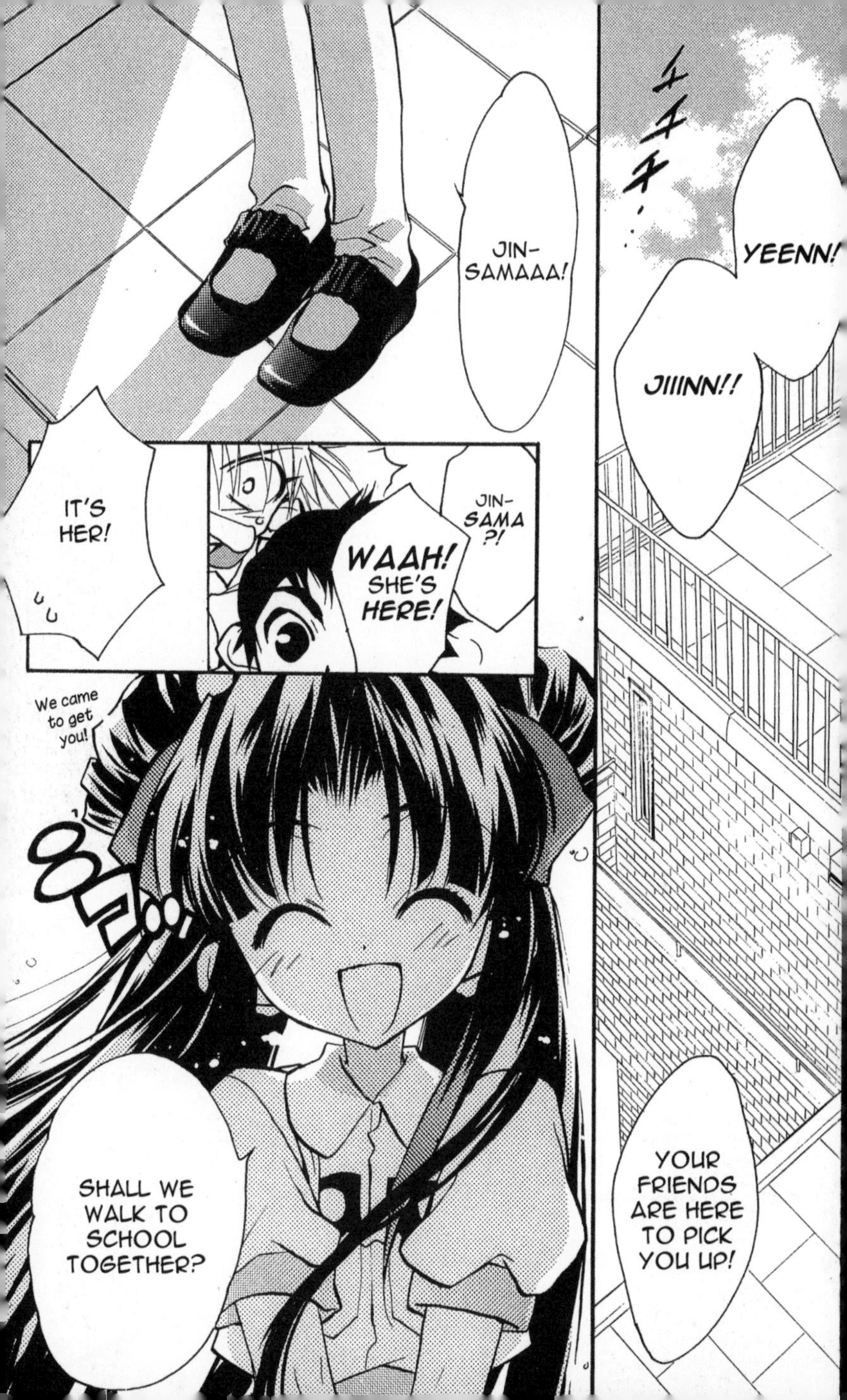
YEENN!
JIIINN!!
YOUR FRIENDS ARE HERE TO PICK YOU UP!
JIN-SAMAAA!
JIN-SAMA?!
WAAH! SHE'S HERE!
IT'S HER!
We came to get you!
SHALL WE WALK TO SCHOOL TOGETHER?

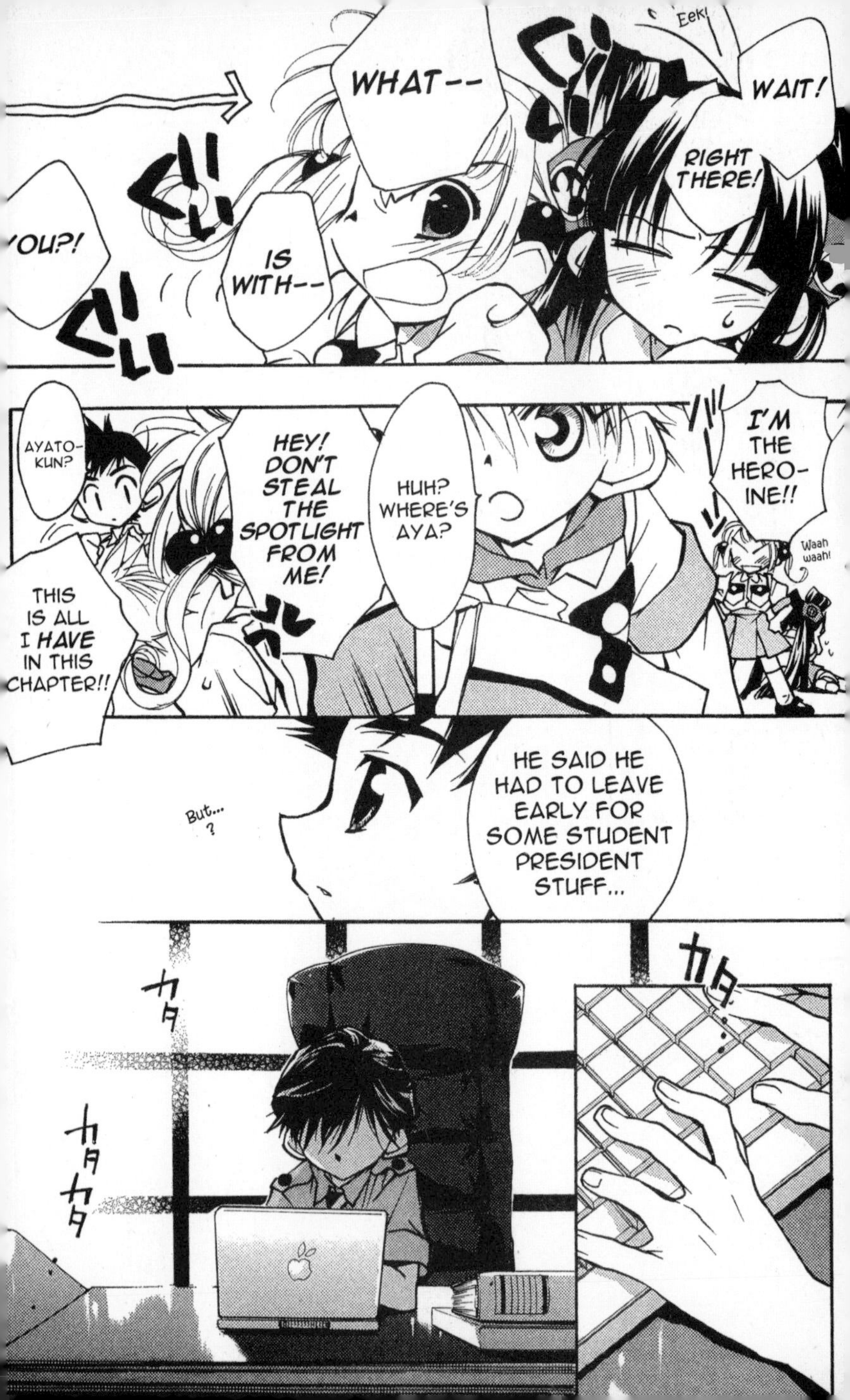
Eek!
WAIT!
RIGHT THERE!
WHAT--
IS WITH--
YOU?!
I'M THE HERO-INE!!
Waah waah!
HUH? WHERE'S AYA?
HEY! DON'T STEAL THE SPOTLIGHT FROM ME!
AYATO-KUN?
THIS IS ALL I *HAVE* IN THIS CHAPTER!!
HE SAID HE HAD TO LEAVE EARLY FOR SOME STUDENT PRESIDENT STUFF...
But... ?
カタ
カタ
カタカタ

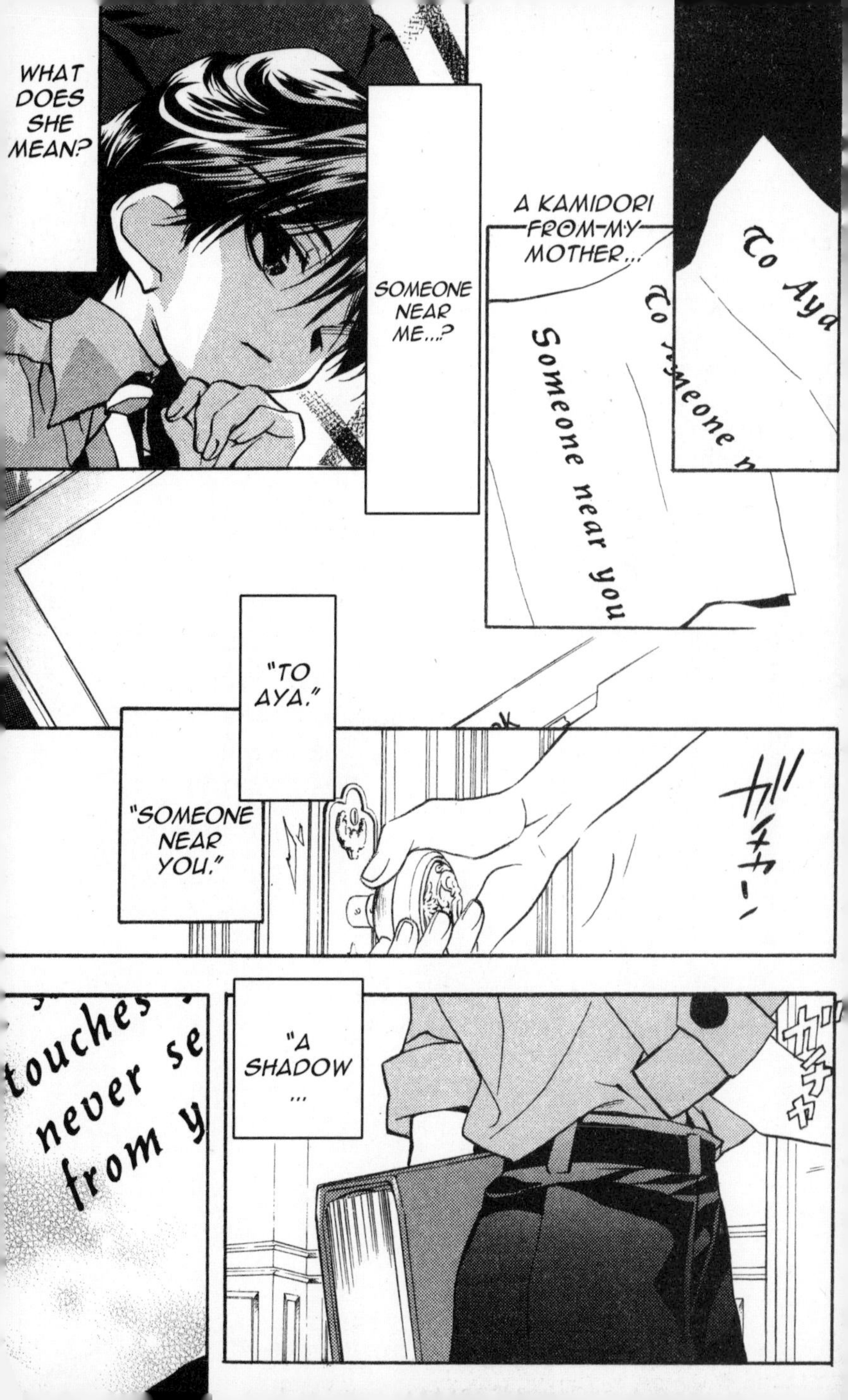
To Aya
Someone near you
A KAMIDORI FROM MY MOTHER...
SOMEONE NEAR ME...?
WHAT DOES SHE MEAN?
ガチャー
"TO AYA."
"SOMEONE NEAR YOU."
ガチャ
"A SHADOW ...
touches
never
from

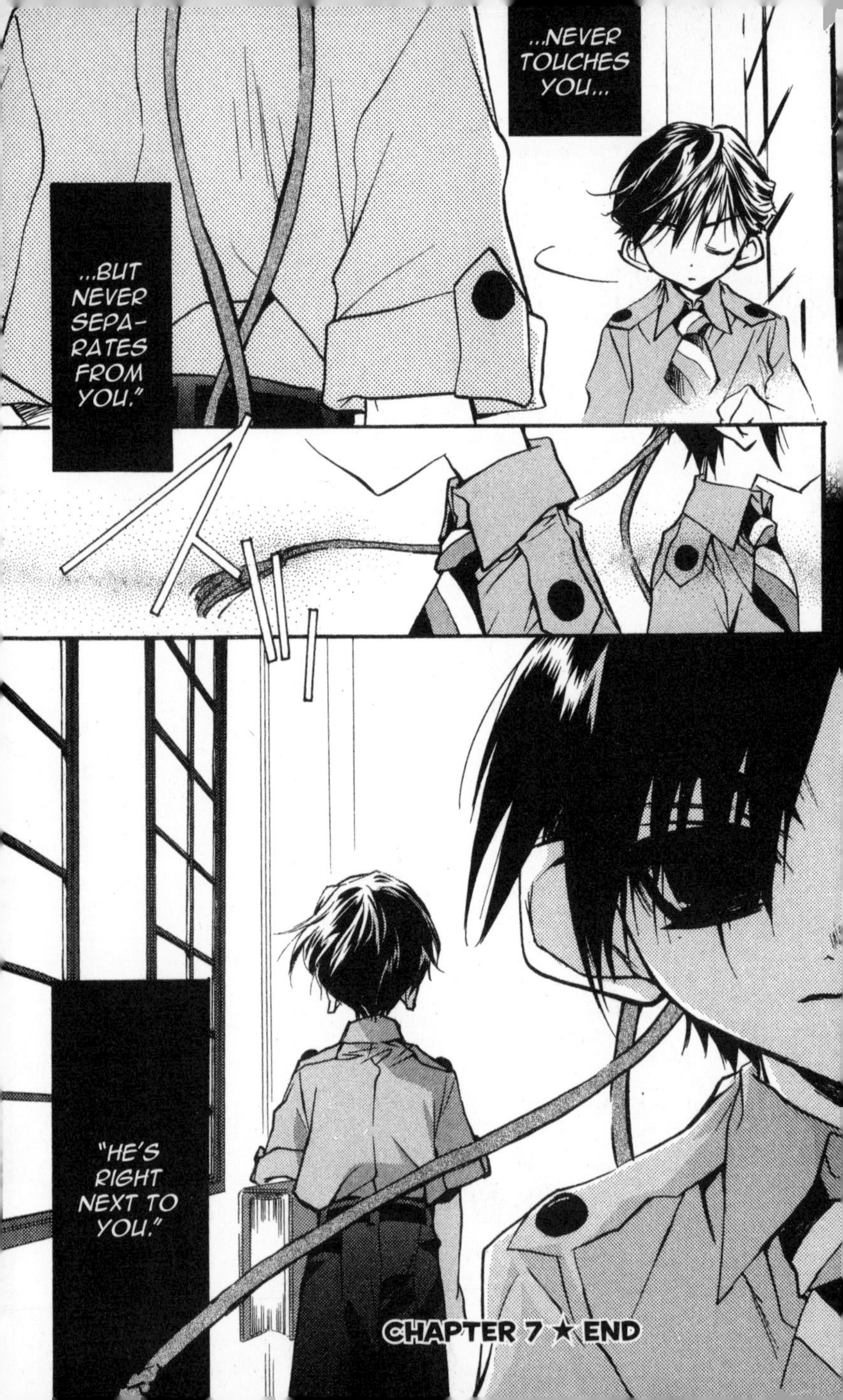
...NEVER TOUCHES YOU...
...BUT NEVER SEPARATES FROM YOU."
"HE'S RIGHT NEXT TO YOU."
CHAPTER 7 ★ END

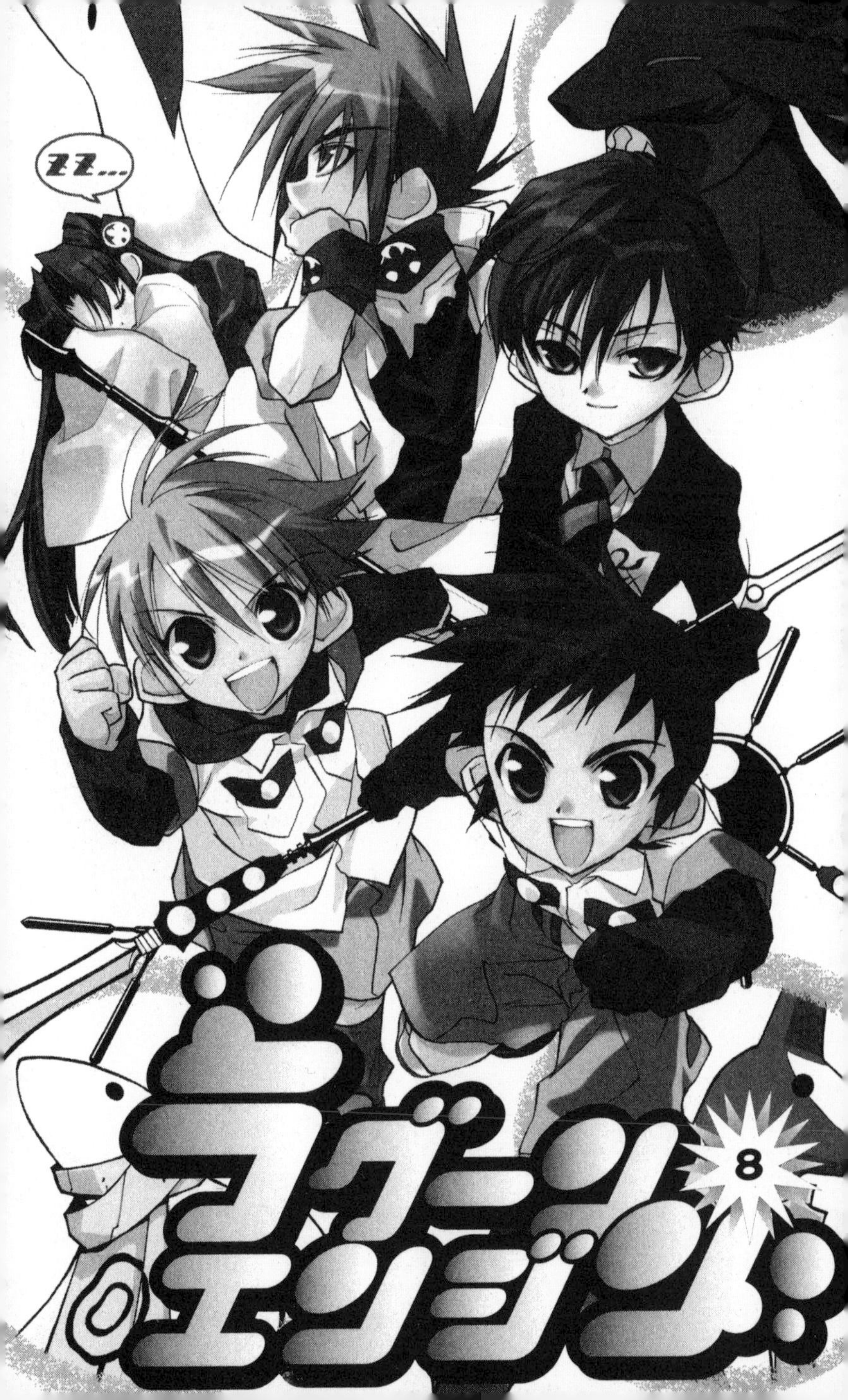
zz...
ラグーンエンジン
8

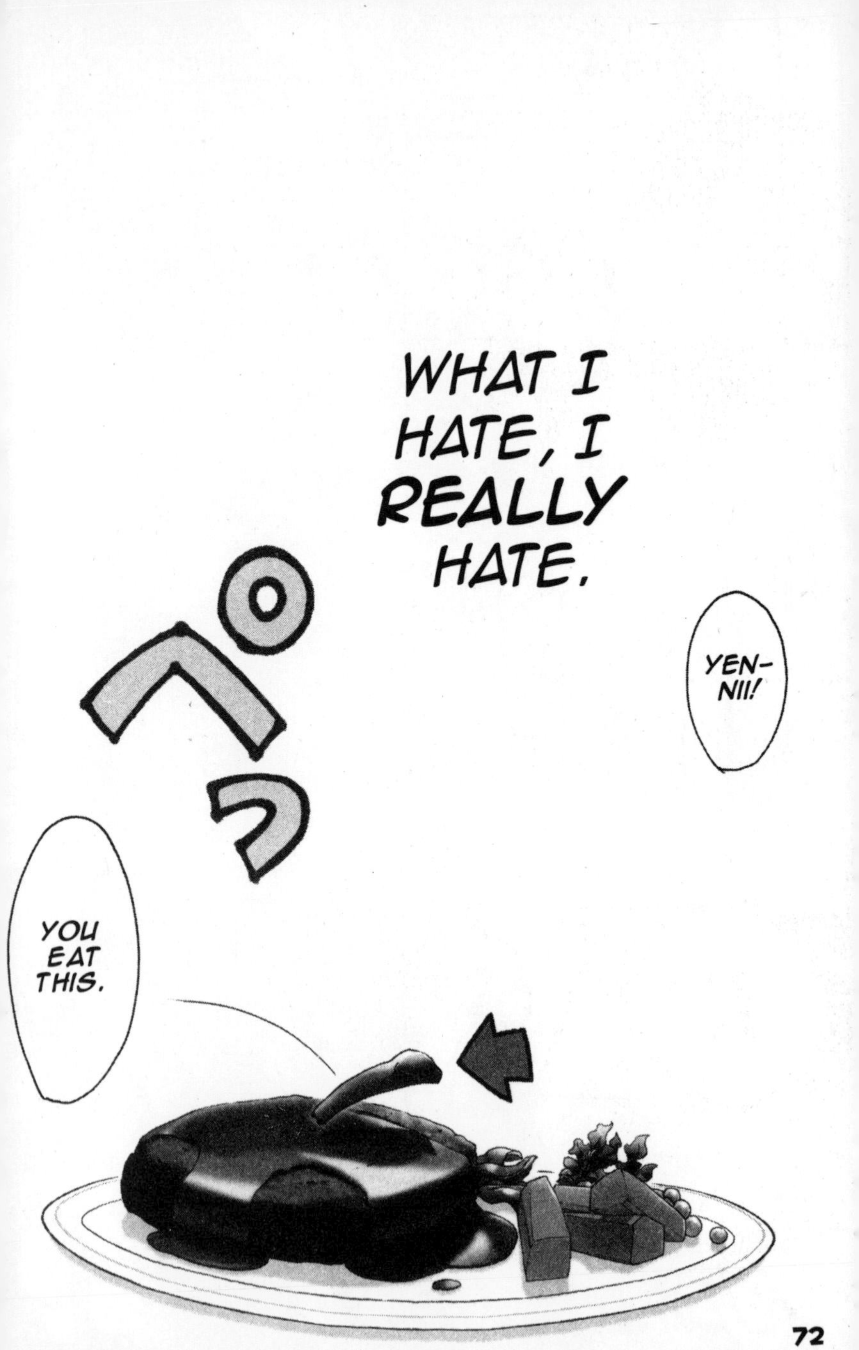
WHAT I HATE, I REALLY HATE.
YEN-NII!
ぺっ
YOU EAT THIS.

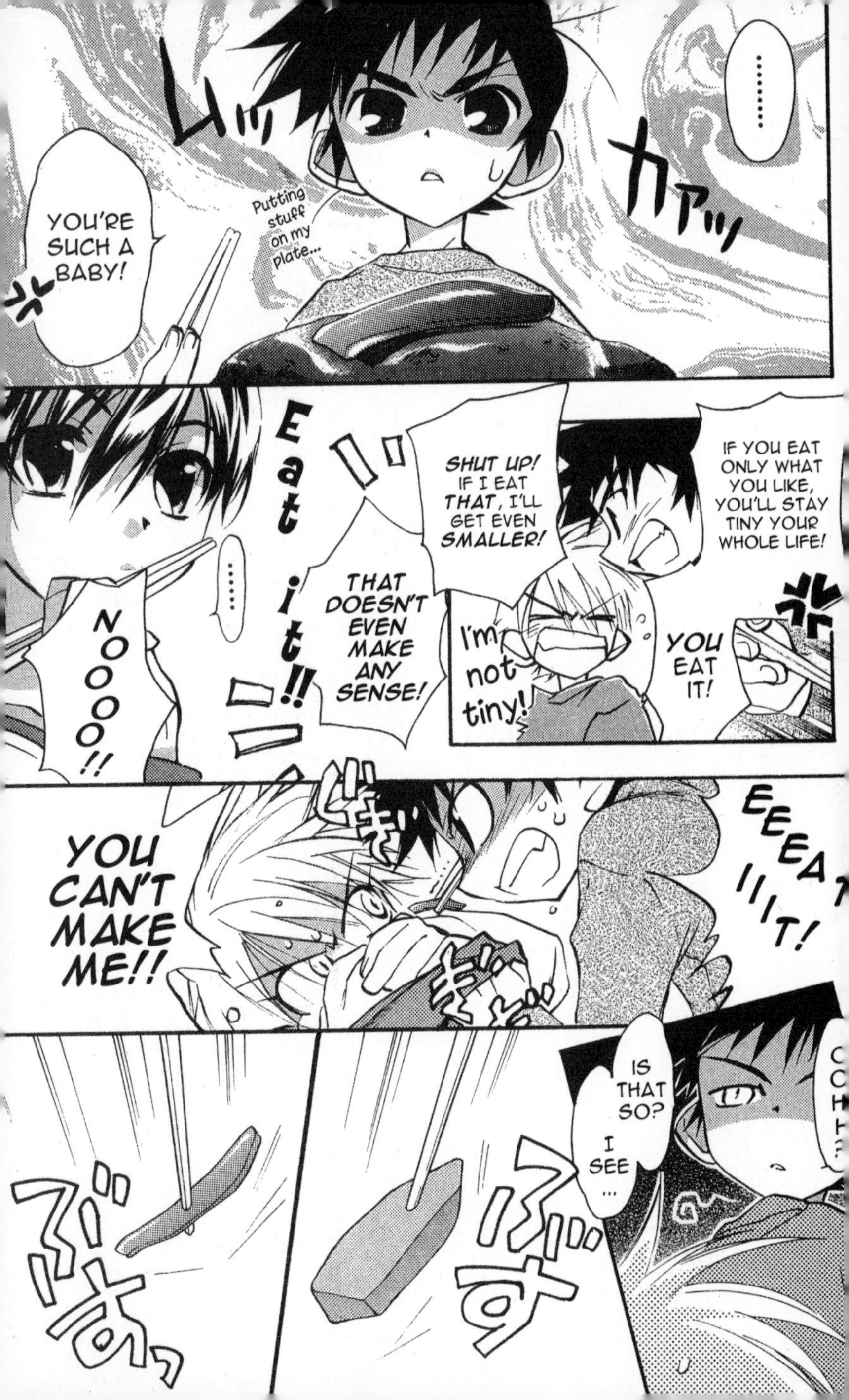
……
カァッ
Putting stuff on my plate...
ムッ
YOU'RE SUCH A BABY!
IF YOU EAT ONLY WHAT YOU LIKE, YOU'LL STAY TINY YOUR WHOLE LIFE!
SHUT UP! IF I EAT THAT, I'LL GET EVEN SMALLER!
YOU EAT IT!
I'm not tiny!
THAT DOESN'T EVEN MAKE ANY SENSE!
Eat it!!
……
NOOOOO!!
EEEAT IIIIT!
YOU CAN'T MAKE ME!!
OOOH?
IS THAT SO?
I SEE …

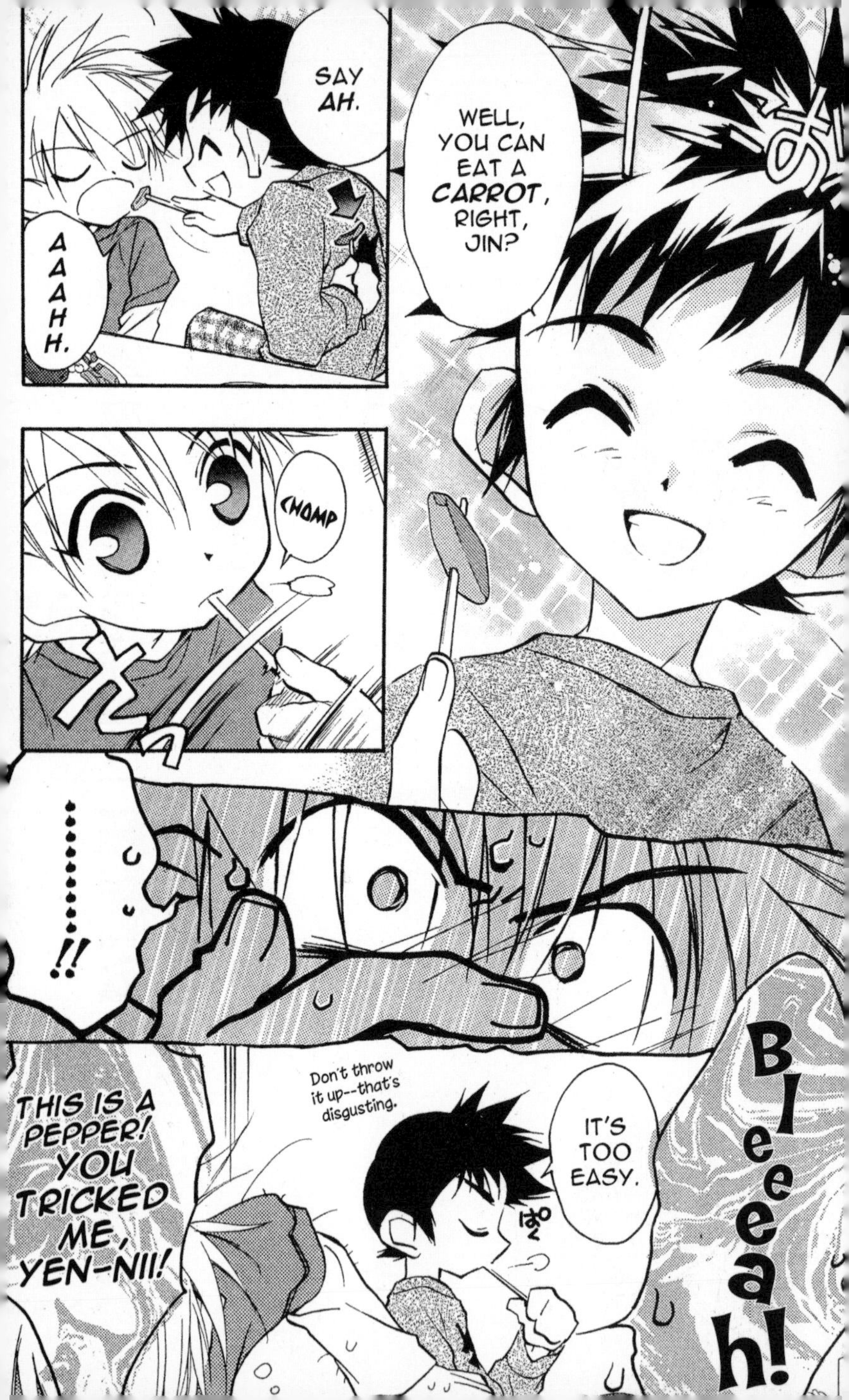
WELL, YOU CAN EAT A CARROT, RIGHT, JIN?
SAY AH.
AAAAHH.
CHOMP
......!!
Bleeeah!
IT'S TOO EASY.
Don't throw it up--that's disgusting.
THIS IS A PEPPER! YOU TRICKED ME, YEN-NII!

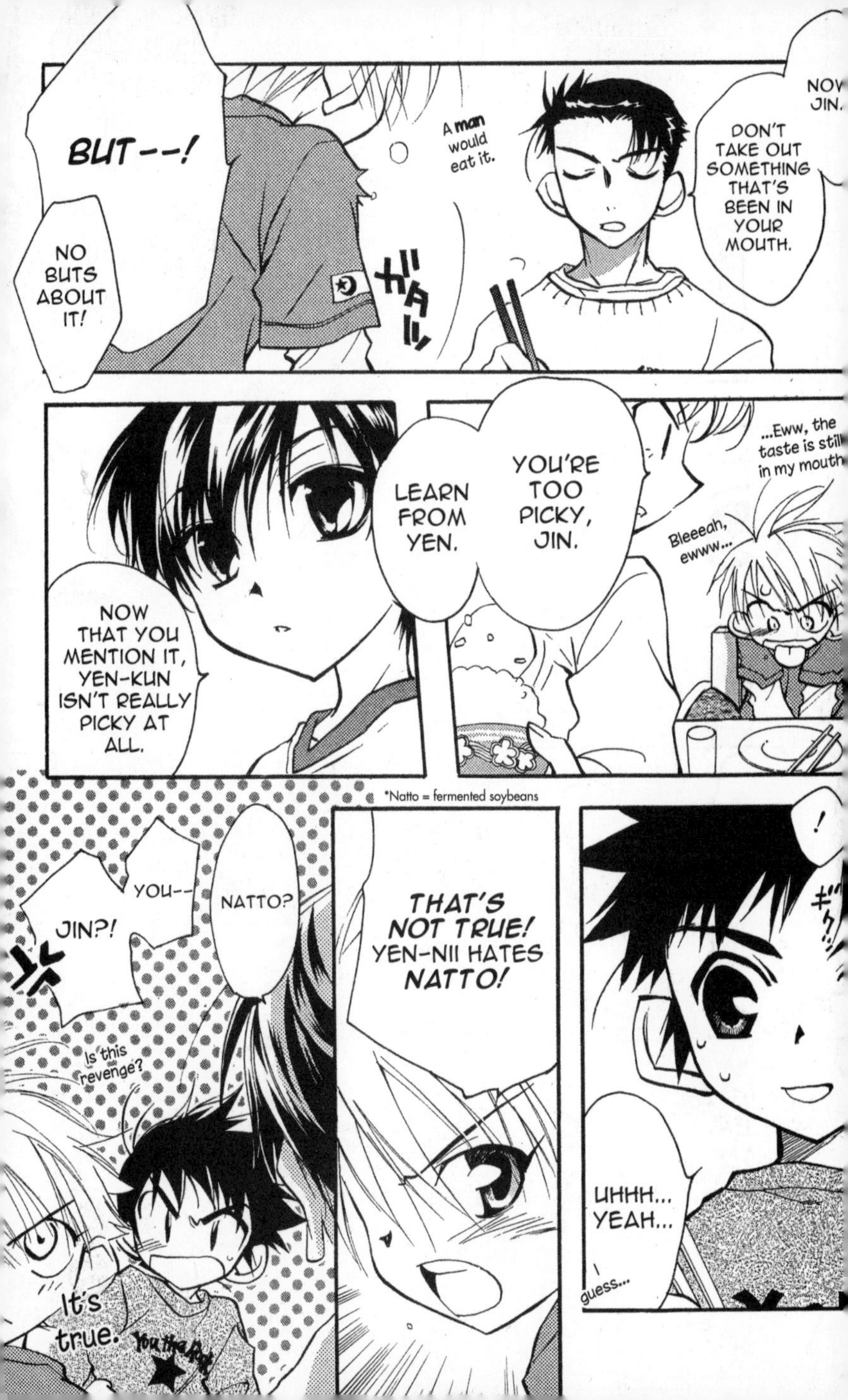
NOW JIN.
DON'T TAKE OUT SOMETHING THAT'S BEEN IN YOUR MOUTH.
A man would eat it.
BUT--!
NO BUTS ABOUT IT!
...Eww, the taste is still in my mouth
Bleeeah, ewww...
YOU'RE TOO PICKY, JIN.
LEARN FROM YEN.
NOW THAT YOU MENTION IT, YEN-KUN ISN'T REALLY PICKY AT ALL.
!
UHHH... YEAH...
I guess...
THAT'S NOT TRUE! YEN-NII HATES NATTO!
NATTO?
YOU--
JIN?!
Is this revenge?
It's true.

*Natto = fermented soybeans

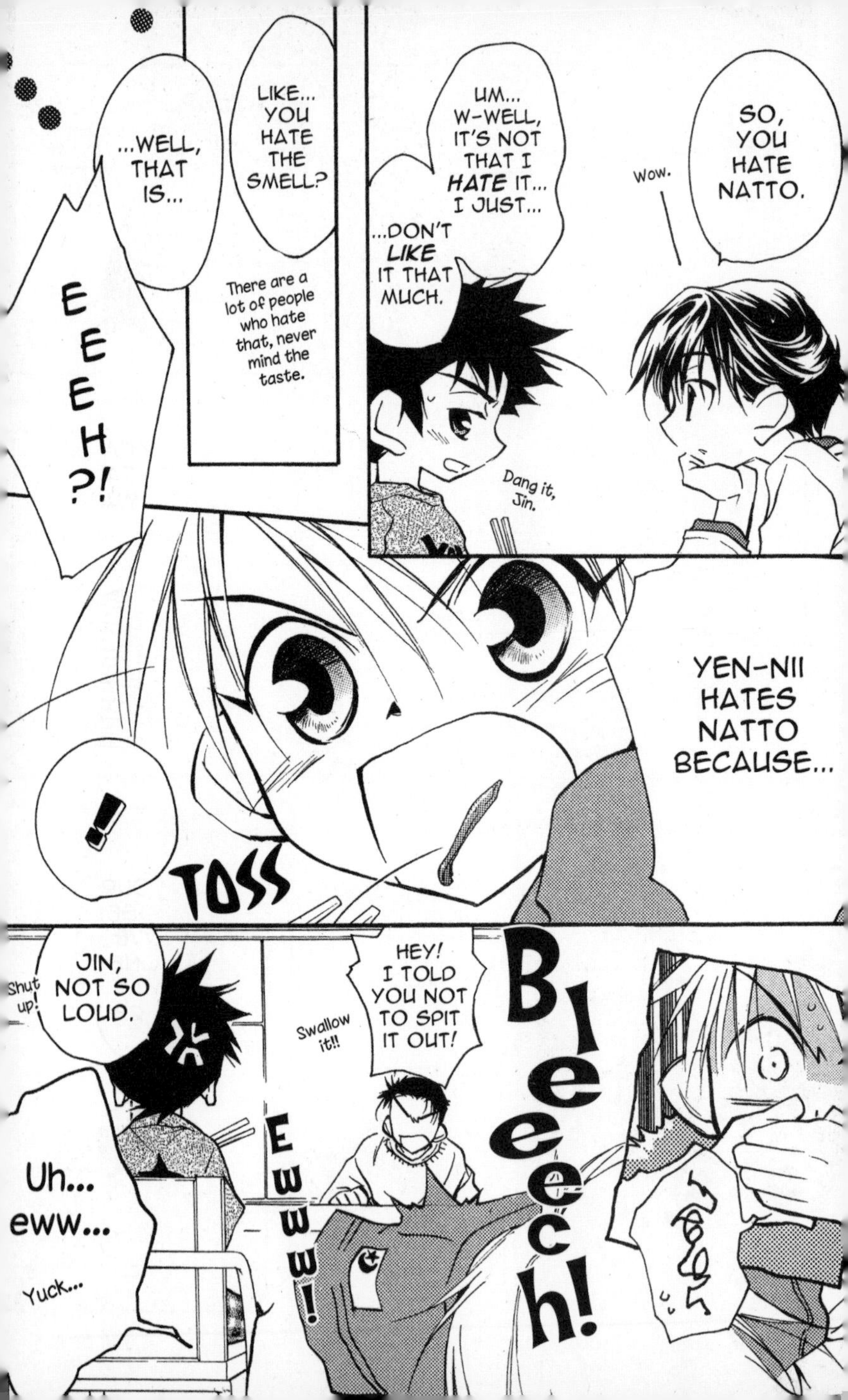

SO, YOU HATE NATTO.
Wow.
UM... W-WELL, IT'S NOT THAT I HATE IT... I JUST...
...DON'T LIKE IT THAT MUCH.
Dang it, Jin.
LIKE... YOU HATE THE SMELL?
There are a lot of people who hate that, never mind the taste.
...WELL, THAT IS...
EEEEH?!
YEN-NII HATES NATTO BECAUSE...
!
TOSS
Bleeeech!
HEY! I TOLD YOU NOT TO SPIT IT OUT!
Swallow it!!
Ewwww!
JIN, NOT SO LOUD.
Shut up!
Uh... eww...
Yuck...

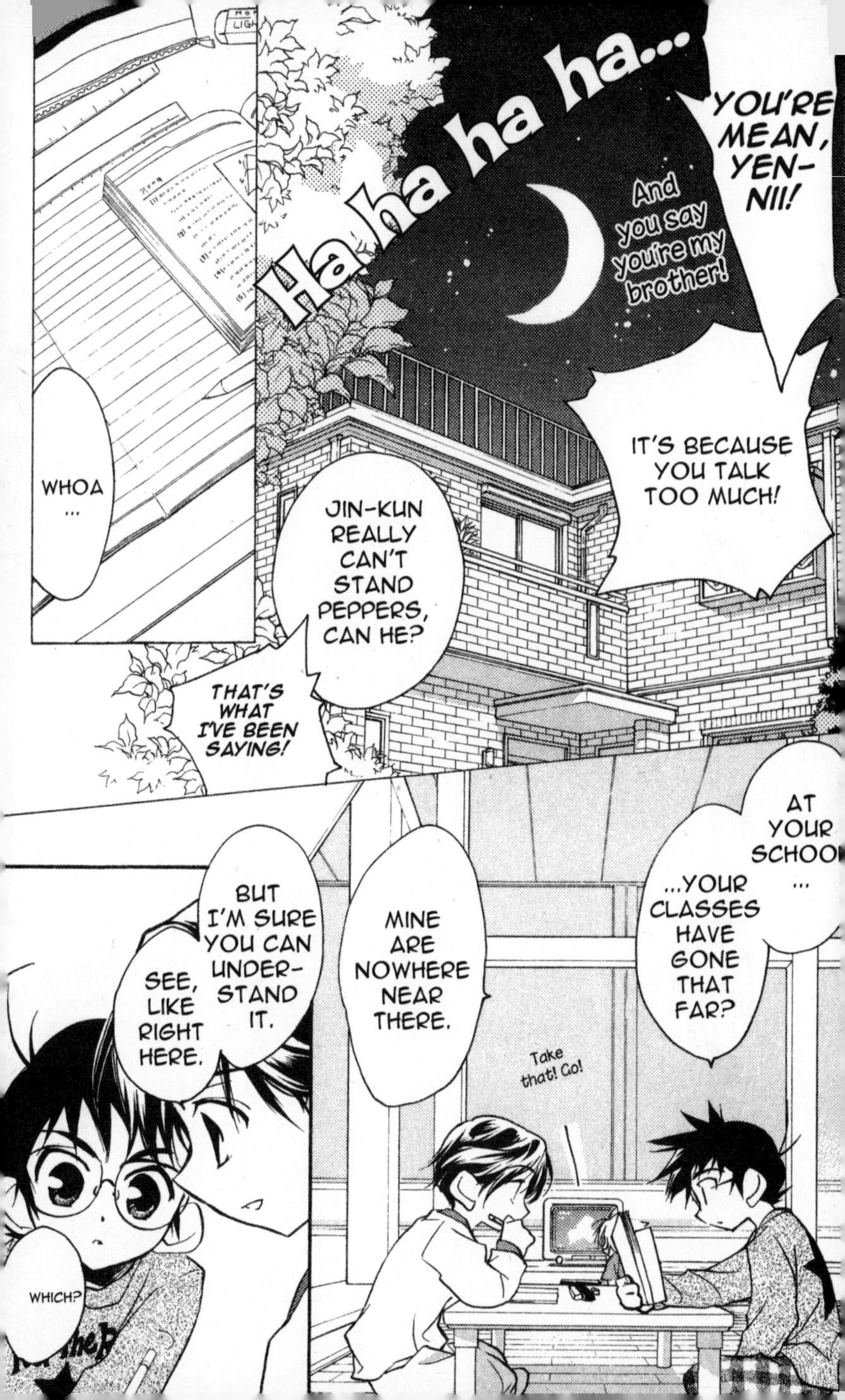
Ha ha ha ha...
YOU'RE MEAN, YEN-NII!
And you say you're my brother!
IT'S BECAUSE YOU TALK TOO MUCH!
JIN-KUN REALLY CAN'T STAND PEPPERS, CAN HE?
THAT'S WHAT I'VE BEEN SAYING!
WHOA ...
AT YOUR SCHOO ...
...YOUR CLASSES HAVE GONE THAT FAR?
Take that! Go!
MINE ARE NOWHERE NEAR THERE.
BUT I'M SURE YOU CAN UNDERSTAND IT.
SEE, LIKE RIGHT HERE.
WHICH?

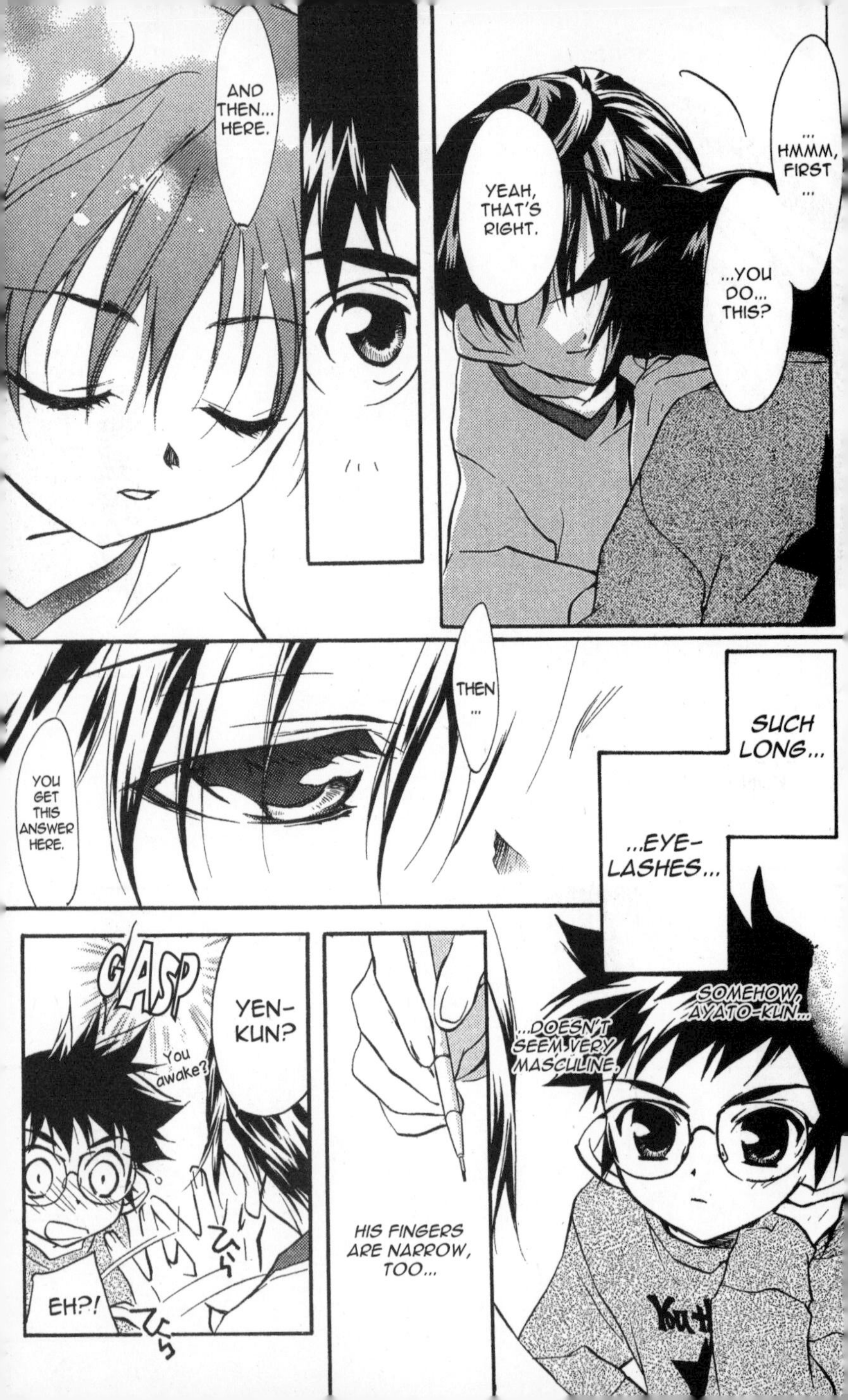
... HMMM, FIRST ...
...YOU DO... THIS?
YEAH, THAT'S RIGHT.
AND THEN... HERE.
SUCH LONG...
...EYE-LASHES...
THEN ...
YOU GET THIS ANSWER HERE.
SOMEHOW, AYATO-KUN...
...DOESN'T SEEM VERY MASCULINE.
HIS FINGERS ARE NARROW, TOO...
YEN-KUN?
GASP
You awake?
EH?!

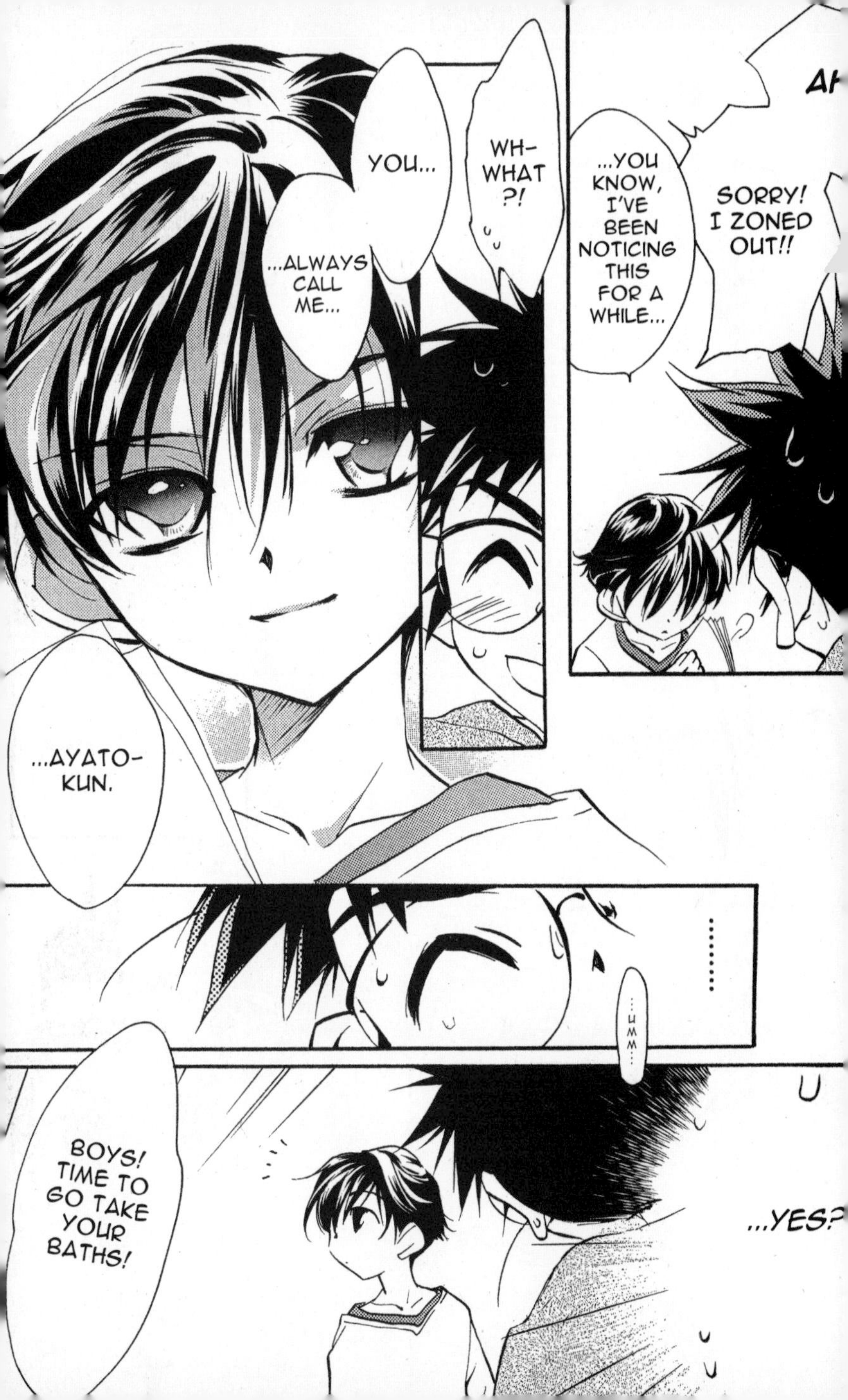
SORRY! I ZONED OUT!!
...YOU KNOW, I'VE BEEN NOTICING THIS FOR A WHILE...
WH-WHAT?!
YOU...
...ALWAYS CALL ME...
...AYATO-KUN.
......
...UMM...
...YES?
BOYS! TIME TO GO TAKE YOUR BATHS!

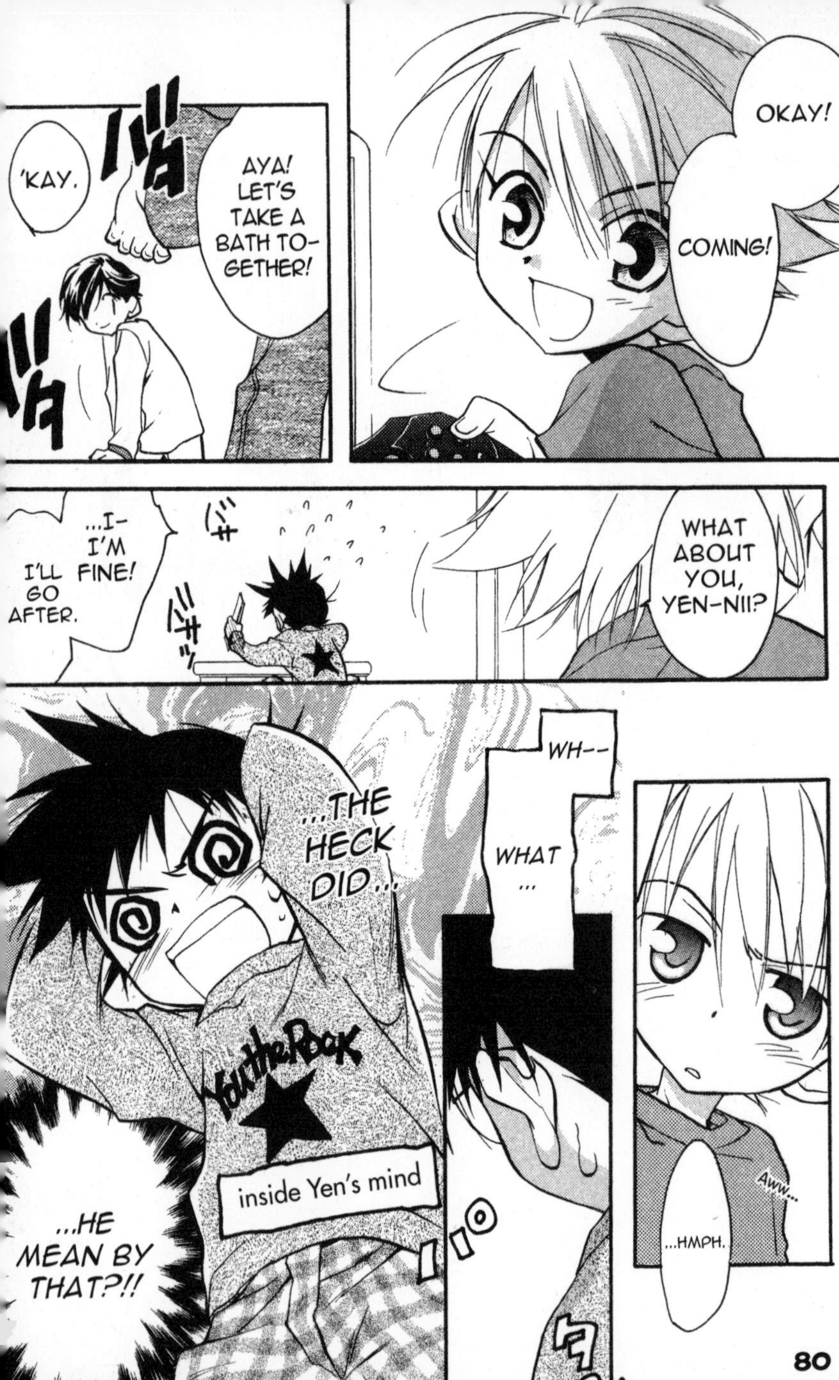
OKAY!
COMING!
AYA! LET'S TAKE A BATH TO-GETHER!
'KAY.
WHAT ABOUT YOU, YEN-NII?
...I- I'M FINE!
I'LL GO AFTER.
Aww...
...HMPH.
WH--
WHAT ...
...THE HECK DID...
...HE MEAN BY THAT?!!
inside Yen's mind
You the Rock

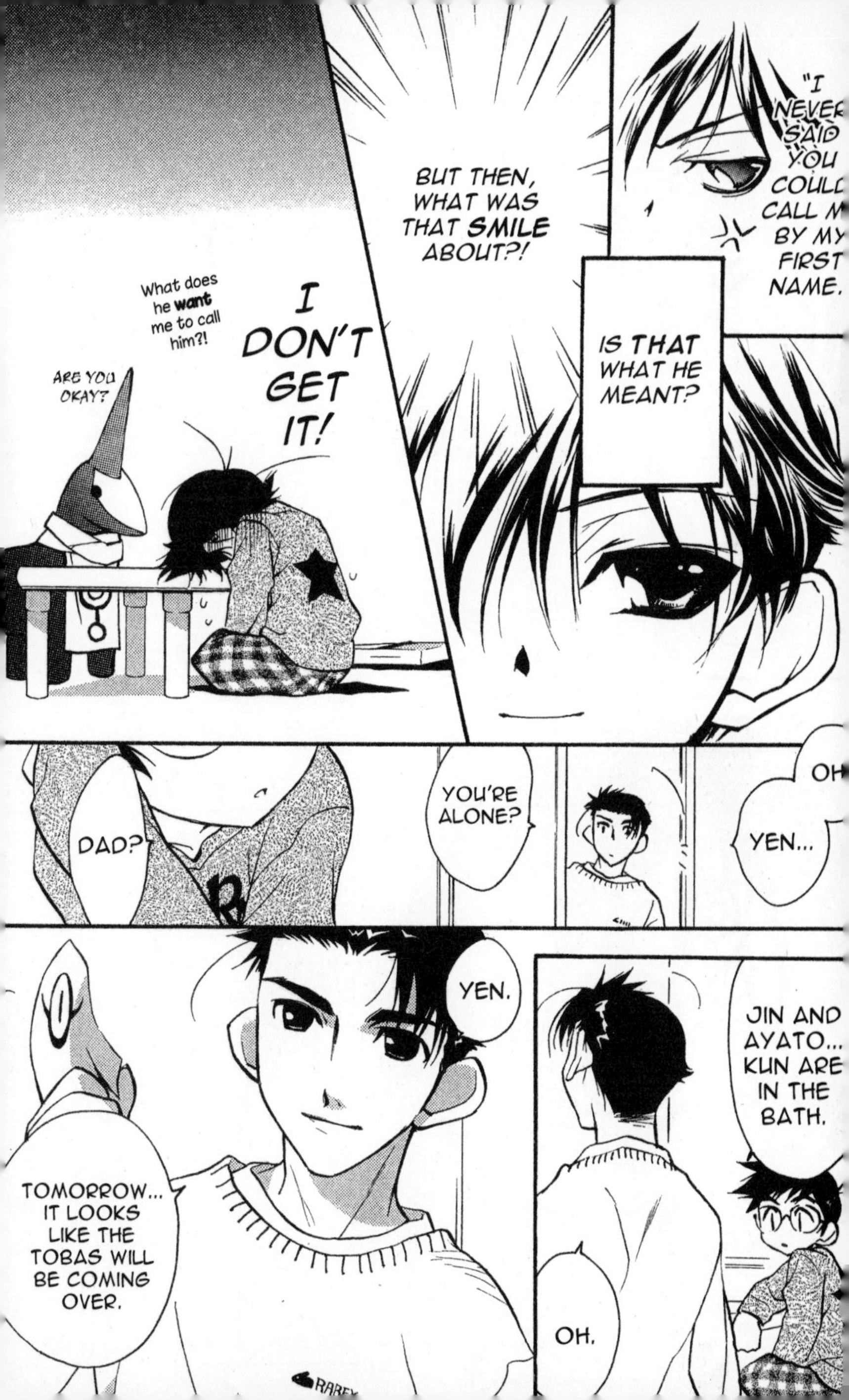
"I NEVER SAID YOU COULD CALL M BY MY FIRST NAME.
IS THAT WHAT HE MEANT?
BUT THEN, WHAT WAS THAT SMILE ABOUT?!
I DON'T GET IT!
What does he want me to call him?!
ARE YOU OKAY?
OH YEN...
YOU'RE ALONE?
DAD?
JIN AND AYATO... KUN ARE IN THE BATH.
OH.
YEN.
TOMORROW... IT LOOKS LIKE THE TOBAS WILL BE COMING OVER.

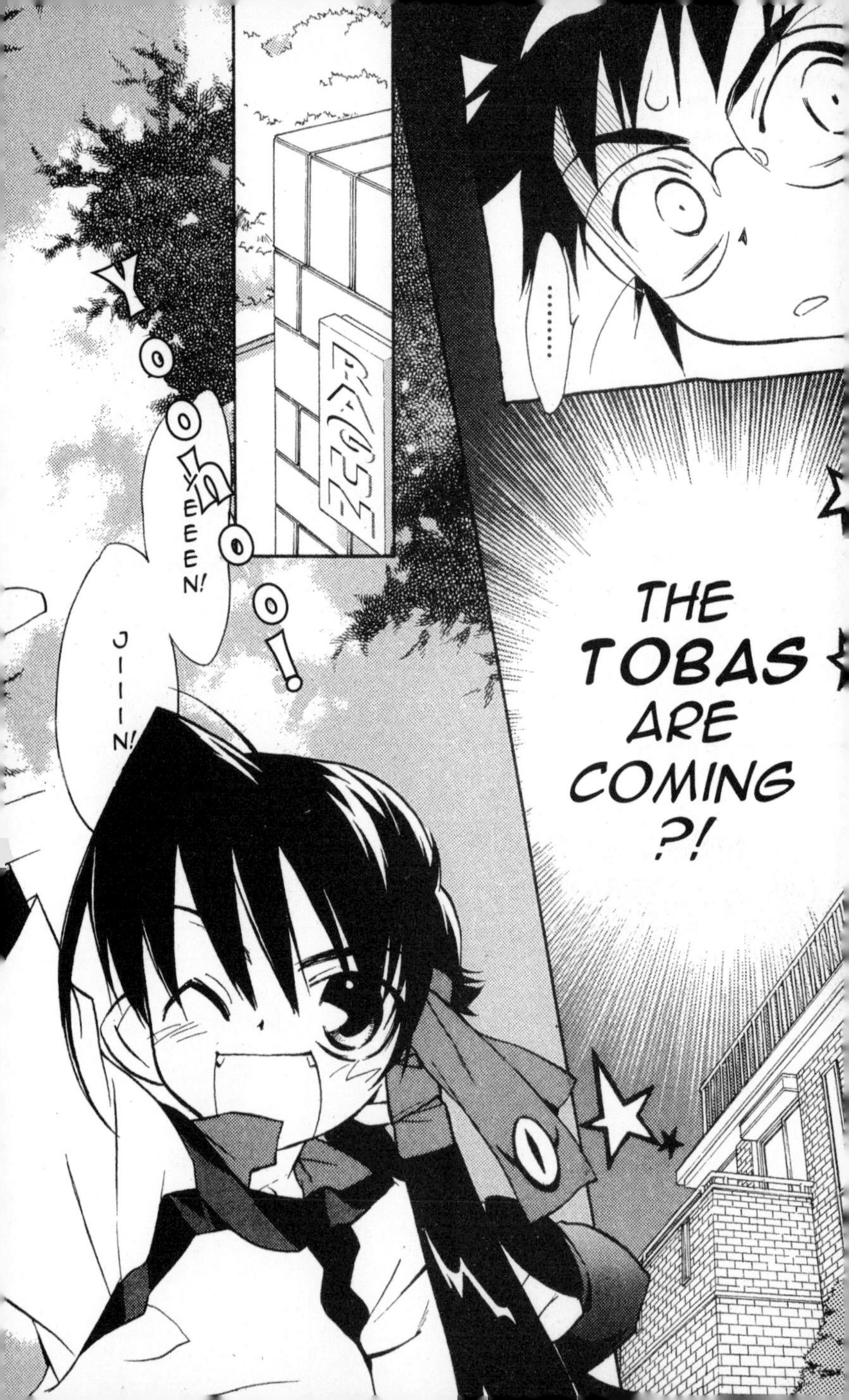
THE TOBAS ARE COMING?!
Yooohooo!
YEEEEN!
JIIIIN!

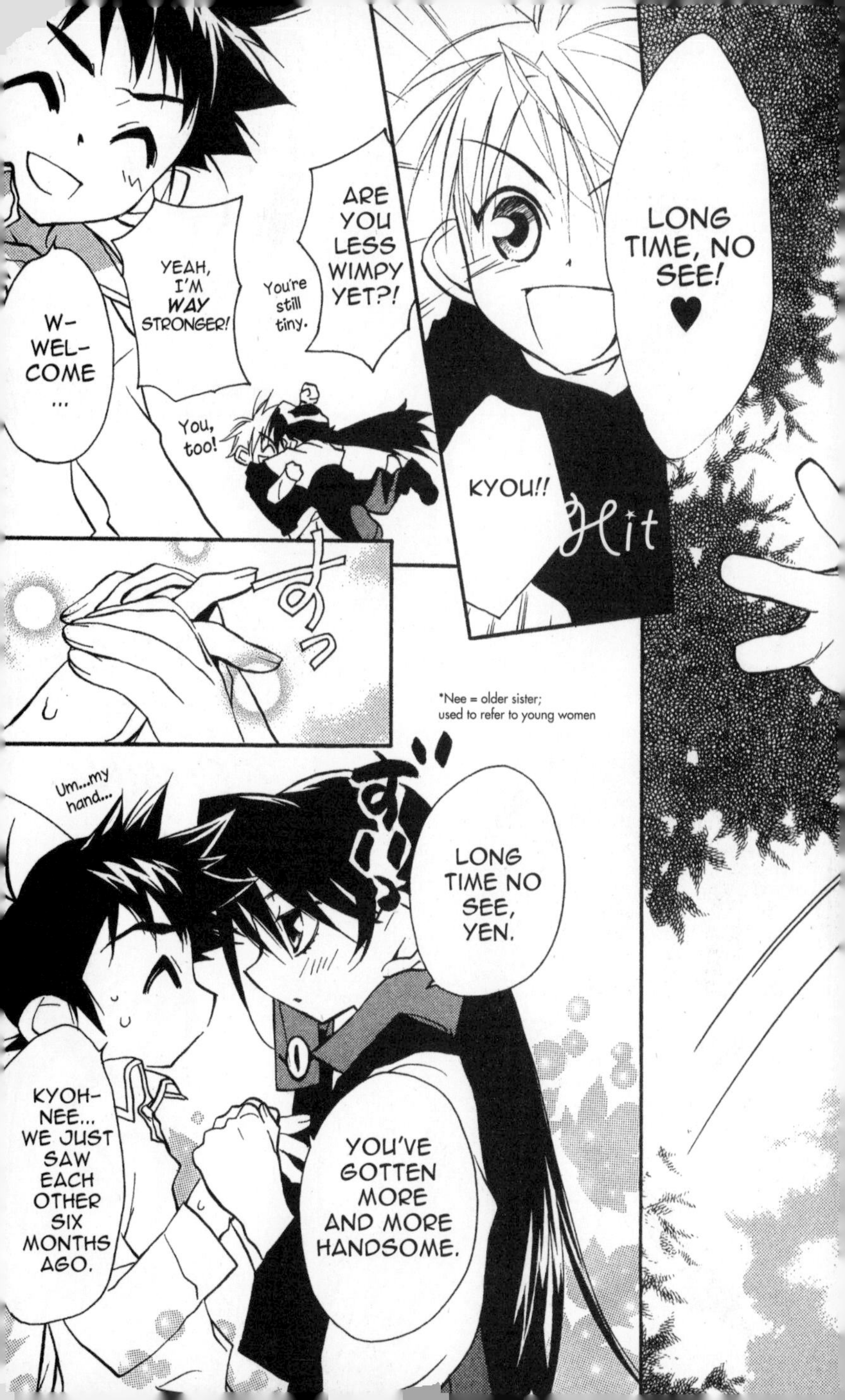
LONG TIME, NO SEE! ♥
KYOU!!
Hit
ARE YOU LESS WIMPY YET?!
You're still tiny.
YEAH, I'M WAY STRONGER!
You, too!
W-WEL-COME ...
*Nee = older sister; used to refer to young women
LONG TIME NO SEE, YEN.
YOU'VE GOTTEN MORE AND MORE HANDSOME.
Um...my hand...
KYOH-NEE... WE JUST SAW EACH OTHER SIX MONTHS AGO.

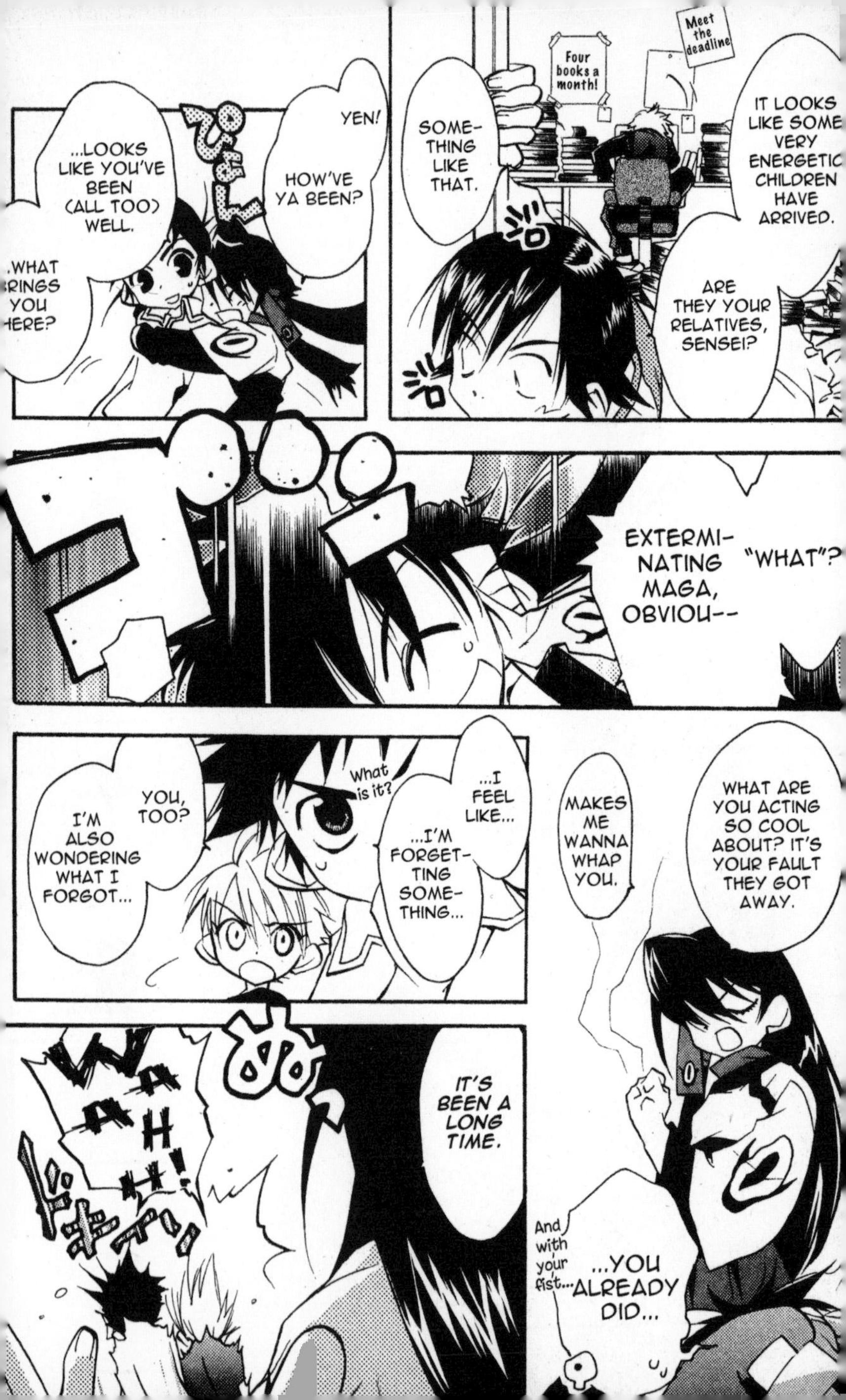
Meet the deadline
Four books a month!
IT LOOKS LIKE SOME VERY ENERGETIC CHILDREN HAVE ARRIVED.
ARE THEY YOUR RELATIVES, SENSEI?
SOME-THING LIKE THAT.
YEN!
HOW'VE YA BEEN?
...LOOKS LIKE YOU'VE BEEN (ALL TOO) WELL.
.WHAT RINGS YOU HERE?
EXTERMI-NATING MAGA, OBVIOU--
"WHAT"?
WHAT ARE YOU ACTING SO COOL ABOUT? IT'S YOUR FAULT THEY GOT AWAY.
MAKES ME WANNA WHAP YOU.
...YOU ALREADY DID...
And with your fist...
...I FEEL LIKE...
What is it?
...I'M FORGET-TING SOME-THING...
YOU, TOO?
I'M ALSO WONDERING WHAT I FORGOT...
IT'S BEEN A LONG TIME.
WAAHH!

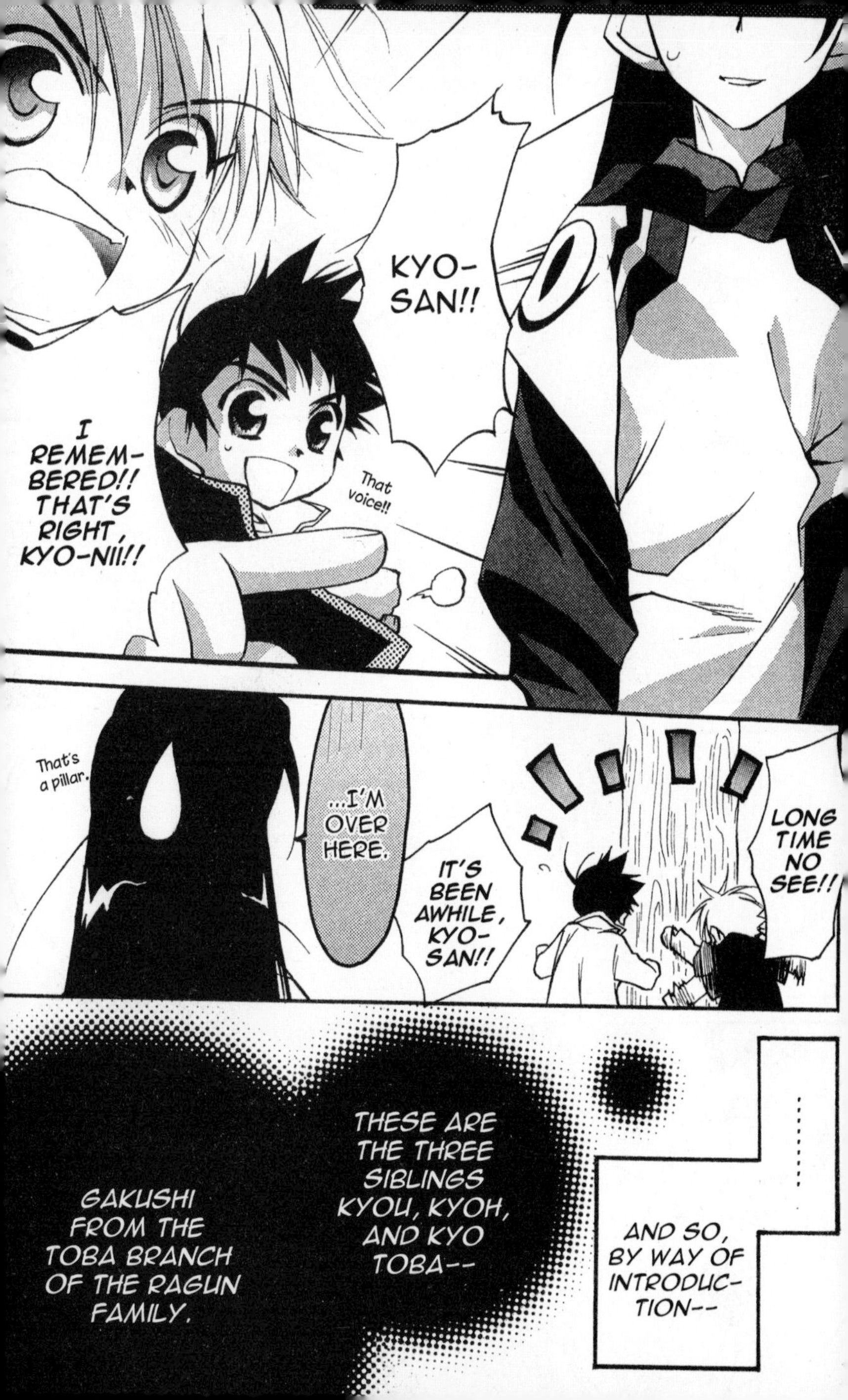
KYO-SAN!!
That voice!!
I REMEMBERED!! THAT'S RIGHT, KYO-NII!!
LONG TIME NO SEE!!
IT'S BEEN AWHILE, KYO-SAN!!
...I'M OVER HERE.
That's a pillar.
AND SO, BY WAY OF INTRODUCTION--
THESE ARE THE THREE SIBLINGS KYOU, KYOH, AND KYO TOBA--
GAKUSHI FROM THE TOBA BRANCH OF THE RAGUN FAMILY.

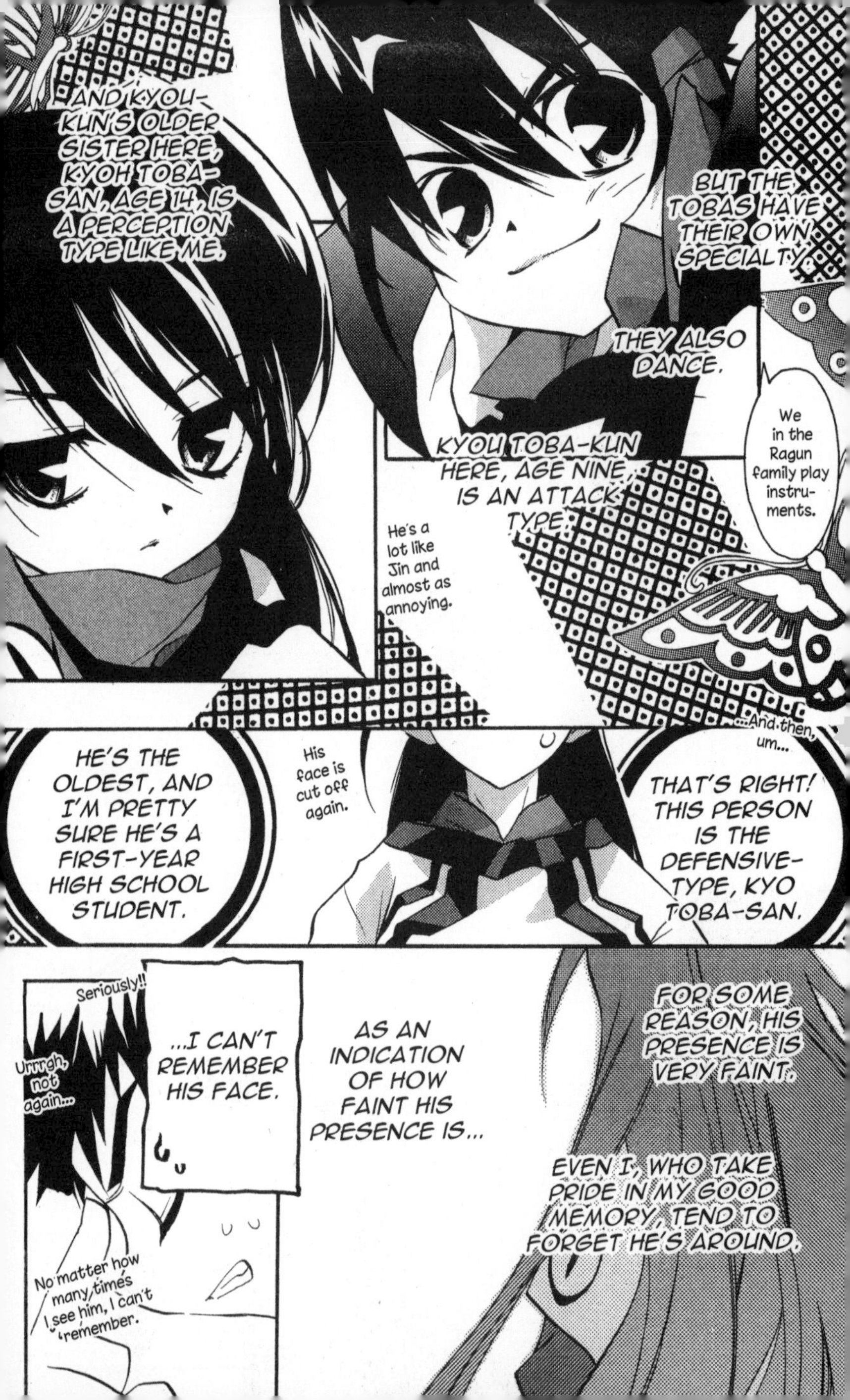
BUT THE TOBAS HAVE THEIR OWN SPECIALTY.
THEY ALSO DANCE.
We in the Ragun family play instruments.
KYOU TOBA-KUN HERE, AGE NINE, IS AN ATTACK TYPE.
He's a lot like Jin and almost as annoying.
AND KYOU-KUN'S OLDER SISTER HERE, KYOH TOBA-SAN, AGE 14, IS A PERCEPTION TYPE LIKE ME.
...And then, um...
THAT'S RIGHT! THIS PERSON IS THE DEFENSIVE-TYPE, KYO TOBA-SAN.
His face is cut off again.
HE'S THE OLDEST, AND I'M PRETTY SURE HE'S A FIRST-YEAR HIGH SCHOOL STUDENT.
FOR SOME REASON, HIS PRESENCE IS VERY FAINT.
EVEN I, WHO TAKE PRIDE IN MY GOOD MEMORY, TEND TO FORGET HE'S AROUND.
AS AN INDICATION OF HOW FAINT HIS PRESENCE IS...
...I CAN'T REMEMBER HIS FACE.
Seriously!!
Urrrgh, not again...
No matter how many times I see him, I can't remember.

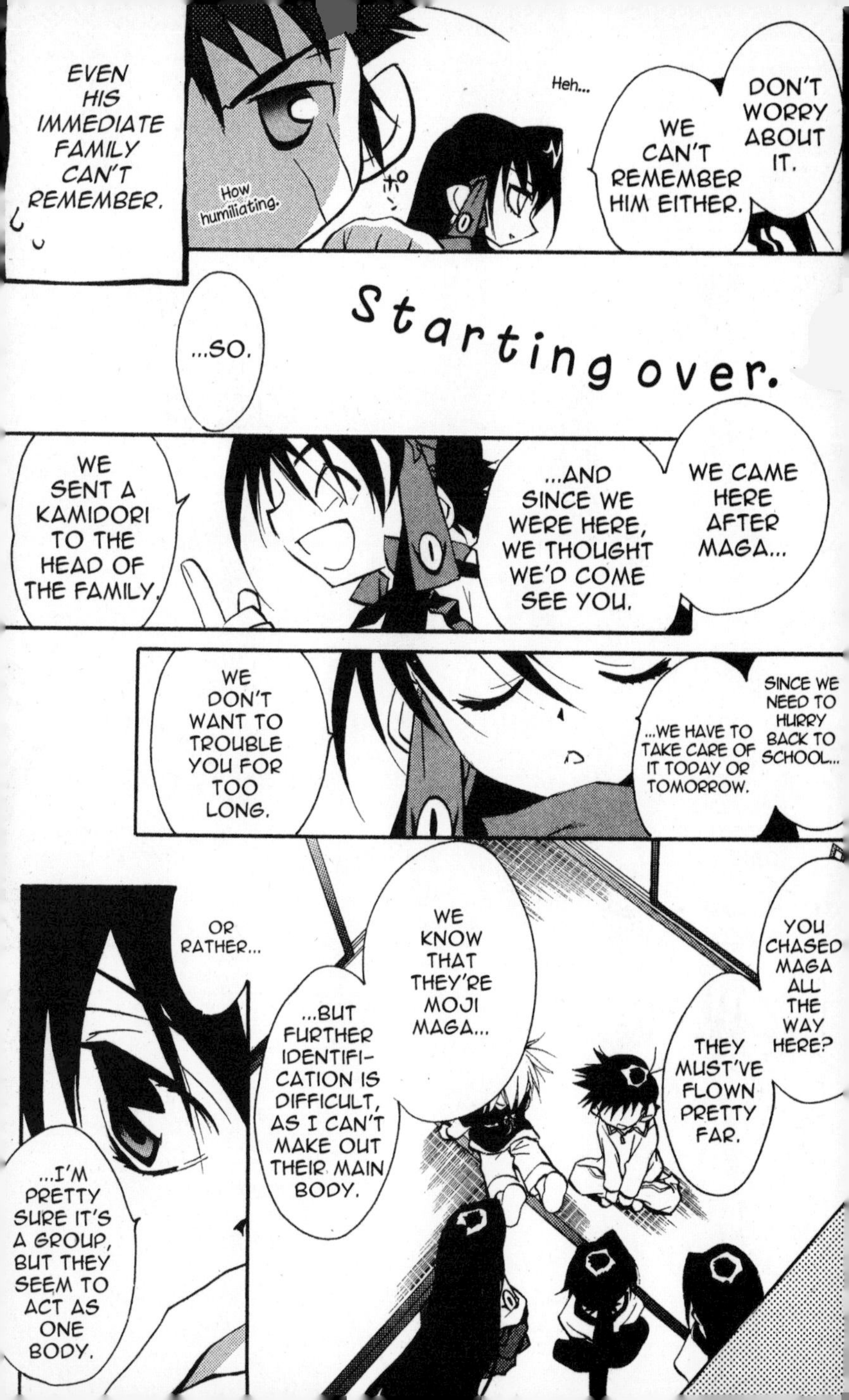
DON'T WORRY ABOUT IT.
WE CAN'T REMEMBER HIM EITHER.
Heh...
How humiliating.
EVEN HIS IMMEDIATE FAMILY CAN'T REMEMBER.
Starting over.
...SO.
WE CAME HERE AFTER MAGA...
...AND SINCE WE WERE HERE, WE THOUGHT WE'D COME SEE YOU.
WE SENT A KAMIDORI TO THE HEAD OF THE FAMILY.
SINCE WE NEED TO HURRY BACK TO SCHOOL...
...WE HAVE TO TAKE CARE OF IT TODAY OR TOMORROW.
WE DON'T WANT TO TROUBLE YOU FOR TOO LONG.
YOU CHASED MAGA ALL THE WAY HERE?
THEY MUST'VE FLOWN PRETTY FAR.
WE KNOW THAT THEY'RE MOJI MAGA...
...BUT FURTHER IDENTIFICATION IS DIFFICULT, AS I CAN'T MAKE OUT THEIR MAIN BODY.
OR RATHER...
...I'M PRETTY SURE IT'S A GROUP, BUT THEY SEEM TO ACT AS ONE BODY.

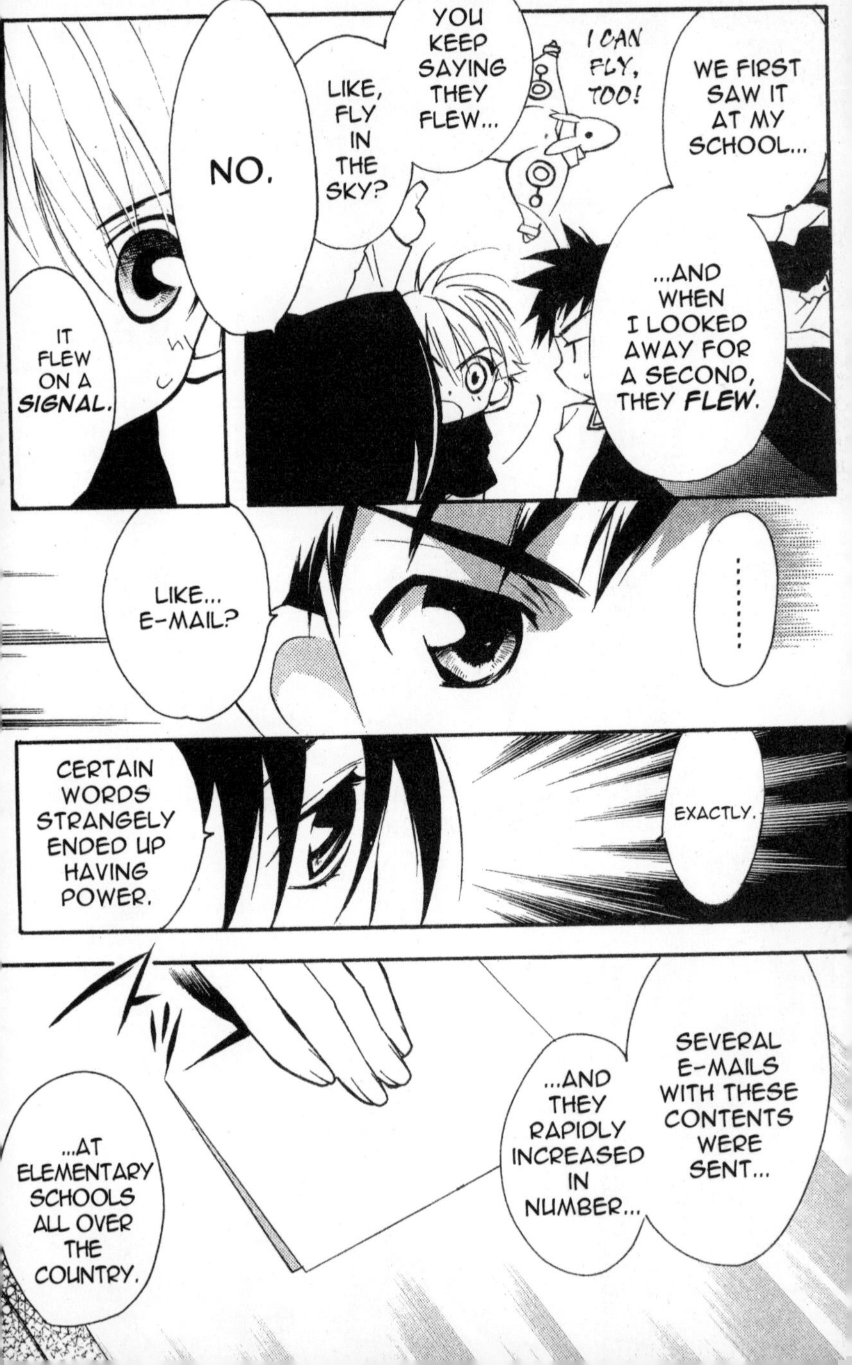
WE FIRST SAW IT AT MY SCHOOL...
...AND WHEN I LOOKED AWAY FOR A SECOND, THEY *FLEW*.
I CAN FLY, TOO!
YOU KEEP SAYING THEY FLEW...
LIKE, FLY IN THE SKY?
NO.
IT FLEW ON A *SIGNAL*.
......
LIKE... E-MAIL?
EXACTLY.
CERTAIN WORDS STRANGELY ENDED UP HAVING POWER.
SEVERAL E-MAILS WITH THESE CONTENTS WERE SENT...
...AND THEY RAPIDLY INCREASED IN NUMBER...
...AT ELEMENTARY SCHOOLS ALL OVER THE COUNTRY.

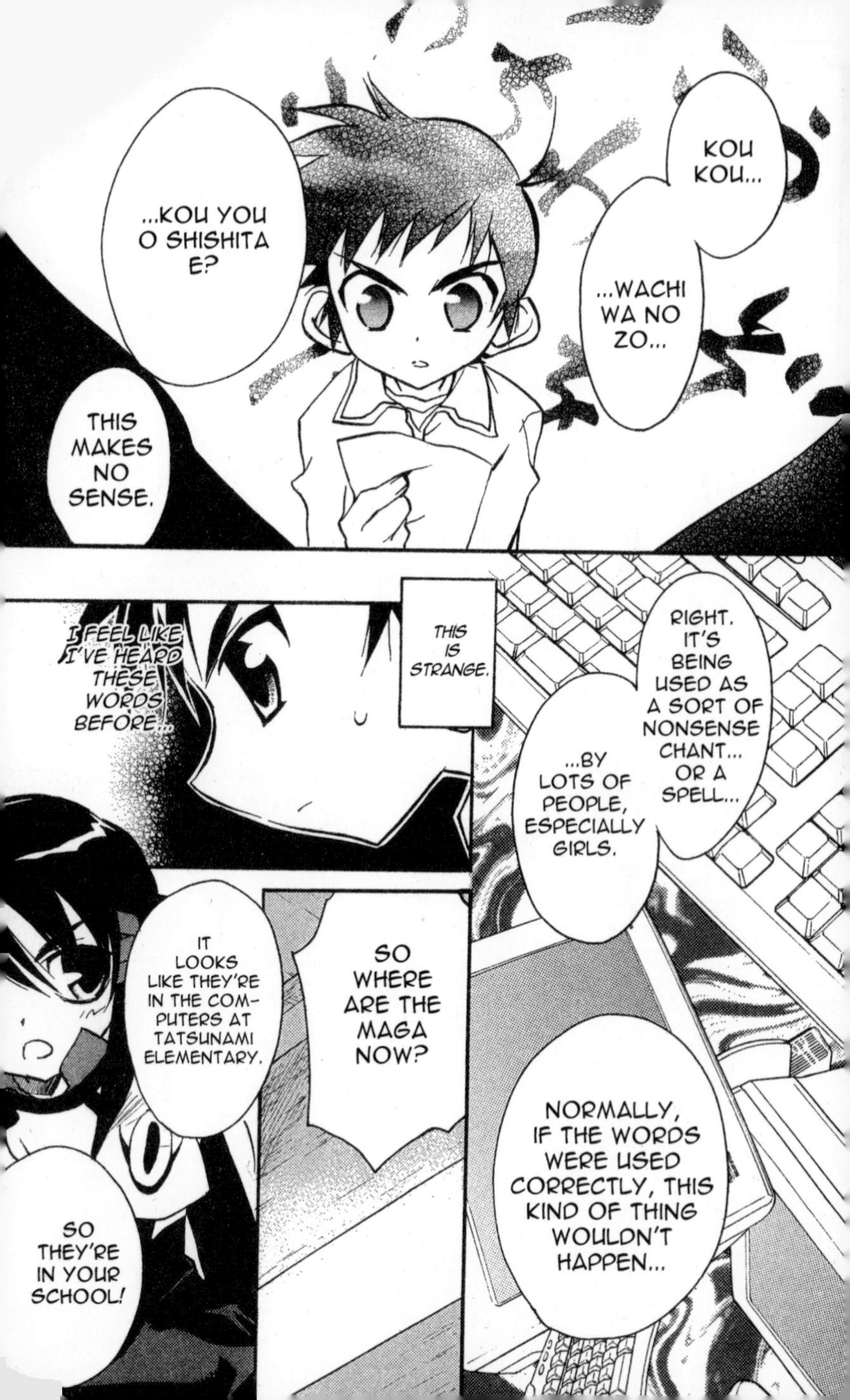
KOU KOU...
...WACHI WA NO ZO...
...KOU YOU O SHISHITA E?
THIS MAKES NO SENSE.
RIGHT. IT'S BEING USED AS A SORT OF NONSENSE CHANT... OR A SPELL...
...BY LOTS OF PEOPLE, ESPECIALLY GIRLS.
NORMALLY, IF THE WORDS WERE USED CORRECTLY, THIS KIND OF THING WOULDN'T HAPPEN...
THIS IS STRANGE.
I FEEL LIKE I'VE HEARD THESE WORDS BEFORE...
SO WHERE ARE THE MAGA NOW?
IT LOOKS LIKE THEY'RE IN THE COM-PUTERS AT TATSUNAMI ELEMENTARY.
SO THEY'RE IN YOUR SCHOOL!

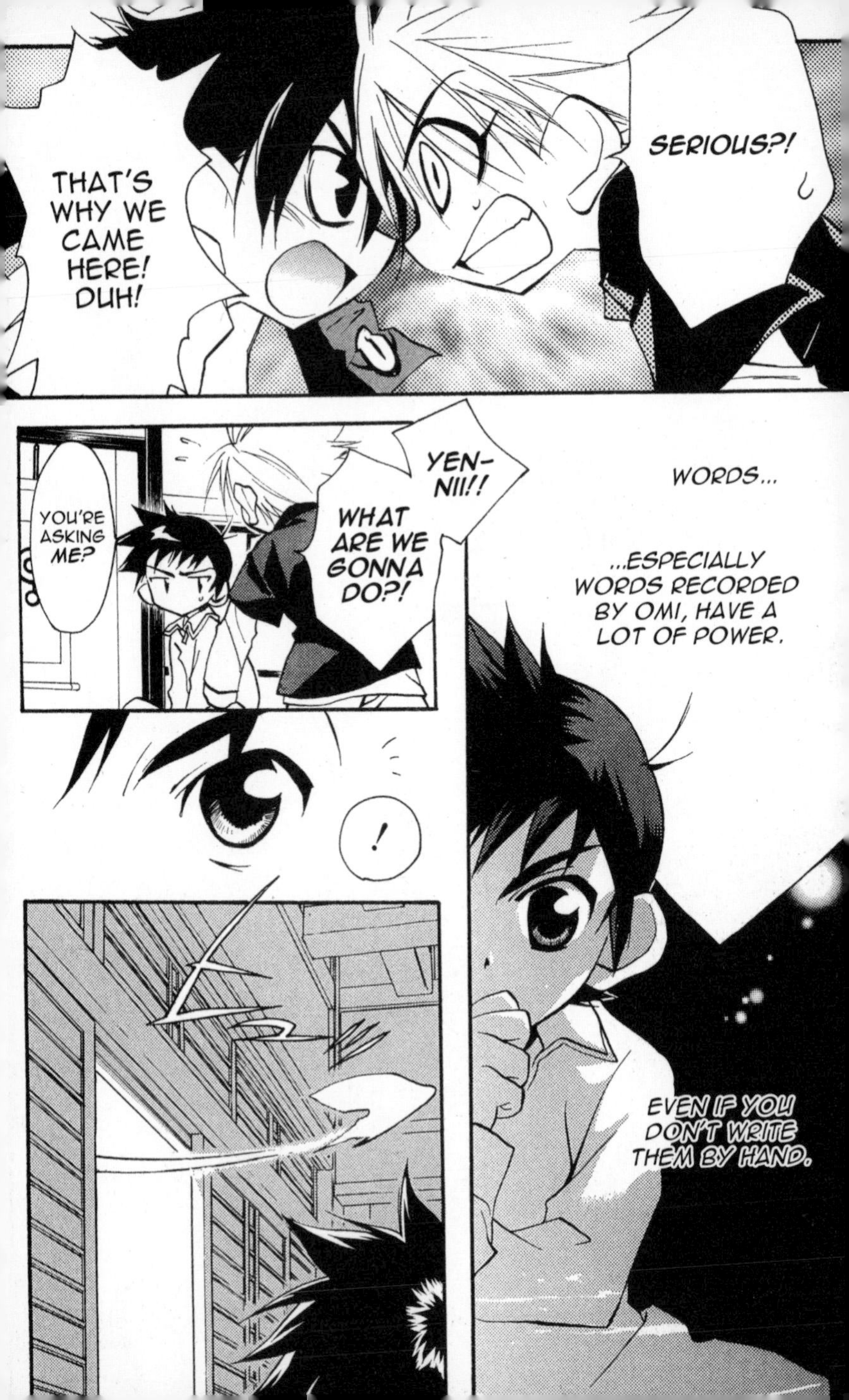
SERIOUS?!
THAT'S WHY WE CAME HERE! DUH!
WORDS...
...ESPECIALLY WORDS RECORDED BY OMI, HAVE A LOT OF POWER.
EVEN IF YOU DON'T WRITE THEM BY HAND.
YEN-NII!!
WHAT ARE WE GONNA DO?!
YOU'RE ASKING ME?
!

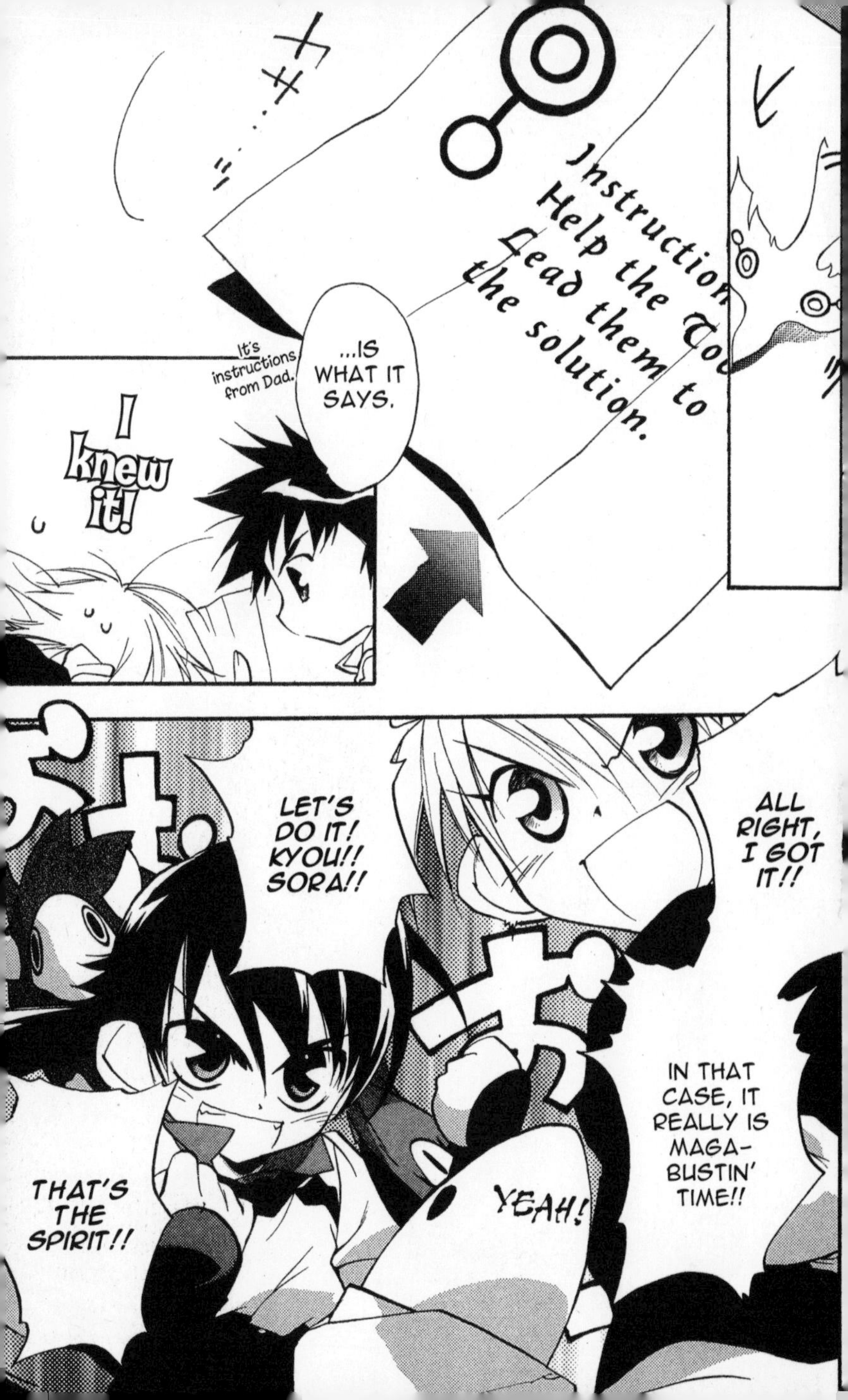
Instruction
Help the To
Lead them to
the solution.
...IS WHAT IT SAYS.
It's instructions from Dad.
I knew it!
ALL RIGHT, I GOT IT!!
LET'S DO IT! KYOU!! SORA!!
IN THAT CASE, IT REALLY IS MAGA-BUSTIN' TIME!!
YEAH!
THAT'S THE SPIRIT!!

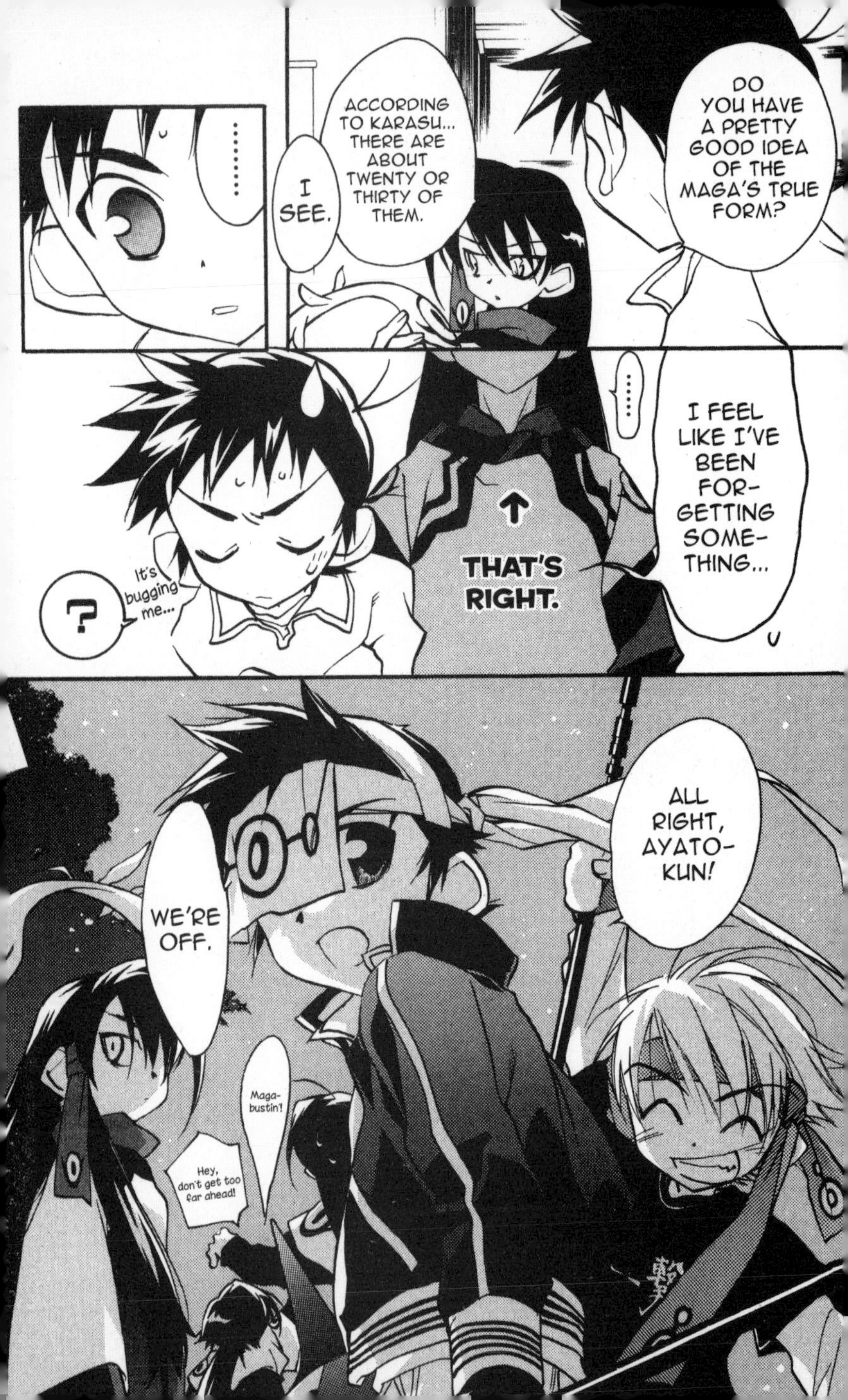
DO YOU HAVE A PRETTY GOOD IDEA OF THE MAGA'S TRUE FORM?
ACCORDING TO KARASU... THERE ARE ABOUT TWENTY OR THIRTY OF THEM.
I SEE.
......
I FEEL LIKE I'VE BEEN FOR-GETTING SOME-THING...
......
THAT'S RIGHT.
It's bugging me...
?
ALL RIGHT, AYATO-KUN!
WE'RE OFF.
Maga-bustin'!
Hey, don't get too far ahead!

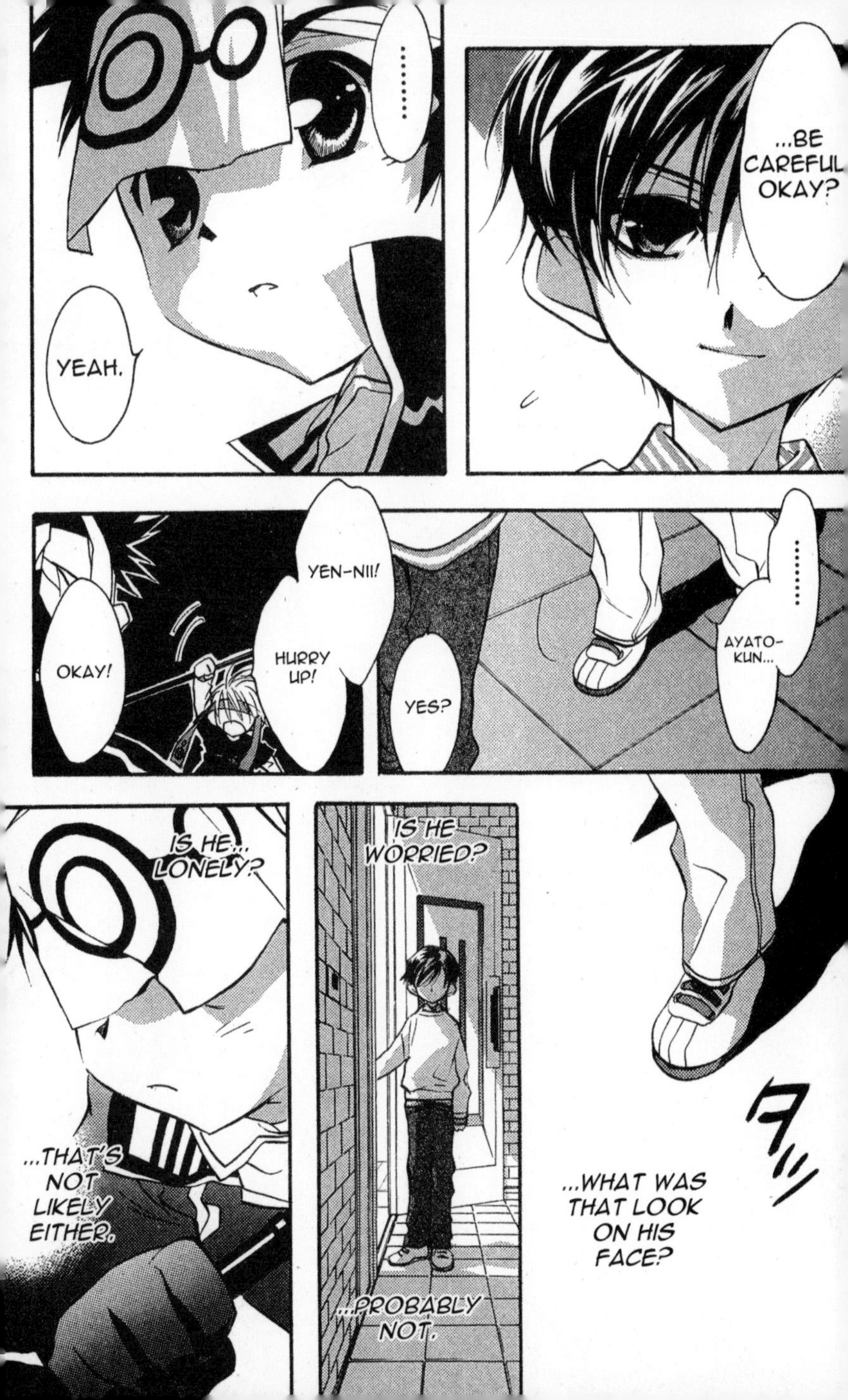
...BE CAREFUL OKAY?
......
YEAH.
......
AYATO-KUN...
YES?
YEN-NII!
HURRY UP!
OKAY!
...WHAT WAS THAT LOOK ON HIS FACE?
ダッ
IS HE WORRIED?
...PROBABLY NOT.
IS HE... LONELY?
...THAT'S NOT LIKELY EITHER.

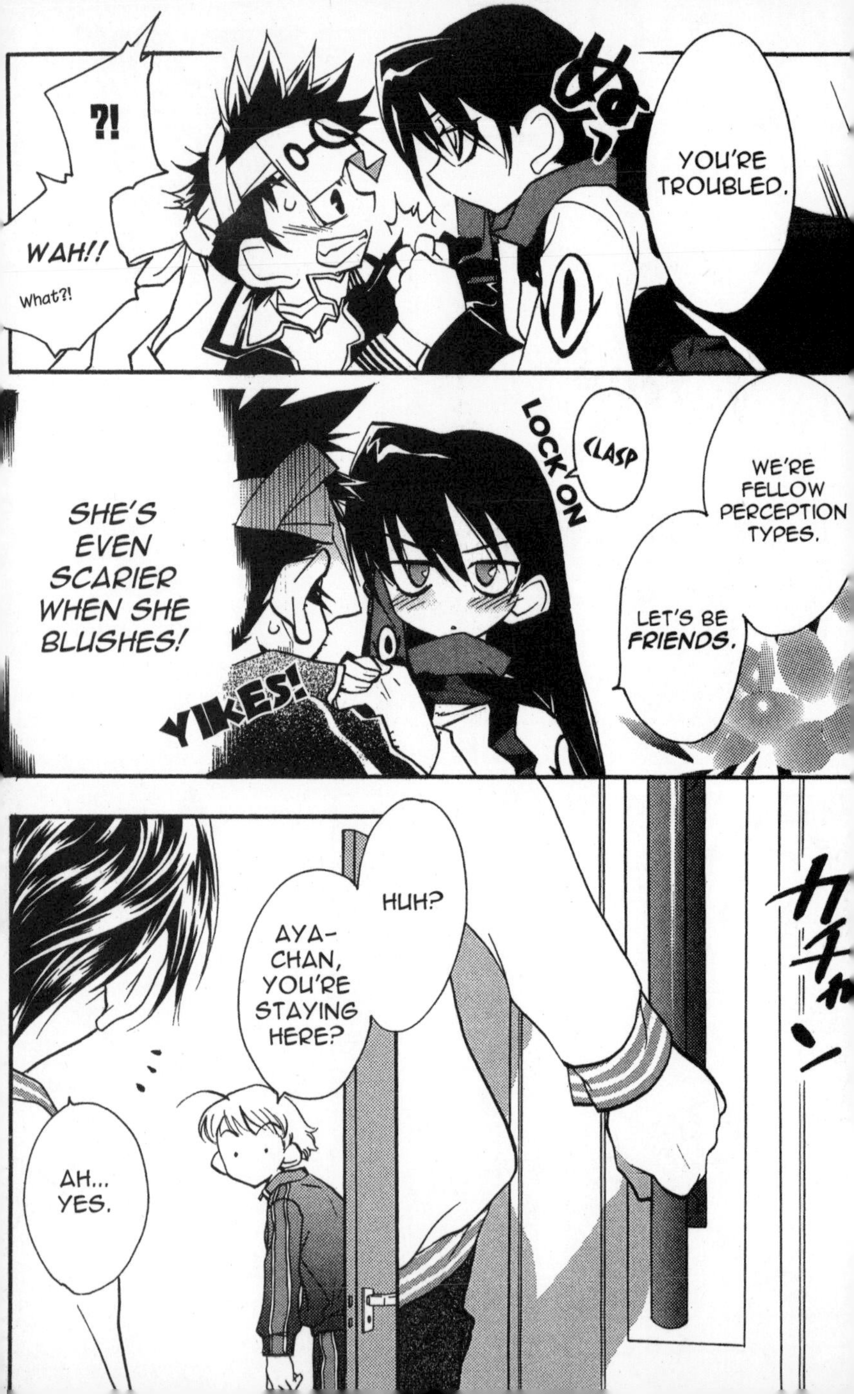
YOU'RE TROUBLED.
ぬっ
?!
WAH!!
What?!
WE'RE FELLOW PERCEPTION TYPES.
LET'S BE FRIENDS.
CLASP
LOCK ON
SHE'S EVEN SCARIER WHEN SHE BLUSHES!
YIKES!
カチャン
HUH?
AYA-CHAN, YOU'RE STAYING HERE?
...
AH... YES.

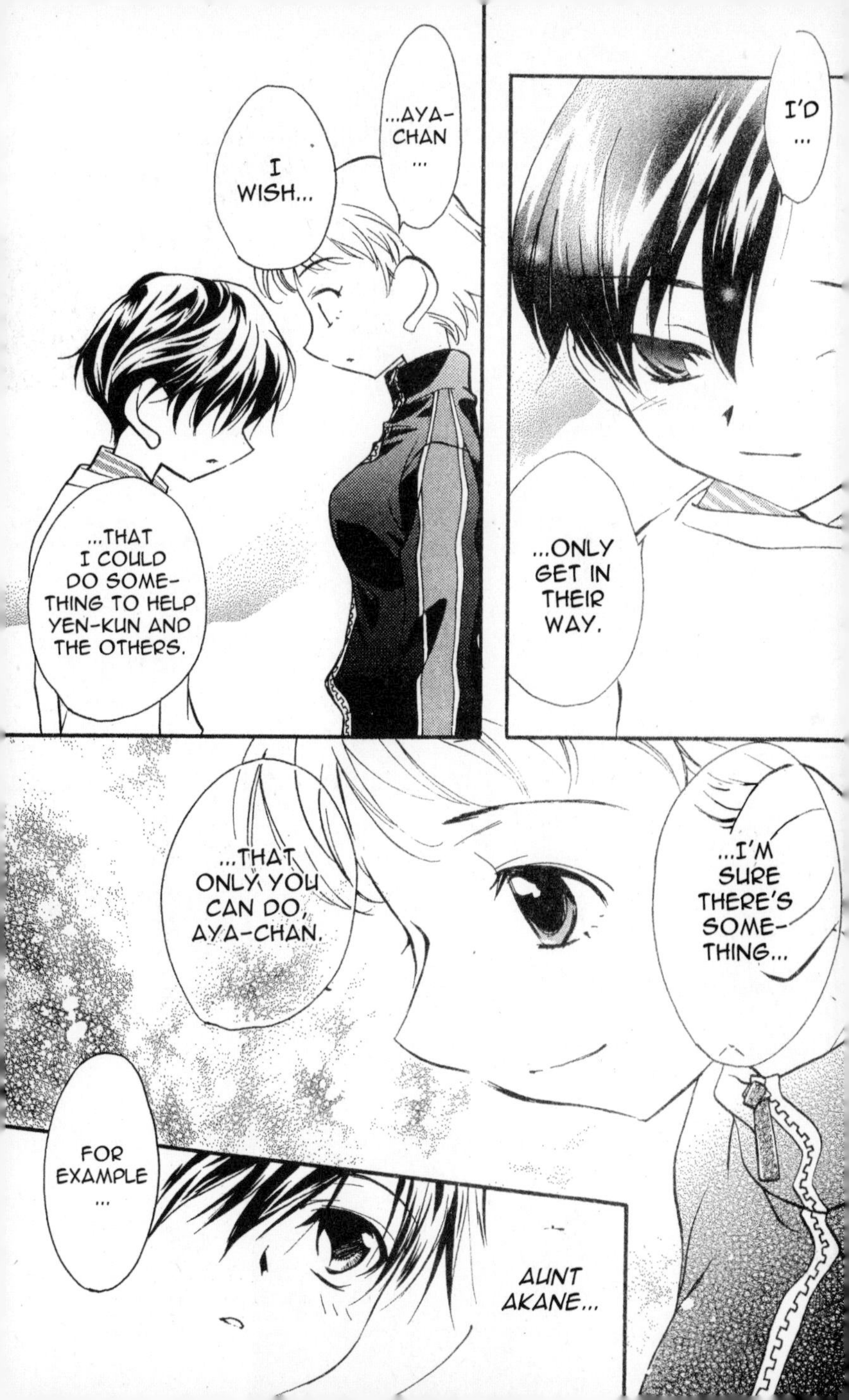
I'D ...
...ONLY GET IN THEIR WAY.
...AYA-CHAN ...
I WISH...
...THAT I COULD DO SOMETHING TO HELP YEN-KUN AND THE OTHERS.
...I'M SURE THERE'S SOMETHING...
...THAT ONLY YOU CAN DO, AYA-CHAN.
FOR EXAMPLE ...
AUNT AKANE...

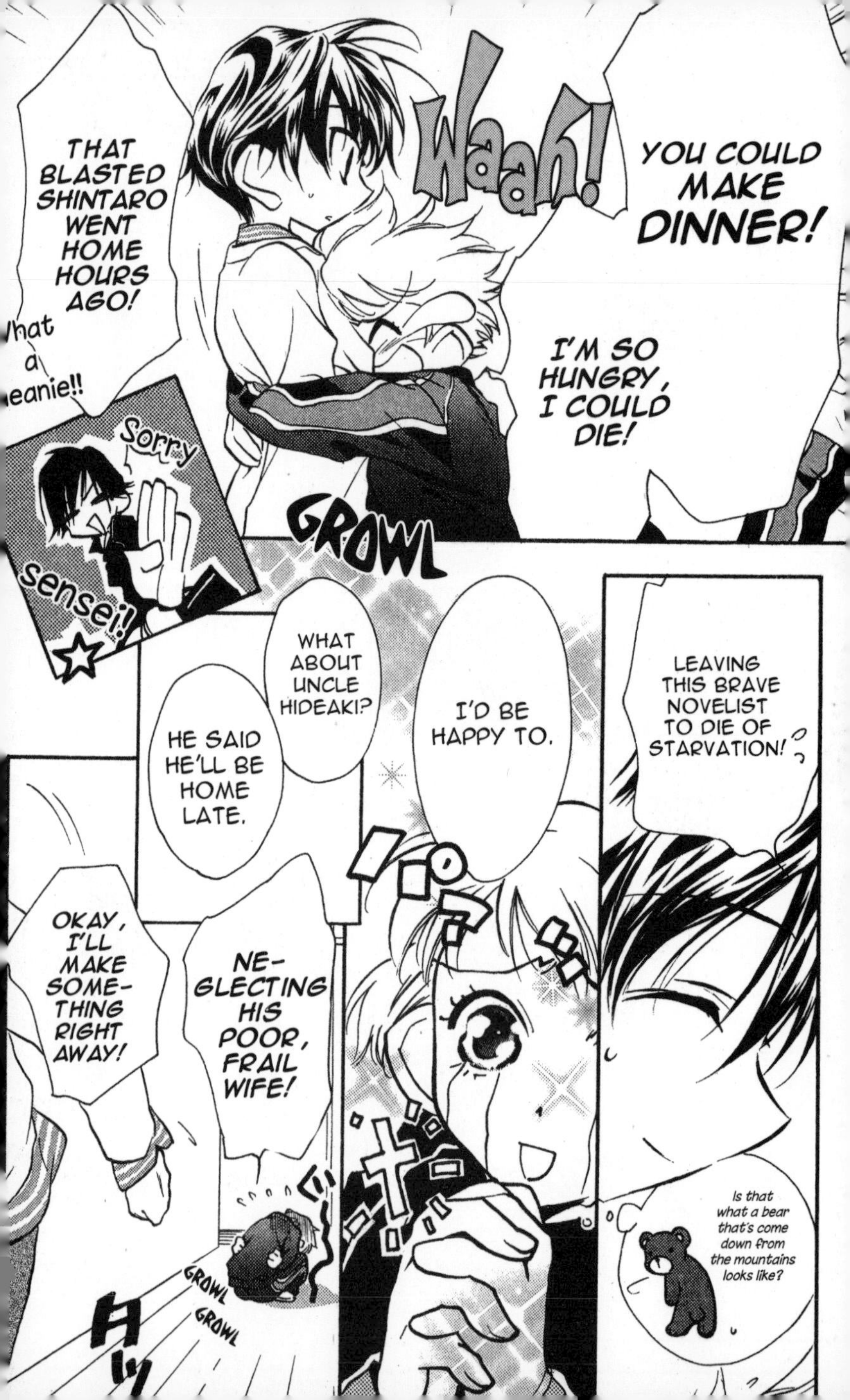
YOU COULD MAKE DINNER!
Waah!
I'M SO HUNGRY, I COULD DIE!
THAT BLASTED SHINTARO WENT HOME HOURS AGO!
hat a eanie!!
Sorry sensei!!
GROWL
LEAVING THIS BRAVE NOVELIST TO DIE OF STARVATION!
I'D BE HAPPY TO.
WHAT ABOUT UNCLE HIDEAKI?
HE SAID HE'LL BE HOME LATE.
Is that what a bear that's come down from the mountains looks like?
NE-GLECTING HIS POOR, FRAIL WIFE!
OKAY, I'LL MAKE SOME-THING RIGHT AWAY!
GROWL
GROWL

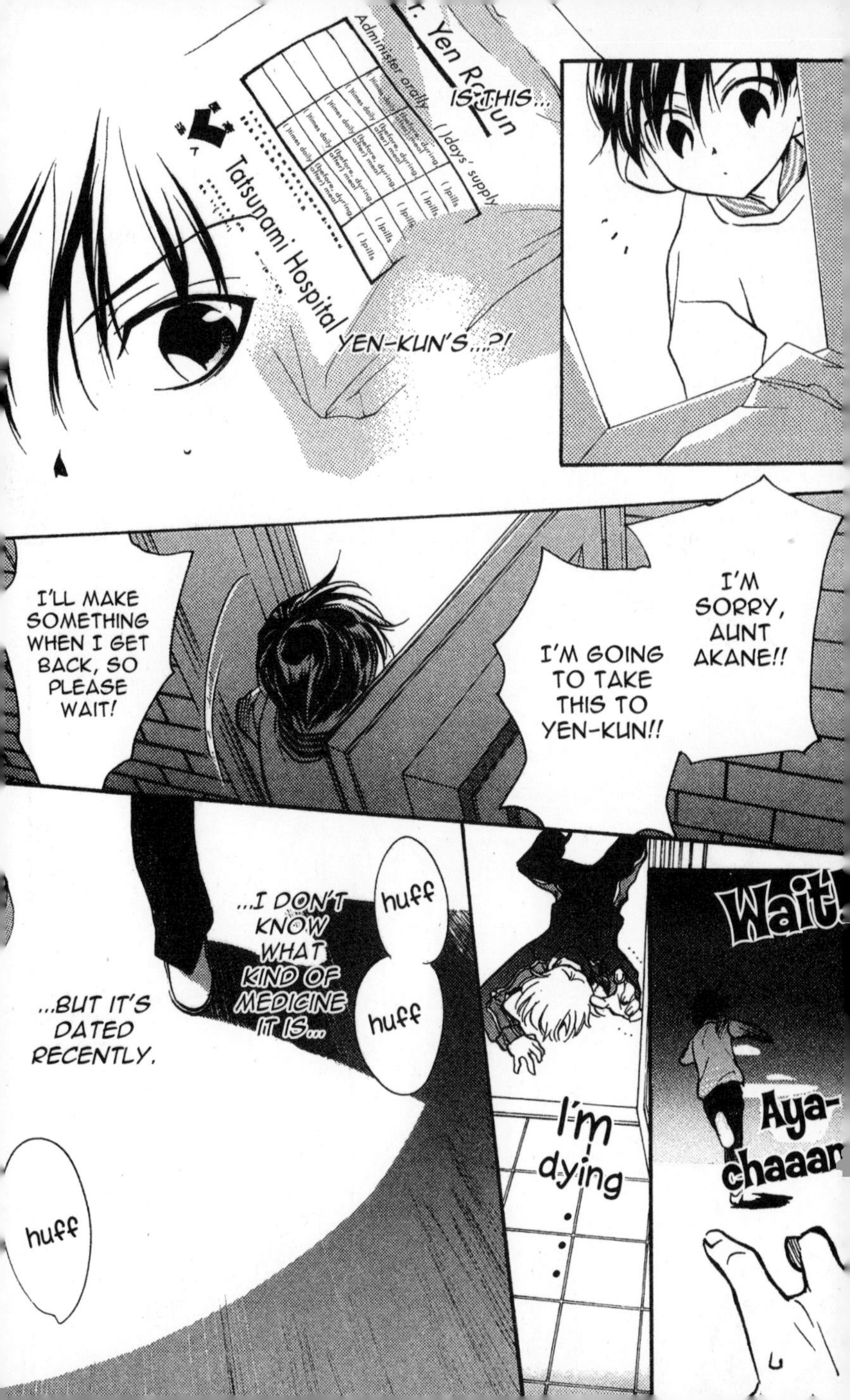
...
Administer orally
( )days' supply
Tatsunami Hospital
IS THIS...
YEN-KUN'S...?!
I'M SORRY, AUNT AKANE!!
I'M GOING TO TAKE THIS TO YEN-KUN!!
I'LL MAKE SOMETHING WHEN I GET BACK, SO PLEASE WAIT!
Wait!
Aya-chaaan
I'm dying...
huff
...I DON'T KNOW WHAT KIND OF MEDICINE IT IS...
huff
...BUT IT'S DATED RECENTLY.
huff

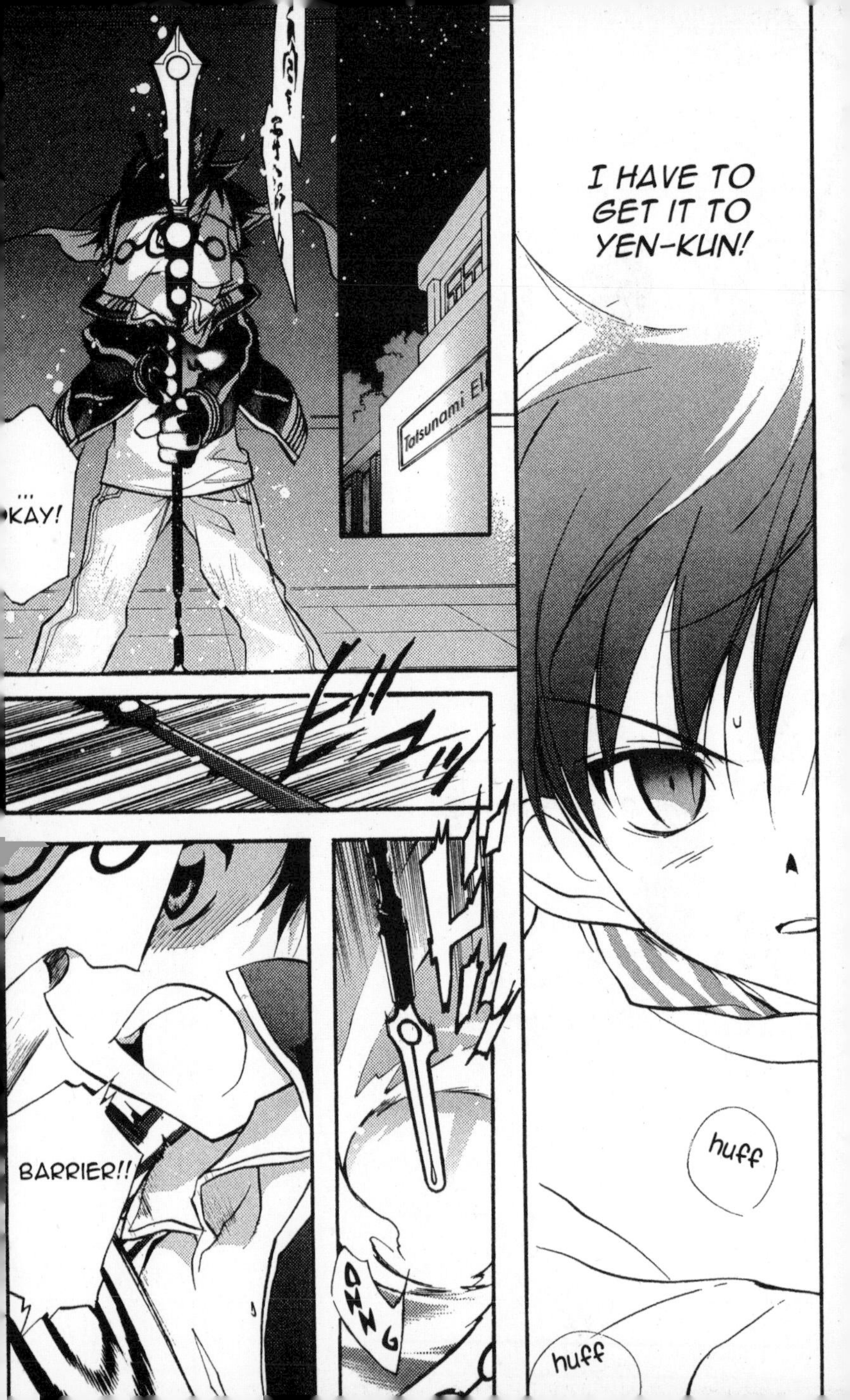
I HAVE TO GET IT TO YEN-KUN!
huff
huff
...
KAY!
BARRIER!!

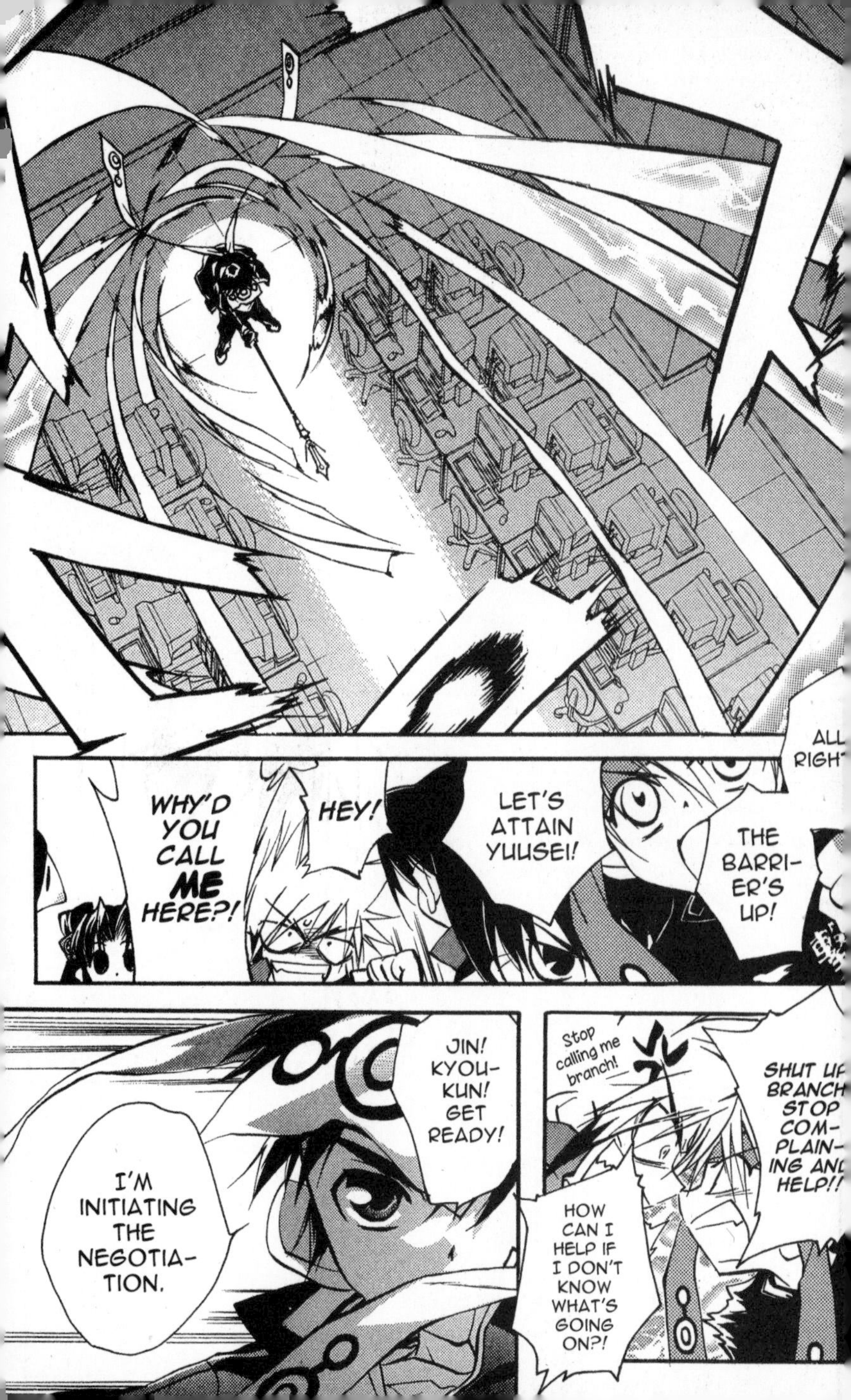

ALL RIGHT
THE BARRIER'S UP!
LET'S ATTAIN YUUSEI!
HEY!
WHY'D YOU CALL **ME** HERE?!
SHUT UP BRANCH STOP COMPLAINING AND HELP!!
Stop calling me branch!
HOW CAN I HELP IF I DON'T KNOW WHAT'S GOING ON?!
JIN! KYOU-KUN! GET READY!
I'M INITIATING THE NEGOTIATION.

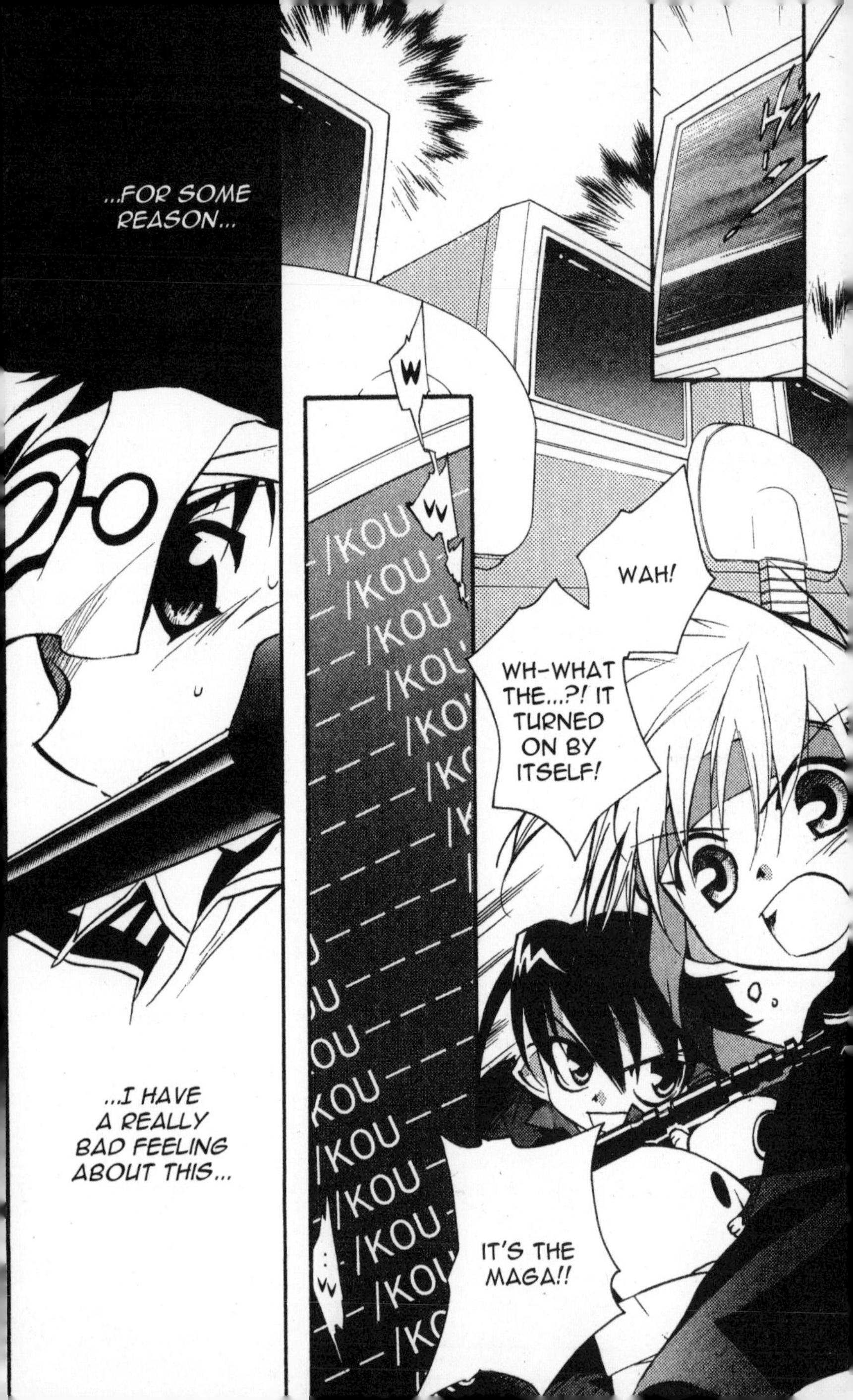
WAH!
WH-WHAT THE...?! IT TURNED ON BY ITSELF!
IT'S THE MAGA!!
/KOU
...FOR SOME REASON...
...I HAVE A REALLY BAD FEELING ABOUT THIS...

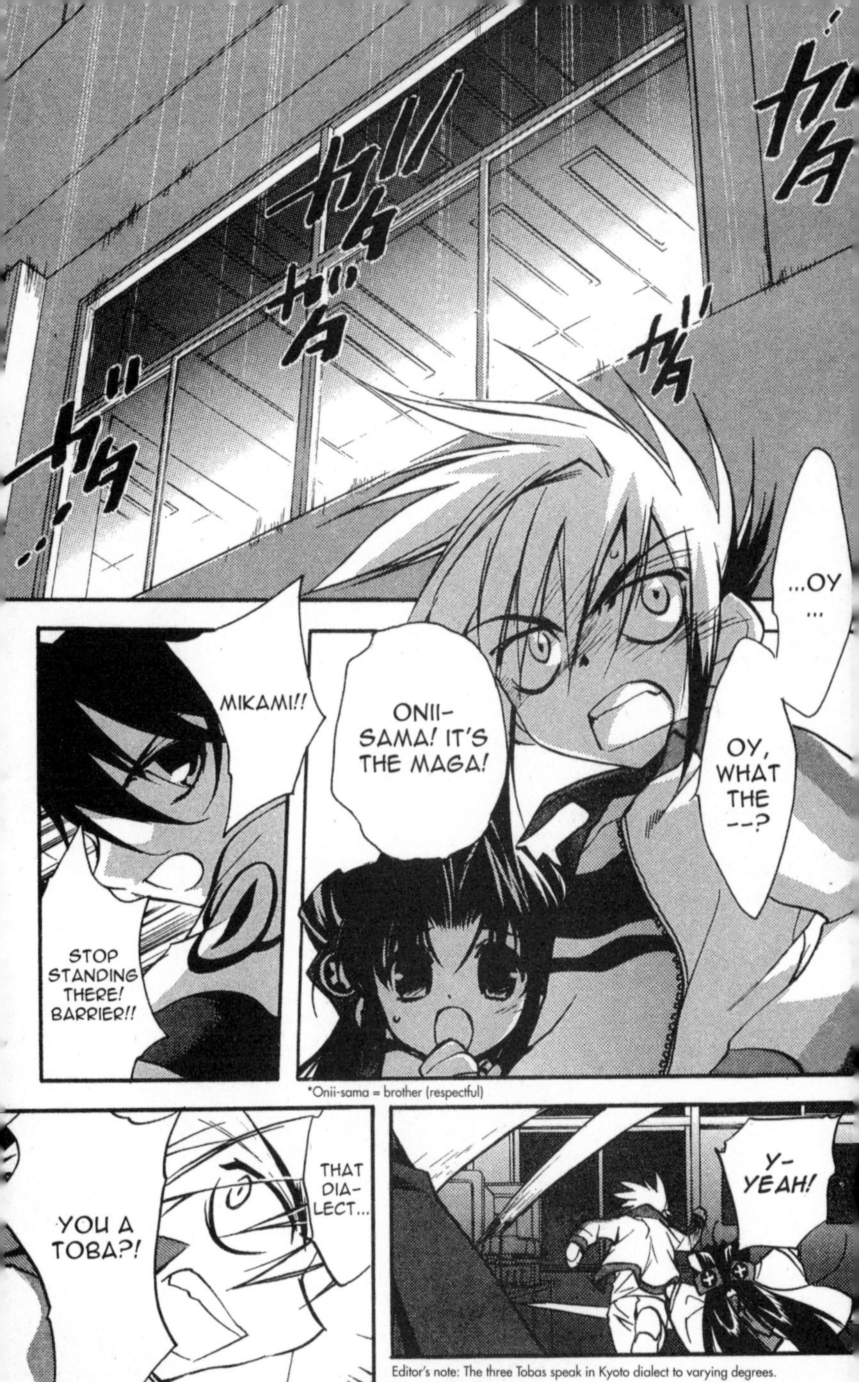
...OY ...
OY, WHAT THE --?
ONII-SAMA! IT'S THE MAGA!
MIKAMI!!
STOP STANDING THERE! BARRIER!!
Y-YEAH!
THAT DIA-LECT...
YOU A TOBA?!

*Onii-sama = brother (respectful)

Editor's note: The three Tobas speak in Kyoto dialect to varying degrees.

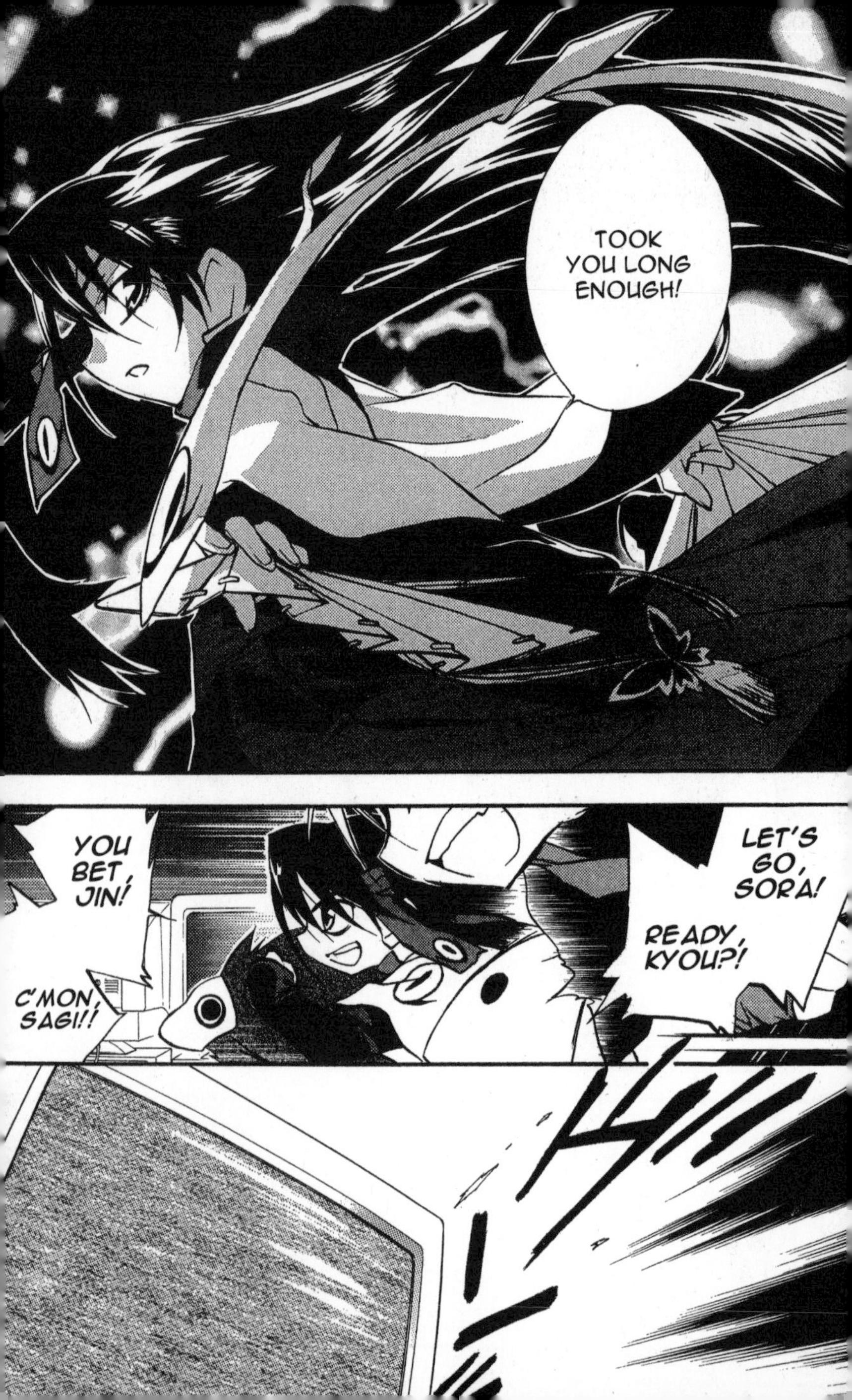
TOOK YOU LONG ENOUGH!
LET'S GO, SORA!
READY, KYOU?!
YOU BET, JIN!
C'MON, SAGI!!

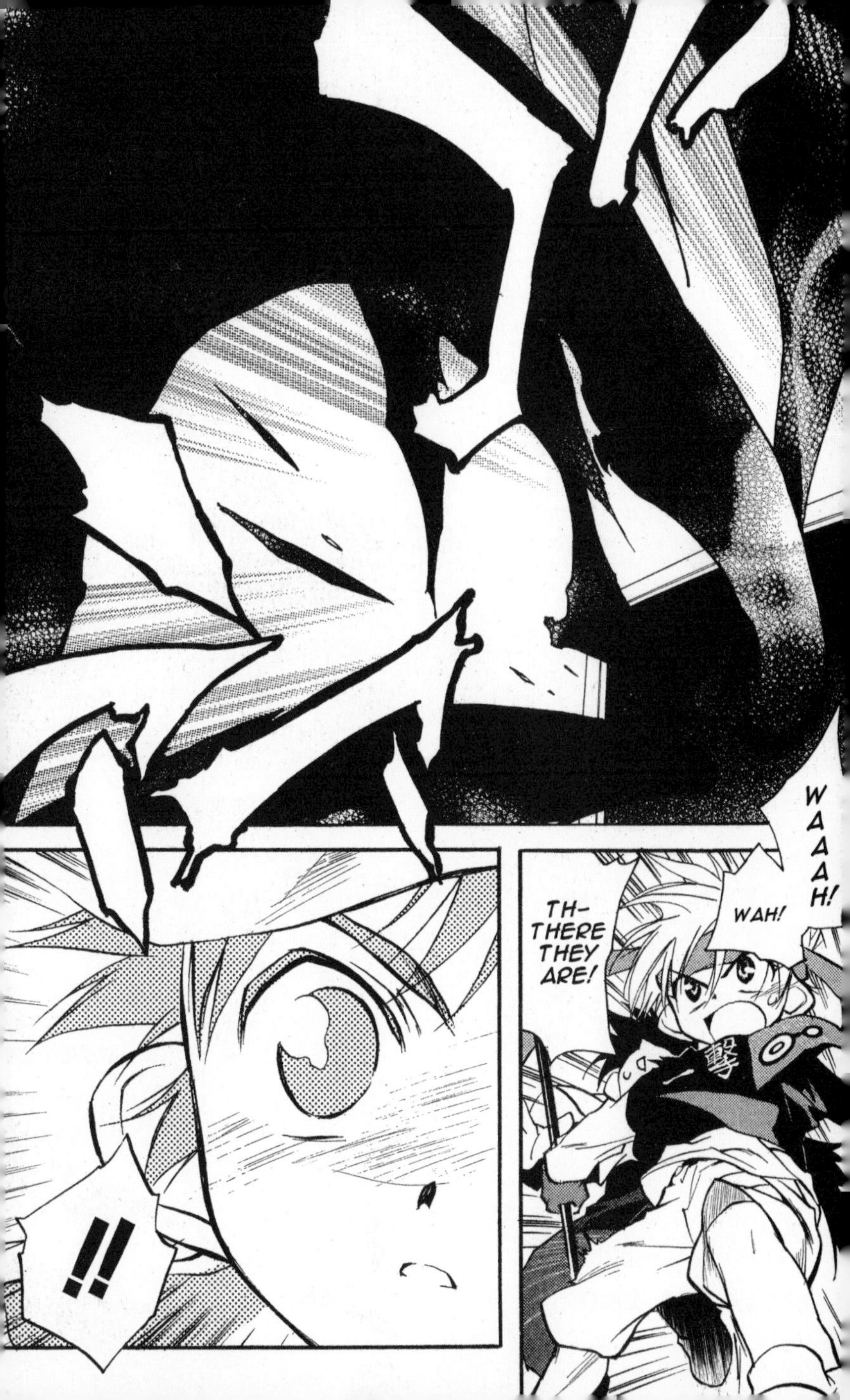
WAAAAH!
WAH!
TH-THERE THEY ARE!
!!

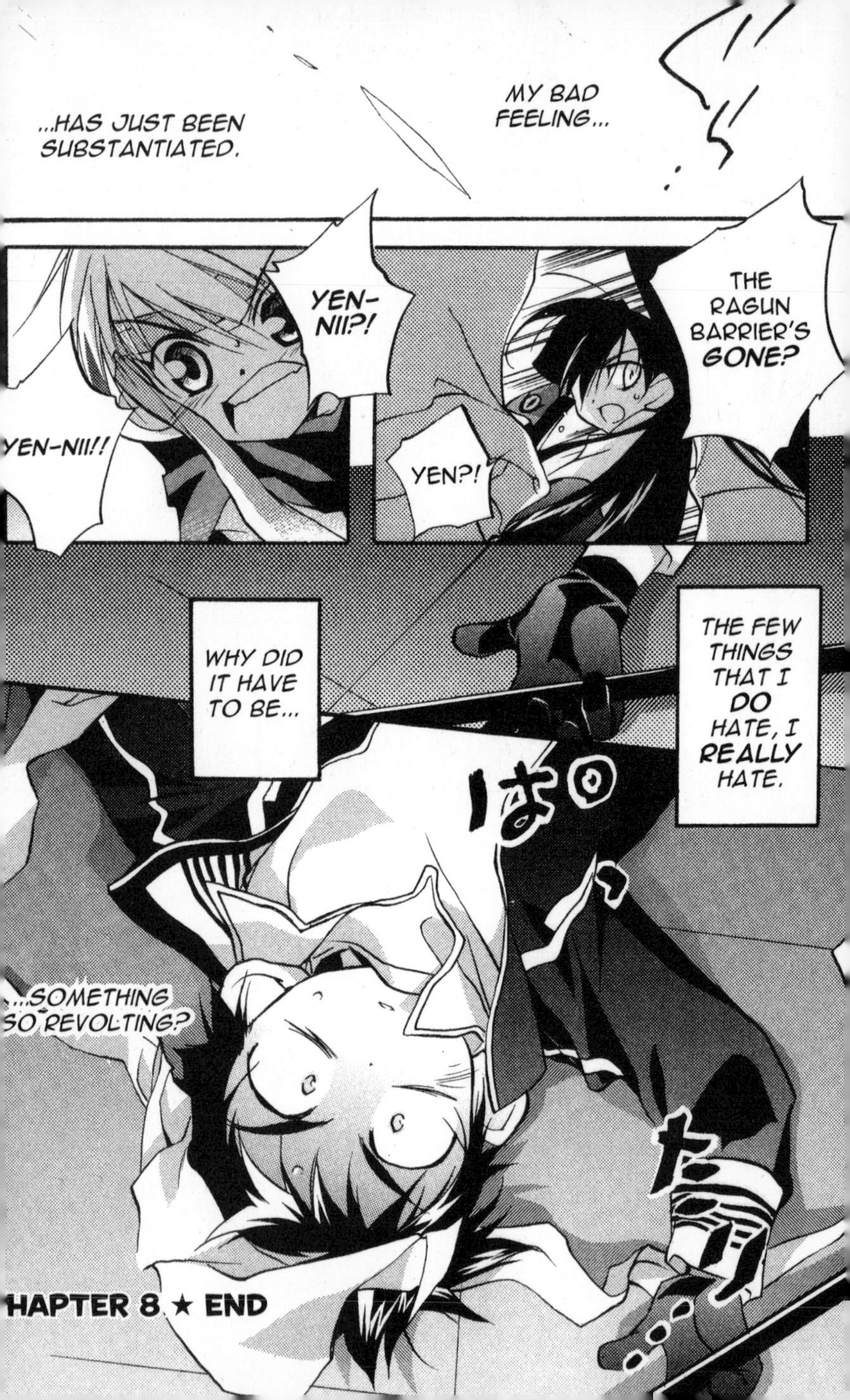
MY BAD FEELING...
...HAS JUST BEEN SUBSTANTIATED.
THE RAGUN BARRIER'S GONE?
YEN?!
YEN-NII?!
YEN-NII!!
THE FEW THINGS THAT I DO HATE, I REALLY HATE.
WHY DID IT HAVE TO BE...
...SOMETHING SO REVOLTING?
HAPTER 8 ★ END

YEN 2002 YUKIRU SUGISAKI
RAGUN LAGOON ENGINE

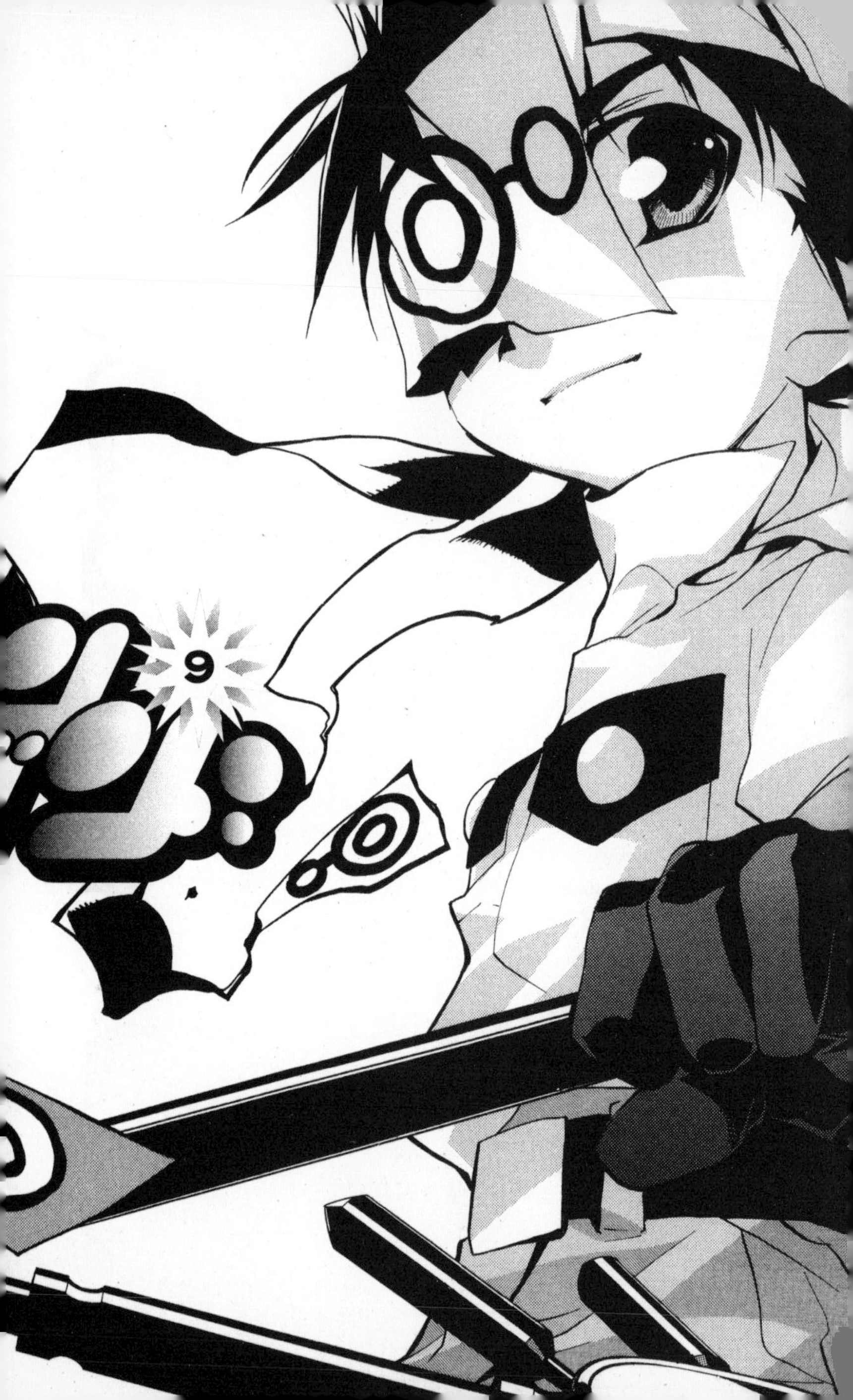

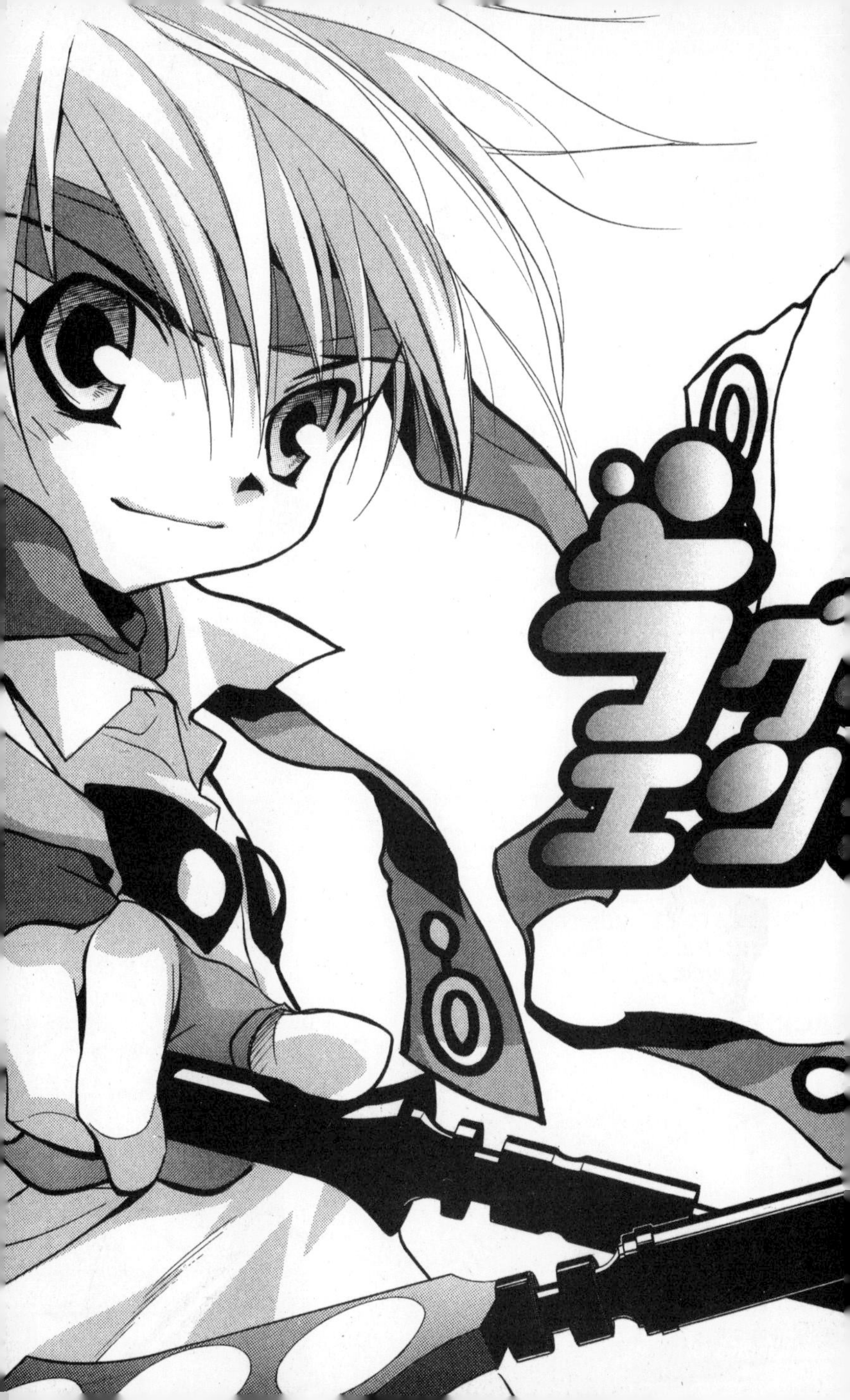

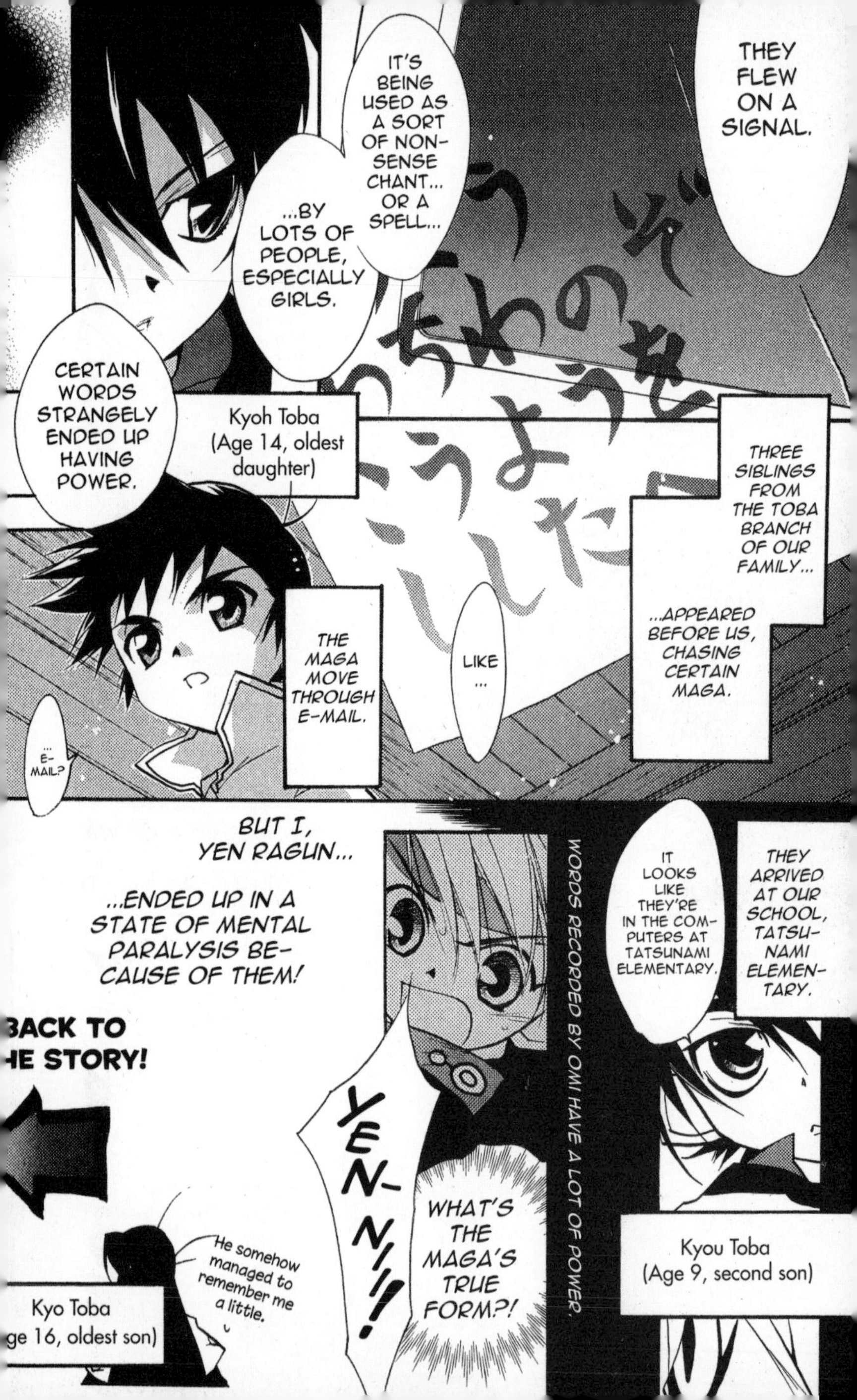
THEY FLEW ON A SIGNAL.
IT'S BEING USED AS A SORT OF NON-SENSE CHANT... OR A SPELL...
...BY LOTS OF PEOPLE, ESPECIALLY GIRLS.
CERTAIN WORDS STRANGELY ENDED UP HAVING POWER.
Kyoh Toba (Age 14, oldest daughter)
THREE SIBLINGS FROM THE TOBA BRANCH OF OUR FAMILY...
...APPEARED BEFORE US, CHASING CERTAIN MAGA.
LIKE ...
THE MAGA MOVE THROUGH E-MAIL.
... E-MAIL?
THEY ARRIVED AT OUR SCHOOL, TATSU-NAMI ELEMEN-TARY.
IT LOOKS LIKE THEY'RE IN THE COM-PUTERS AT TATSUNAMI ELEMENTARY.
Kyou Toba (Age 9, second son)
WORDS RECORDED BY OMI HAVE A LOT OF POWER.
YEN-NI!!
WHAT'S THE MAGA'S TRUE FORM?!
BUT I, YEN RAGUN...
...ENDED UP IN A STATE OF MENTAL PARALYSIS BE-CAUSE OF THEM!
BACK TO
HE STORY!
He somehow managed to remember me a little.
Kyo Toba
ge 16, oldest son)

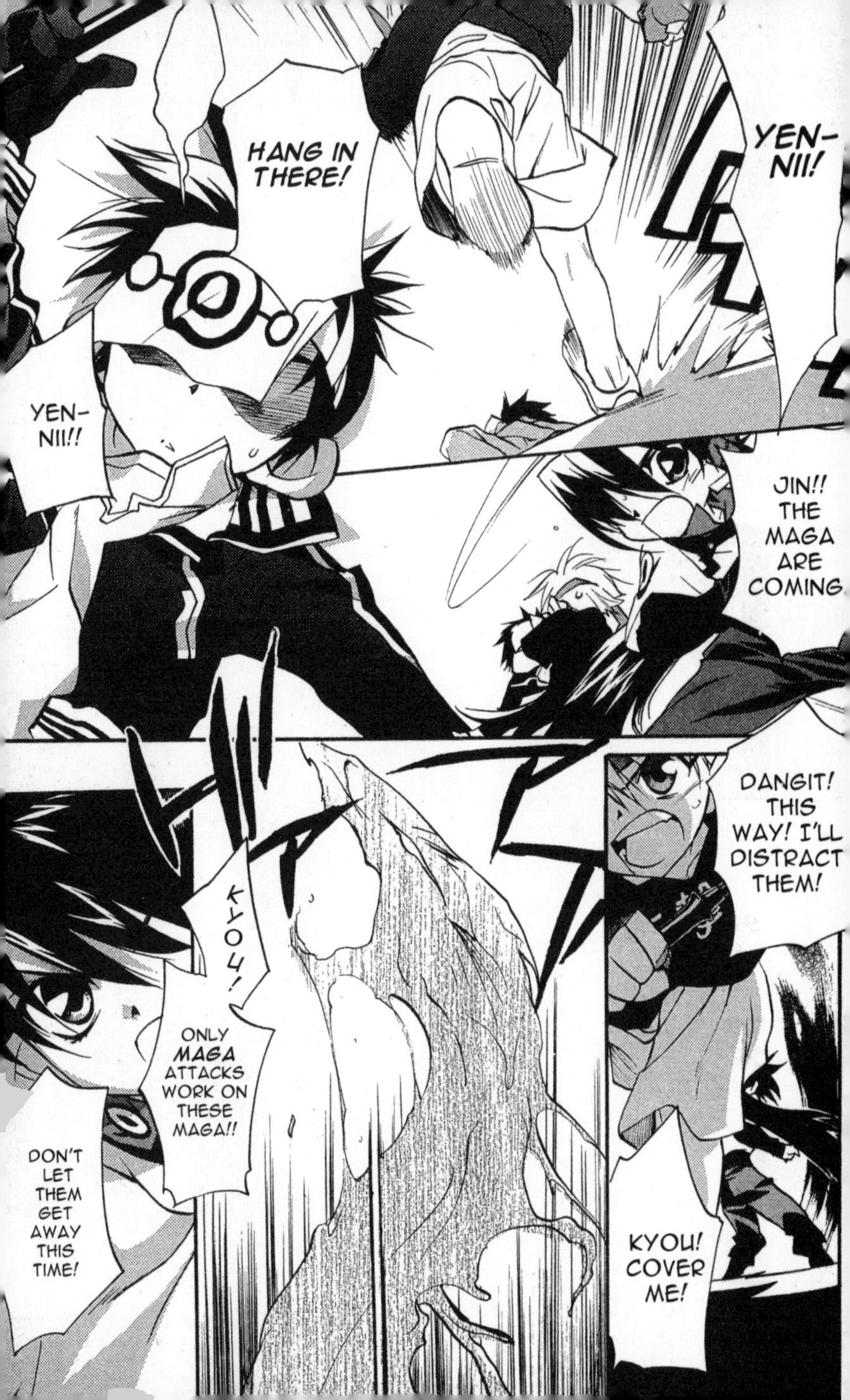
YEN-NII!
HANG IN THERE!
YEN-NII!!
JIN!! THE MAGA ARE COMING
DANGIT! THIS WAY! I'LL DISTRACT THEM!
KYOU! COVER ME!
KYOU!
ONLY MAGA ATTACKS WORK ON THESE MAGA!!
DON'T LET THEM GET AWAY THIS TIME!

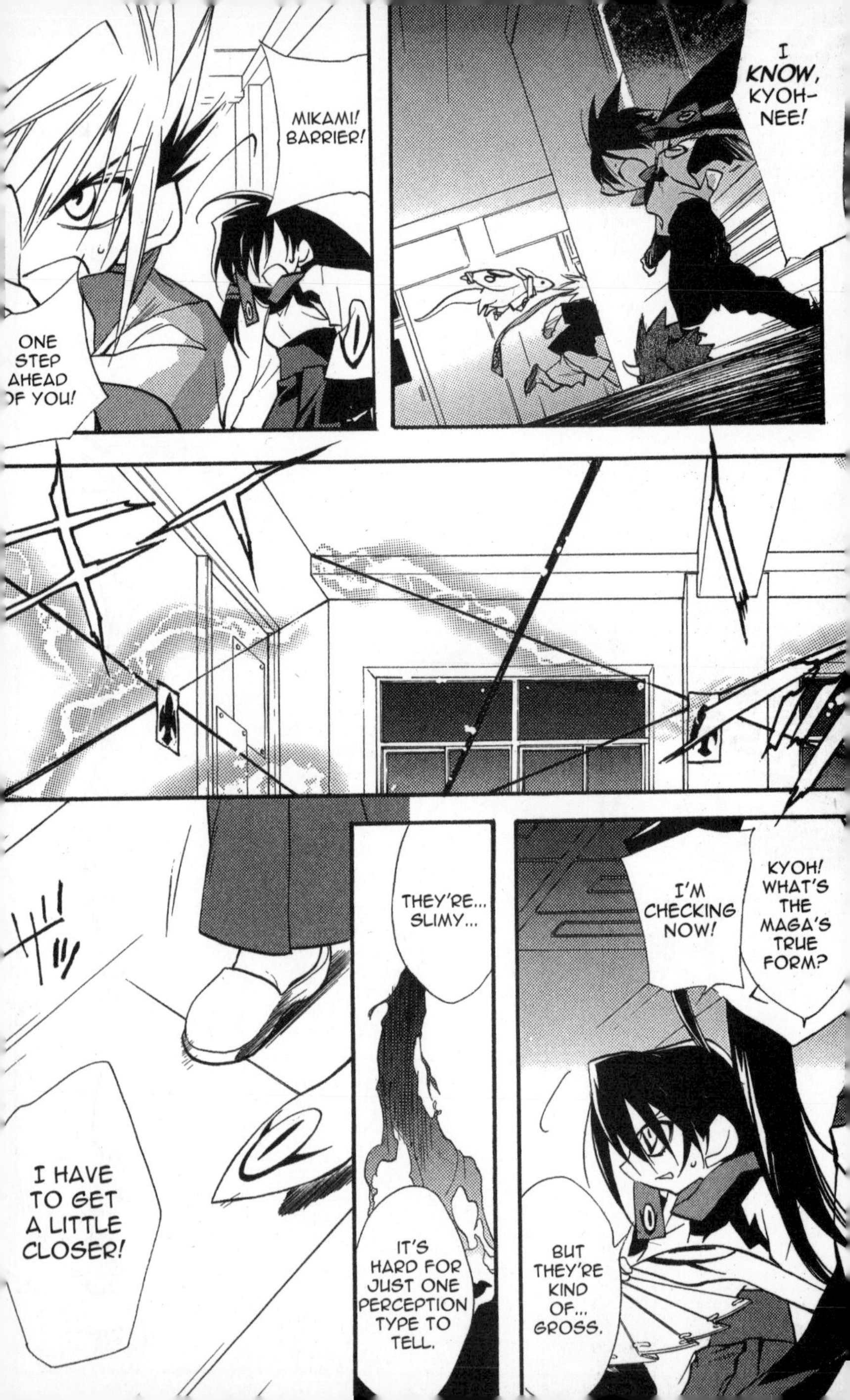
I KNOW, KYOH-NEE!
MIKAMI! BARRIER!
ONE STEP AHEAD OF YOU!
KYOH! WHAT'S THE MAGA'S TRUE FORM?
I'M CHECKING NOW!
BUT THEY'RE KIND OF... GROSS.
THEY'RE... SLIMY...
IT'S HARD FOR JUST ONE PERCEPTION TYPE TO TELL.
I HAVE TO GET A LITTLE CLOSER!

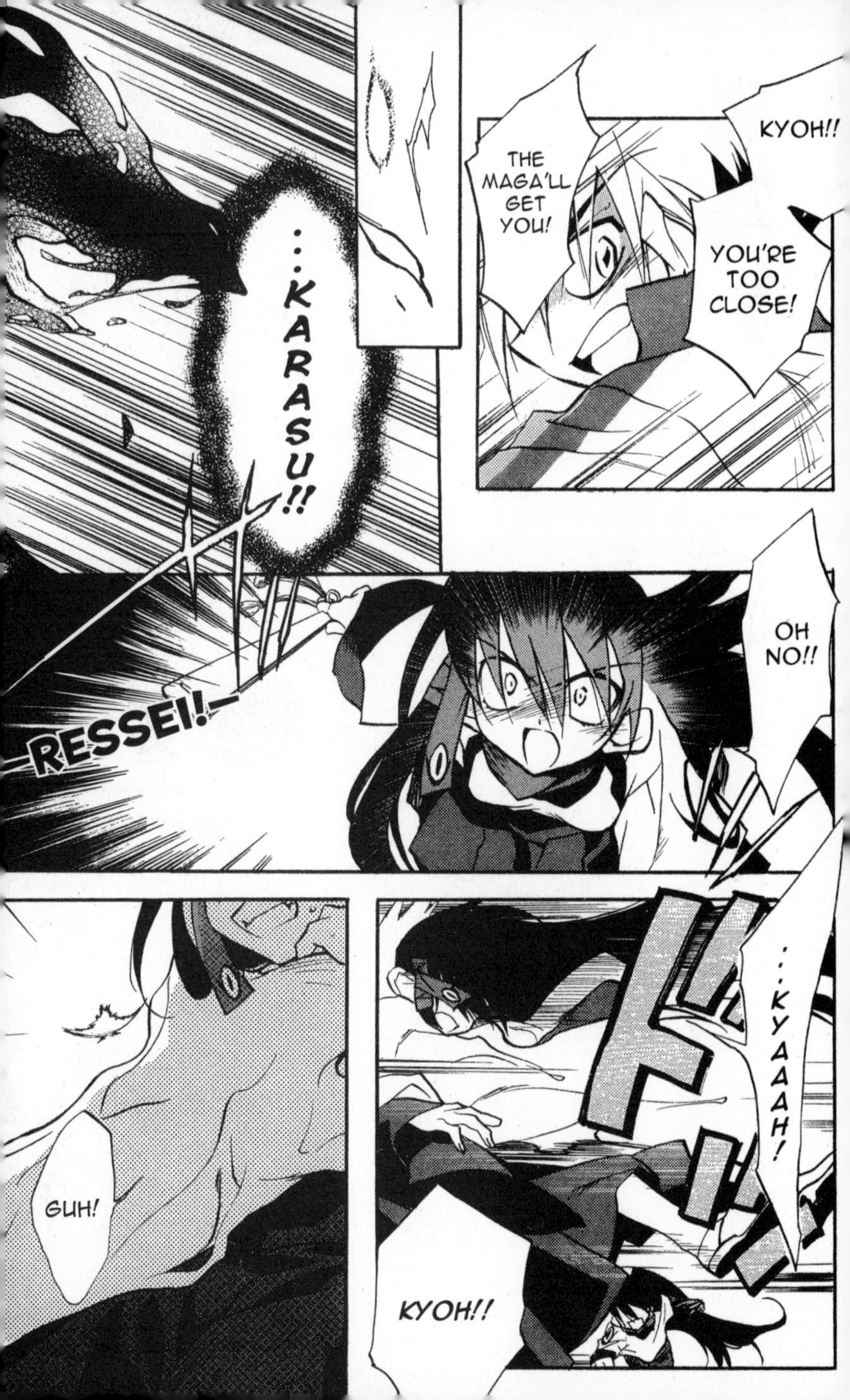
KYOH!!
THE MAGA'LL GET YOU!
YOU'RE TOO CLOSE!
...KARASU!!
OH NO!!
RESSEI!
...KYAAAAH!
KYOH!!
GUH!

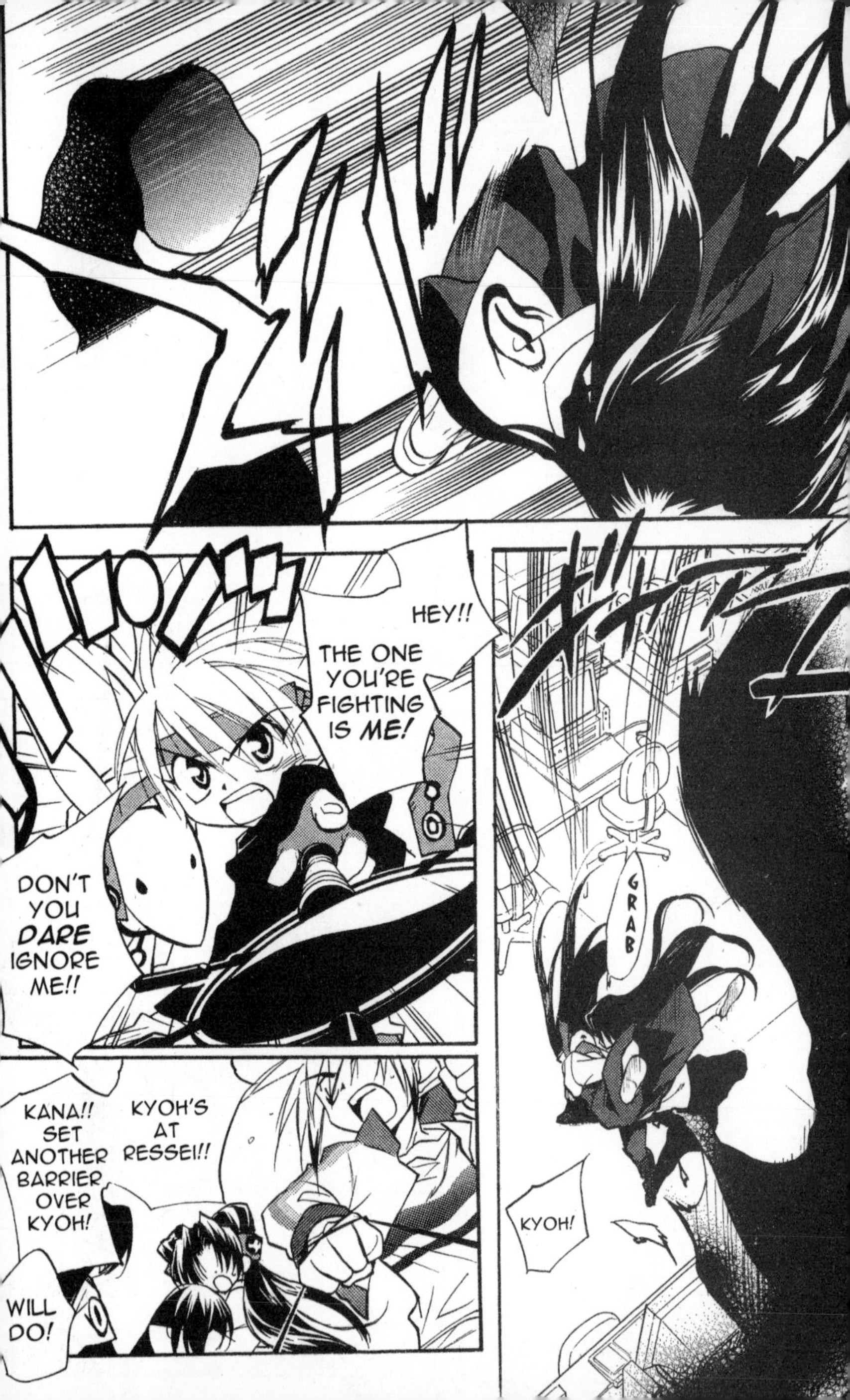
GRAB
KYOH!
HEY!!
THE ONE YOU'RE FIGHTING IS *ME!*
DON'T YOU ***DARE*** IGNORE ME!!
KYOH'S AT RESSEI!!
KANA!! SET ANOTHER BARRIER OVER KYOH!
WILL DO!

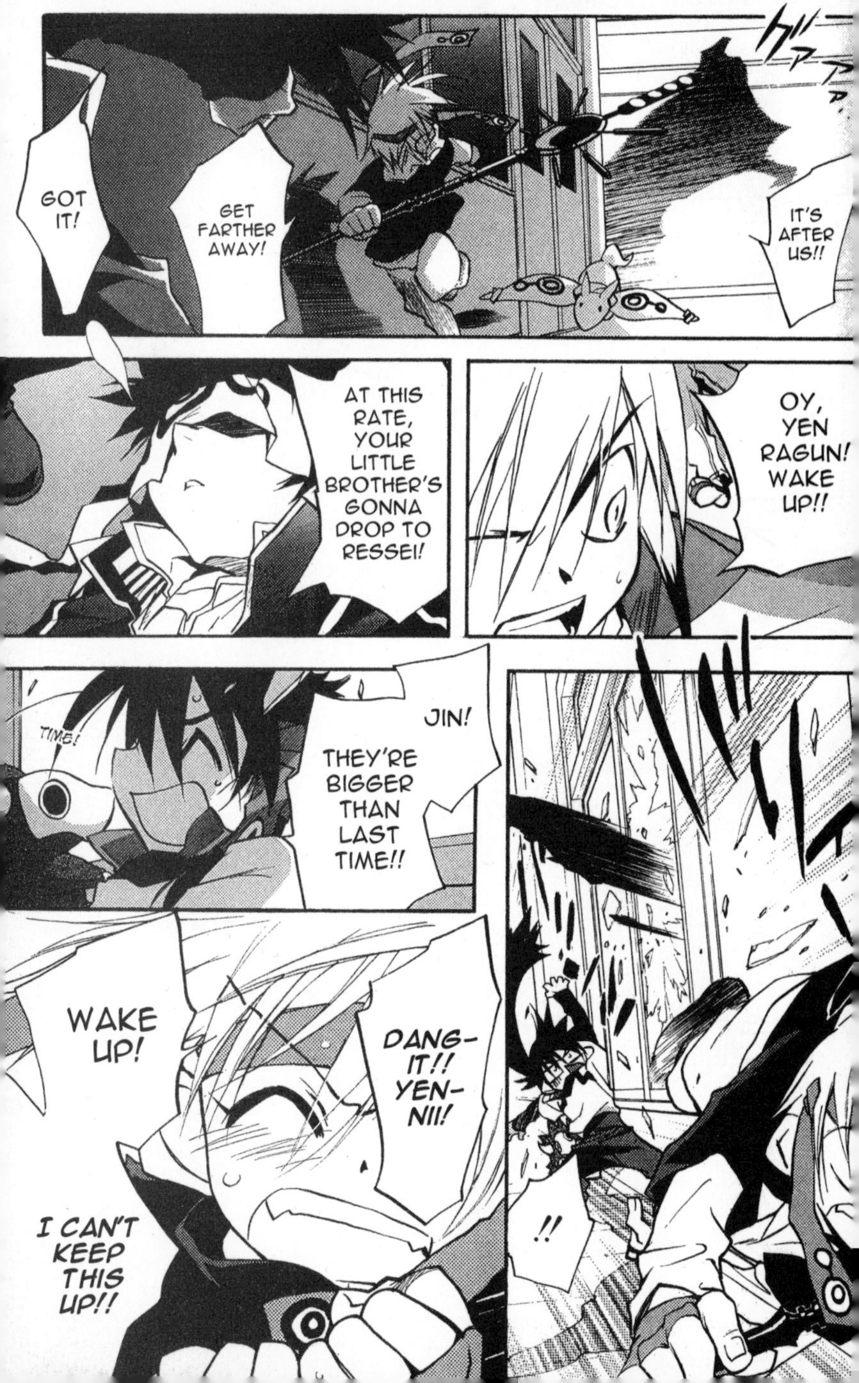
IT'S AFTER US!!
GET FARTHER AWAY!
GOT IT!
OY, YEN RAGUN! WAKE UP!!
AT THIS RATE, YOUR LITTLE BROTHER'S GONNA DROP TO RESSEI!
!!
JIN!
THEY'RE BIGGER THAN LAST TIME!!
TIME!
DANG-IT!! YEN-NII!
WAKE UP!
I CAN'T KEEP THIS UP!!

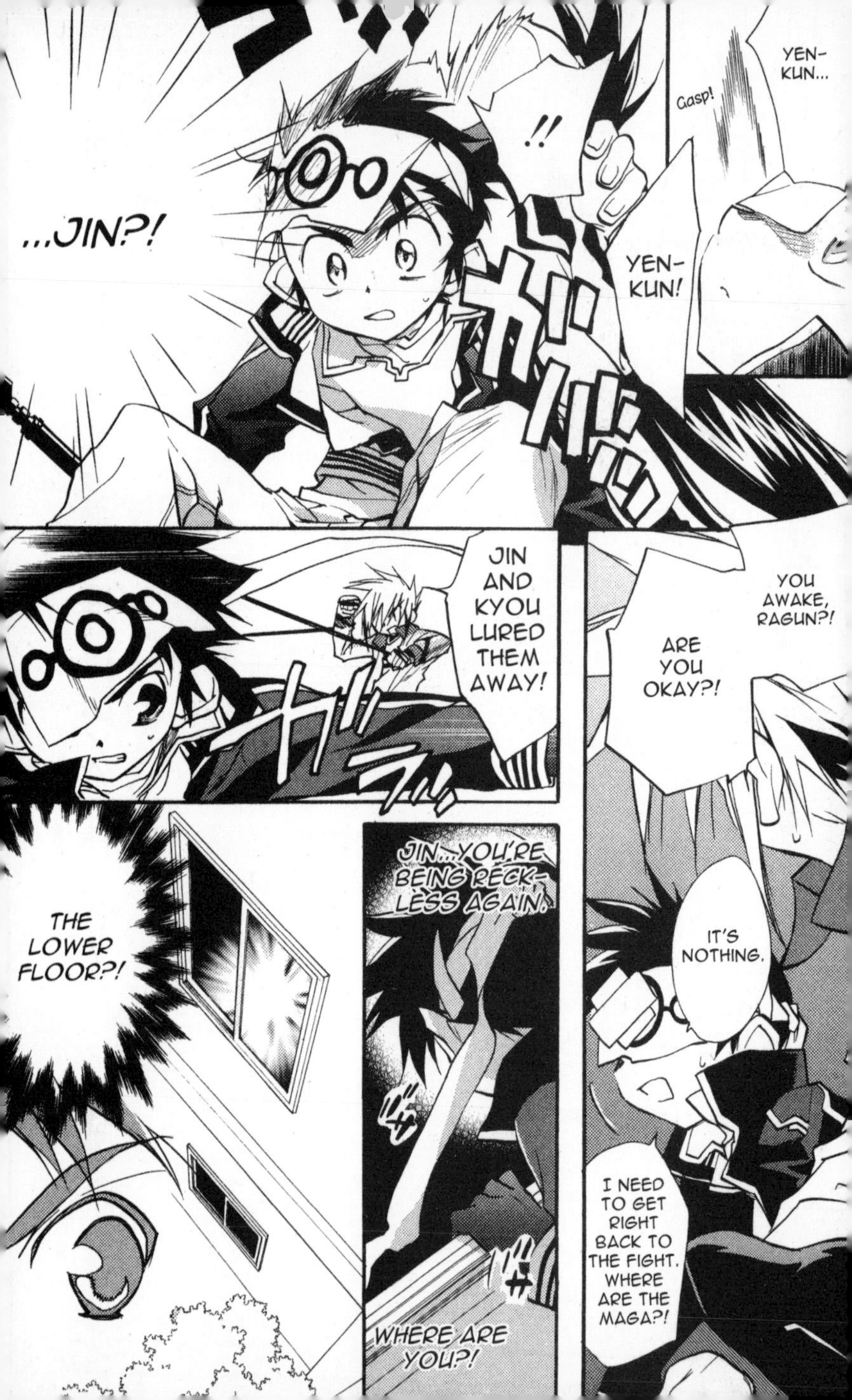
YEN-KUN...
Gasp!
YEN-KUN!
!!
...JIN?!
YOU AWAKE, RAGUN?!
ARE YOU OKAY?!
IT'S NOTHING.
I NEED TO GET RIGHT BACK TO THE FIGHT. WHERE ARE THE MAGA?!
JIN AND KYOU LURED THEM AWAY!
JIN... YOU'RE BEING RECK-LESS AGAIN.
WHERE ARE YOU?!
THE LOWER FLOOR?!

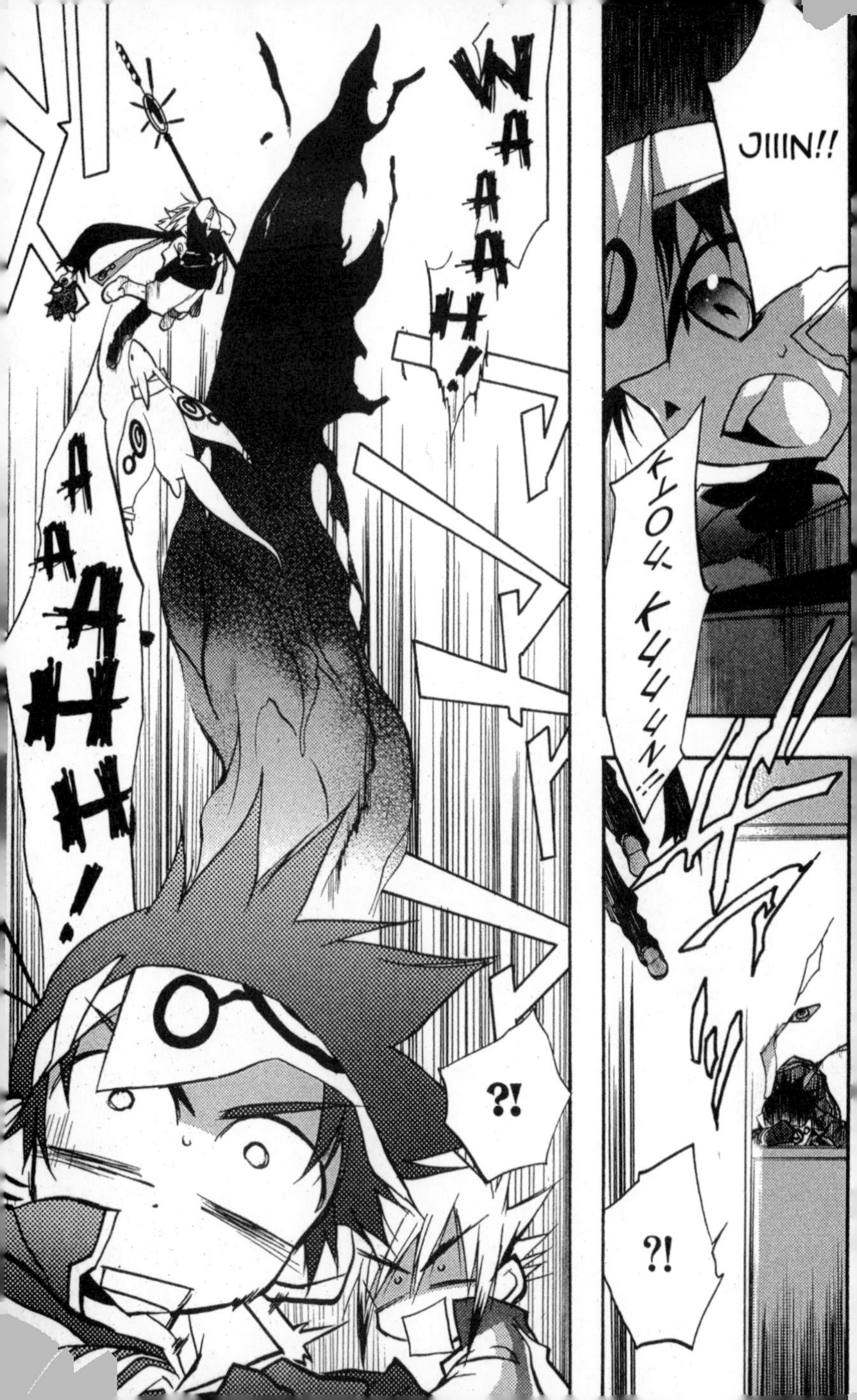
JIIIN!!
KYOU KUUUUN!!
?!
WAAAH!
AAAHH!!
?!

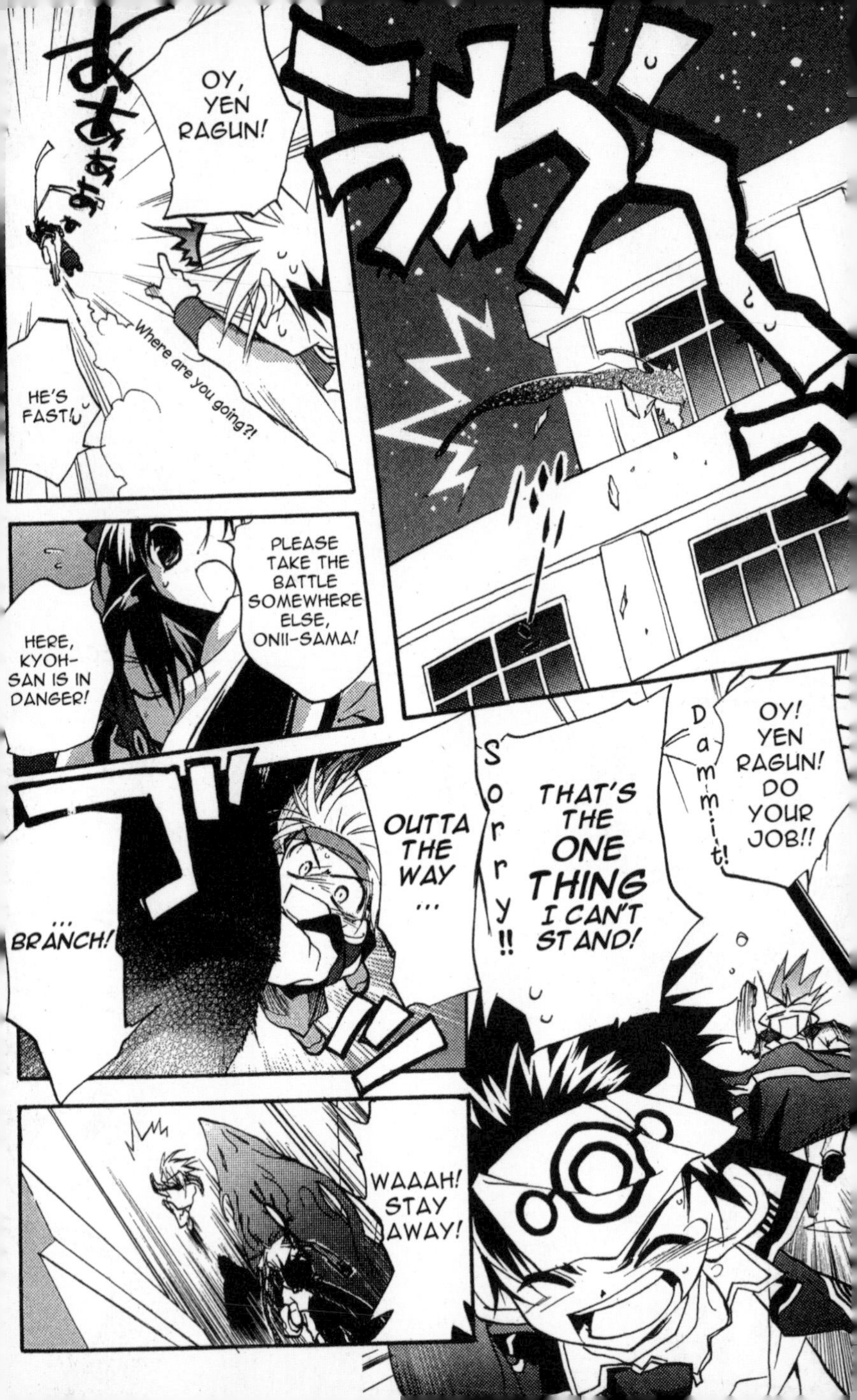
OY, YEN RAGUN!
Where are you going?!
HE'S FAST!
PLEASE TAKE THE BATTLE SOMEWHERE ELSE, ONII-SAMA!
HERE, KYOH-SAN IS IN DANGER!
OY! YEN RAGUN! DO YOUR JOB!!
Dammit!
THAT'S THE ONE THING I CAN'T STAND!
Sorry!!
OUTTA THE WAY ...
... BRANCH!
WAAAH! STAY AWAY!

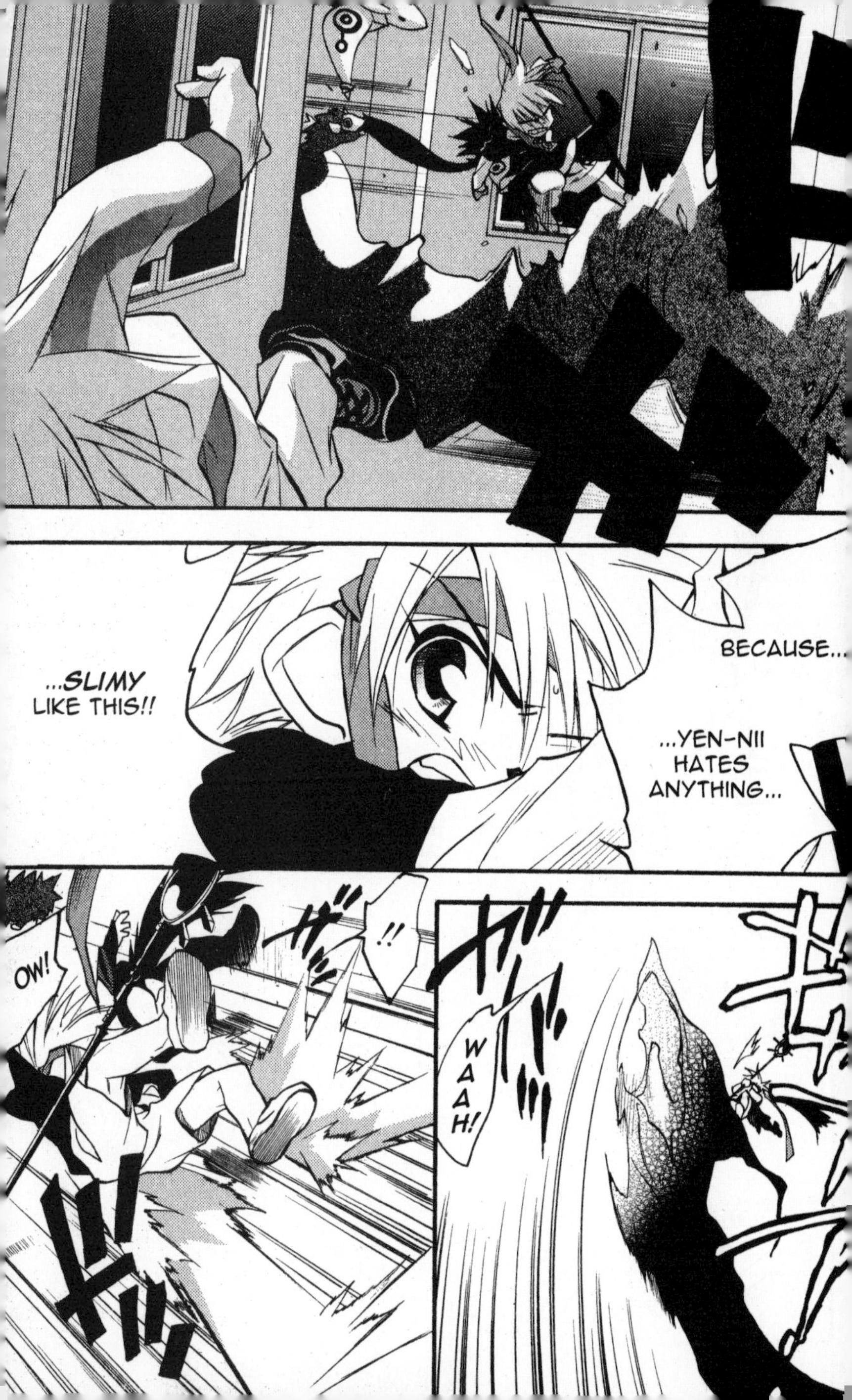
BECAUSE...
...YEN-NII HATES ANYTHING...
...SLIMY LIKE THIS!!
WAAH!
!!
OW!

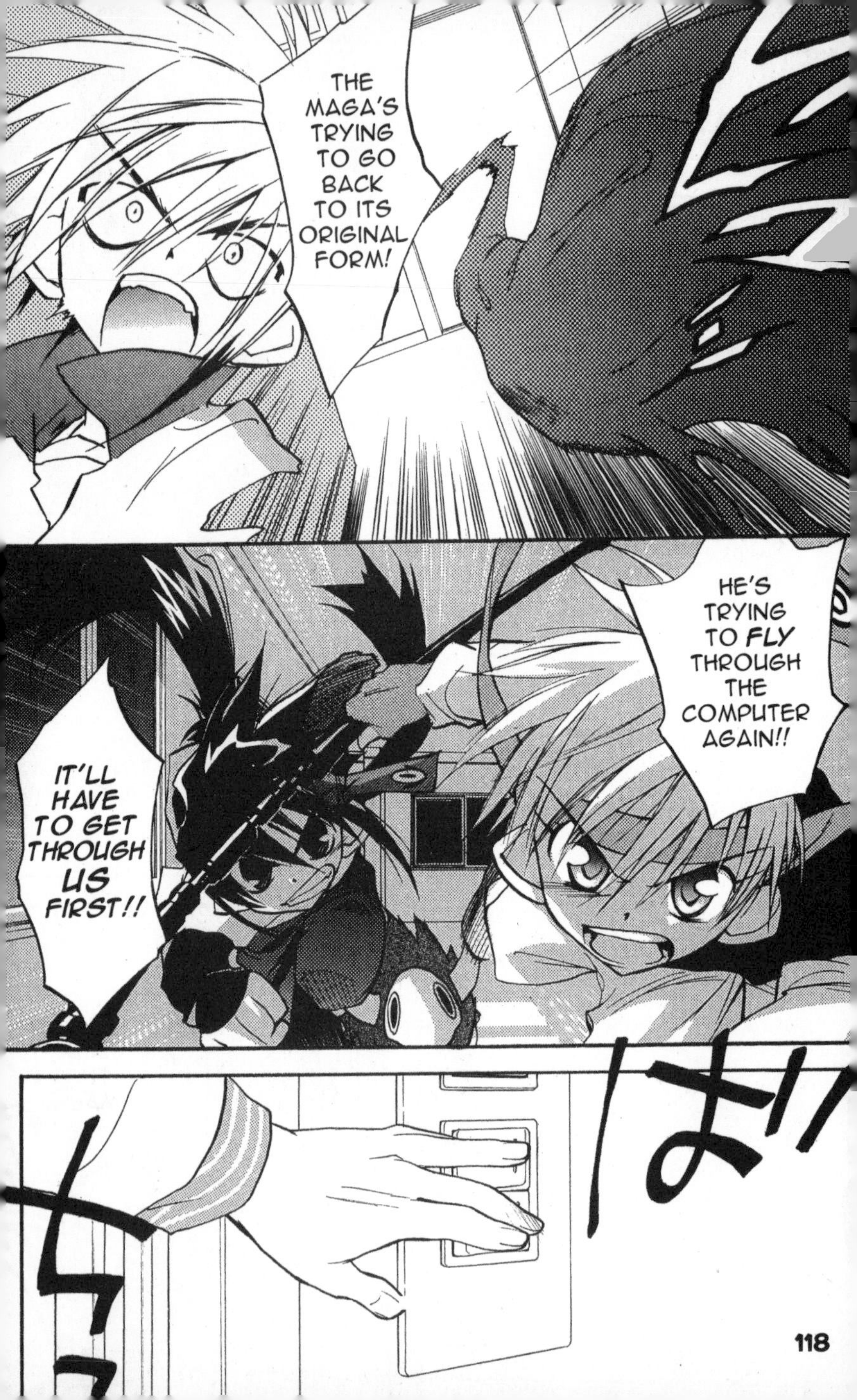
THE MAGA'S TRYING TO GO BACK TO ITS ORIGINAL FORM!
HE'S TRYING TO FLY THROUGH THE COMPUTER AGAIN!!
IT'LL HAVE TO GET THROUGH US FIRST!!

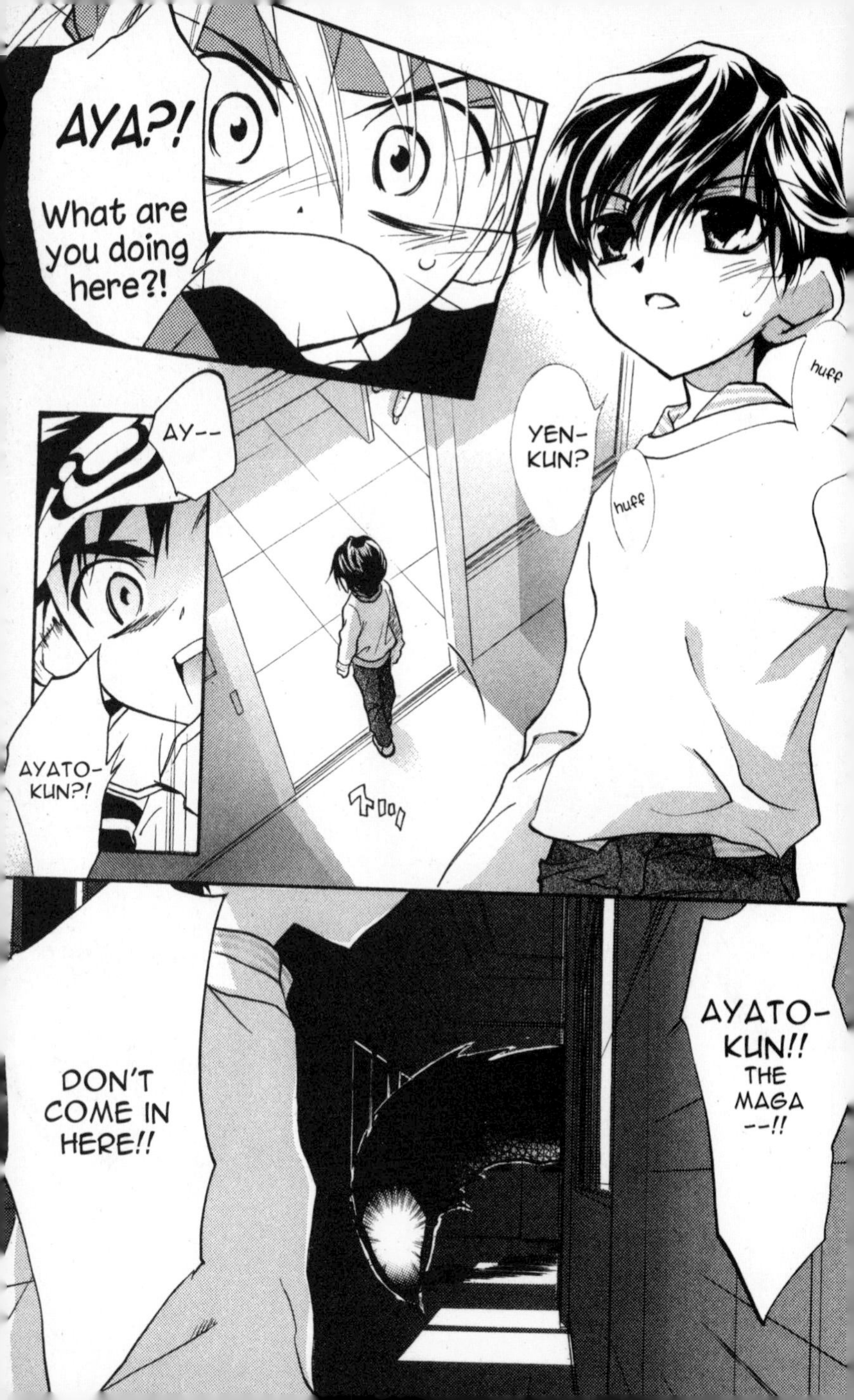
huff
huff
YEN-KUN?
AYA?!
What are you doing here?!
AY--
AYATO-KUN?!
AYATO-KUN!! THE MAGA--!!
DON'T COME IN HERE!!

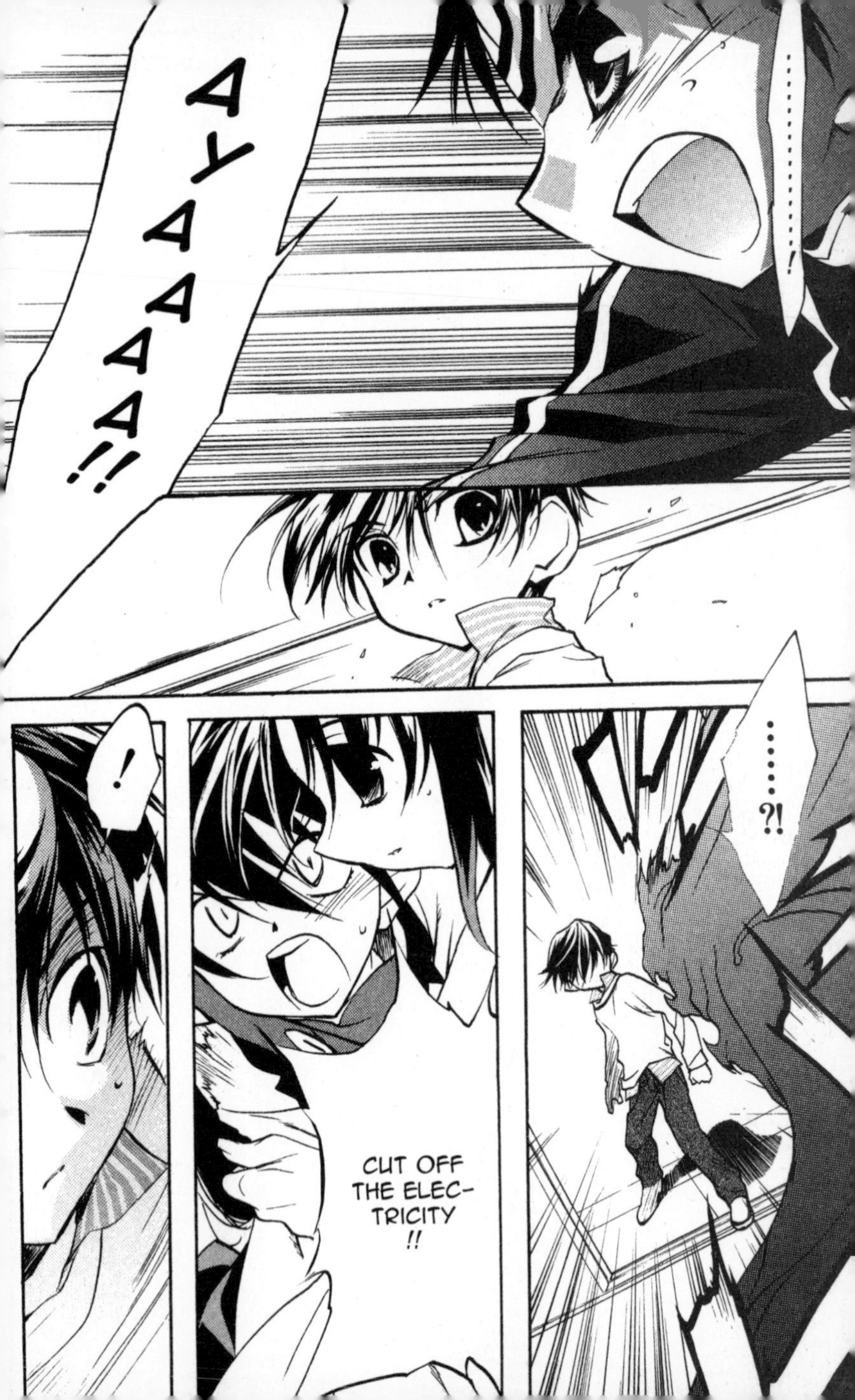

......!
AYAAAA!!
......?!
CUT OFF THE ELEC-TRICITY!!
!

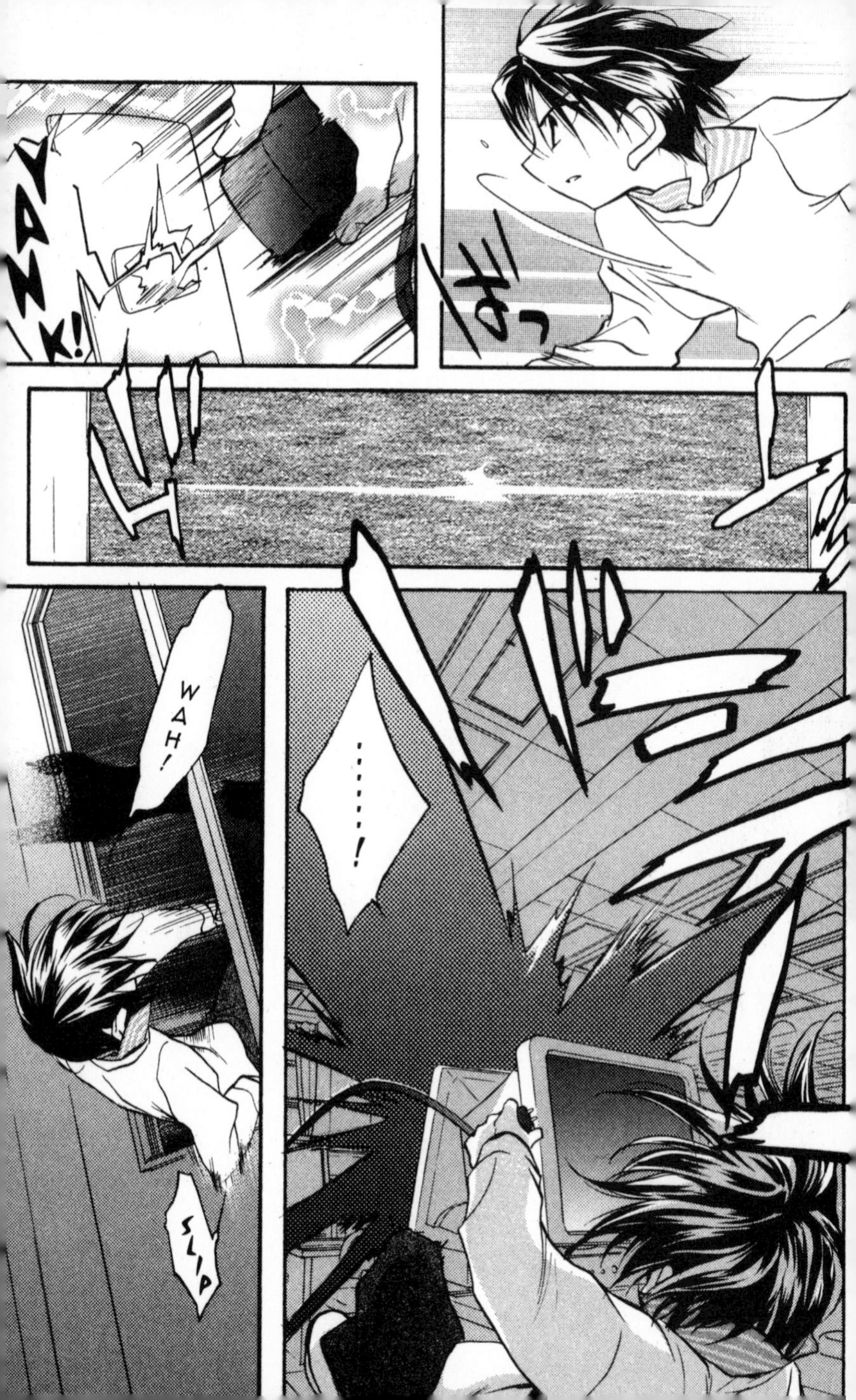
YANK!
......!
WAH!
SLIP

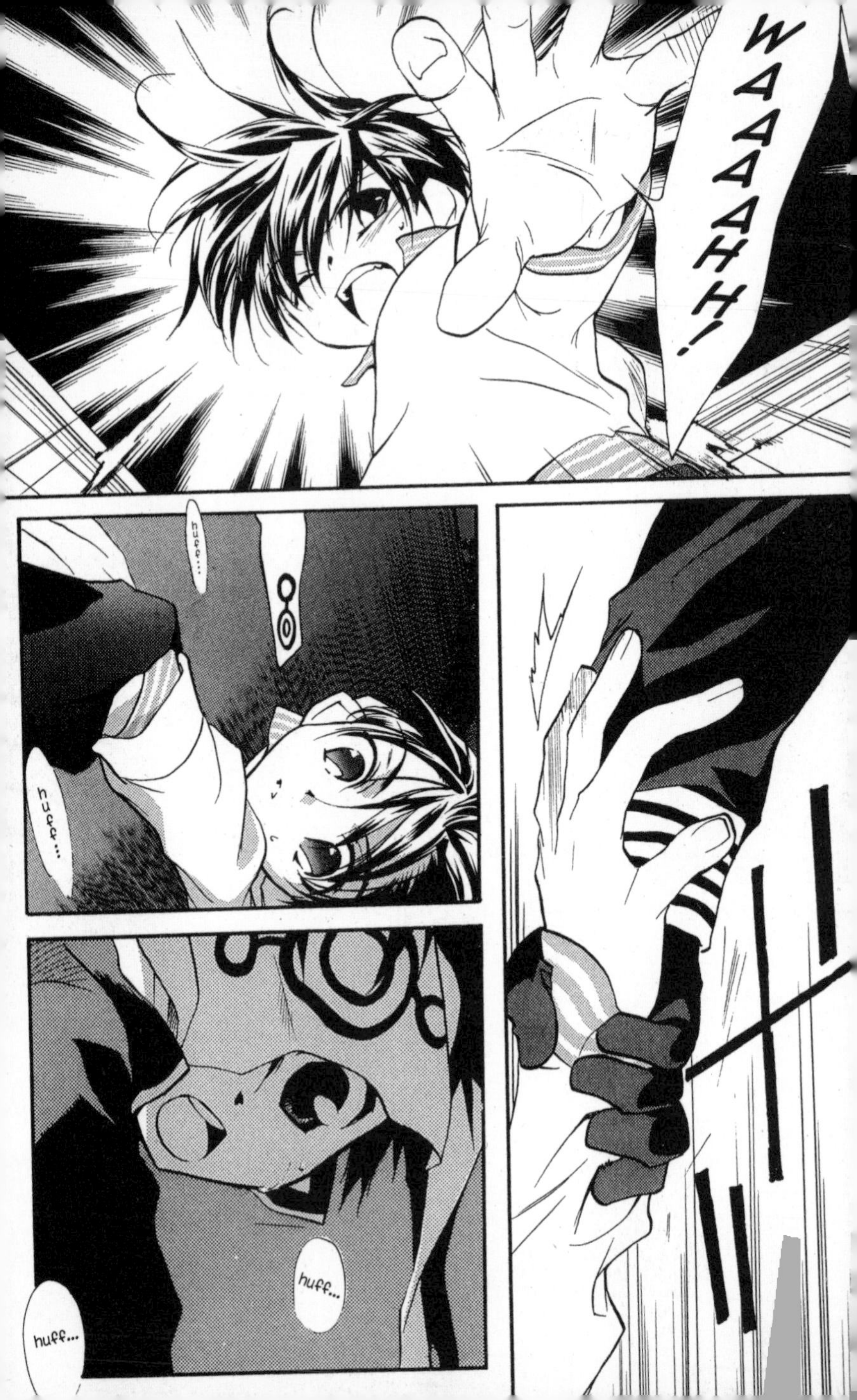
WAAAAAHH!
huff...
huff...
huff...
huff...

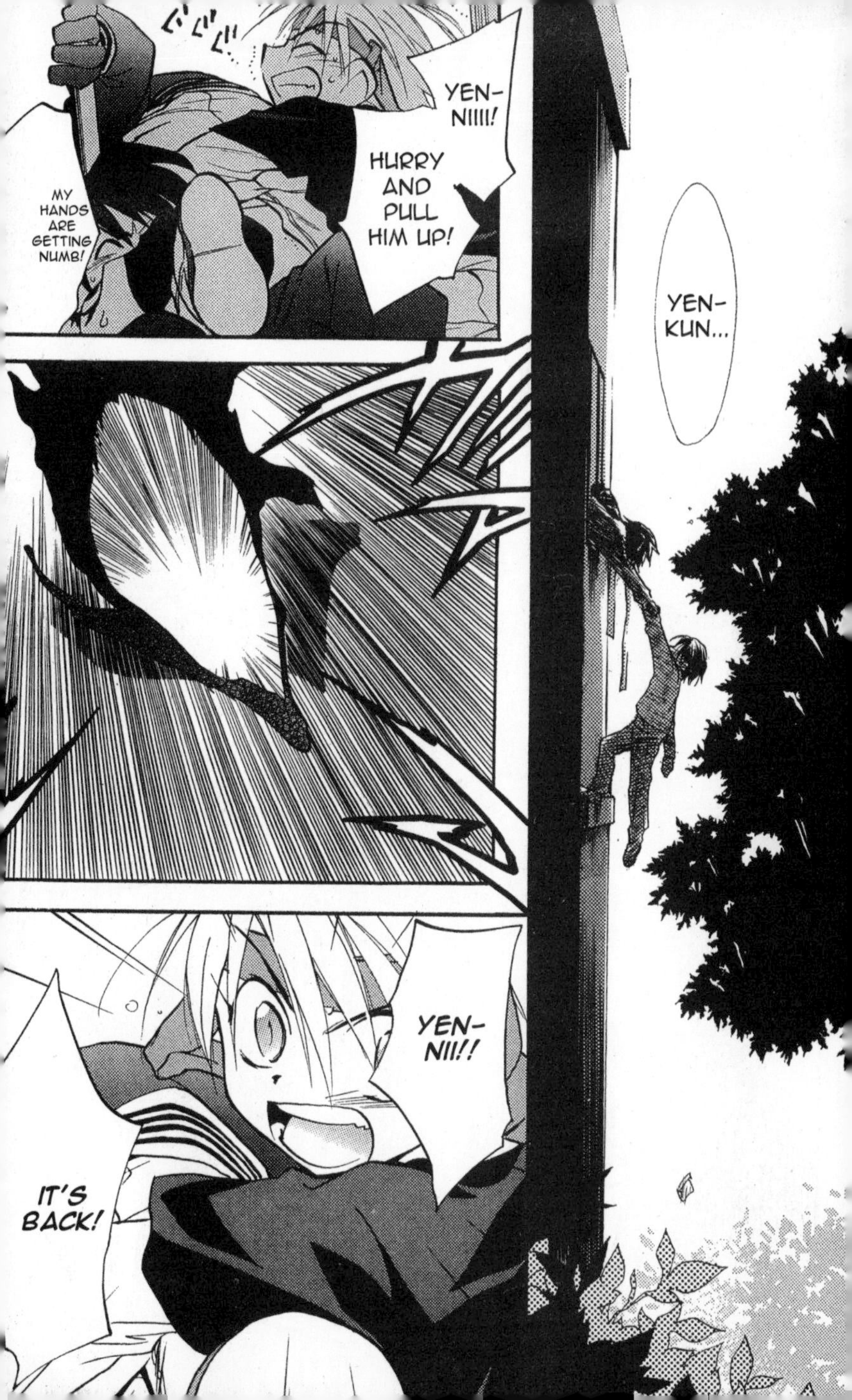
YEN-KUN...
YEN-NIIII!
HURRY AND PULL HIM UP!
MY HANDS ARE GETTING NUMB!
YEN-NII!!
IT'S BACK!

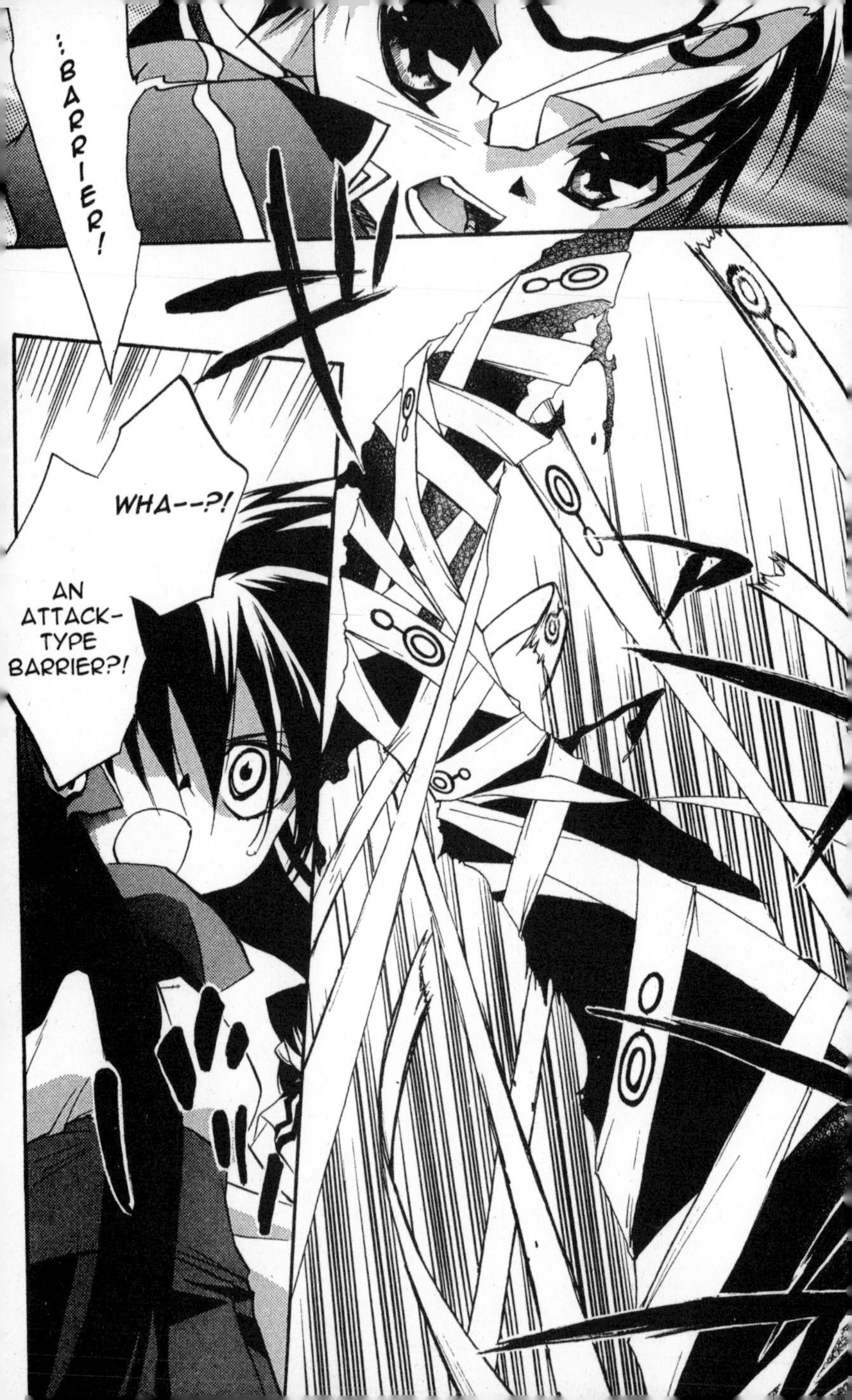
...BARRIER!
WHA--?!
AN ATTACK-TYPE BARRIER?!

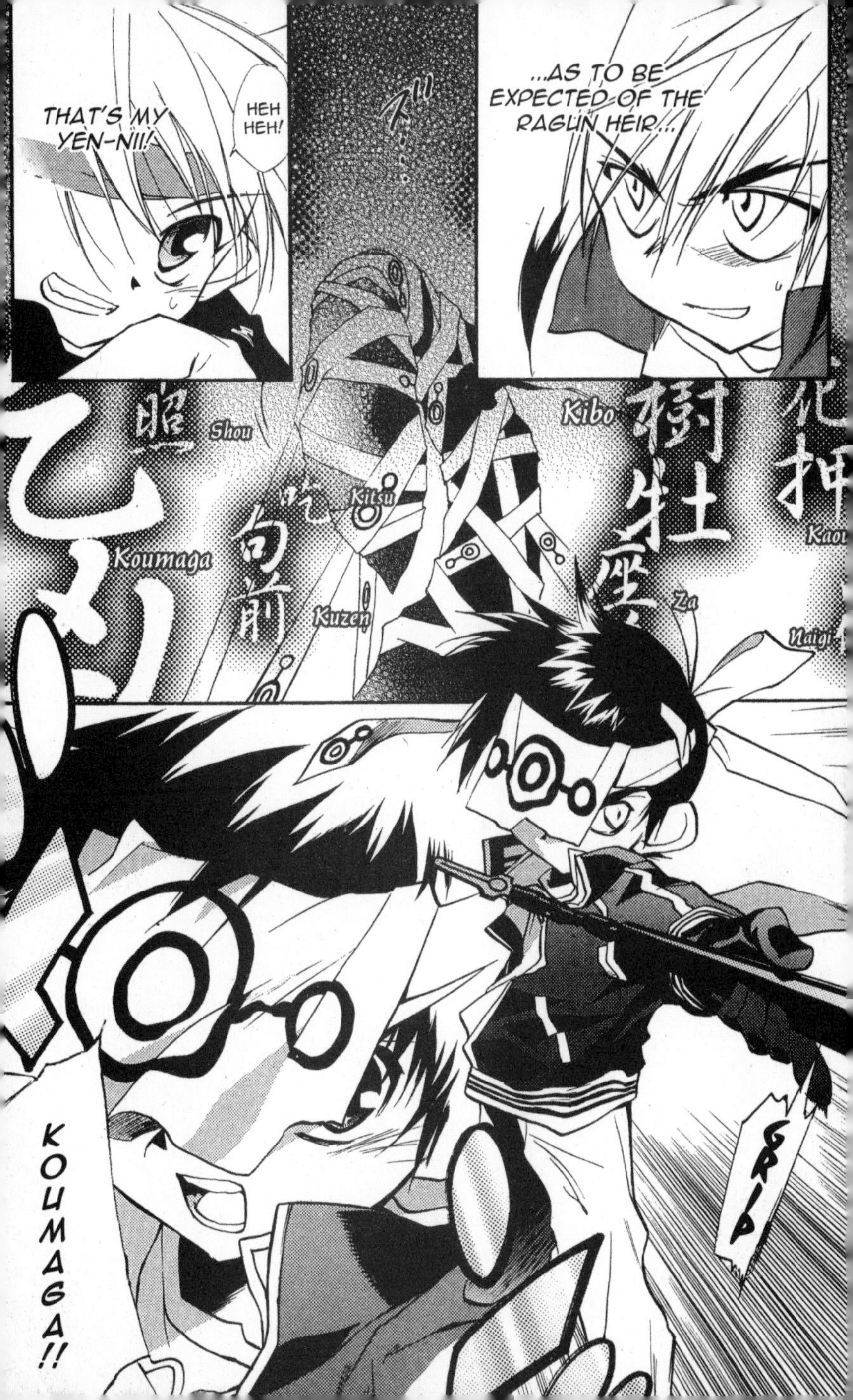

...AS TO BE EXPECTED OF THE RAGUN HEIR...
HEH HEH!
THAT'S MY YEN-NII!
Kao
Kibo
Za
Naigi
Kitsu
Kuzen
Shou
Koumaga
GRIP
KOUMAGA!!

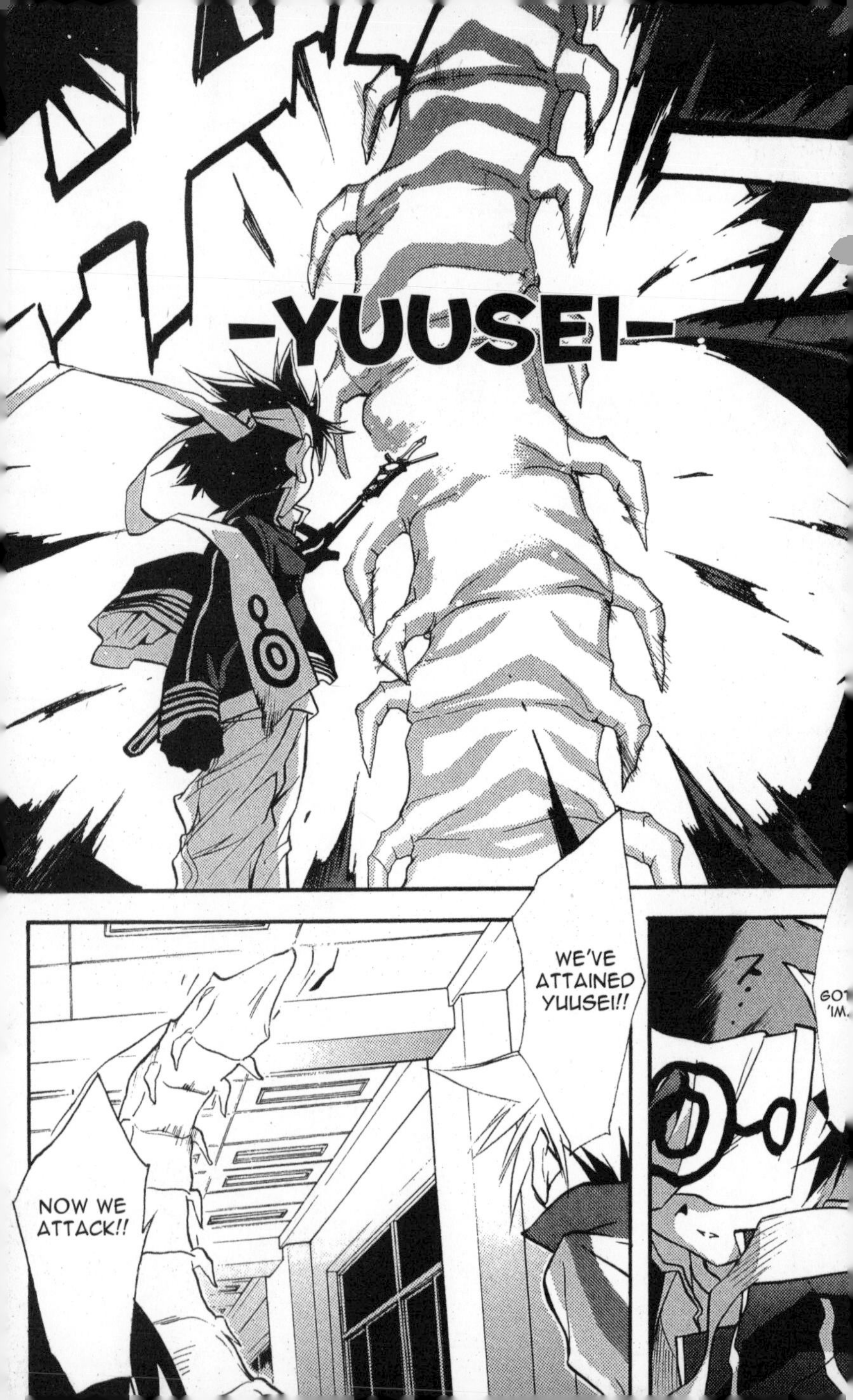
-YUUSEI-
GOT 'IM.
WE'VE ATTAINED YUUSEI!!
NOW WE ATTACK!!

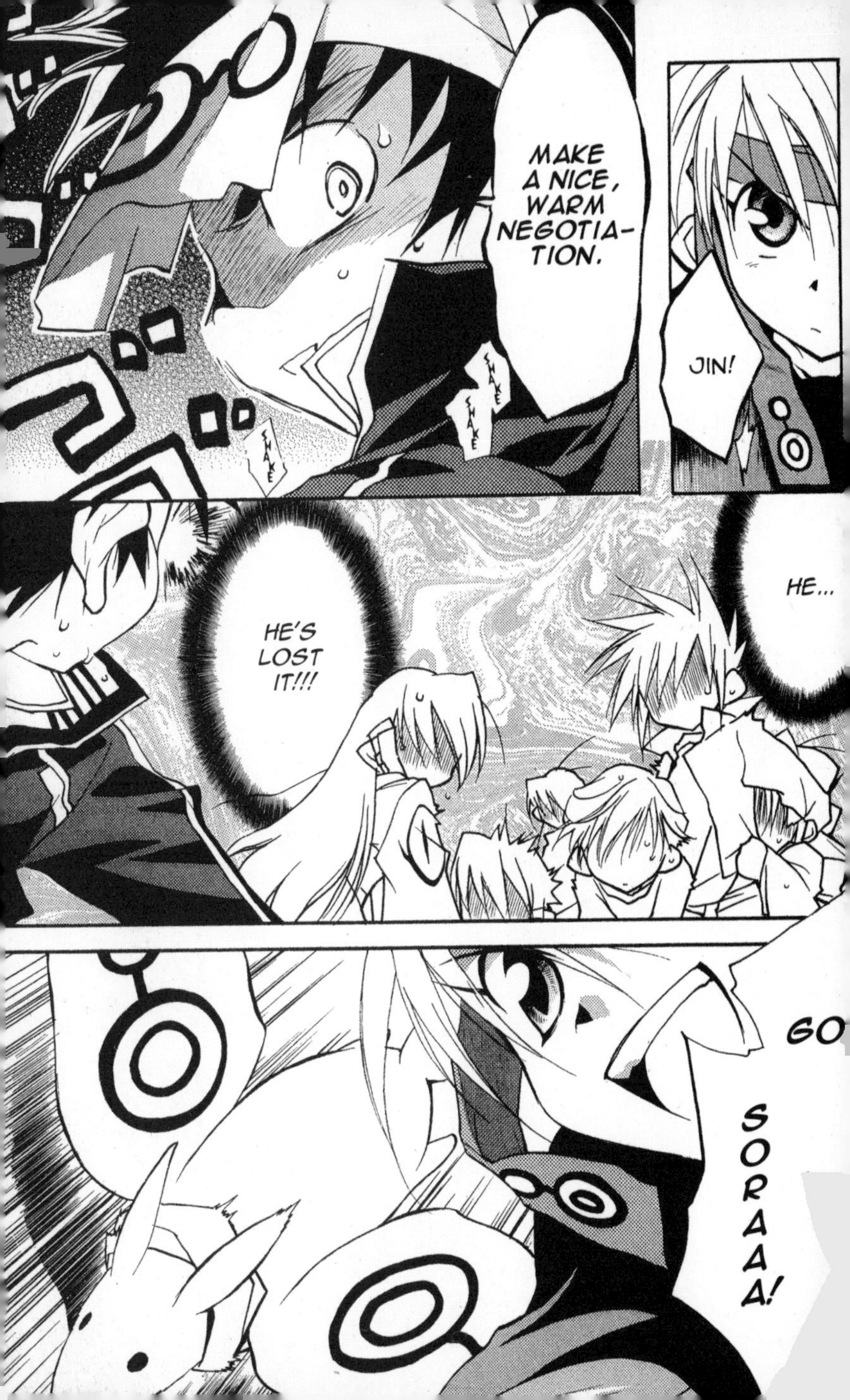

MAKE A NICE, WARM NEGOTIATION.
JIN!
SHAKE
SHAKE
SHAKE
HE...
HE'S LOST IT!!!
GO SORAAA!

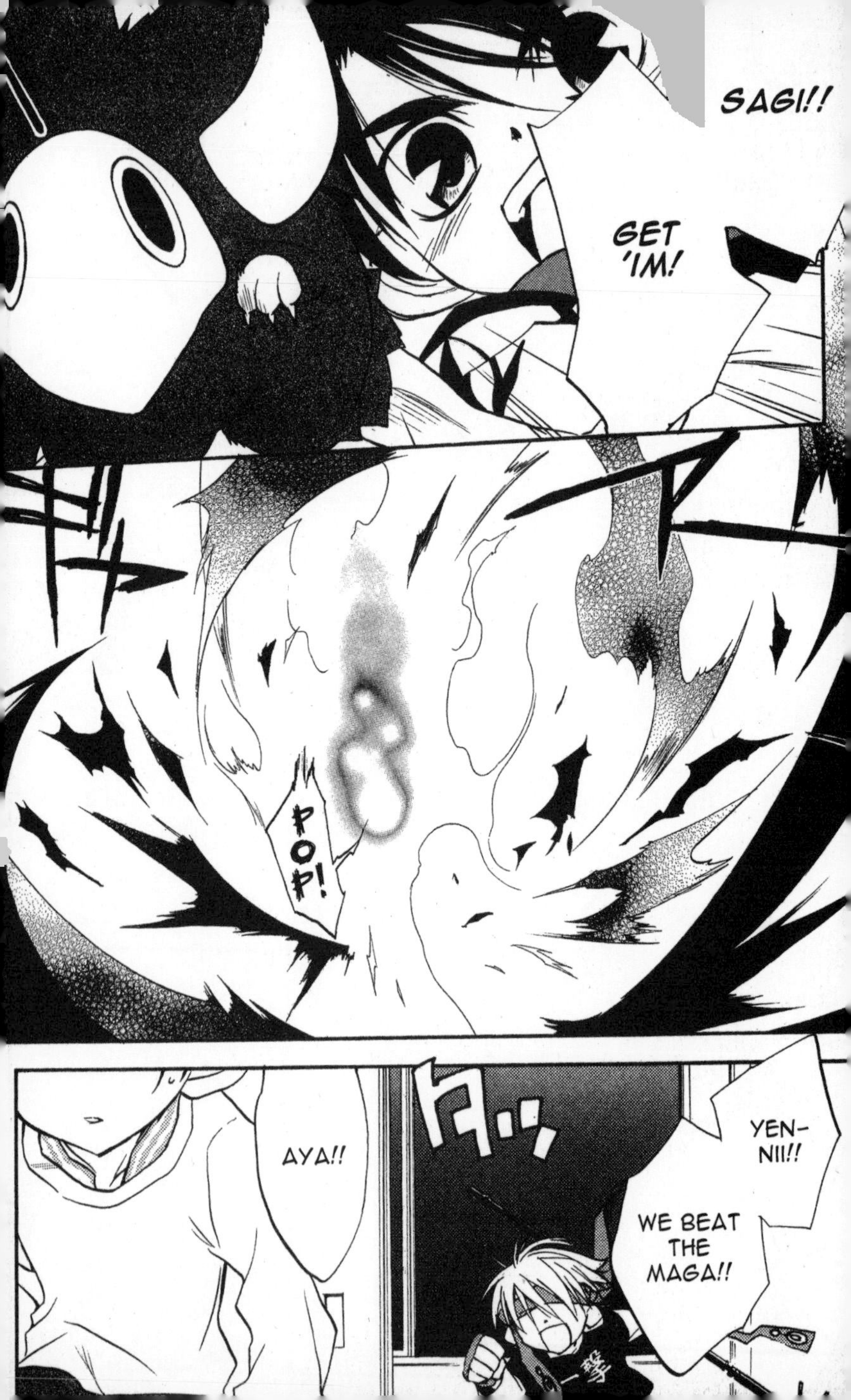
SAGI!!
GET 'IM!
POP!
YEN-NII!!
WE BEAT THE MAGA!!
AYA!!

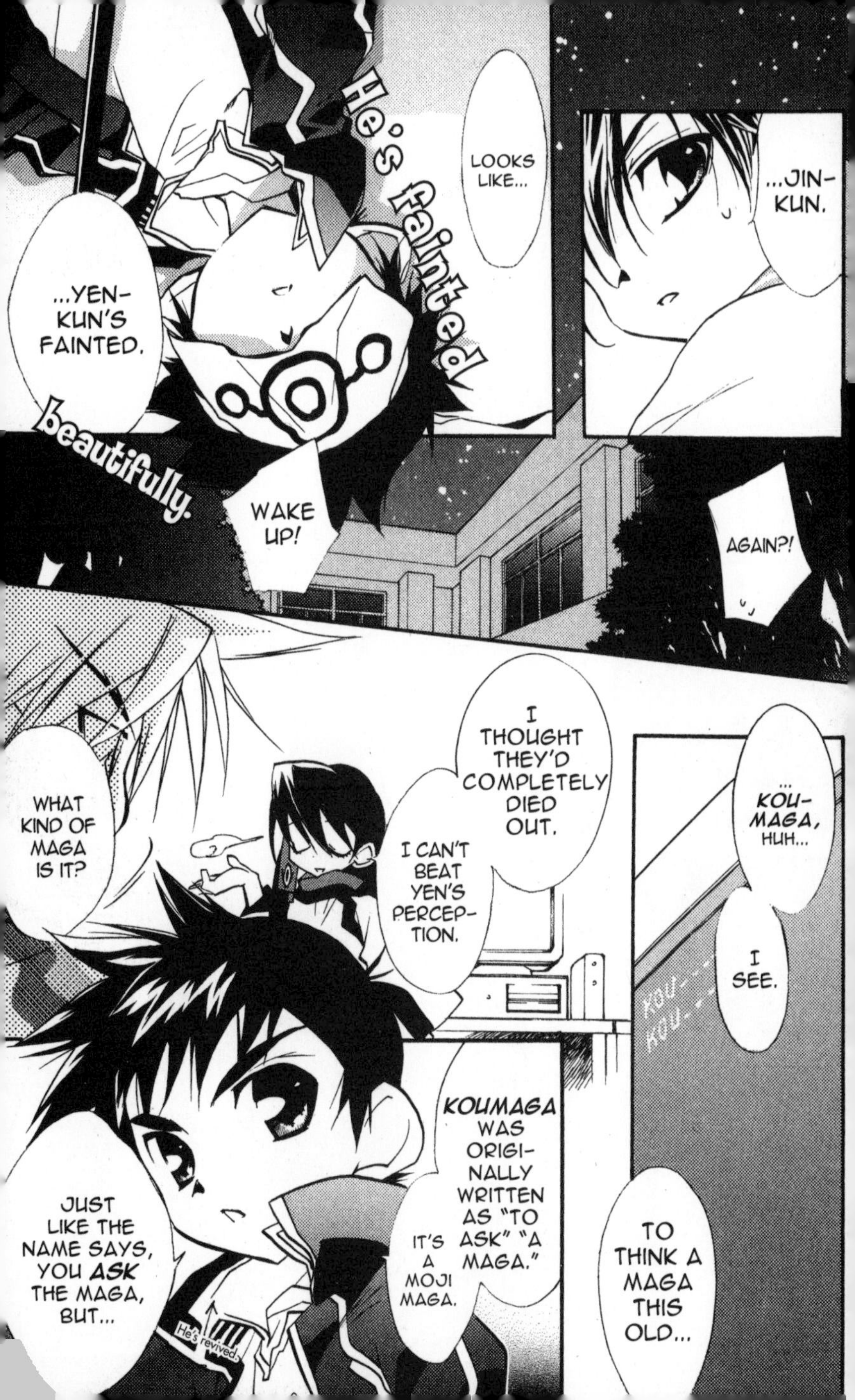
...JIN-KUN.
LOOKS LIKE...
...YEN-KUN'S FAINTED.
He's fainted beautifully.
AGAIN?!
WAKE UP!
...KOUMAGA, HUH...
I SEE.
KOU-- KOU--
I THOUGHT THEY'D COMPLETELY DIED OUT.
I CAN'T BEAT YEN'S PERCEPTION.
WHAT KIND OF MAGA IS IT?
TO THINK A MAGA THIS OLD...
KOUMAGA WAS ORIGINALLY WRITTEN AS "TO ASK" "A MAGA."
IT'S A MOJI MAGA.
JUST LIKE THE NAME SAYS, YOU ASK THE MAGA, BUT...
He's revived.

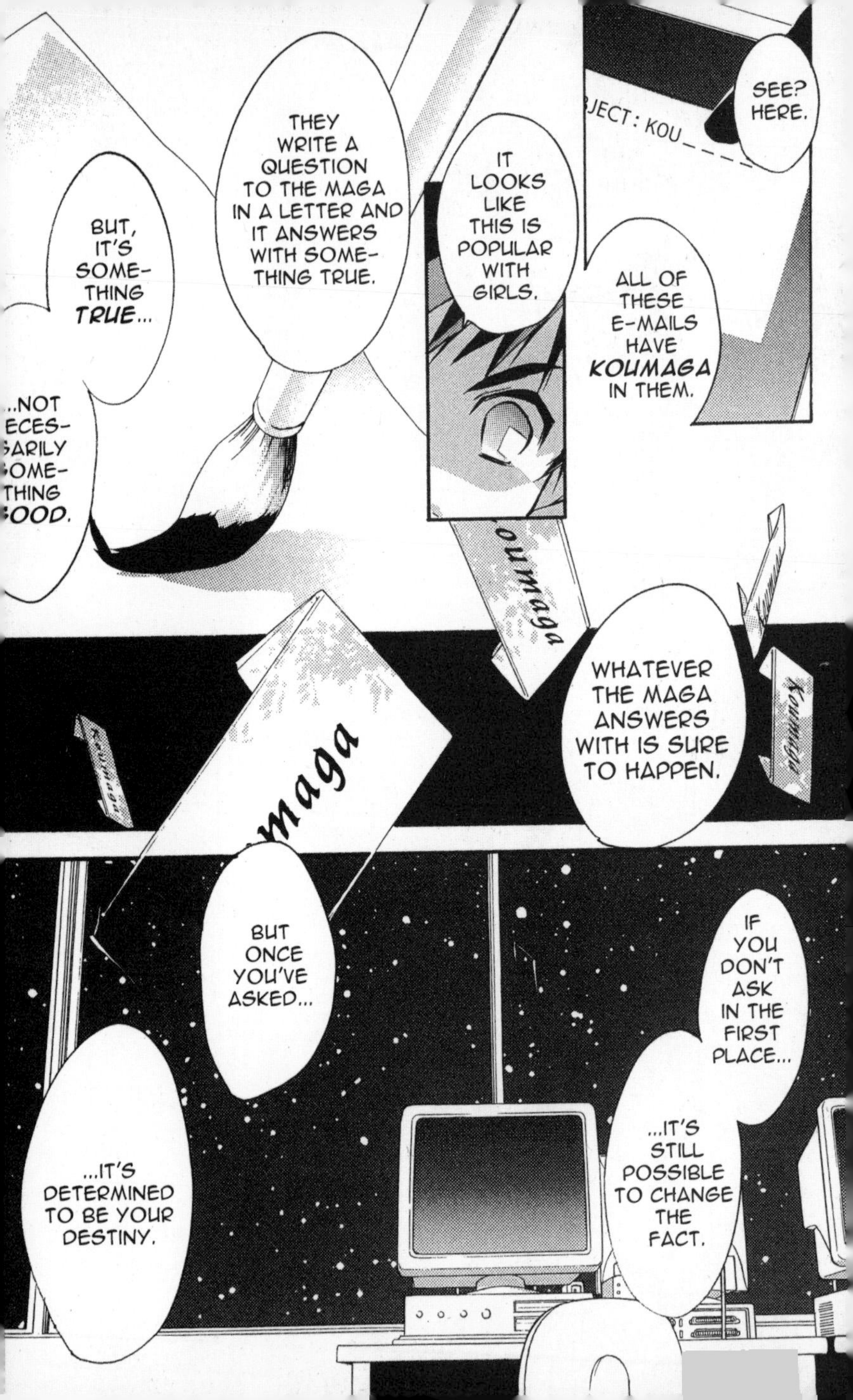
SEE? HERE.
JECT : KOU
IT LOOKS LIKE THIS IS POPULAR WITH GIRLS.
ALL OF THESE E-MAILS HAVE **KOUMAGA** IN THEM.
THEY WRITE A QUESTION TO THE MAGA IN A LETTER AND IT ANSWERS WITH SOME-THING TRUE.
BUT, IT'S SOME-THING ***TRUE***...
..NOT ECES- ARILY OME- THING ***OOD***.
oumaga
Koumaga
WHATEVER THE MAGA ANSWERS WITH IS SURE TO HAPPEN.
maga
IF YOU DON'T ASK IN THE FIRST PLACE...
...IT'S STILL POSSIBLE TO CHANGE THE FACT.
BUT ONCE YOU'VE ASKED...
...IT'S DETERMINED TO BE YOUR DESTINY.

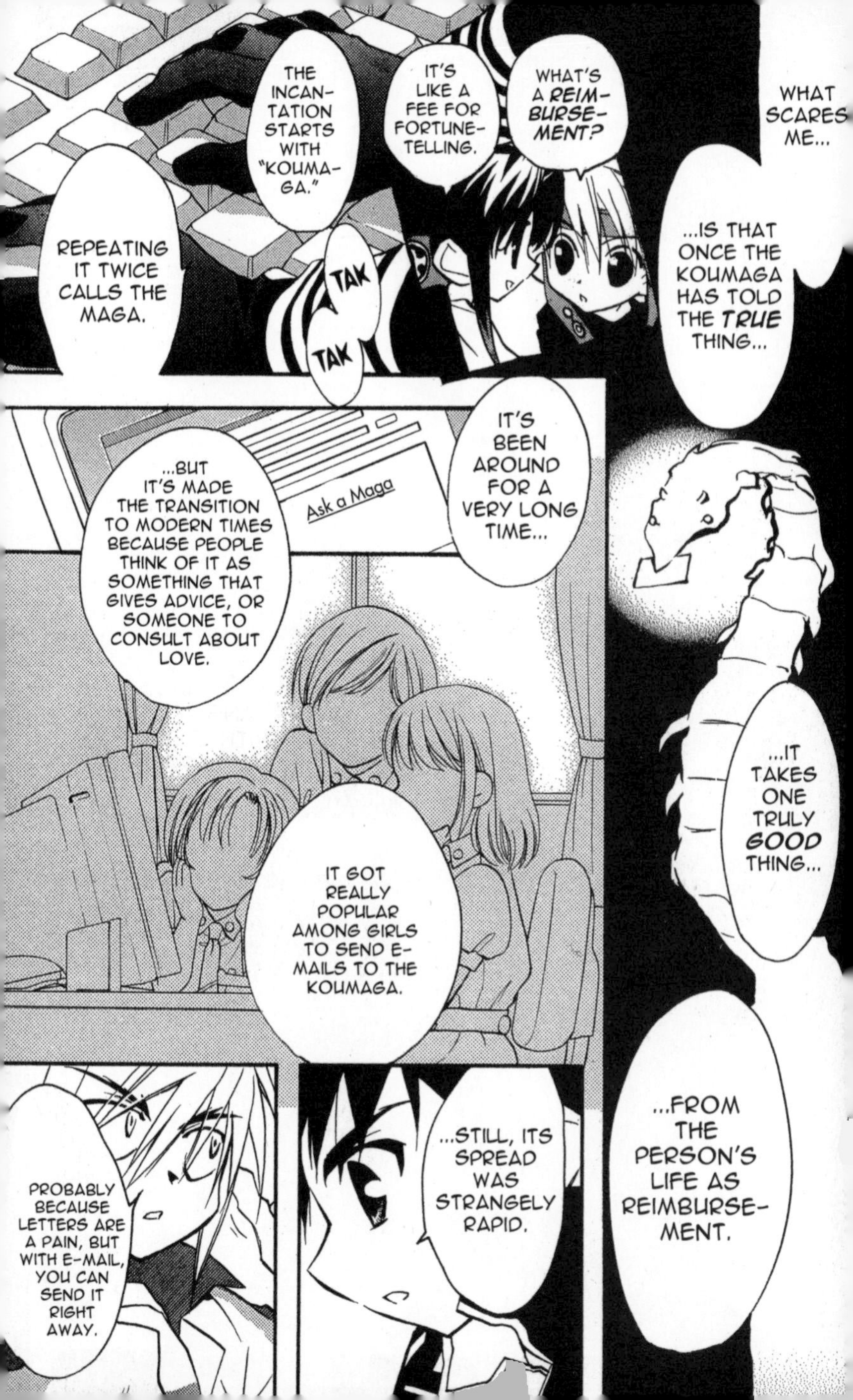
WHAT'S A *REIMBURSEMENT?*
IT'S LIKE A FEE FOR FORTUNE-TELLING.
THE INCANTATION STARTS WITH "KOUMAGA."
REPEATING IT TWICE CALLS THE MAGA.
TAK
TAK
WHAT SCARES ME...
...IS THAT ONCE THE KOUMAGA HAS TOLD THE *TRUE* THING...
...IT TAKES ONE TRULY *GOOD* THING...
...FROM THE PERSON'S LIFE AS REIMBURSEMENT.
IT'S BEEN AROUND FOR A VERY LONG TIME...
...BUT IT'S MADE THE TRANSITION TO MODERN TIMES BECAUSE PEOPLE THINK OF IT AS SOMETHING THAT GIVES ADVICE, OR SOMEONE TO CONSULT ABOUT LOVE.
Ask a Maga
IT GOT REALLY POPULAR AMONG GIRLS TO SEND E-MAILS TO THE KOUMAGA.
...STILL, ITS SPREAD WAS STRANGELY RAPID.
PROBABLY BECAUSE LETTERS ARE A PAIN, BUT WITH E-MAIL, YOU CAN SEND IT RIGHT AWAY.

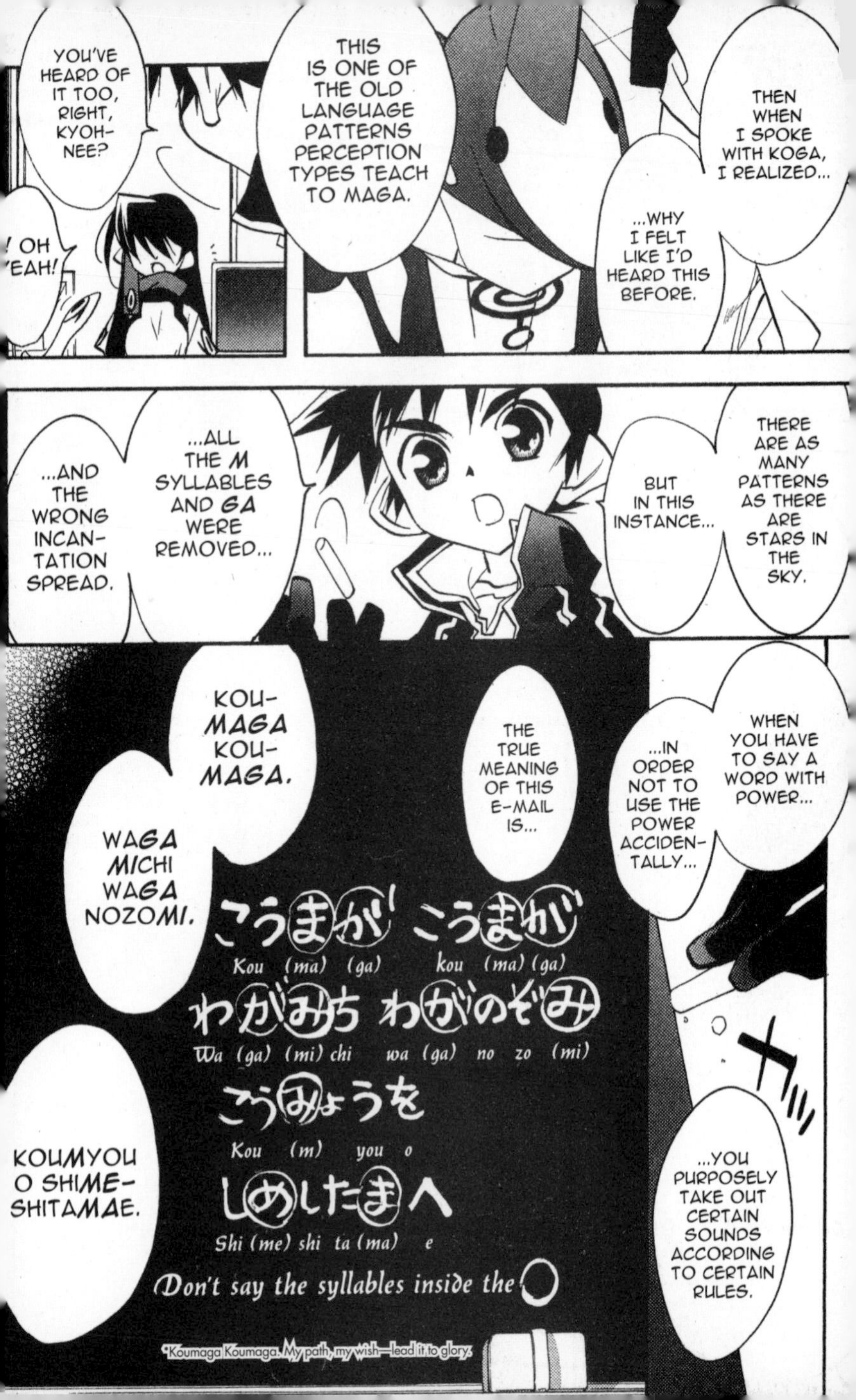
THEN WHEN I SPOKE WITH KOGA, I REALIZED...
...WHY I FELT LIKE I'D HEARD THIS BEFORE.
THIS IS ONE OF THE OLD LANGUAGE PATTERNS PERCEPTION TYPES TEACH TO MAGA.
YOU'VE HEARD OF IT TOO, RIGHT, KYOH-NEE?
! OH 'EAH!
THERE ARE AS MANY PATTERNS AS THERE ARE STARS IN THE SKY.
BUT IN THIS INSTANCE...
...ALL THE *M* SYLLABLES AND *GA* WERE REMOVED...
...AND THE WRONG INCANTATION SPREAD.
WHEN YOU HAVE TO SAY A WORD WITH POWER...
...IN ORDER NOT TO USE THE POWER ACCIDENTALLY...
...YOU PURPOSELY TAKE OUT CERTAIN SOUNDS ACCORDING TO CERTAIN RULES.
THE TRUE MEANING OF THIS E-MAIL IS...
KOU-MAGA KOU-MAGA.
WAGA MICHI WAGA NOZOMI.
KOUMYOU O SHIME-SHITAMAE.
こうまが こうまが
Kou (ma) (ga) kou (ma) (ga)
わがみち わがのぞみ
Wa (ga) (mi) chi wa (ga) no zo (mi)
こうみょうを
Kou (m) you o
しめしたまへ
Shi (me) shi ta (ma) e
Don't say the syllables inside the ○
*Koumaga Koumaga. My path, my wish—lead it to glory.

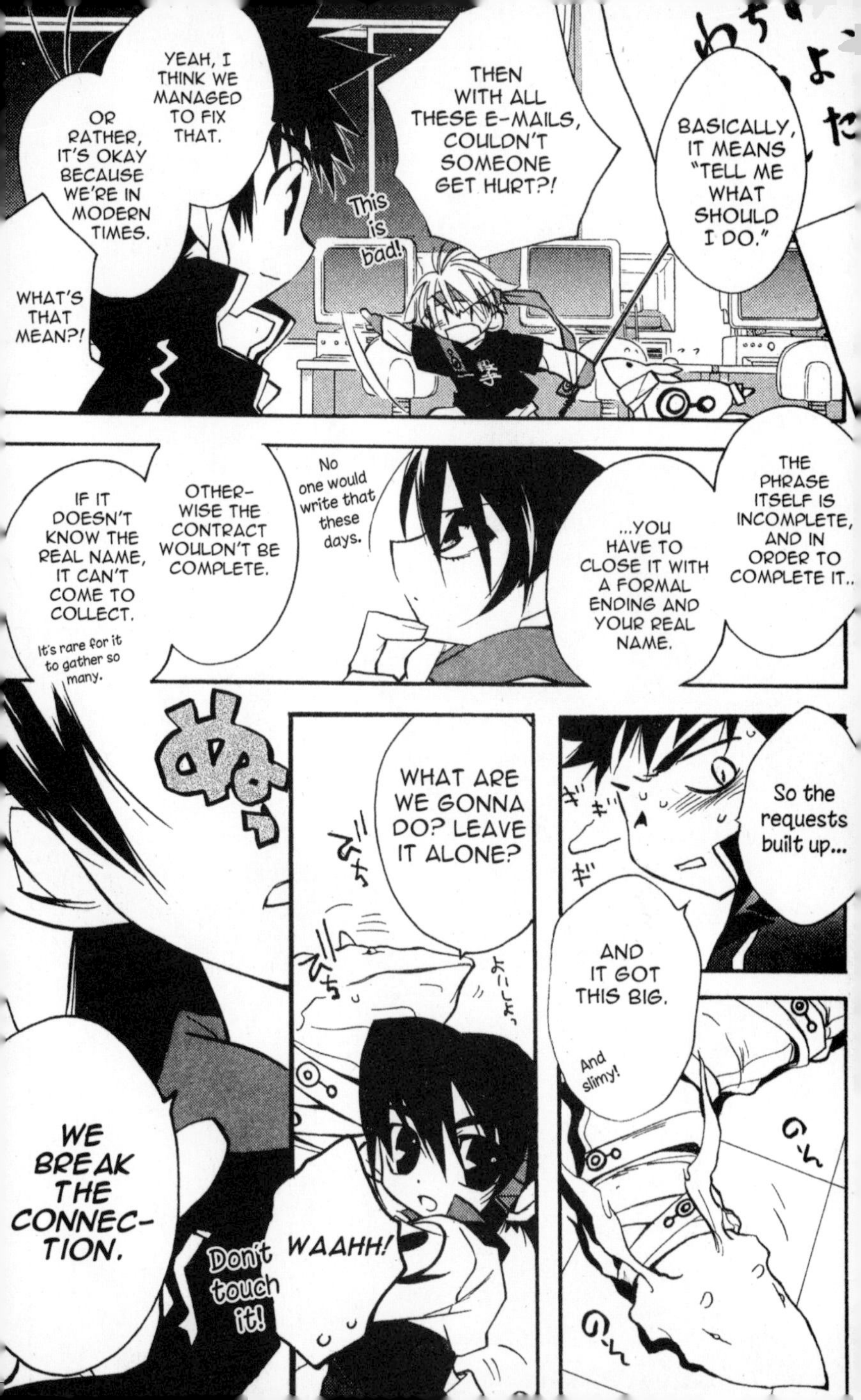
BASICALLY, IT MEANS "TELL ME WHAT SHOULD I DO."
THEN WITH ALL THESE E-MAILS, COULDN'T SOMEONE GET HURT?!
This is bad!
YEAH, I THINK WE MANAGED TO FIX THAT.
OR RATHER, IT'S OKAY BECAUSE WE'RE IN MODERN TIMES.
WHAT'S THAT MEAN?!
THE PHRASE ITSELF IS INCOMPLETE, AND IN ORDER TO COMPLETE IT..
...YOU HAVE TO CLOSE IT WITH A FORMAL ENDING AND YOUR REAL NAME.
No one would write that these days.
OTHER-WISE THE CONTRACT WOULDN'T BE COMPLETE.
IF IT DOESN'T KNOW THE REAL NAME, IT CAN'T COME TO COLLECT.
It's rare for it to gather so many.
So the requests built up...
AND IT GOT THIS BIG.
And slimy!
WHAT ARE WE GONNA DO? LEAVE IT ALONE?
WAAHH!
Don't touch it!
WE BREAK THE CONNECTION.

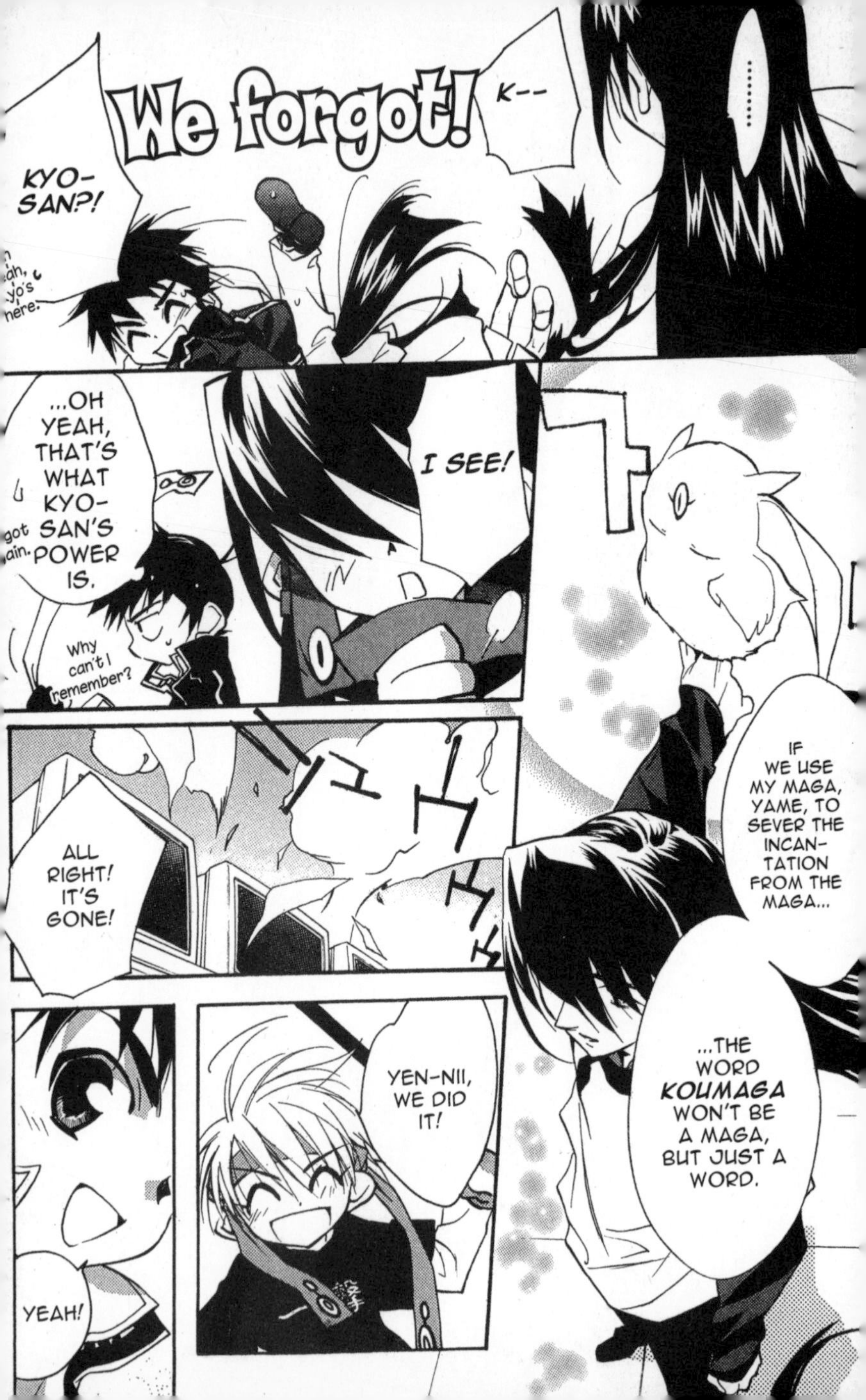
……
K--
We forgot!
KYO-SAN?!
IF WE USE MY MAGA, YAME, TO SEVER THE INCANTATION FROM THE MAGA...
...THE WORD **KOUMAGA** WON'T BE A MAGA, BUT JUST A WORD.
I SEE!
...OH YEAH, THAT'S WHAT KYO-SAN'S POWER IS.
Why can't I remember?
ALL RIGHT! IT'S GONE!
YEN-NII, WE DID IT!
YEAH!

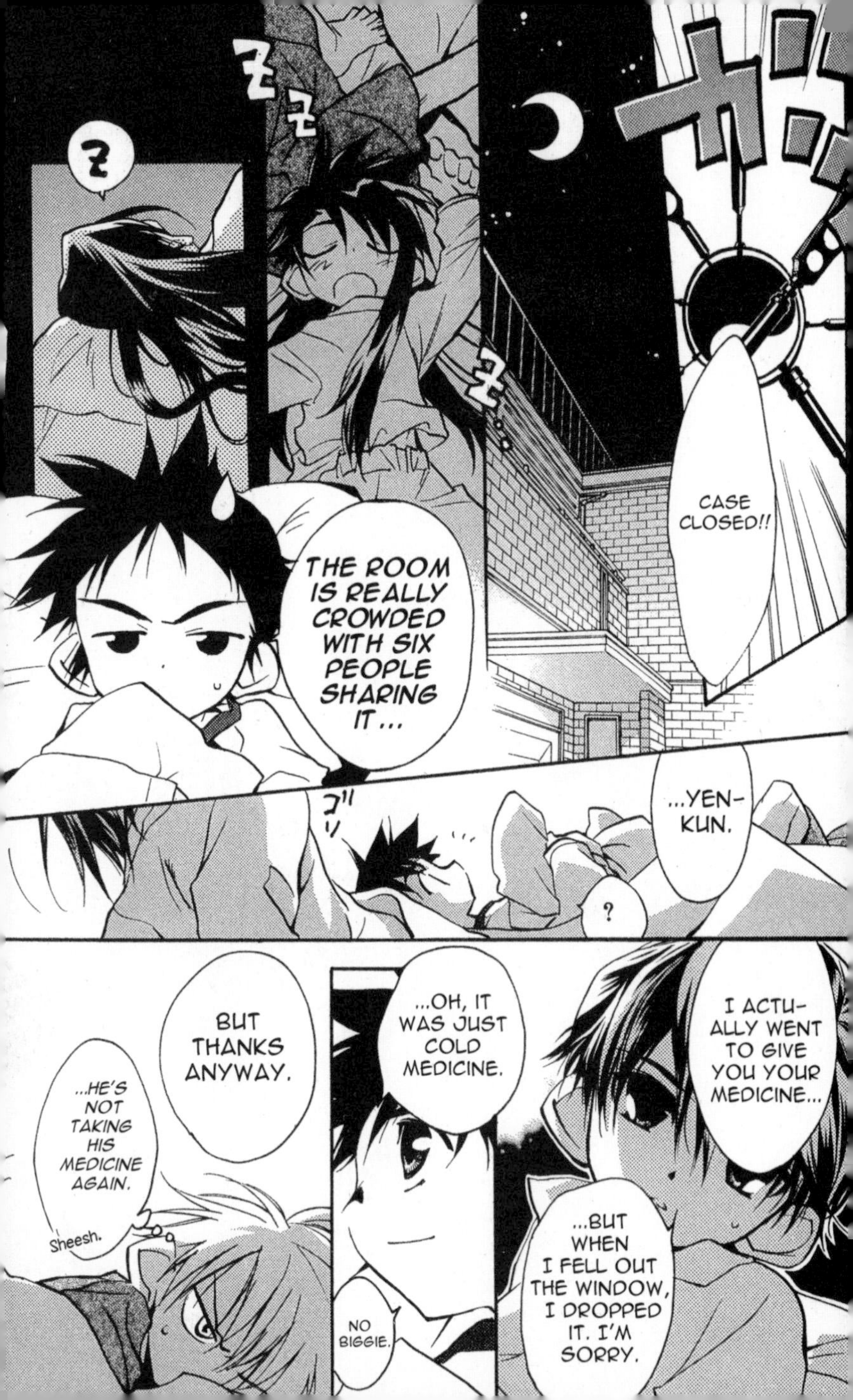
CASE CLOSED!!
THE ROOM IS REALLY CROWDED WITH SIX PEOPLE SHARING IT...
...YEN-KUN.
?
I ACTUALLY WENT TO GIVE YOU YOUR MEDICINE...
...BUT WHEN I FELL OUT THE WINDOW, I DROPPED IT. I'M SORRY.
...OH, IT WAS JUST COLD MEDICINE.
NO BIGGIE.
BUT THANKS ANYWAY.
...HE'S NOT TAKING HIS MEDICINE AGAIN.
Sheesh.

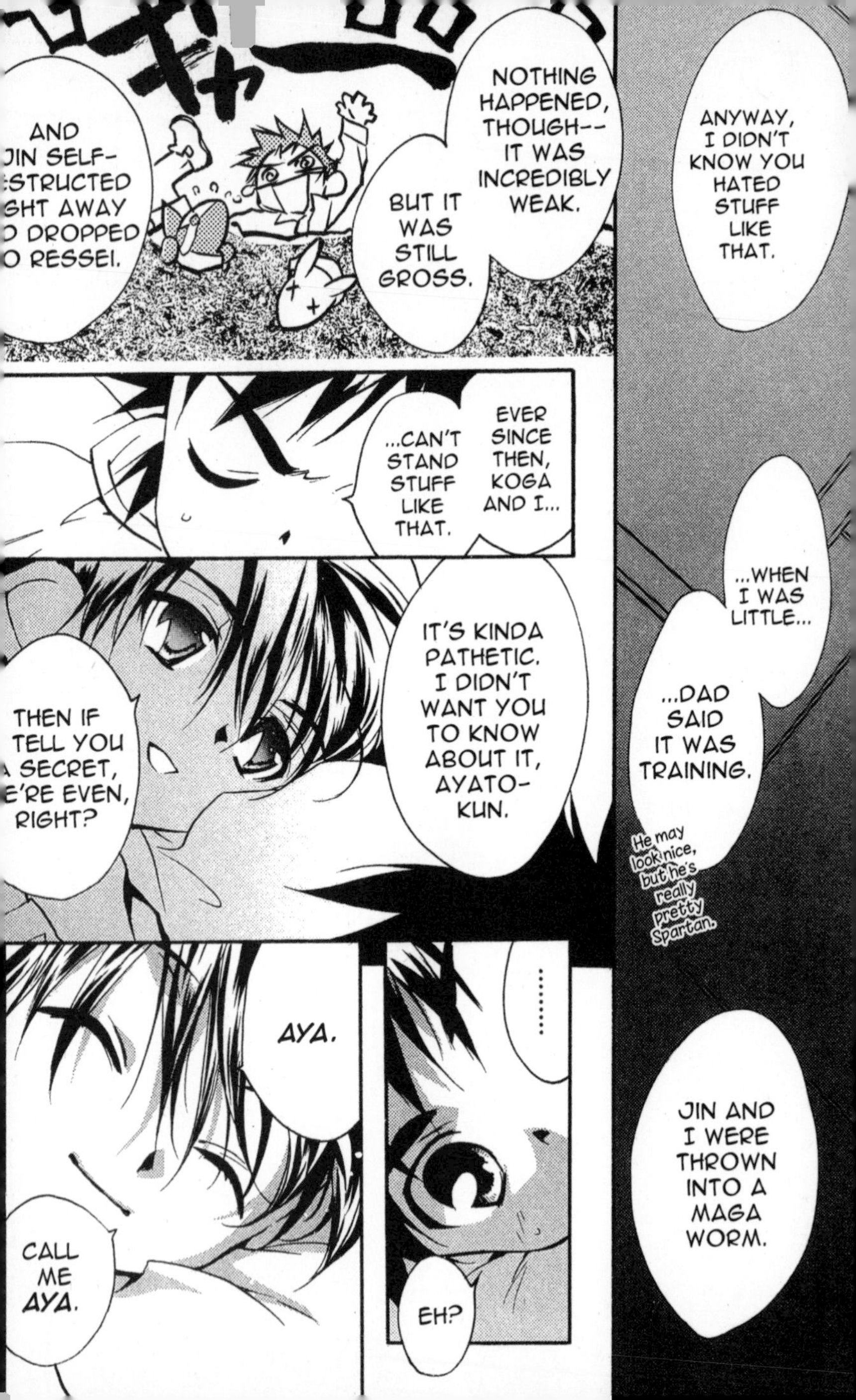
ANYWAY, I DIDN'T KNOW YOU HATED STUFF LIKE THAT.
...WHEN I WAS LITTLE...
...DAD SAID IT WAS TRAINING.
He may look nice, but he's really pretty Spartan.
JIN AND I WERE THROWN INTO A MAGA WORM.
NOTHING HAPPENED, THOUGH-- IT WAS INCREDIBLY WEAK.
BUT IT WAS STILL GROSS.
AND JIN SELF-
STRUCTED GHT AWAY D DROPPED O RESSEI.
EVER SINCE THEN, KOGA AND I...
...CAN'T STAND STUFF LIKE THAT.
IT'S KINDA PATHETIC. I DIDN'T WANT YOU TO KNOW ABOUT IT, AYATO-KUN.
THEN IF TELL YOU SECRET, 'RE EVEN, RIGHT?
....
EH?
AYA.
CALL ME AYA.

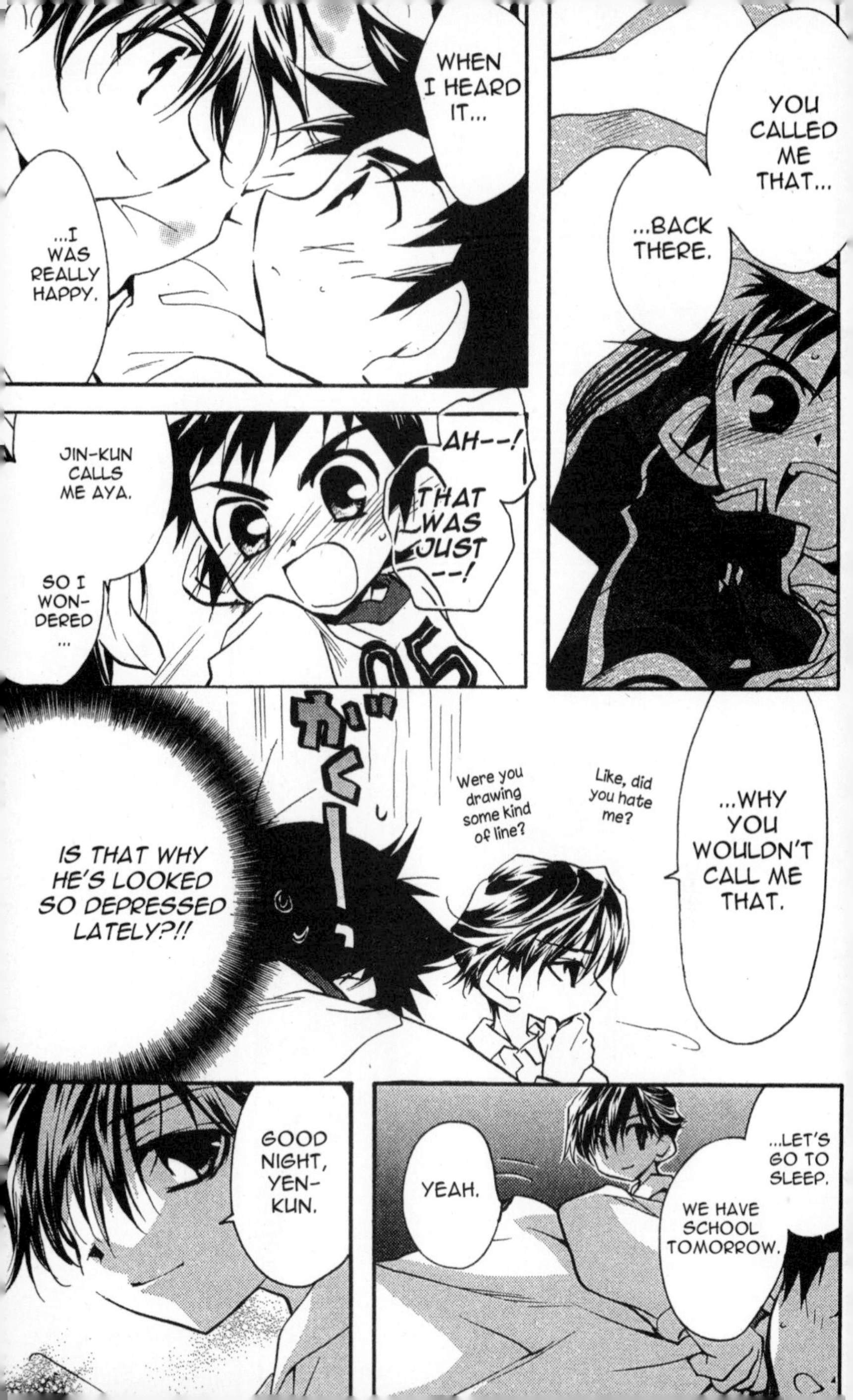
YOU CALLED ME THAT...
...BACK THERE.
WHEN I HEARD IT...
...I WAS REALLY HAPPY.
AH--! THAT WAS JUST--!
JIN-KUN CALLS ME AYA.
SO I WONDERED...
...WHY YOU WOULDN'T CALL ME THAT.
Like, did you hate me?
Were you drawing some kind of line?
がくー
IS THAT WHY HE'S LOOKED SO DEPRESSED LATELY?!!
...LET'S GO TO SLEEP.
WE HAVE SCHOOL TOMORROW.
YEAH.
GOOD NIGHT, YEN-KUN.

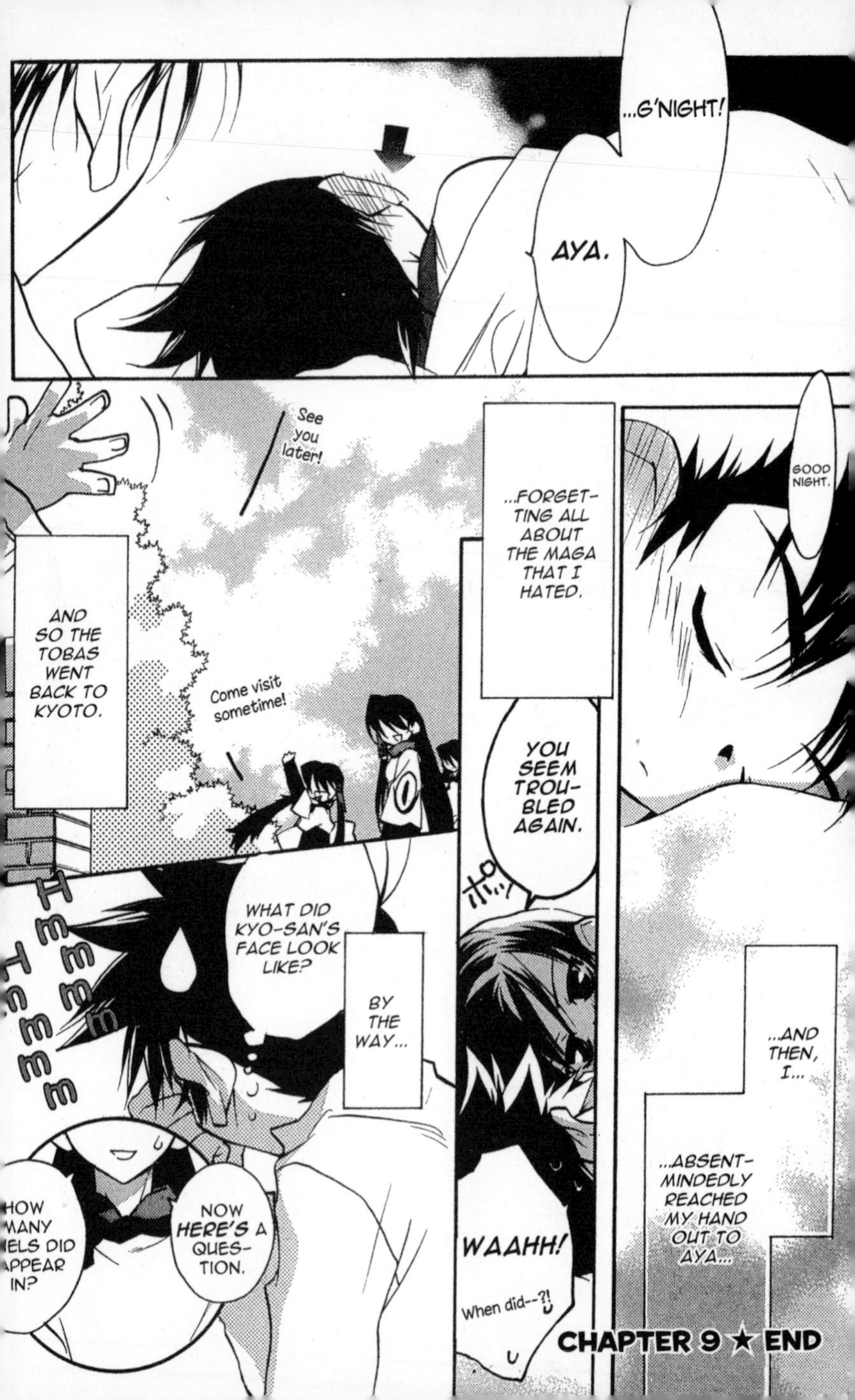
...G'NIGHT!
AYA.
GOOD NIGHT.
...AND THEN, I...
...ABSENT-MINDEDLY REACHED MY HAND OUT TO AYA...
...FORGETTING ALL ABOUT THE MAGA THAT I HATED.
YOU SEEM TROUBLED AGAIN.
ポッ
WAAHH!
When did--?!
See you later!
Come visit sometime!
AND SO THE TOBAS WENT BACK TO KYOTO.
BY THE WAY...
WHAT DID KYO-SAN'S FACE LOOK LIKE?
NOW HERE'S A QUESTION.
CHAPTER 9 ★ END

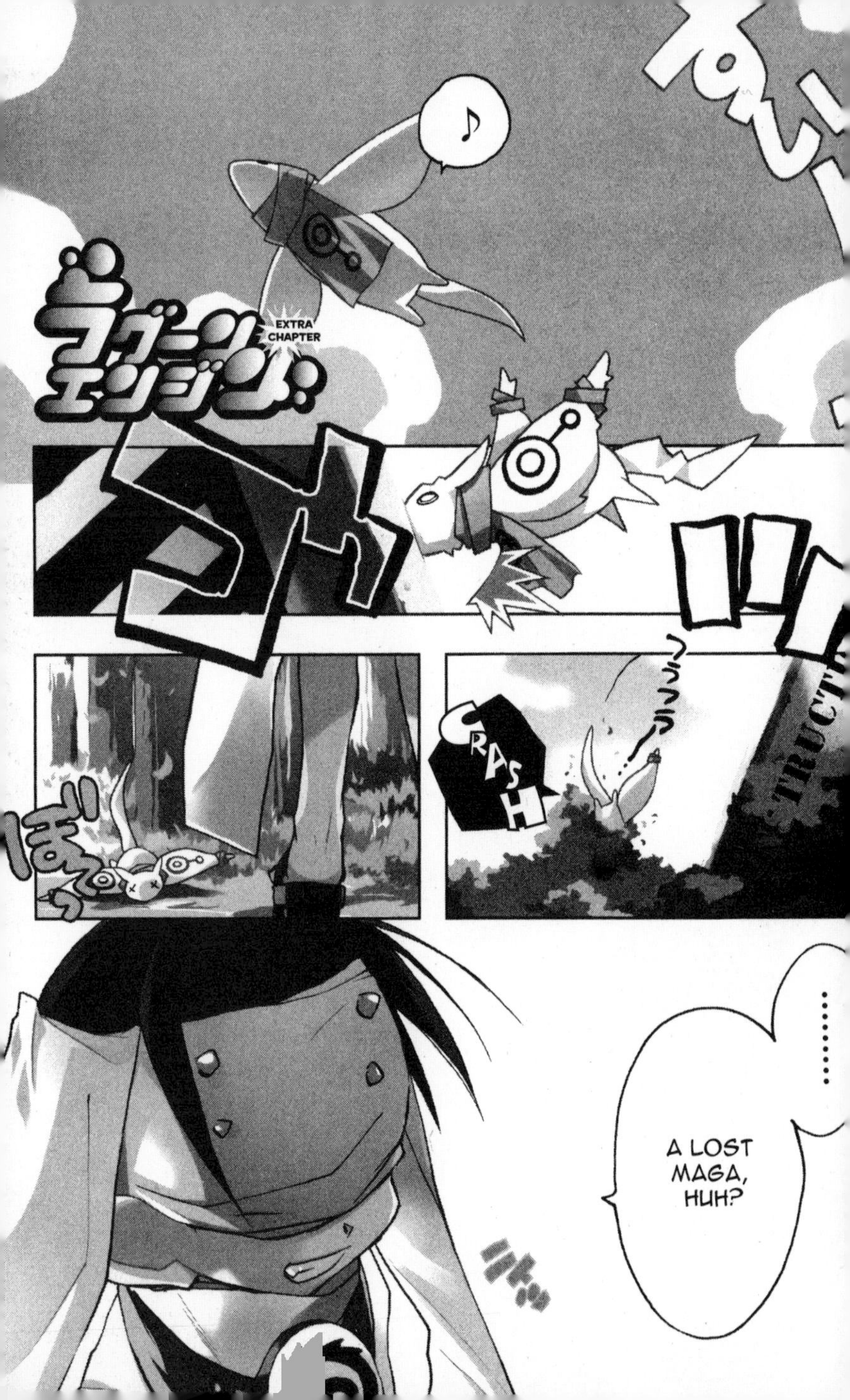
♪
EXTRA CHAPTER
CRASH
....
A LOST MAGA, HUH?

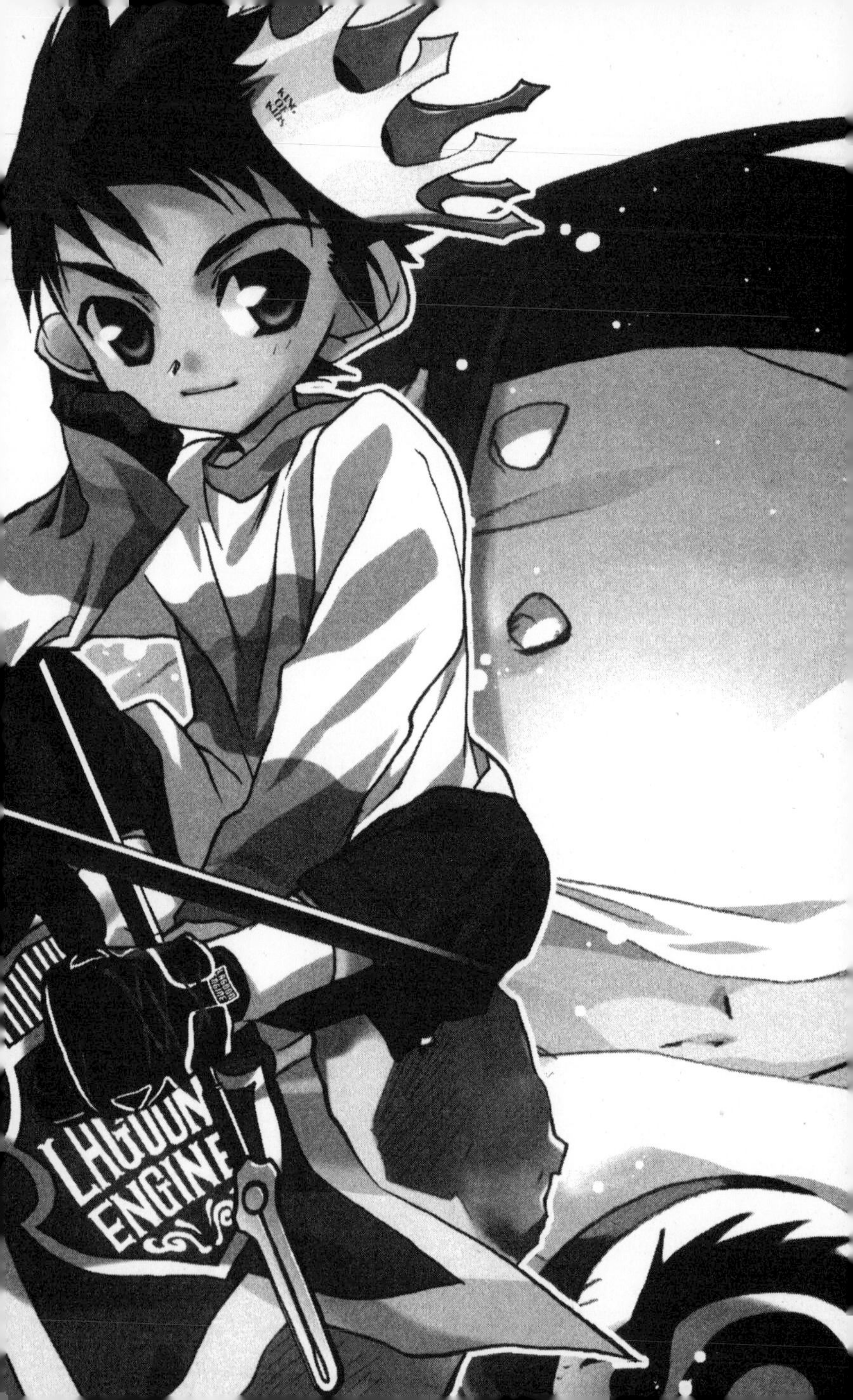

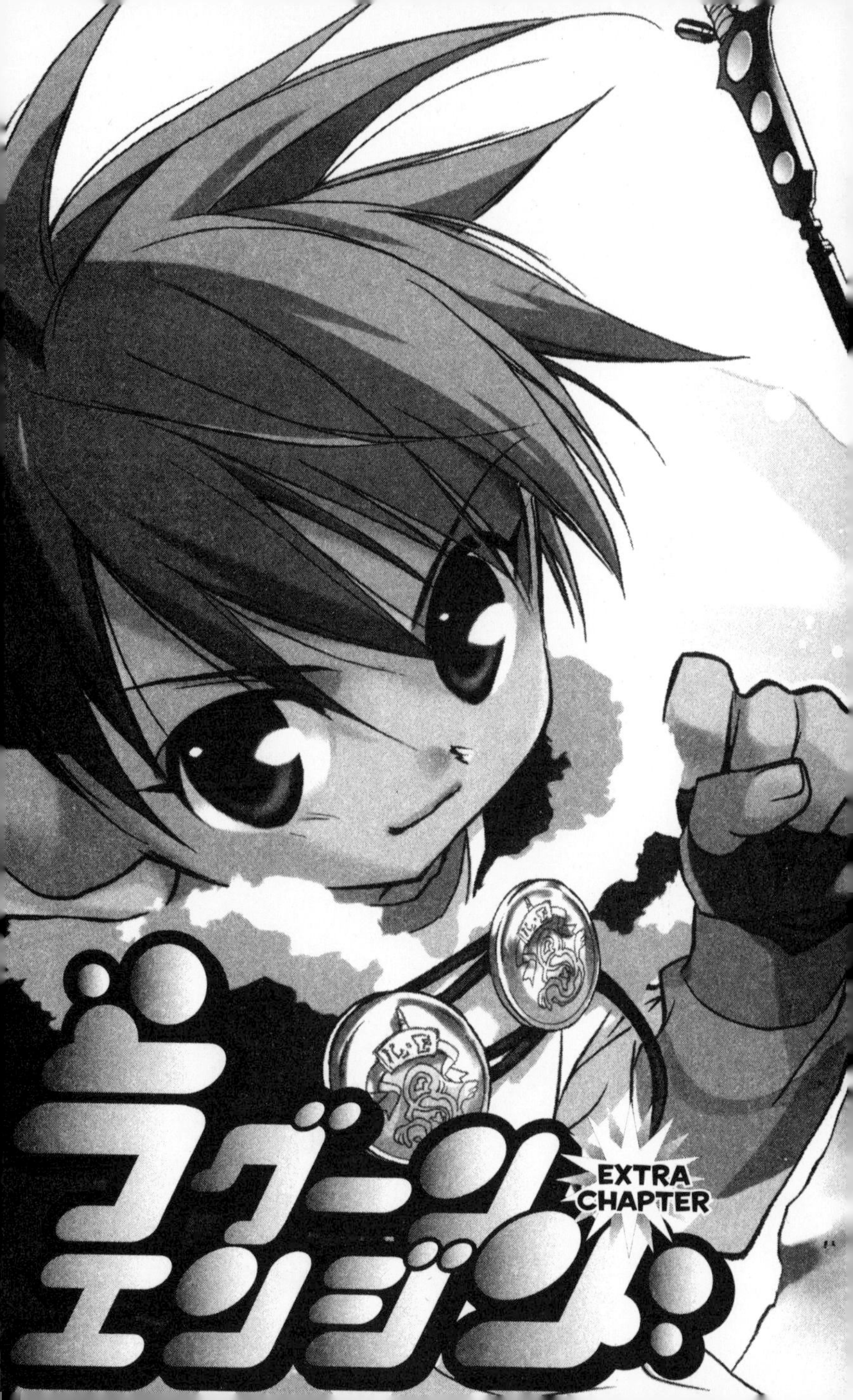
ラグーンエンジン
EXTRA CHAPTER

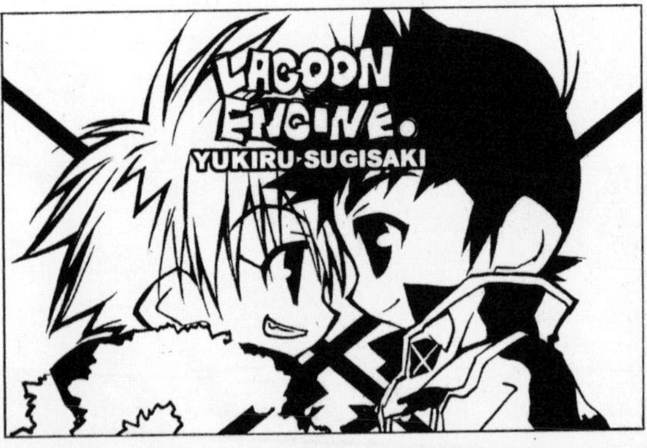
LAGOON ENGINE.
YUKIRU·SUGISAKI

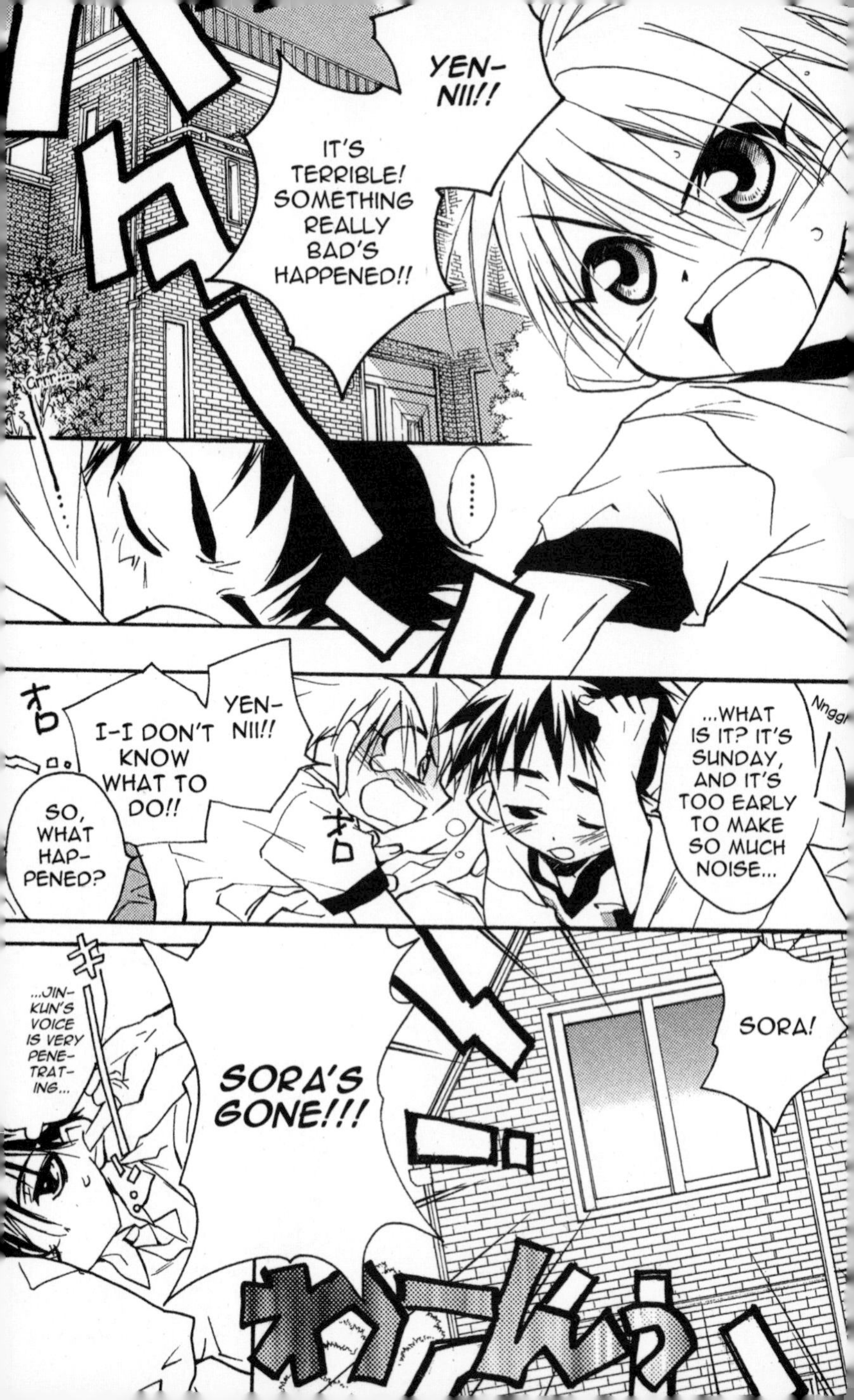
YEN-NII!!
IT'S TERRIBLE! SOMETHING REALLY BAD'S HAPPENED!!
Grrr...
......
...WHAT IS IT? IT'S SUNDAY, AND IT'S TOO EARLY TO MAKE SO MUCH NOISE...
YEN-NII!!
I-I DON'T KNOW WHAT TO DO!!
SO, WHAT HAPPENED?
SORA!
SORA'S GONE!!!
...JIN-KUN'S VOICE IS VERY PENETRATING...

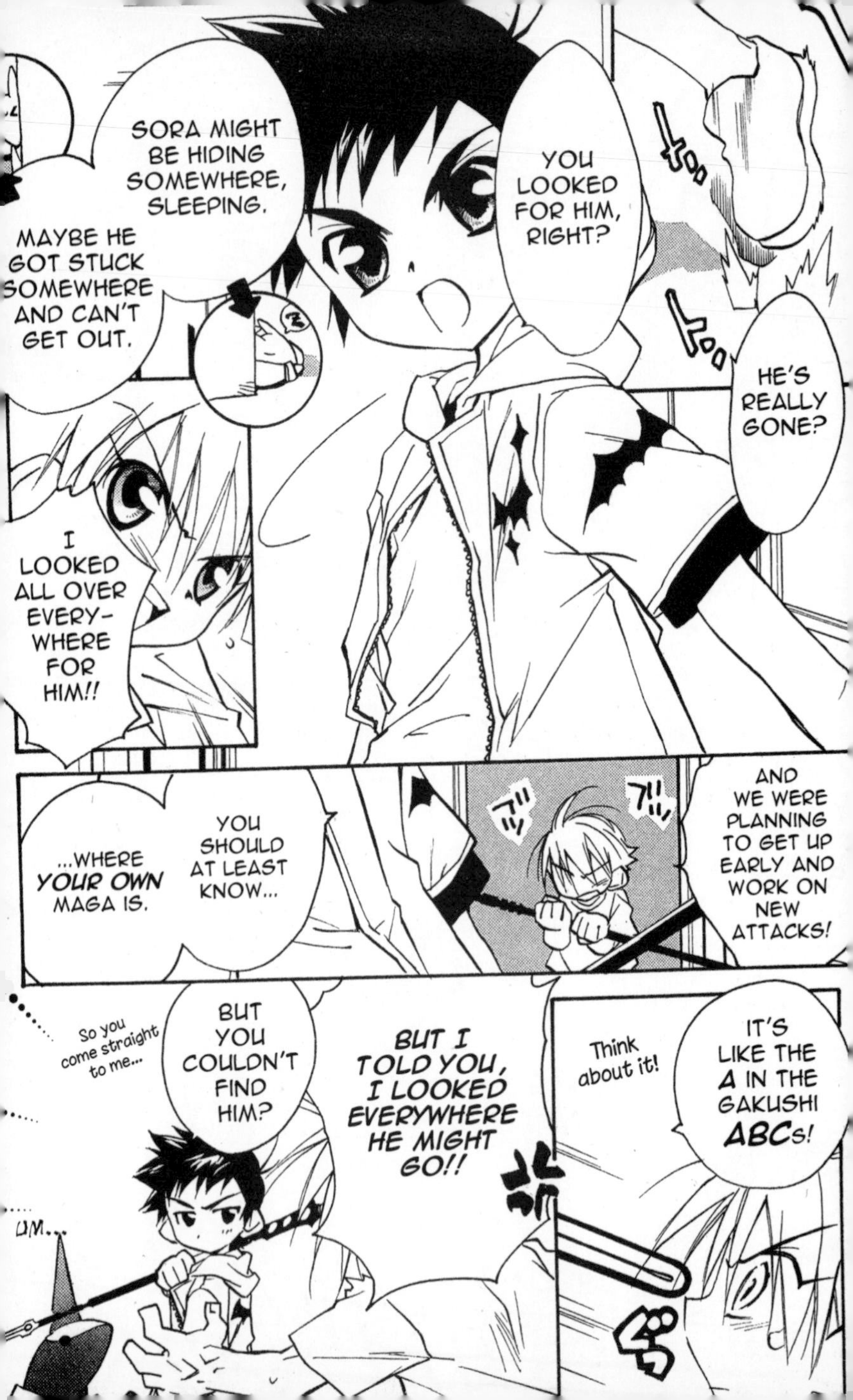
YOU LOOKED FOR HIM, RIGHT?
HE'S REALLY GONE?
SORA MIGHT BE HIDING SOMEWHERE, SLEEPING.
MAYBE HE GOT STUCK SOMEWHERE AND CAN'T GET OUT.
I LOOKED ALL OVER EVERY-WHERE FOR HIM!!
AND WE WERE PLANNING TO GET UP EARLY AND WORK ON NEW ATTACKS!
YOU SHOULD AT LEAST KNOW...
...WHERE YOUR OWN MAGA IS.
IT'S LIKE THE A IN THE GAKUSHI ABCs!
Think about it!
BUT I TOLD YOU, I LOOKED EVERYWHERE HE MIGHT GO!!
BUT YOU COULDN'T FIND HIM?
So you come straight to me...
UM...

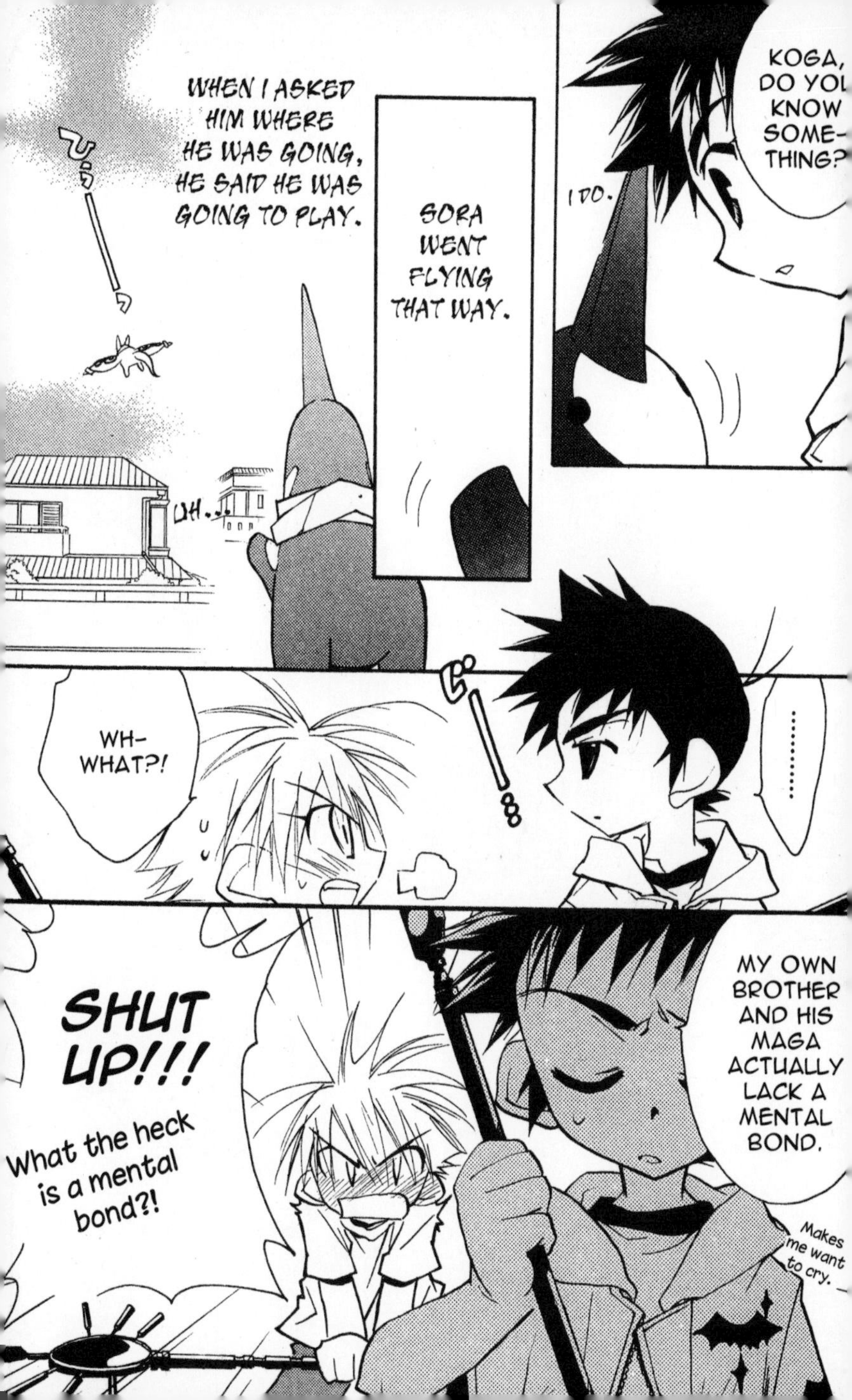

KOGA, DO YOU KNOW SOMETHING?
I DO.
SORA WENT FLYING THAT WAY.
WHEN I ASKED HIM WHERE HE WAS GOING, HE SAID HE WAS GOING TO PLAY.
UH...
......
WH-WHAT?!
MY OWN BROTHER AND HIS MAGA ACTUALLY LACK A MENTAL BOND.
Makes me want to cry.
SHUT UP!!!
What the heck is a mental bond?!

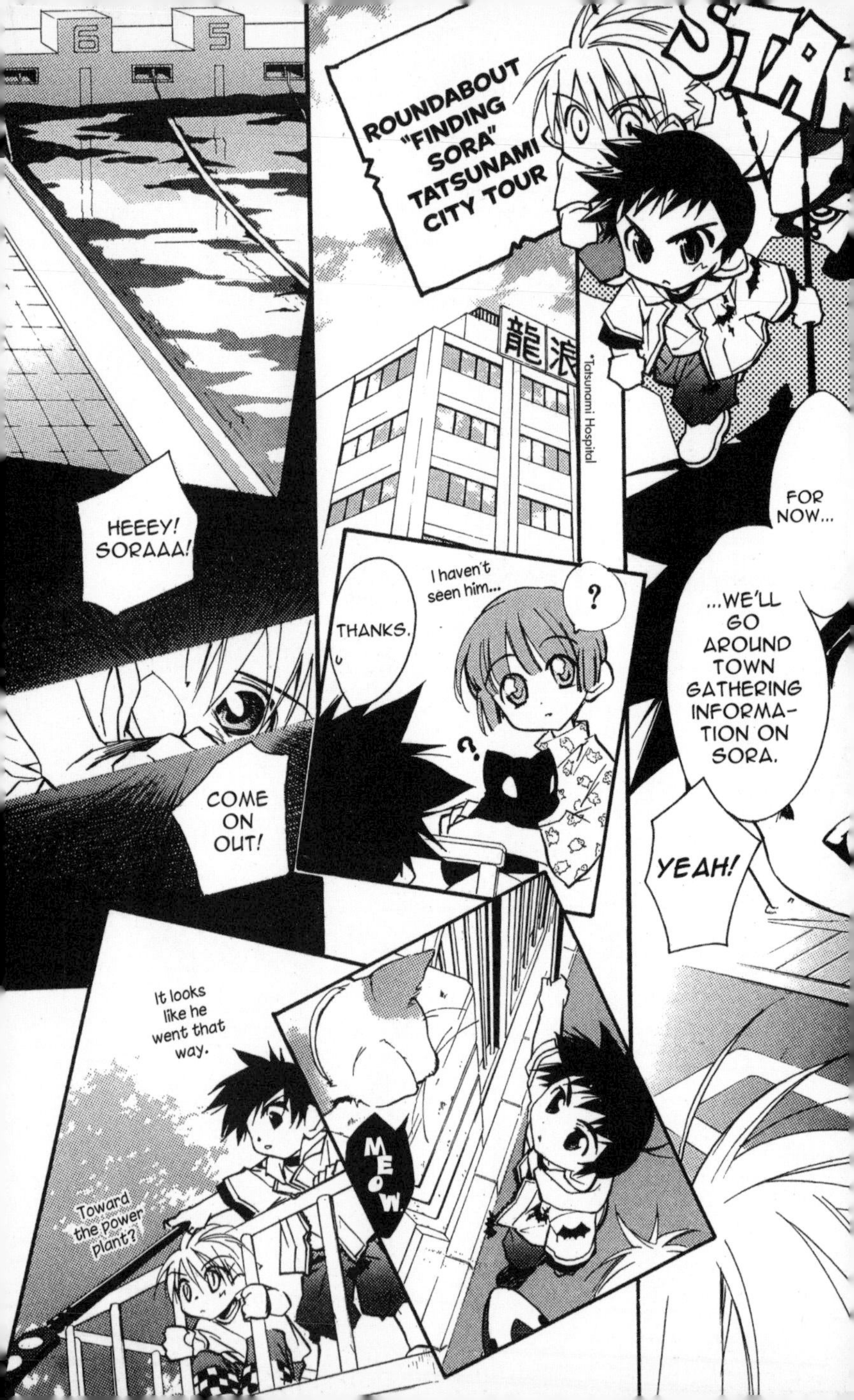
STA
ROUNDABOUT "FINDING SORA" TATSUNAMI CITY TOUR
龍浪
*Tatsunami Hospital
FOR NOW...
...WE'LL GO AROUND TOWN GATHERING INFORMATION ON SORA.
YEAH!
?
I haven't seen him...
THANKS.
HEEEY! SORAAA!
COME ON OUT!
MEOW
It looks like he went that way.
Toward the power plant?

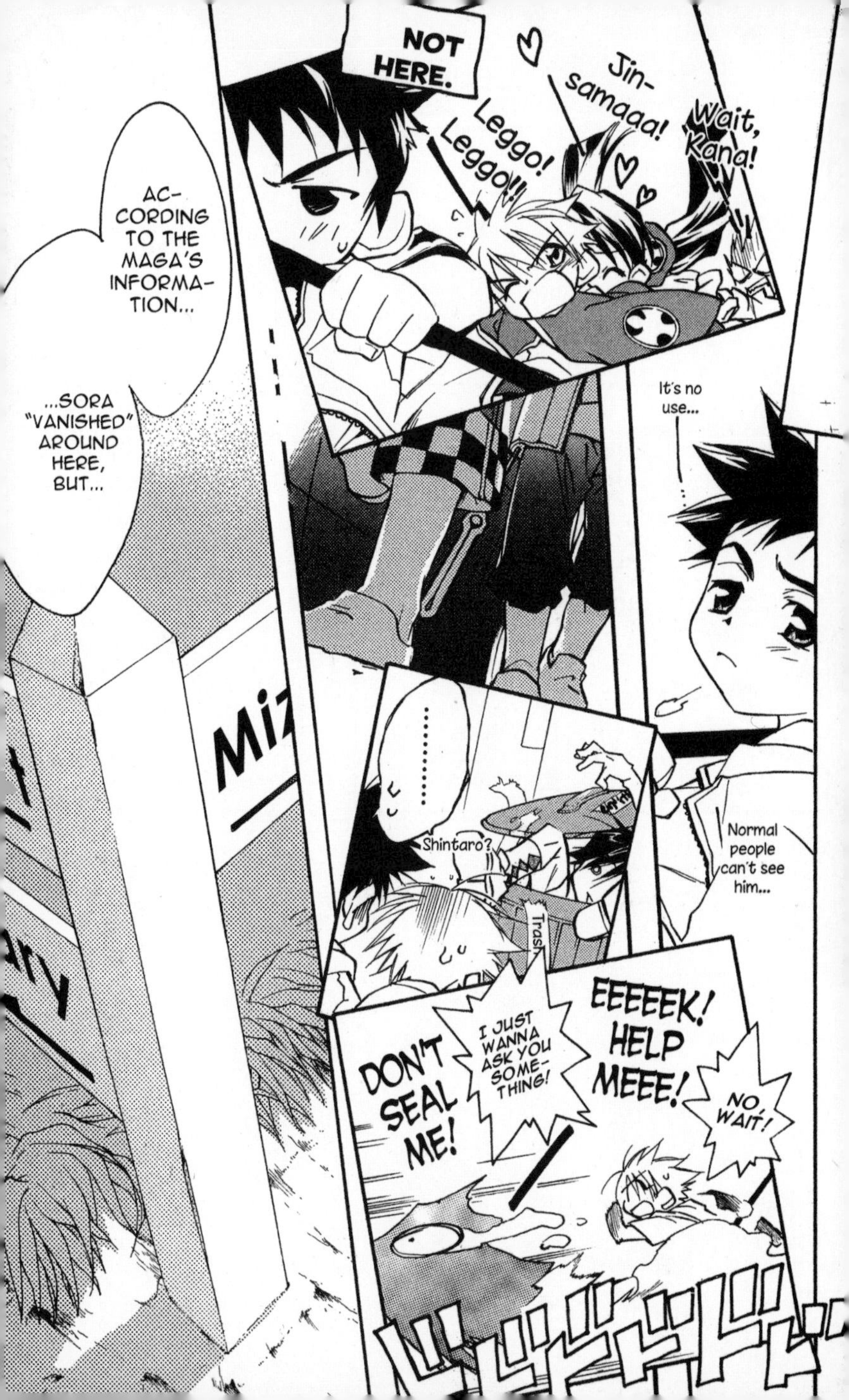
Wait, Kana!
Jin-samaaa!
Leggo! Leggo!!
NOT HERE.
It's no use...
Normal people can't see him...
......
Shintaro?
Trash
NO WAIT!
EEEEEK! HELP MEEE!
I JUST WANNA ASK YOU SOME-THING!
DON'T SEAL ME!
AC-CORDING TO THE MAGA'S INFORMA-TION...
...SORA "VANISHED" AROUND HERE, BUT...

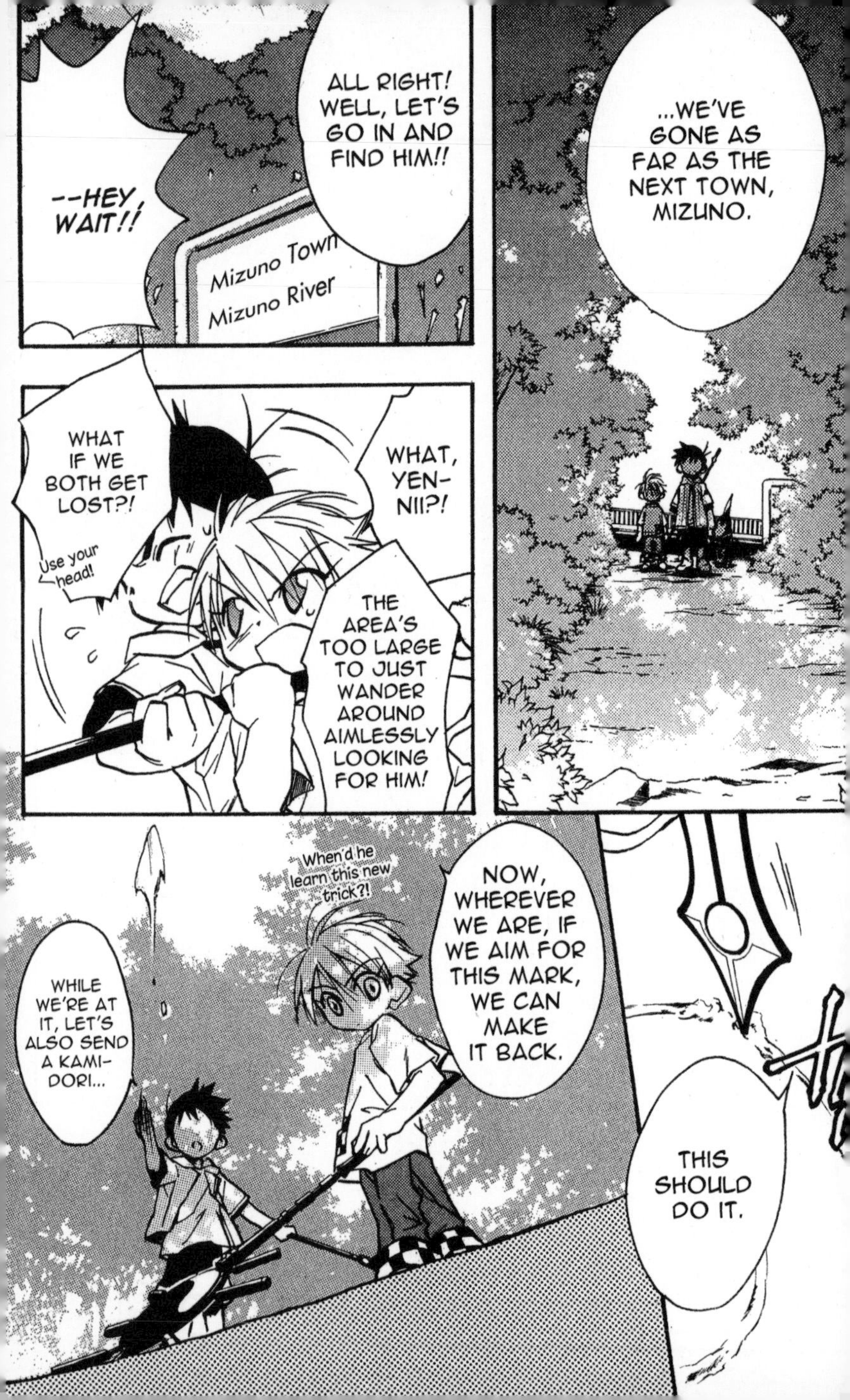
...WE'VE GONE AS FAR AS THE NEXT TOWN, MIZUNO.
ALL RIGHT! WELL, LET'S GO IN AND FIND HIM!!
--HEY, WAIT!!
Mizuno Town
Mizuno River
WHAT, YEN-NII?!
THE AREA'S TOO LARGE TO JUST WANDER AROUND AIMLESSLY LOOKING FOR HIM!
WHAT IF WE BOTH GET LOST?!
Use your head!
THIS SHOULD DO IT.
NOW, WHEREVER WE ARE, IF WE AIM FOR THIS MARK, WE CAN MAKE IT BACK.
When'd he learn this new trick?!
WHILE WE'RE AT IT, LET'S ALSO SEND A KAMI-DORI...

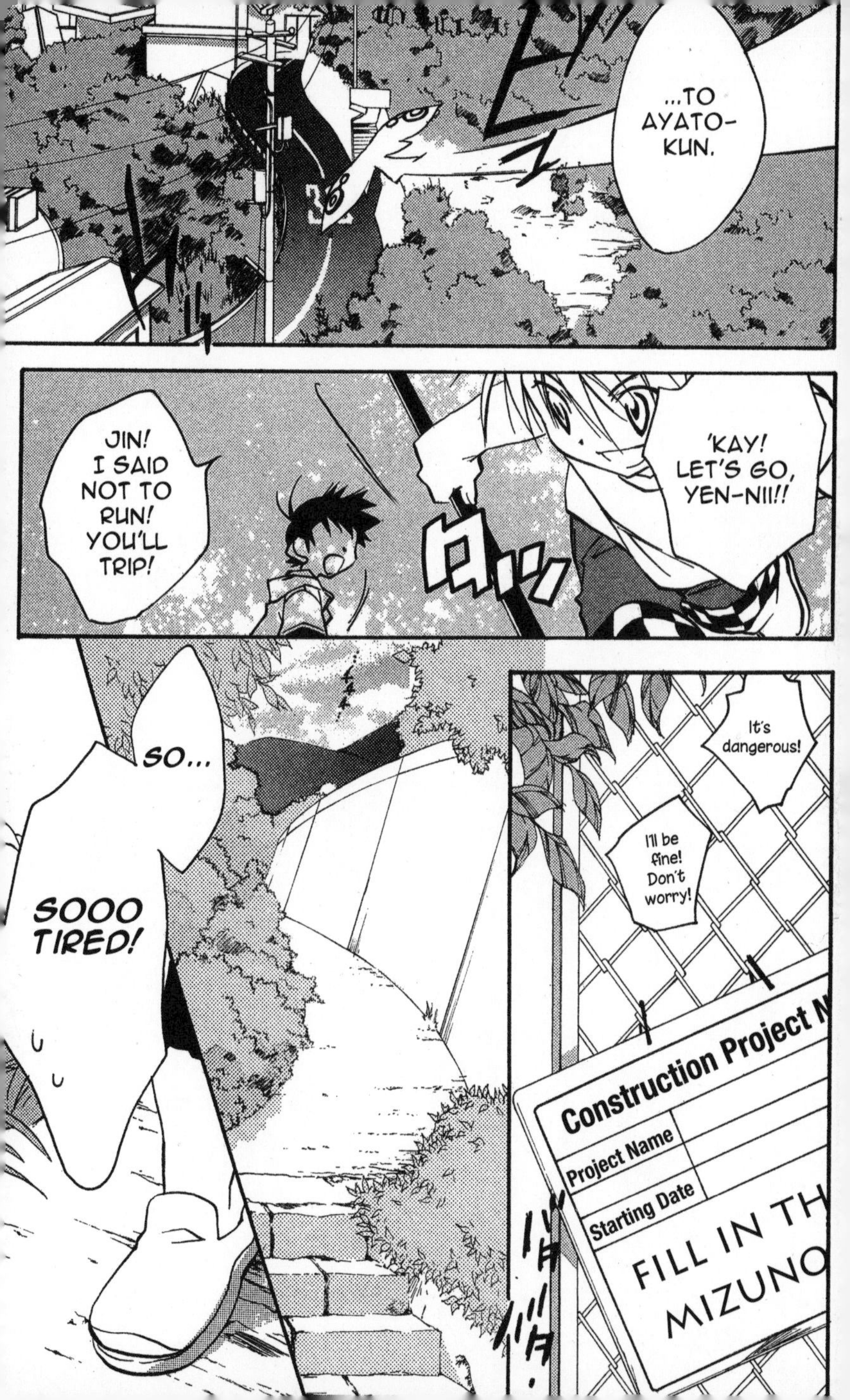
...TO AYATO-KUN.
'KAY! LET'S GO, YEN-NII!!
JIN! I SAID NOT TO RUN! YOU'LL TRIP!
It's dangerous!
I'll be fine! Don't worry!
Construction Project N
Construction
Project Name
Starting Date
FILL IN TH
MIZUNO
SO...
SOOO TIRED!

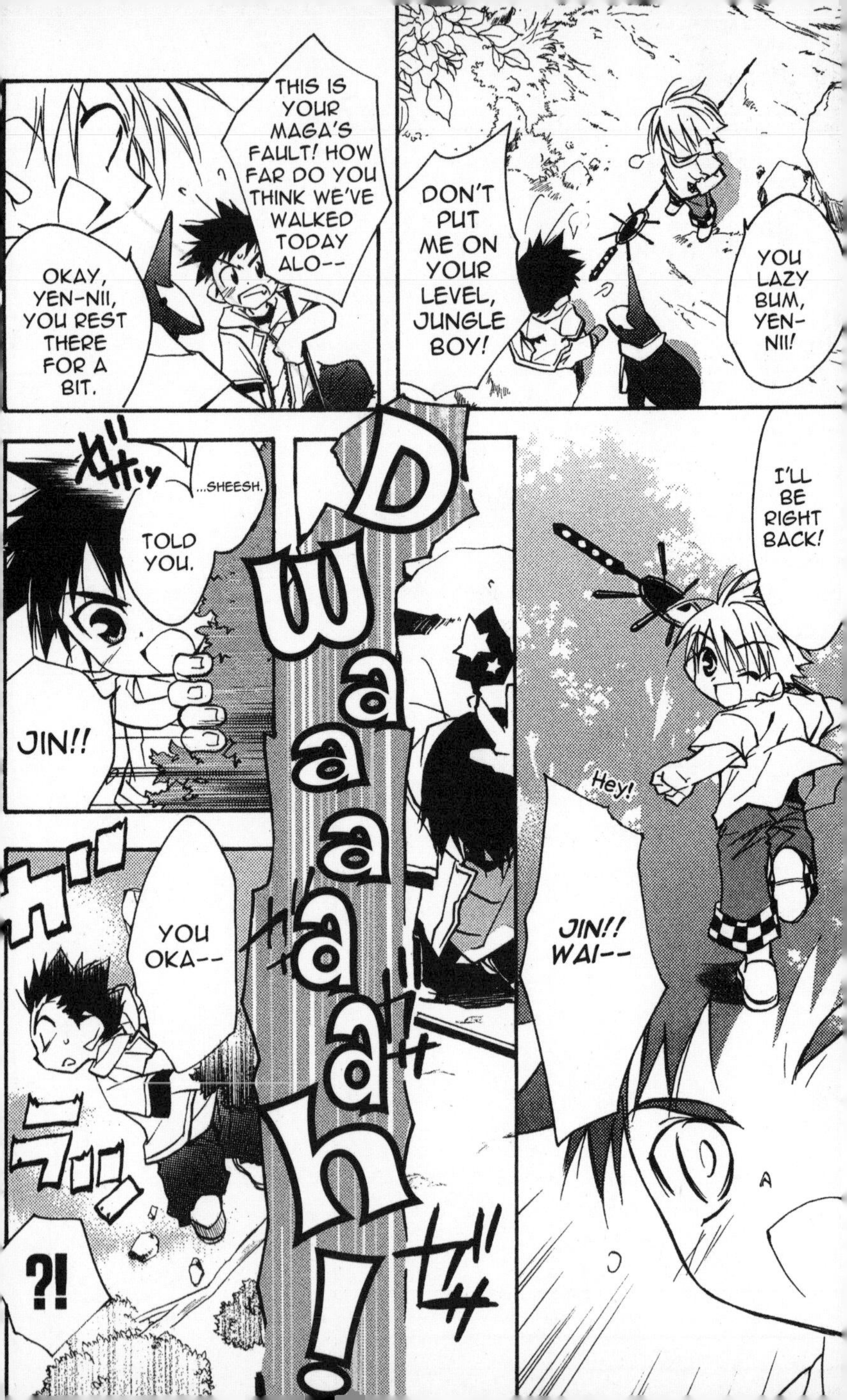
YOU LAZY BUM, YEN-NII!
DON'T PUT ME ON YOUR LEVEL, JUNGLE BOY!
THIS IS YOUR MAGA'S FAULT! HOW FAR DO YOU THINK WE'VE WALKED TODAY ALO--
OKAY, YEN-NII, YOU REST THERE FOR A BIT.
I'LL BE RIGHT BACK!
Hey!
JIN!! WAI--
DWaaaaaaah!
...SHEESH.
TOLD YOU.
JIN!!
YOU OKA--
?!

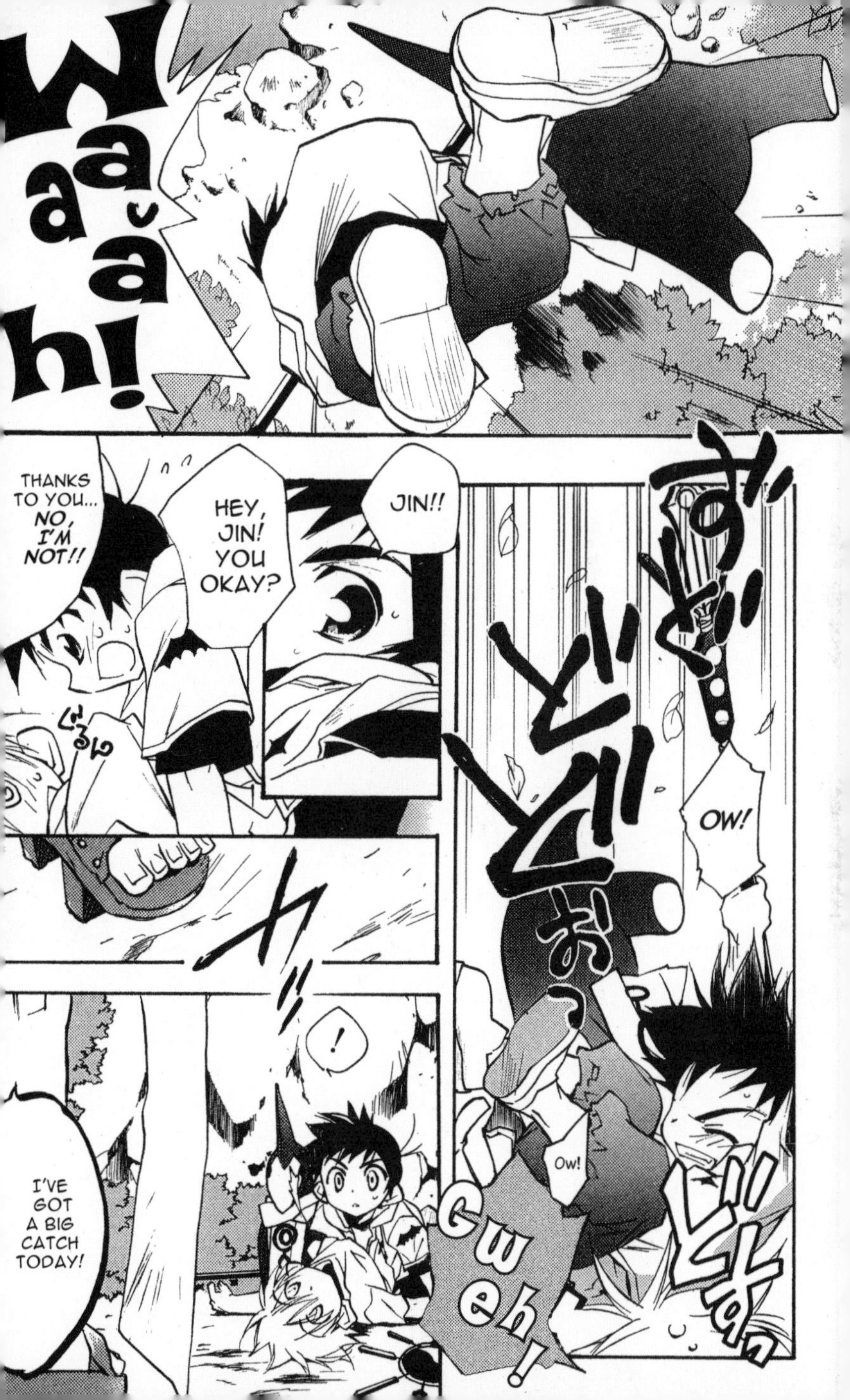
Waaaah!
OW!
Ow!
Gweh!
JIN!!
HEY, JIN! YOU OKAY?
THANKS TO YOU... NO, I'M NOT!!
!
I'VE GOT A BIG CATCH TODAY!

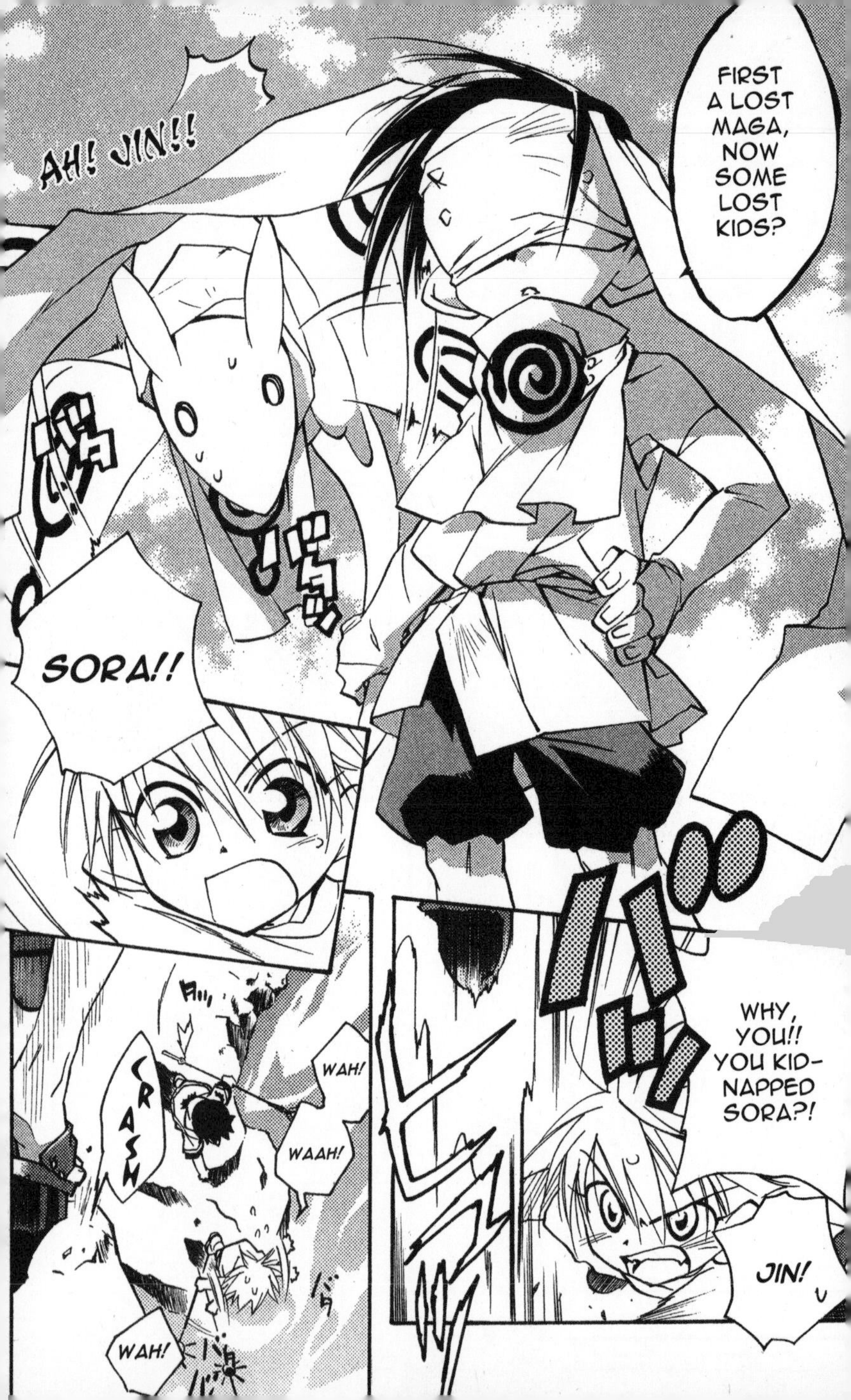
FIRST A LOST MAGA, NOW SOME LOST KIDS?
AH! JIN!!
SORA!!
WHY, YOU!! YOU KID-NAPPED SORA?!
JIN!
WAH!
WAAH!
CRASH
WAH!

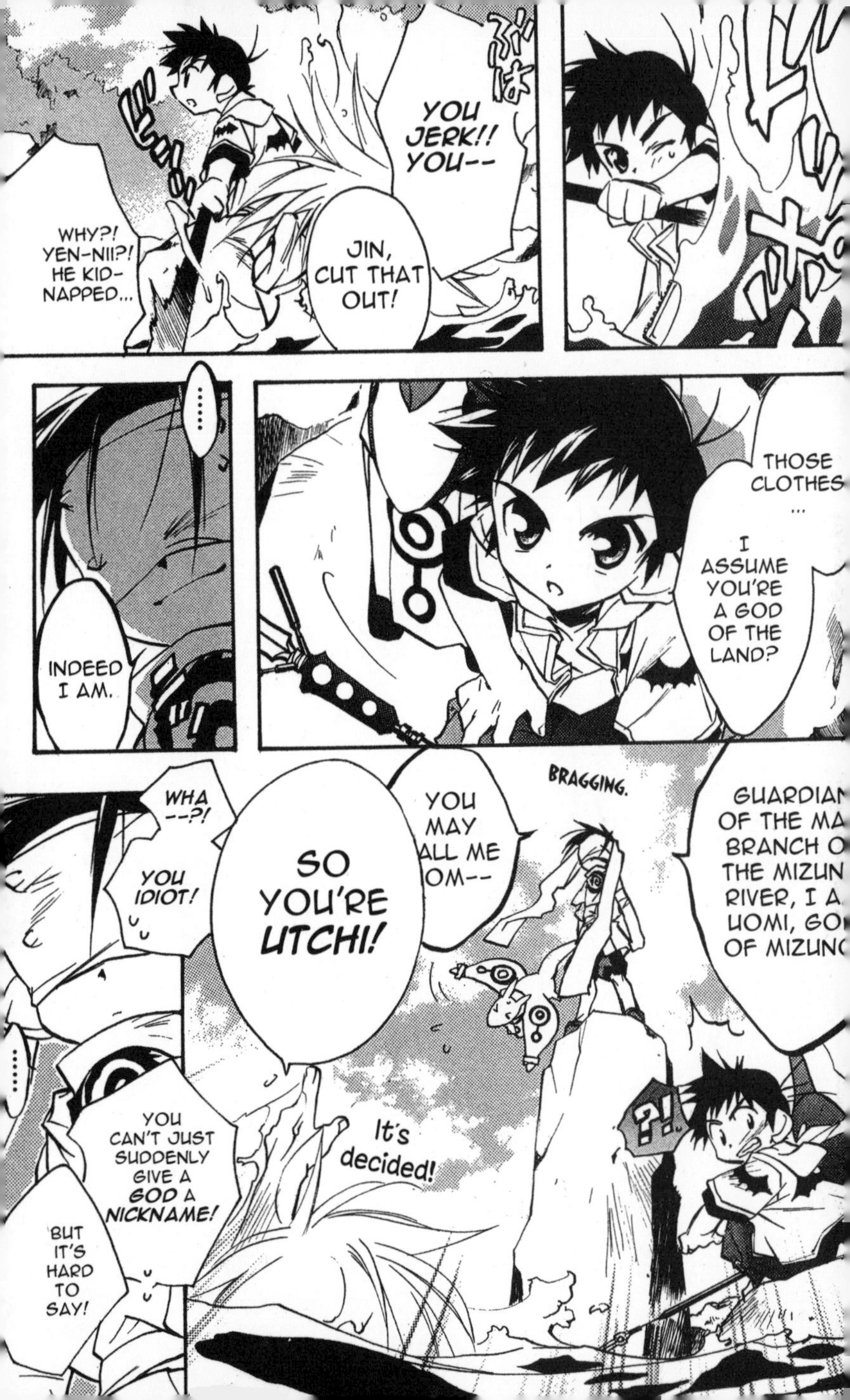
ぷは
YOU JERK!! YOU--
JIN, CUT THAT OUT!
WHY?! YEN-NII?! HE KID-NAPPED...
THOSE CLOTHES ...
I ASSUME YOU'RE A GOD OF THE LAND?
......
INDEED I AM.
GUARDIAN OF THE MA BRANCH O THE MIZUN RIVER, I A UOMI, GO OF MIZUN
BRAGGING.
YOU MAY ALL ME OM--
SO YOU'RE UTCHI!
?!
It's decided!
WHA--?!
YOU IDIOT!
......
YOU CAN'T JUST SUDDENLY GIVE A GOD A NICKNAME!
BUT IT'S HARD TO SAY!

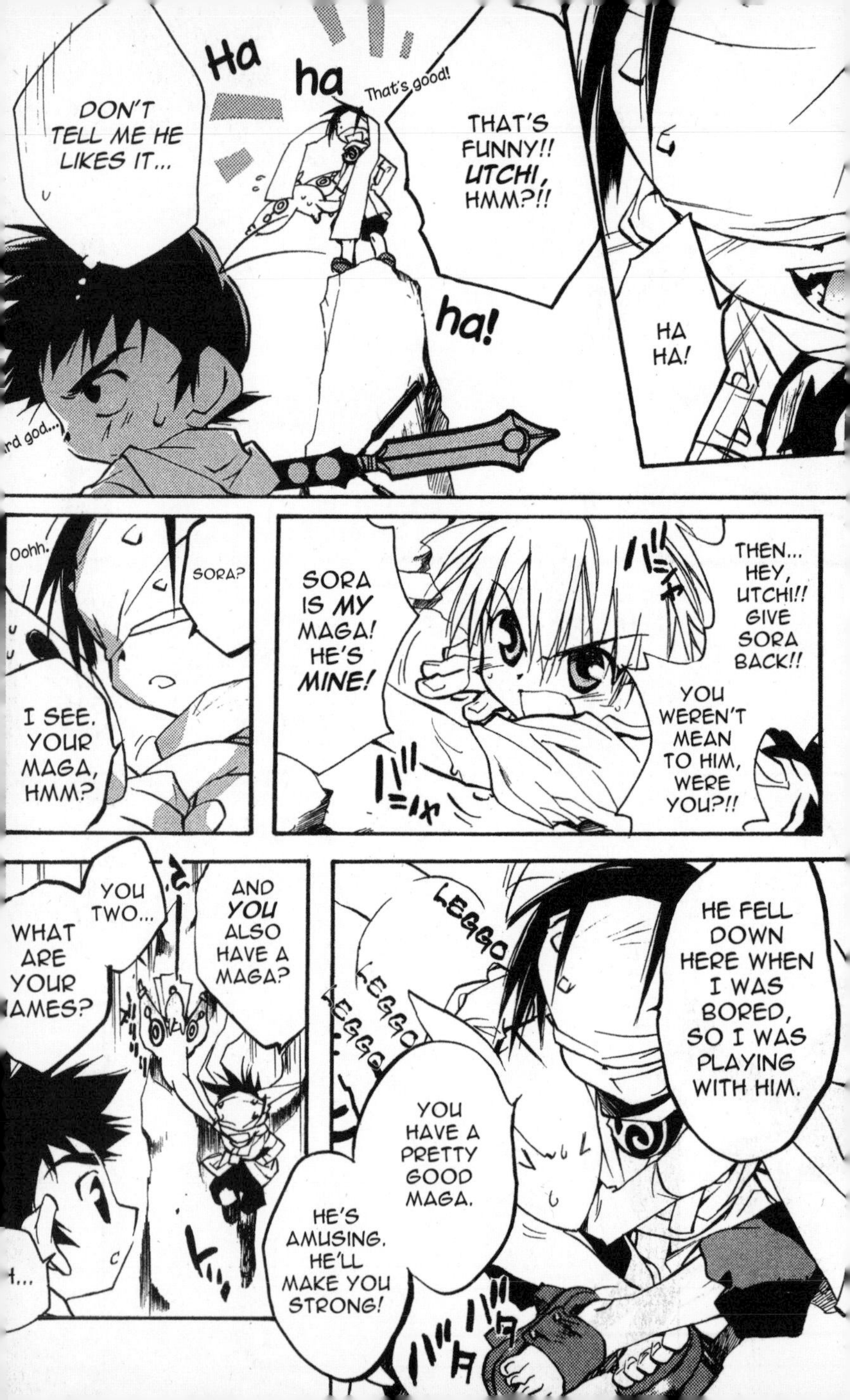
THAT'S FUNNY!! UTCHI, HMM?!!
That's good!
Ha ha ha!
HA HA!
DON'T TELL ME HE LIKES IT...
rd god...
THEN... HEY, UTCHI!! GIVE SORA BACK!!
YOU WEREN'T MEAN TO HIM, WERE YOU?!!
SORA IS MY MAGA! HE'S MINE!
SORA?
Oohh,
I SEE. YOUR MAGA, HMM?
HE FELL DOWN HERE WHEN I WAS BORED, SO I WAS PLAYING WITH HIM.
LEGGO LEGGO LEGGO
YOU HAVE A PRETTY GOOD MAGA.
HE'S AMUSING. HE'LL MAKE YOU STRONG!
AND YOU ALSO HAVE A MAGA?
YOU TWO...
WHAT ARE YOUR AMES?

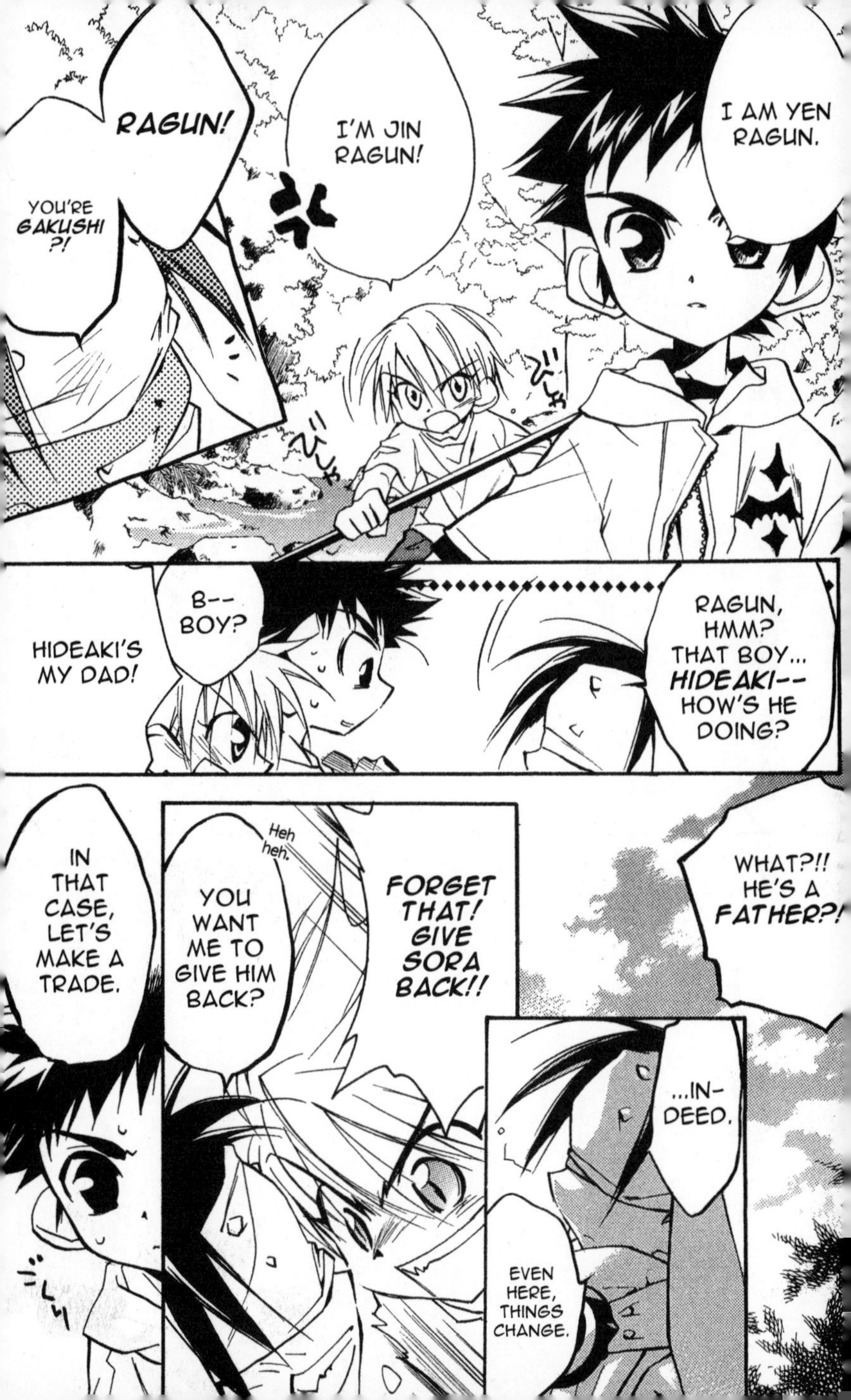
I AM YEN RAGUN.
I'M JIN RAGUN!
RAGUN!
YOU'RE GAKUSHI?!
RAGUN, HMM? THAT BOY... HIDEAKI--HOW'S HE DOING?
B--BOY?
HIDEAKI'S MY DAD!
WHAT?!! HE'S A FATHER?!
...IN-DEED.
EVEN HERE, THINGS CHANGE.
FORGET THAT! GIVE SORA BACK!!
Heh heh.
YOU WANT ME TO GIVE HIM BACK?
IN THAT CASE, LET'S MAKE A TRADE.

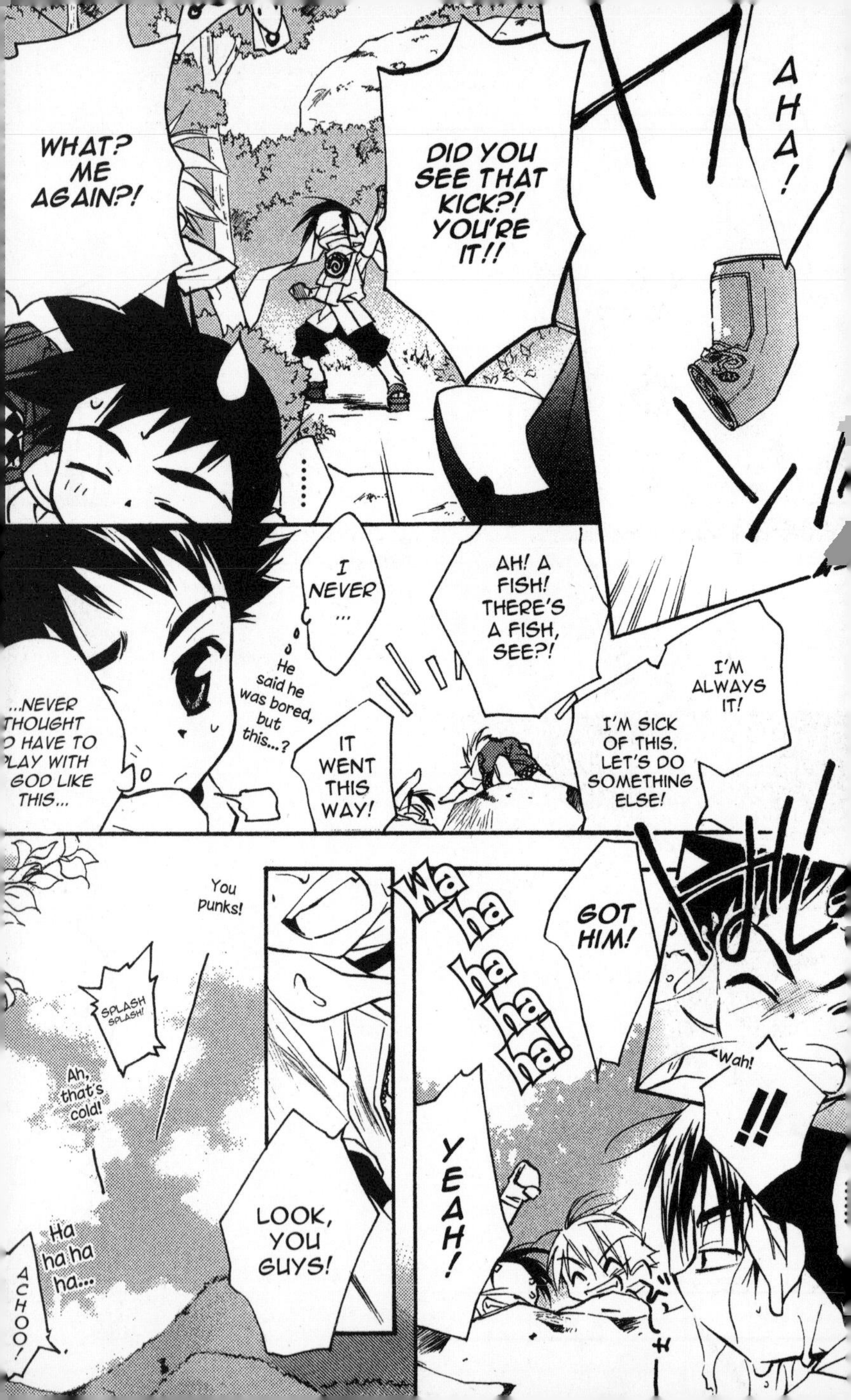
AHA!
DID YOU SEE THAT KICK?! YOU'RE IT!!
WHAT? ME AGAIN?!
......
I'M ALWAYS IT!
I'M SICK OF THIS. LET'S DO SOMETHING ELSE!
AH! A FISH! THERE'S A FISH, SEE?!
IT WENT THIS WAY!
I NEVER ...
He said he was bored, but this...?
...NEVER THOUGHT O HAVE TO LAY WITH GOD LIKE THIS...
Wah!
!!
GOT HIM!
Wa ha ha ha ha ha!
YEAH!
LOOK, YOU GUYS!
You punks!
SPLASH SPLASH!
Ah, that's cold!
Ha ha ha ha...
ACHOO!

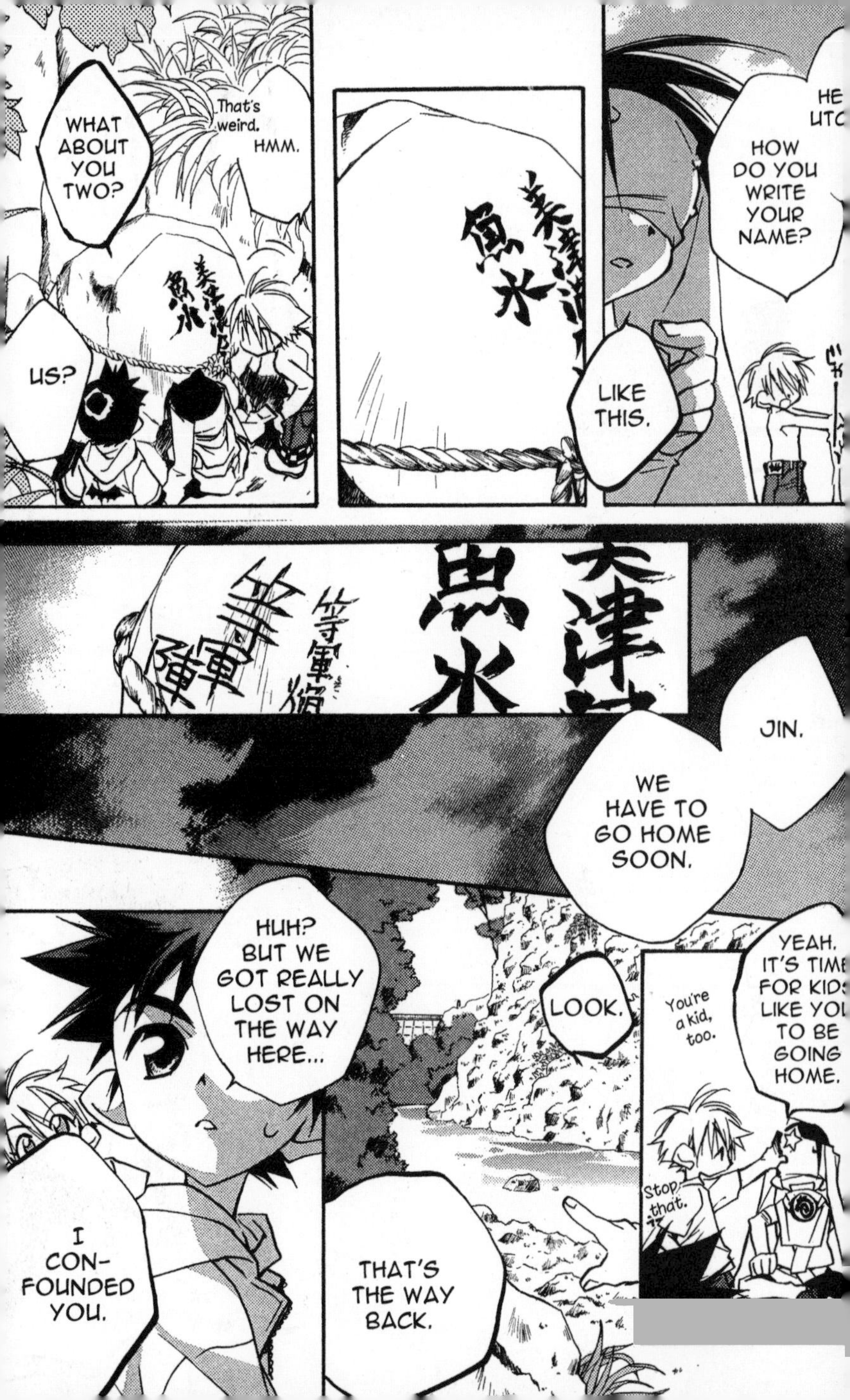

HE UTC
HOW DO YOU WRITE YOUR NAME?
LIKE THIS.
That's weird.
HMM.
WHAT ABOUT YOU TWO?
US?
JIN.
WE HAVE TO GO HOME SOON.
YEAH. IT'S TIME FOR KIDS LIKE YOU TO BE GOING HOME.
You're a kid, too.
Stop that.
LOOK.
HUH? BUT WE GOT REALLY LOST ON THE WAY HERE...
THAT'S THE WAY BACK.
I CON-FOUNDED YOU.

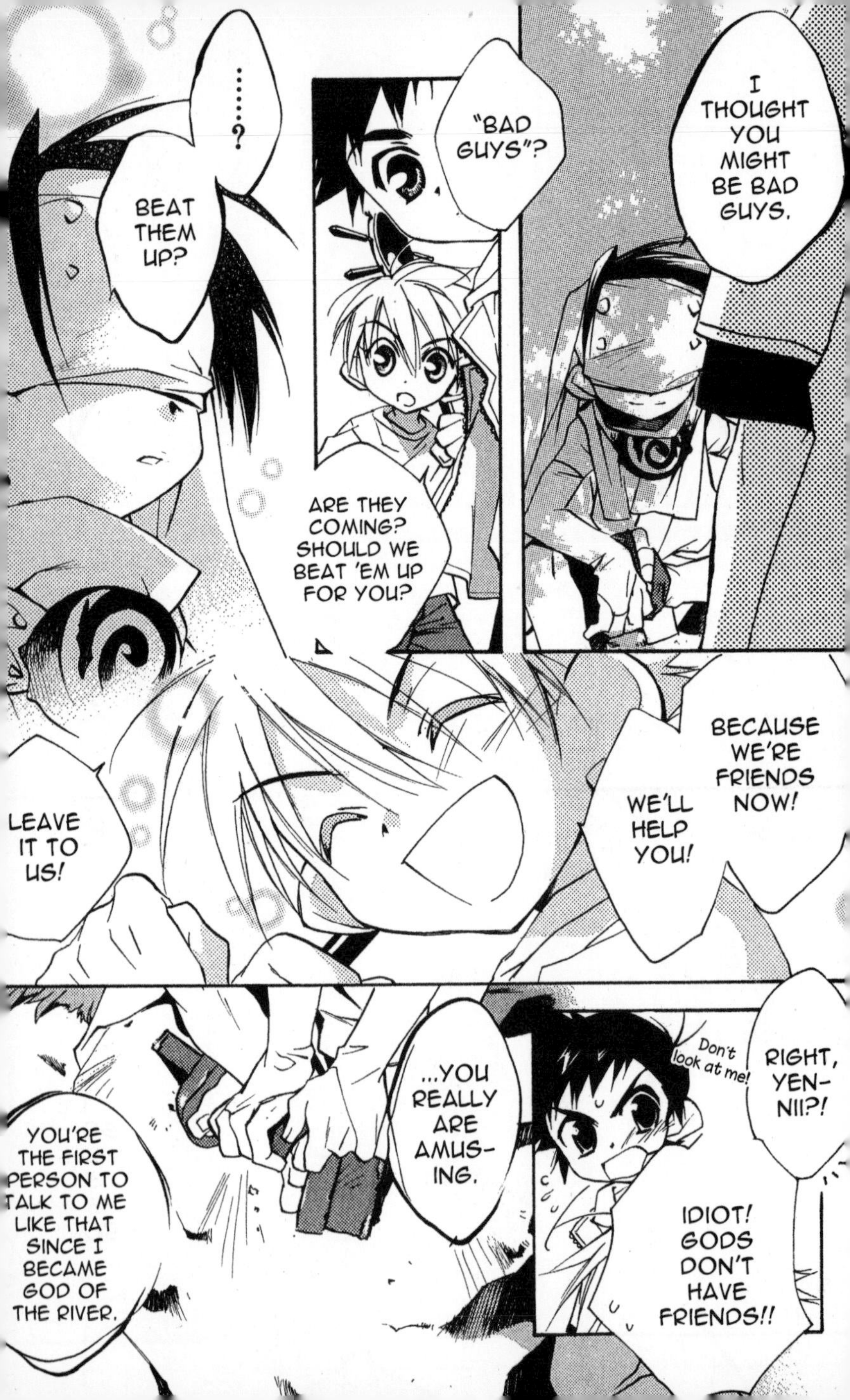
I THOUGHT YOU MIGHT BE BAD GUYS.
"BAD GUYS"?
ARE THEY COMING? SHOULD WE BEAT 'EM UP FOR YOU?
.....?
BEAT THEM UP?
BECAUSE WE'RE FRIENDS NOW!
WE'LL HELP YOU!
LEAVE IT TO US!
RIGHT, YEN-NII?!
Don't look at me!
IDIOT! GODS DON'T HAVE FRIENDS!!
...YOU REALLY ARE AMUS-ING.
YOU'RE THE FIRST PERSON TO TALK TO ME LIKE THAT SINCE I BECAME GOD OF THE RIVER.

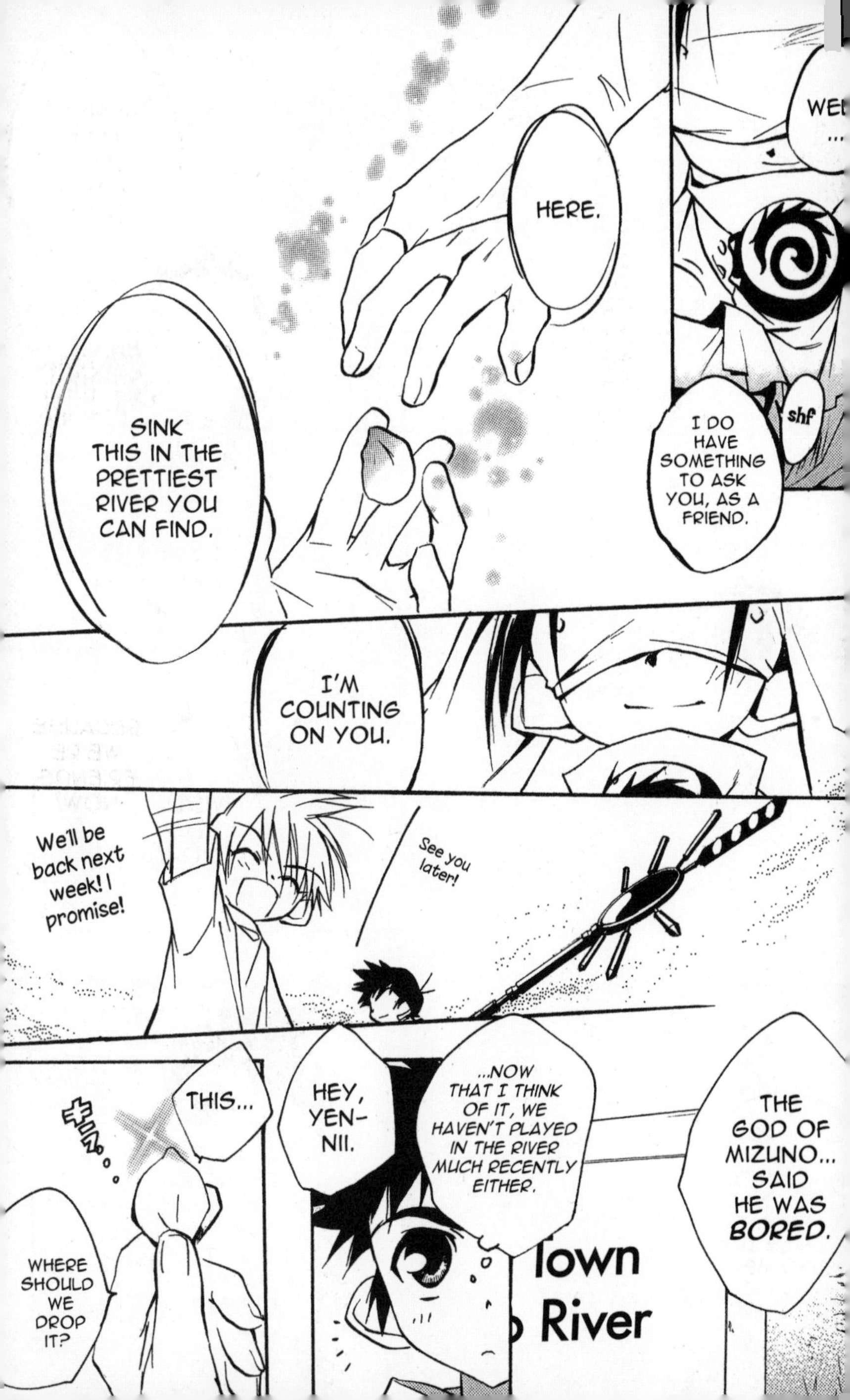
WEL ...
shf
I DO HAVE SOMETHING TO ASK YOU, AS A FRIEND.
HERE.
SINK THIS IN THE PRETTIEST RIVER YOU CAN FIND.
I'M COUNTING ON YOU.
See you later!
We'll be back next week! I promise!
THE GOD OF MIZUNO... SAID HE WAS BORED.
...NOW THAT I THINK OF IT, WE HAVEN'T PLAYED IN THE RIVER MUCH RECENTLY EITHER.
HEY, YEN-NII.
Town
River
THIS...
WHERE SHOULD WE DROP IT?

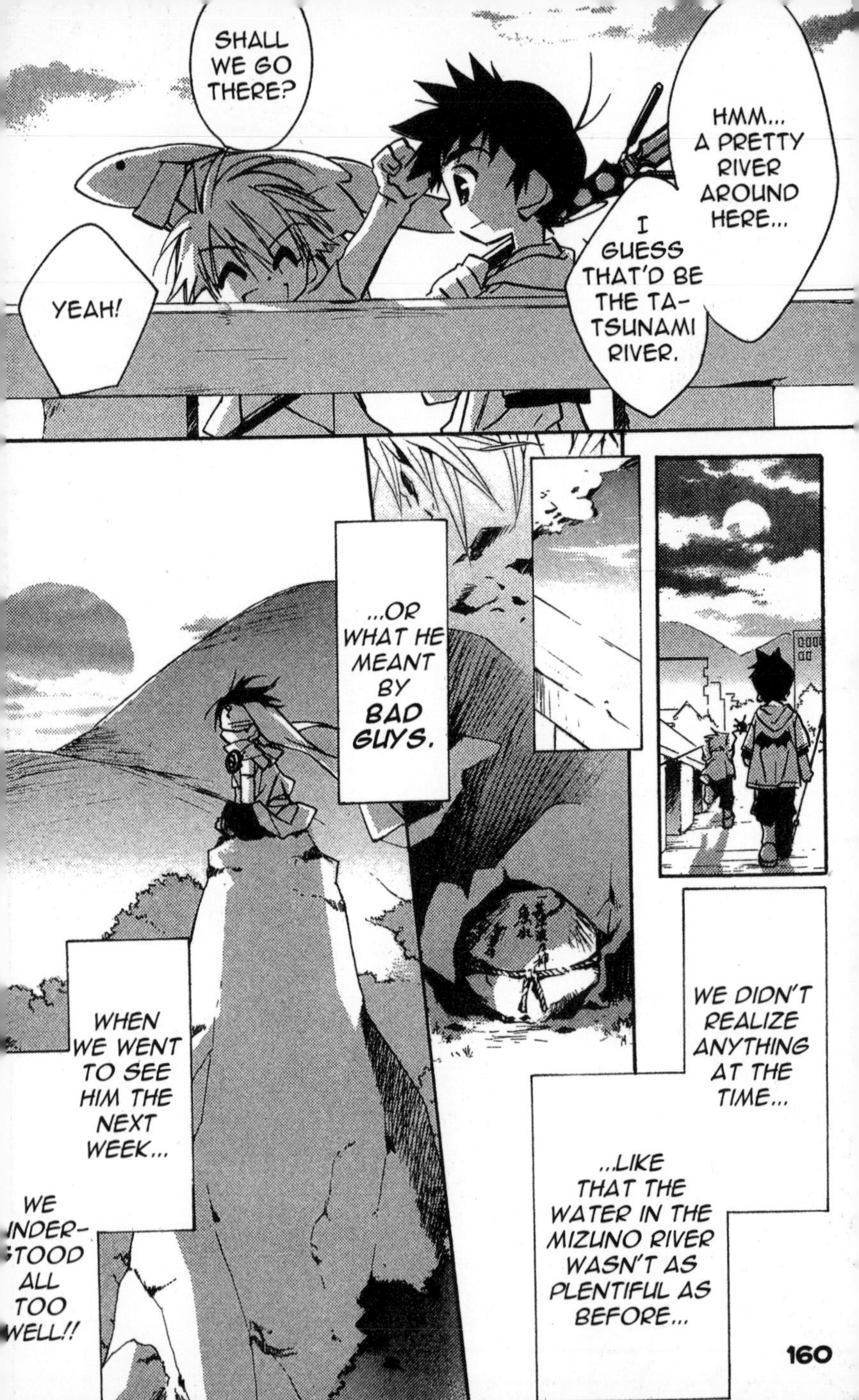
HMM... A PRETTY RIVER AROUND HERE...
I GUESS THAT'D BE THE TA-TSUNAMI RIVER.
SHALL WE GO THERE?
YEAH!
WE DIDN'T REALIZE ANYTHING AT THE TIME...
...LIKE THAT THE WATER IN THE MIZUNO RIVER WASN'T AS PLENTIFUL AS BEFORE...
...OR WHAT HE MEANT BY BAD GUYS.
WHEN WE WENT TO SEE HIM THE NEXT WEEK...
WE UNDER-STOOD ALL TOO WELL!!

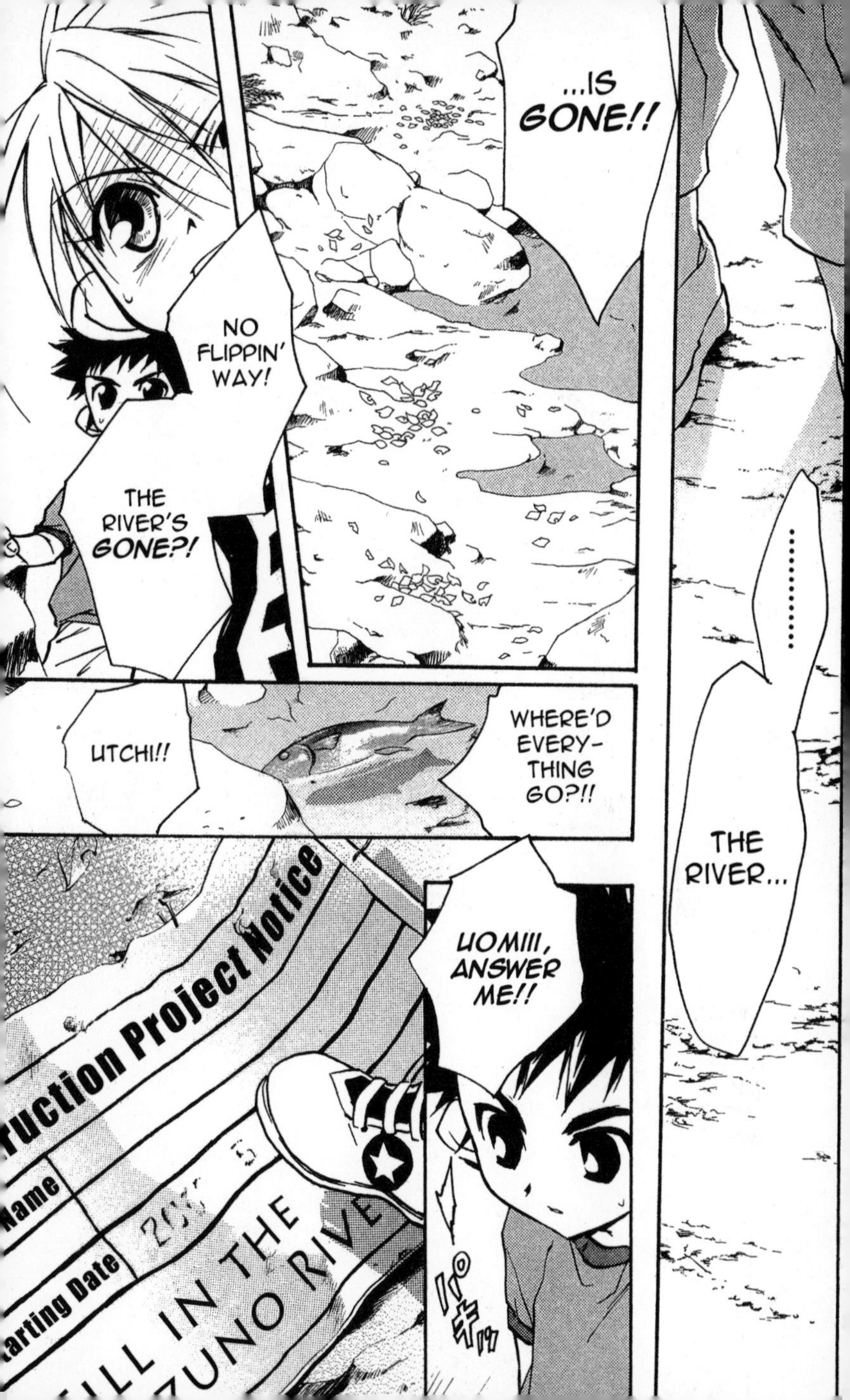

....
THE RIVER...
...IS GONE!!
NO FLIPPIN' WAY!
THE RIVER'S GONE?!
WHERE'D EVERY-THING GO?!!
UTCHI!!
UOMIII, ANSWER ME!!
パキッ
ruction Project Notice
Name
tarting Date
ILL IN THE
ZUNO RIVE

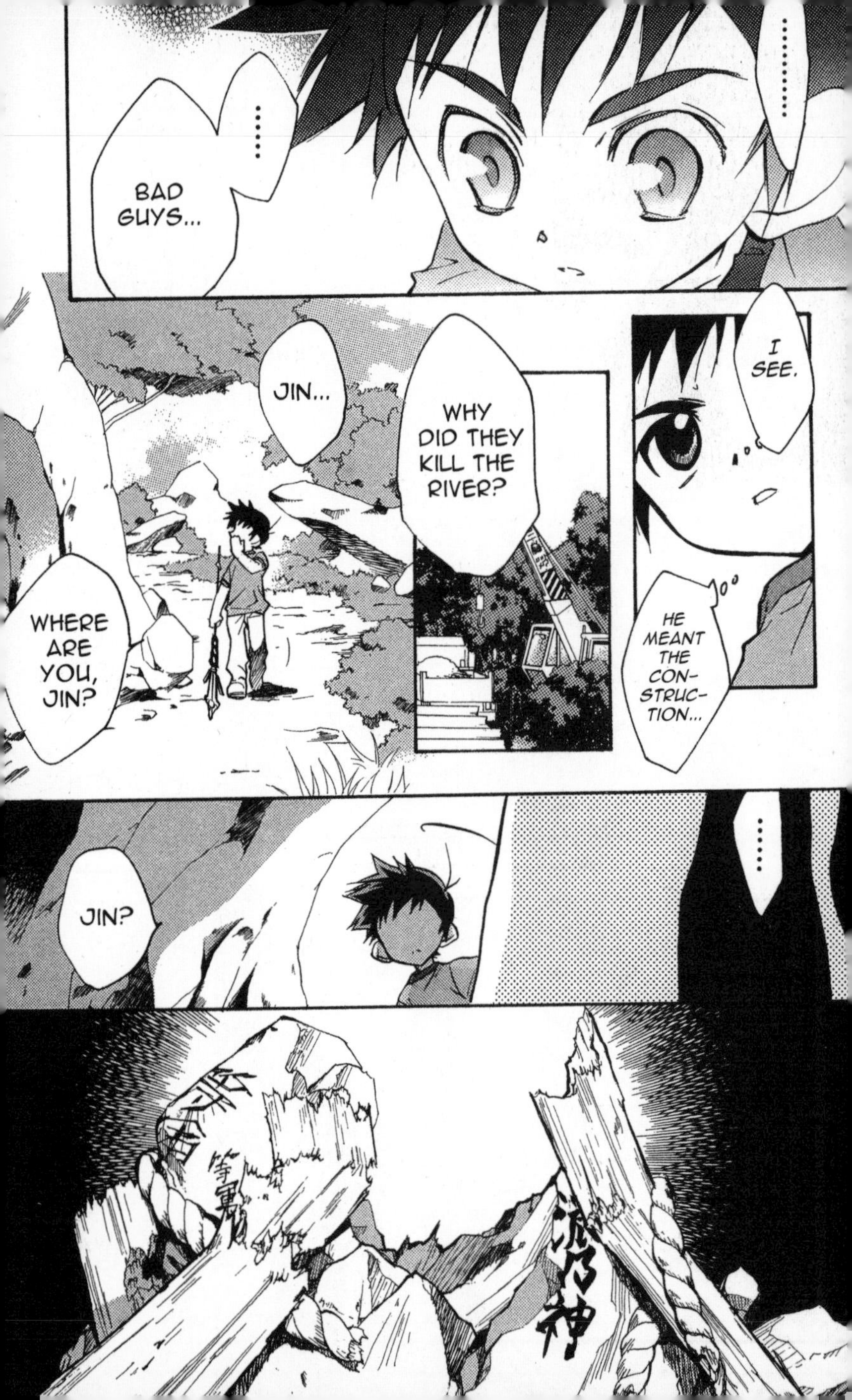
......
...... BAD GUYS...
I SEE.
HE MEANT THE CON-STRUC-TION...
WHY DID THEY KILL THE RIVER?
JIN...
WHERE ARE YOU, JIN?
......
JIN?

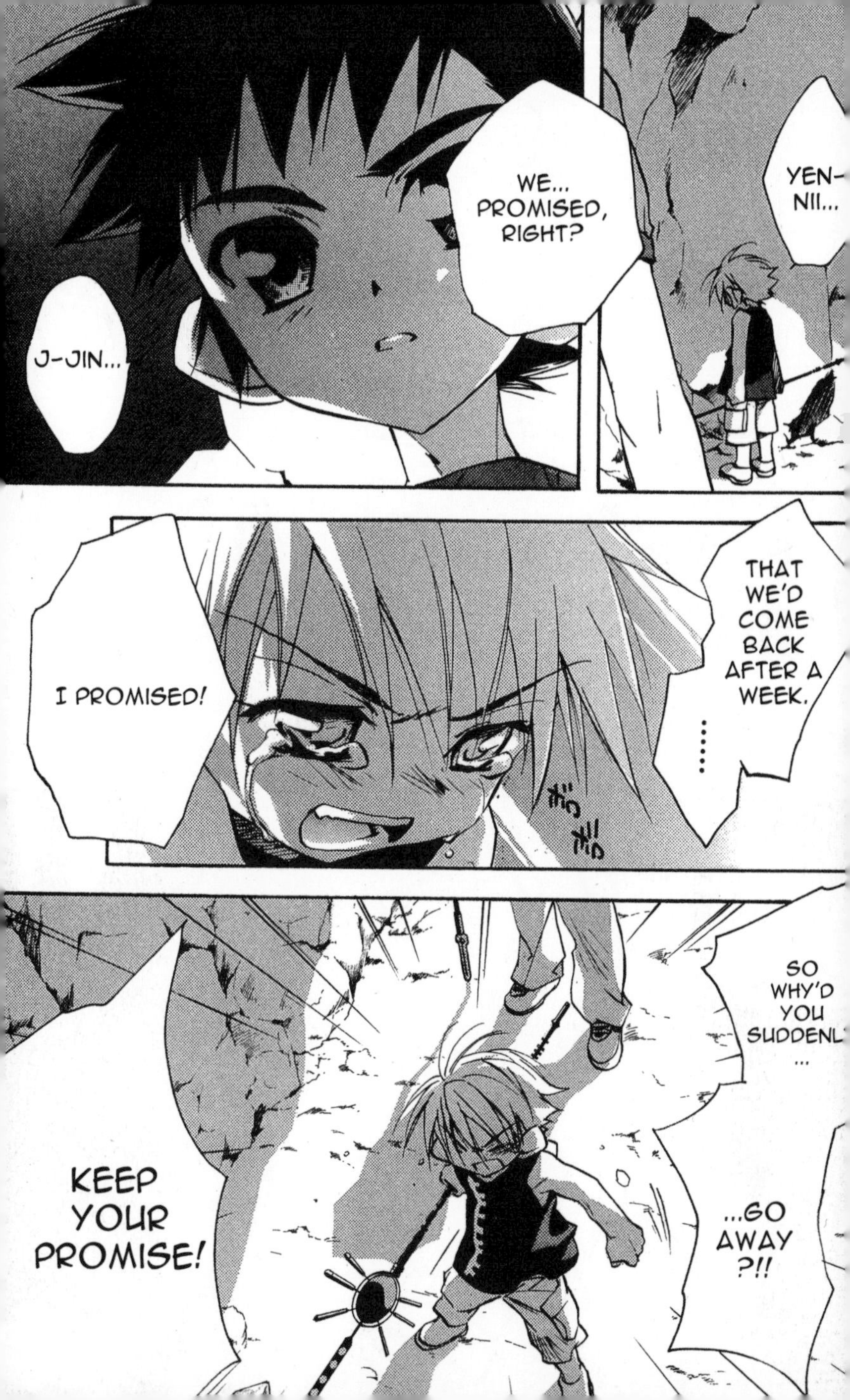
YEN-NII...
WE... PROMISED, RIGHT?
J-JIN...
THAT WE'D COME BACK AFTER A WEEK.
......
I PROMISED!
SO WHY'D YOU SUDDENL ...
...GO AWAY ?!!
KEEP YOUR PROMISE!

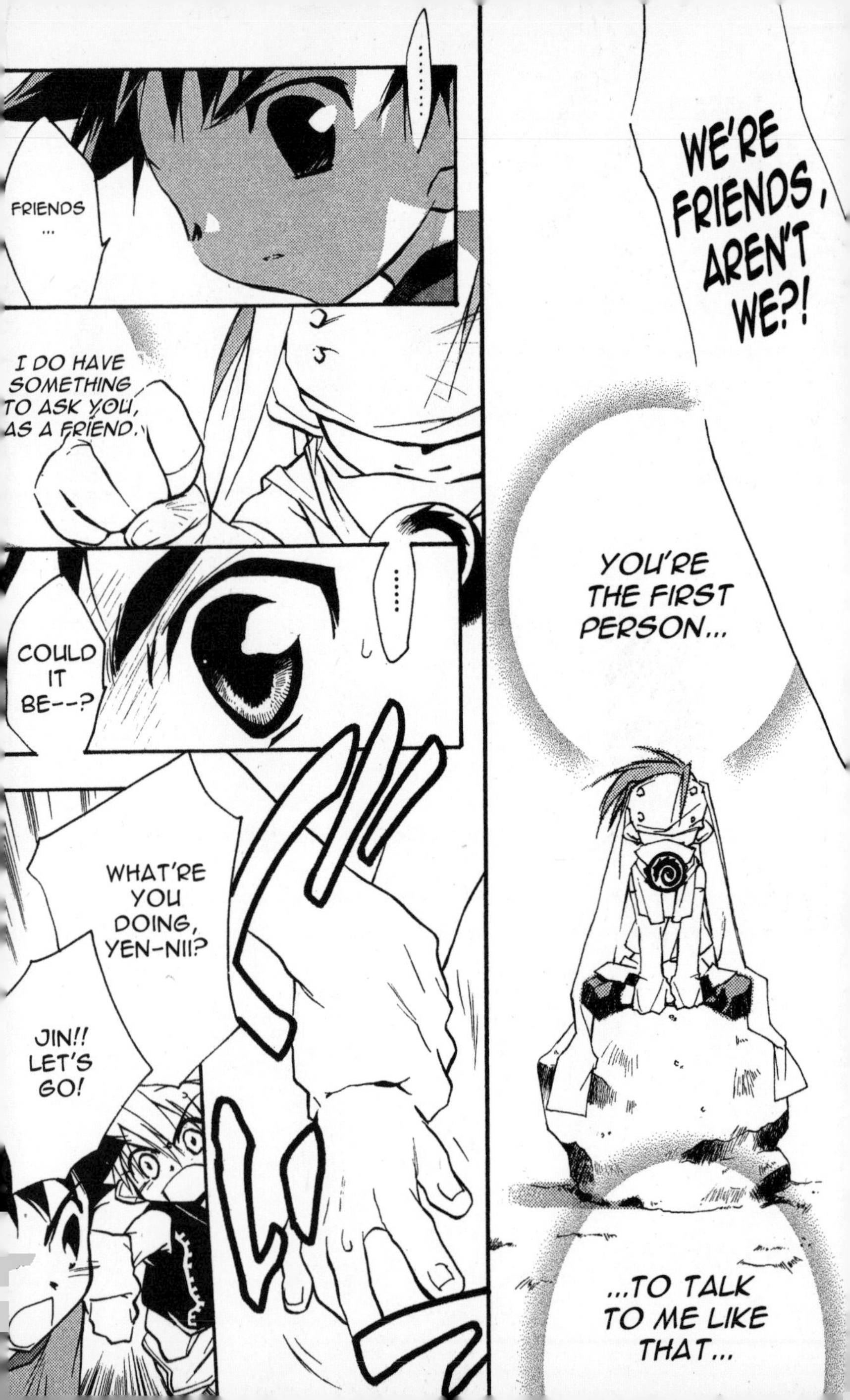
WE'RE FRIENDS, AREN'T WE?!
YOU'RE THE FIRST PERSON...
...TO TALK TO ME LIKE THAT...
......
FRIENDS ...
I DO HAVE SOMETHING TO ASK YOU, AS A FRIEND.
......
COULD IT BE--?
WHAT'RE YOU DOING, YEN-NII?
JIN!! LET'S GO!

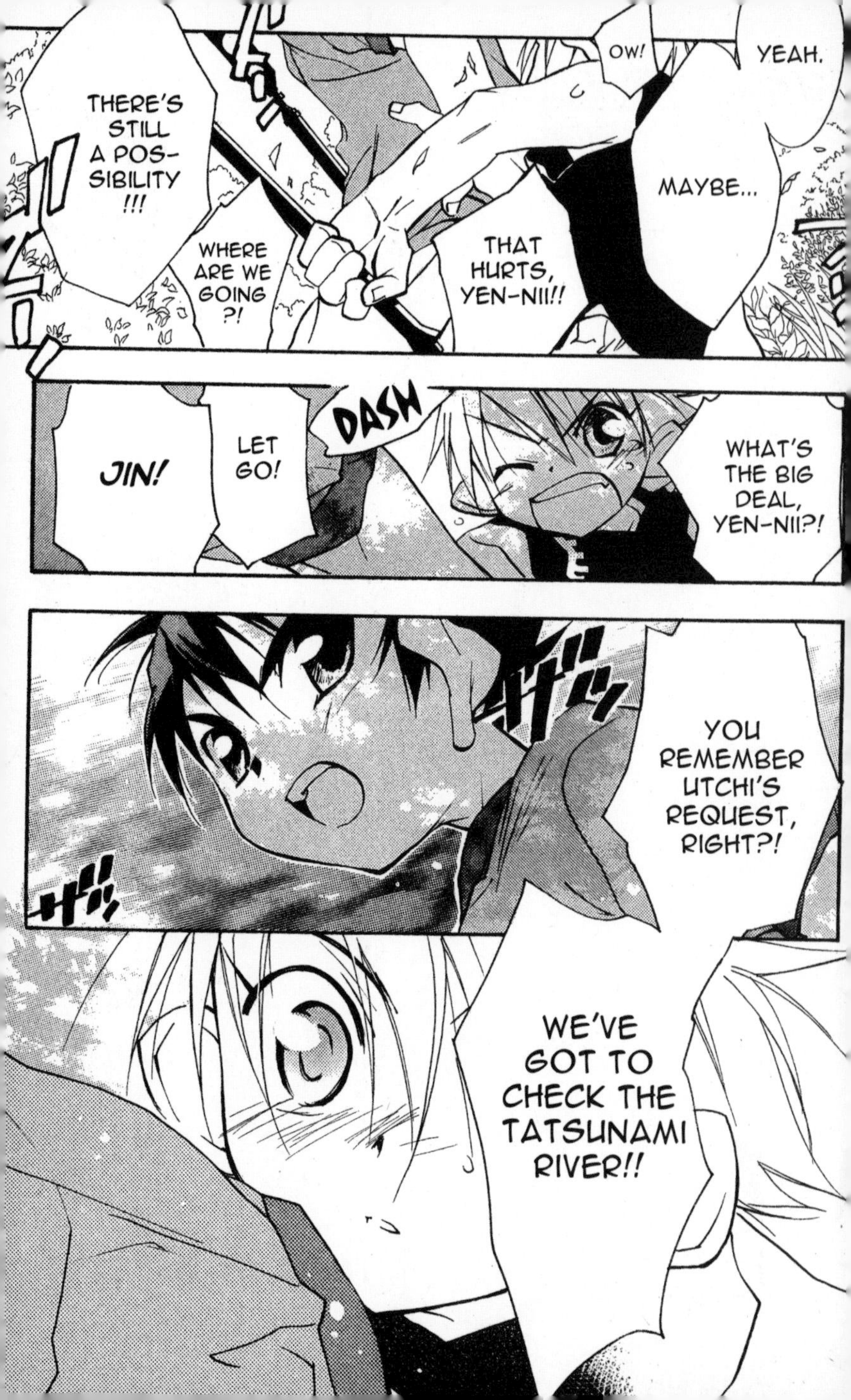
YEAH.
MAYBE...
OW!
THAT HURTS, YEN-NII!!
THERE'S STILL A POS-SIBILITY!!!
WHERE ARE WE GOING?!
WHAT'S THE BIG DEAL, YEN-NII?!
DASH
LET GO!
JIN!
YOU REMEMBER UTCHI'S REQUEST, RIGHT?!
WE'VE GOT TO CHECK THE TATSUNAMI RIVER!!

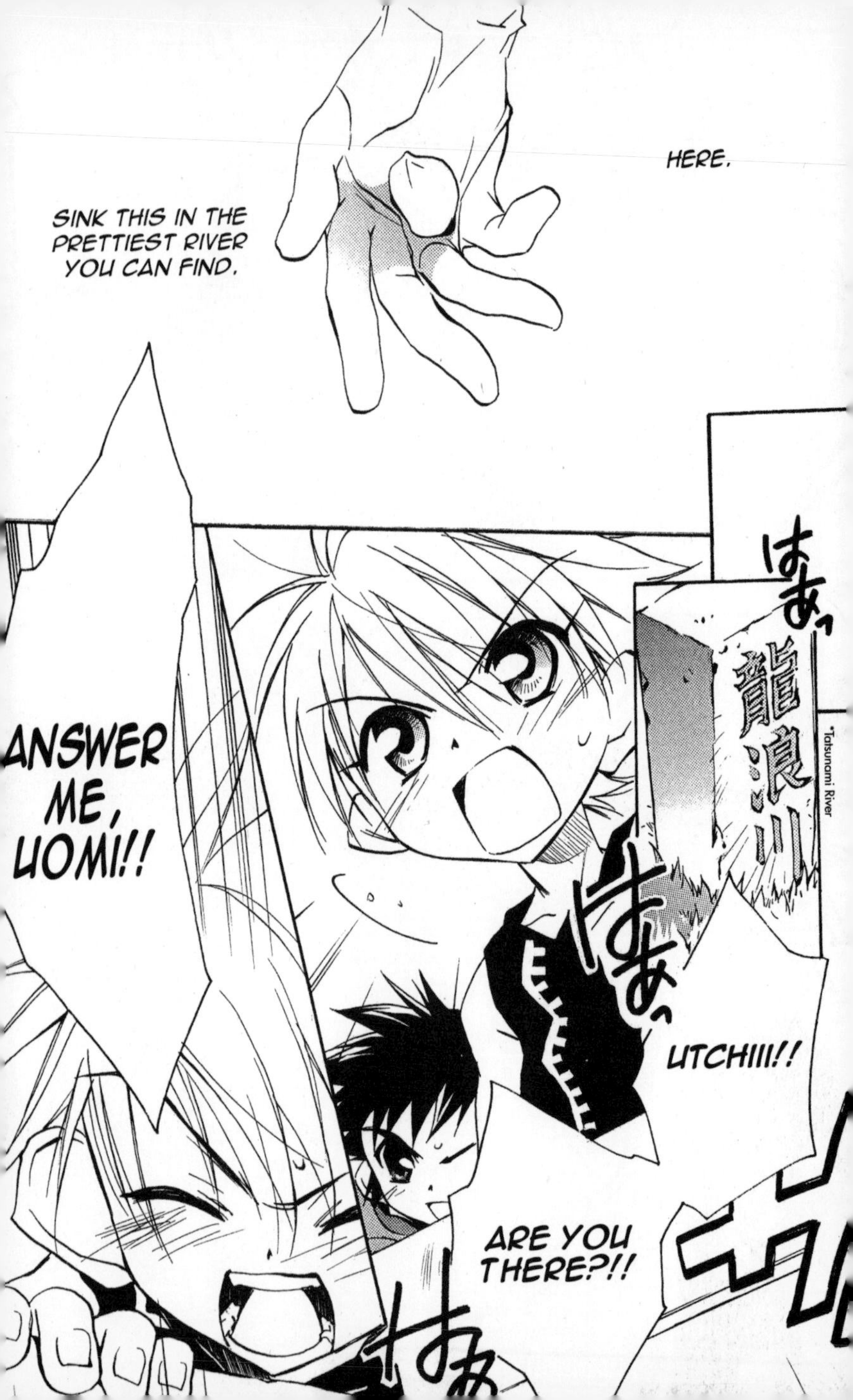
HERE.
SINK THIS IN THE PRETTIEST RIVER YOU CAN FIND.
はあっ
龍浪川
*Tatsunami River
はあっ
UTCHIII!!
ARE YOU THERE?!!
ANSWER ME, UOMI!!
はあ

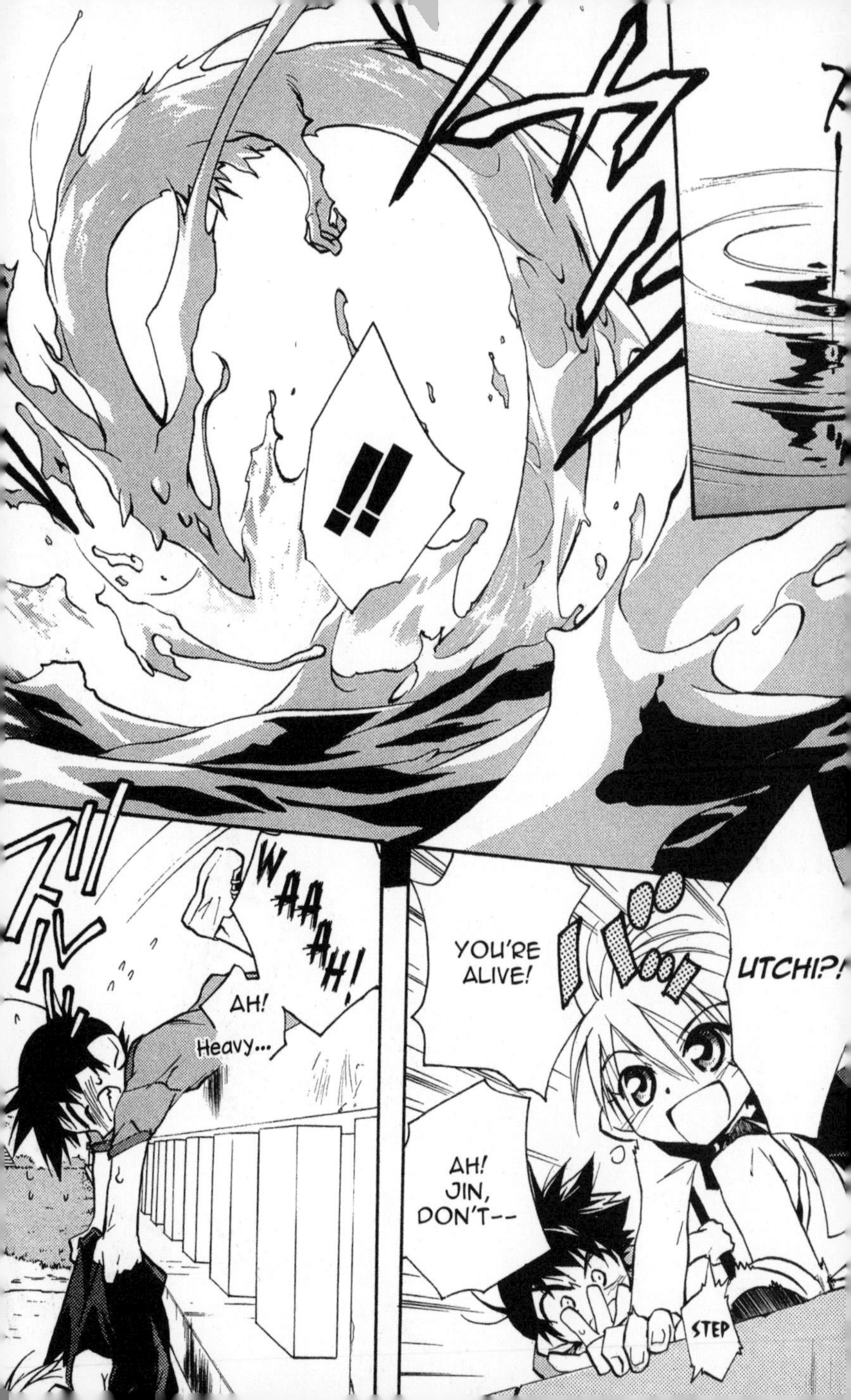

!!
UTCHI?!
YOU'RE ALIVE!
AH! JIN, DON'T--
STEP
WAAAAAH!
AH!
Heavy...

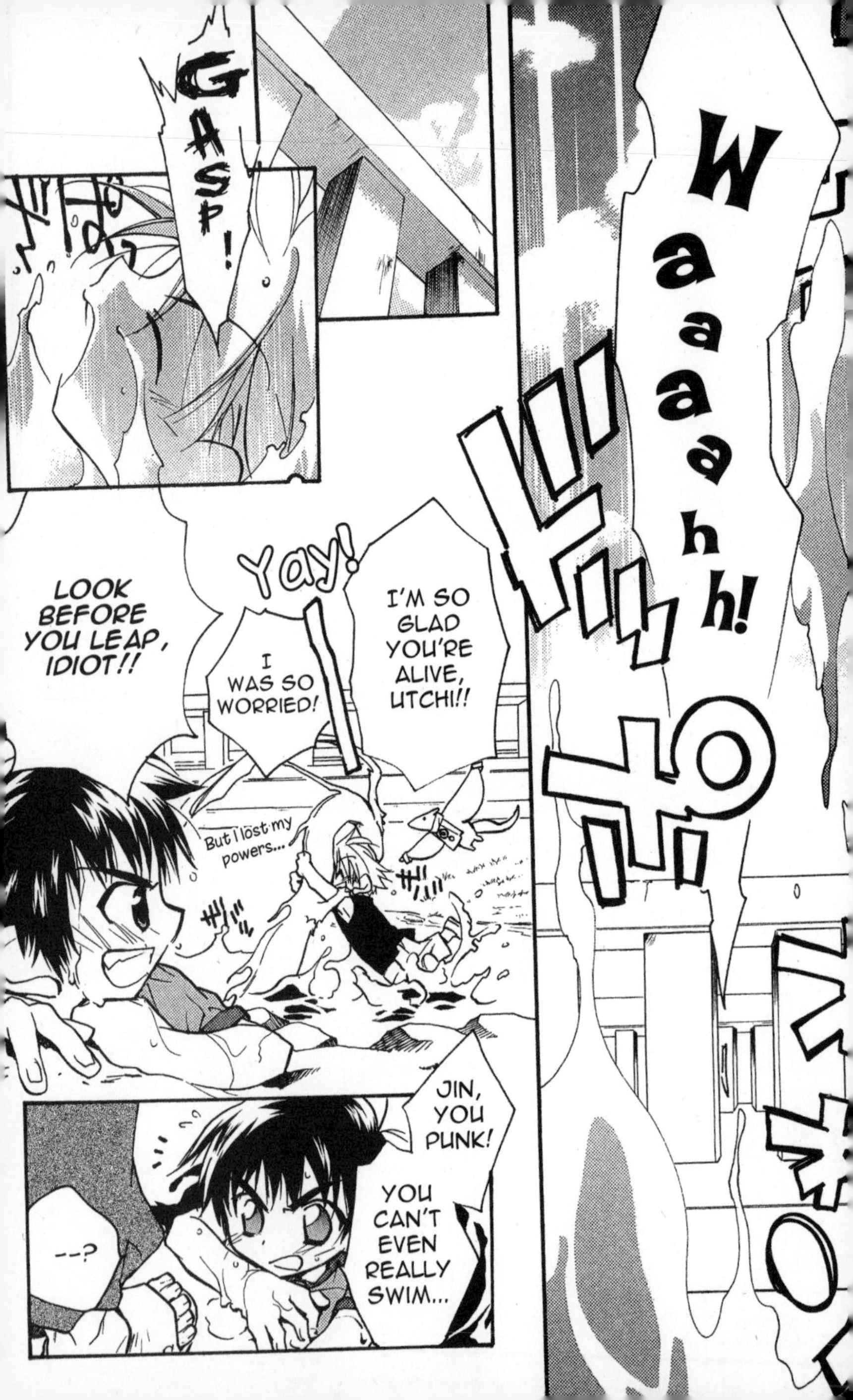
Waaaaahh!
GASP!
I'M SO GLAD YOU'RE ALIVE, UTCHI!!
Yay!
I WAS SO WORRIED!
LOOK BEFORE YOU LEAP, IDIOT!!
But I lost my powers...
JIN, YOU PUNK!
YOU CAN'T EVEN REALLY SWIM...
--?

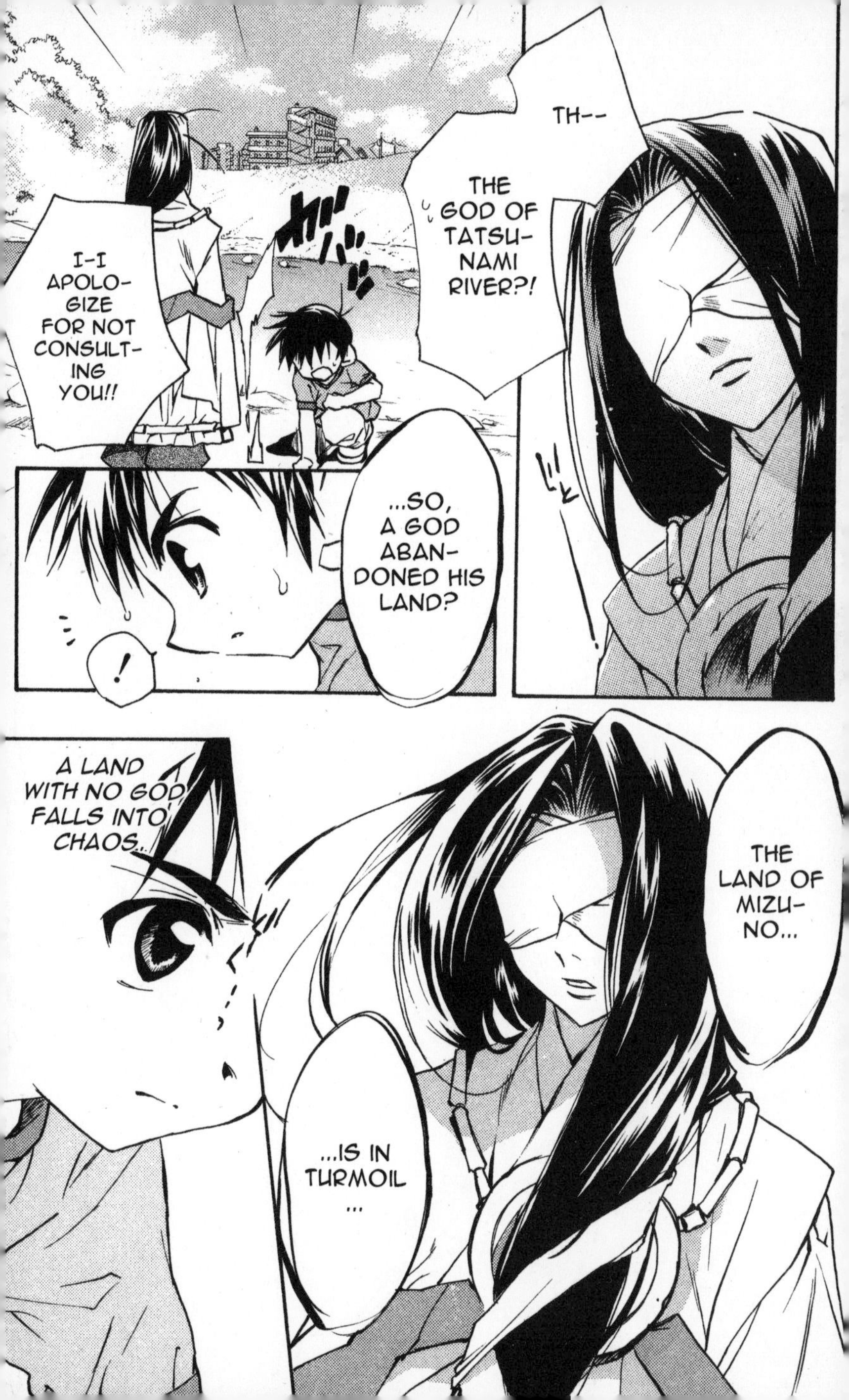
TH--
THE GOD OF TATSU-NAMI RIVER?!
I-I APOLO-GIZE FOR NOT CONSULT-ING YOU!!
...SO, A GOD ABAN-DONED HIS LAND?
!
THE LAND OF MIZU-NO...
...IS IN TURMOIL ...
A LAND WITH NO GOD FALLS INTO CHAOS..

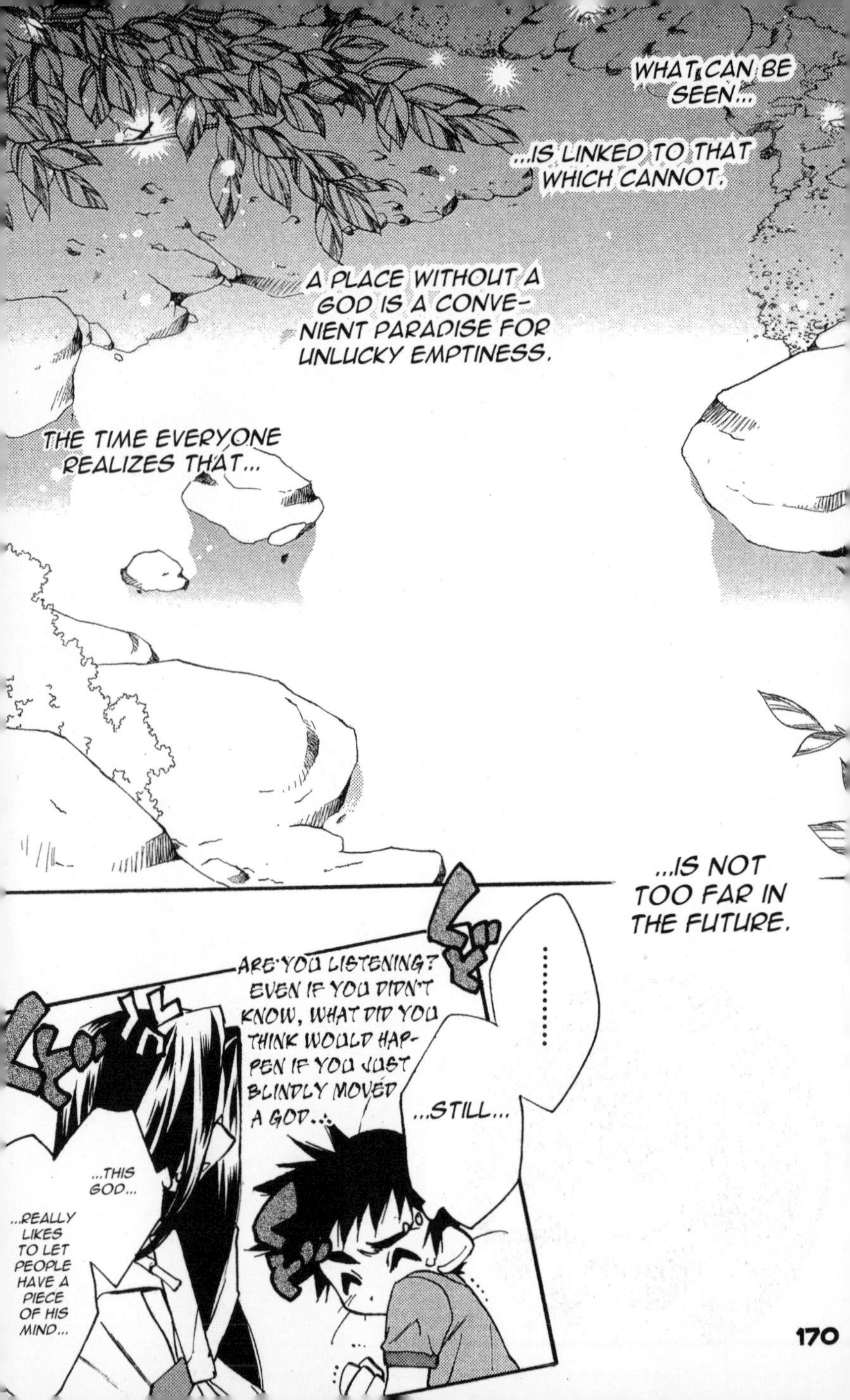
WHAT CAN BE SEEN...
...IS LINKED TO THAT WHICH CANNOT.
A PLACE WITHOUT A GOD IS A CONVENIENT PARADISE FOR UNLUCKY EMPTINESS.
THE TIME EVERYONE REALIZES THAT...
...IS NOT TOO FAR IN THE FUTURE.
......
...STILL...
ARE YOU LISTENING? EVEN IF YOU DIDN'T KNOW, WHAT DID YOU THINK WOULD HAPPEN IF YOU JUST BLINDLY MOVED A GOD...
...THIS GOD...
...REALLY LIKES TO LET PEOPLE HAVE A PIECE OF HIS MIND...

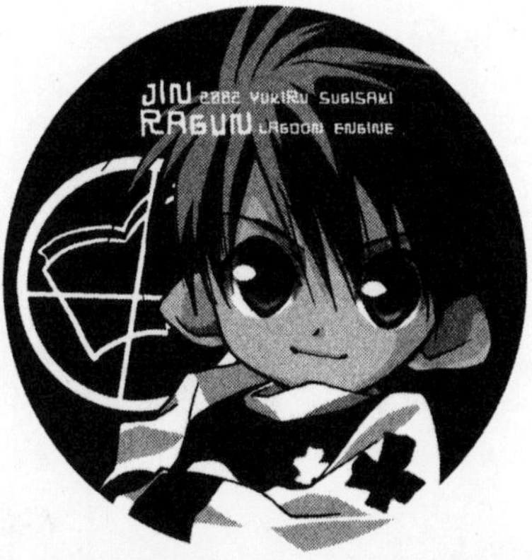
JIN 2002 YUKIRU SUGISAKI
RAGUN LAGOON ENGINE

LAGOON ENGINE

GLOSSARY OF TERMS

In this corner, we will explain the Gakushi terms used by Yen and the others. If you can just remember these, maybe you can fight with them?!

GAKUSHI 楽師 がくし

People who specialize in exorcising and subduing evil spirits and ghosts, referred to as *Maga*. The Ragun family has been Gakushi for generations, and currently Yen and Jin's father is the head of the family.

MAGA 凶 まが

Spirits, ghosts, etc. that do evil in the world are collectively known as Maga. Gakushi are all born with a Maga as their ally, and by negotiating with other Maga and making them into allies, they can gain strength as Gakushi.

OMI 臣 おみ

Maga call humans *Omi*. Also, Gakushi have names other than the ones their parents gave them—names they've had since birth, known as Omi names. Those names are for personal knowledge only, and they are to tell them to no one.

Yeah!
Let's go, Jin!

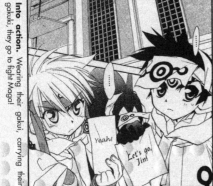

Into action. Wearing their gakui, carrying their gakuki, they go to fight Maga!

GAKUI 楽衣 がくい

Work clothes worn when confronting Maga. They have the family crest on them.

GAKUKI 楽祈 がくき

Tools that amplify power, used when confronting Maga. Passed down as family heirlooms in Gakushi families. When other people touch them, they receive a dangerous shock.

BARRIER (KEKKAI)

結界 けっかい

When confronting Maga, a barrier is first set up. The person who set up the barrier decides on a *stipulation* that is effective only inside the barrier. A stipulation can be anything that would be advantageous in battle, from a large amplification of attack power to preventing death, but it can only be made according to the abilities of the one who set up the barrier.

O GOD TAT-SUNA-MI...
MAGA LAN-GUAGE
FOR WHAT REASON HAVE YOU INTERVENED IN OUR NEGOTIATION?
—BILINGUAL YEN & KOGA—
DON'T TALK IN WORDS I CAN'T UNDERSTAND!!
TRANS-LATION
"IF IT PLEASES YOU, FAVOR ME AND SPEAK IN A MANNER SUCH THAT I WHO AM FOOLISH, THOUGHTLESS, AND POWER-LESS MAY COMPREHEND."
GOT IT?! SAY IT SO I CAN UNDER-STAND!!
TRANS-LATION
"I HUMBLY PETITION YOUR GRACIOUS EXPLANA-TION."
He says.

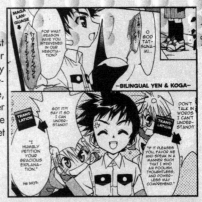

Interpreting. Yen's Maga, Koga, can also interpret. After Yen changes Jin's vulgar language into polite Japanese (laugh).

BARRIER (CONT'D)

When a strong Gakushi sets up a barrier around a human that person is already in a state of *yuusei* in the presence o a Maga. But there are types of barriers that will disappear i that person speaks.

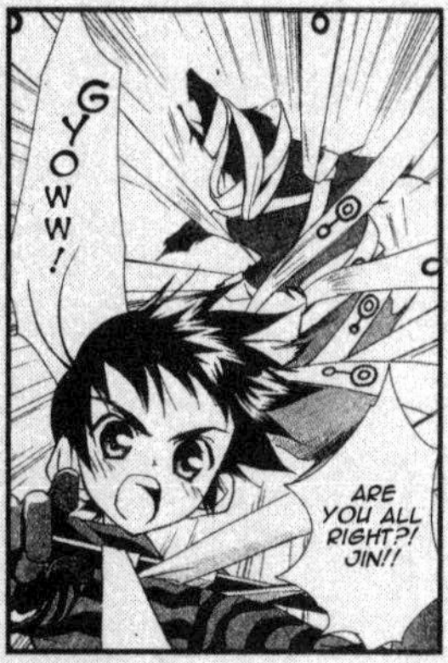

GYOWW!
ARE YOU ALL RIGHT?! JIN!!

Barrier. It's Yen's job to set up the barrier. Bandage-like things with the family crest on them cover the Maga.

YUUSEI 優勢 ゆうせい
RESSEI 劣勢 れっせい

If a Gakushi is able to analyze a Maga and correctly guess its name, they attain *yuusei*. Yuusei is a state of having superiority in battle, and attacks on the opponent are one hundred percent effective. On the other hand, if the Gakushi's name is guessed, they drop to *ressei* and take damage.

MISEI 未勢 みせい

The initial battle conditions before yuusei or ressei is reached.

KAMIDORI 紙鳥 かみどり

Paper cut into the shape of a bird, used by Gakushi for communication. They write a message on it, and it will fly to the other party like a carrier pigeon. It will reach anywhere in the world, and is more reliable than a cell phone.

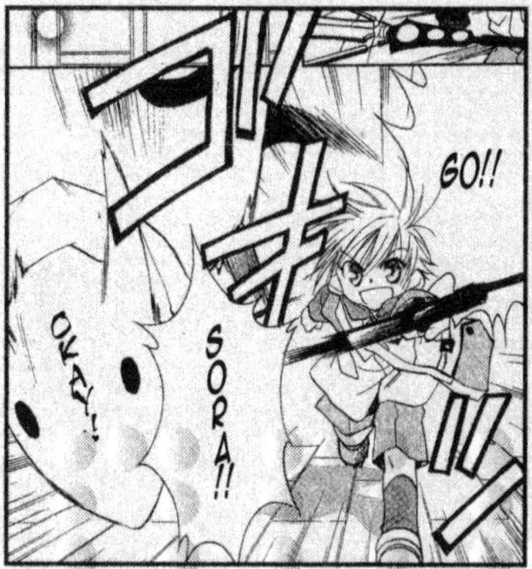

GO!!
SORA!!
OKAY!!

Attack. It's Jin's job to attack. He directs Sora, whose attack power is outstanding.

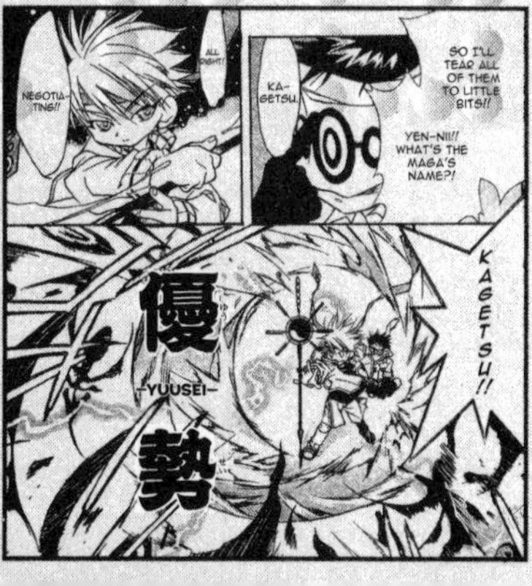

SO I'LL TEAR ALL OF THEM TO LITTLE BITS!!
KA-GETSU.
YEN-NII!! WHAT'S THE MAGA'S NAME?!
ALL RIGHT!
NEGOTIATING!!
KAGETSU!!
優勢
-YUUSEI-

Negotiation. Once they've guessed the Maga's name and attain yuusei, they start a negotiation to see if the Maga will join them or fight.

NAGI NO ENGI
凪の炎儀 なぎのえんぎ

Defeated Maga are sealed into books called *zousho.* The ceremony where zousho are burned is called the *Nagi no Engi*.

KAMEN KUGUTSUSHI
仮面傀儡師 かめんくぐつし

The opposite of Gakushi—who exorcise and subdue Maga—Kamen Kugutsushi are "anti-Gakushi" who stir Maga to anger. Another job of Gakushi is to stop Kamen Kugutsushi.

YUKIRU SUGISAKI

SPECIAL THANKS

MAMORU SUGISAKI

A.NAKAMURA   S.SHIMOZATO
Y.HONZAWA   J.OKU
R.IZUMI   M.NAKAMURA
Y.HISHINUMA   A.KASUGA

T.SHINODA(MEDIAWAVE)   K.MIZUNO(MEDIAWAVE)
MY FAMILY&RABBIT&READERS

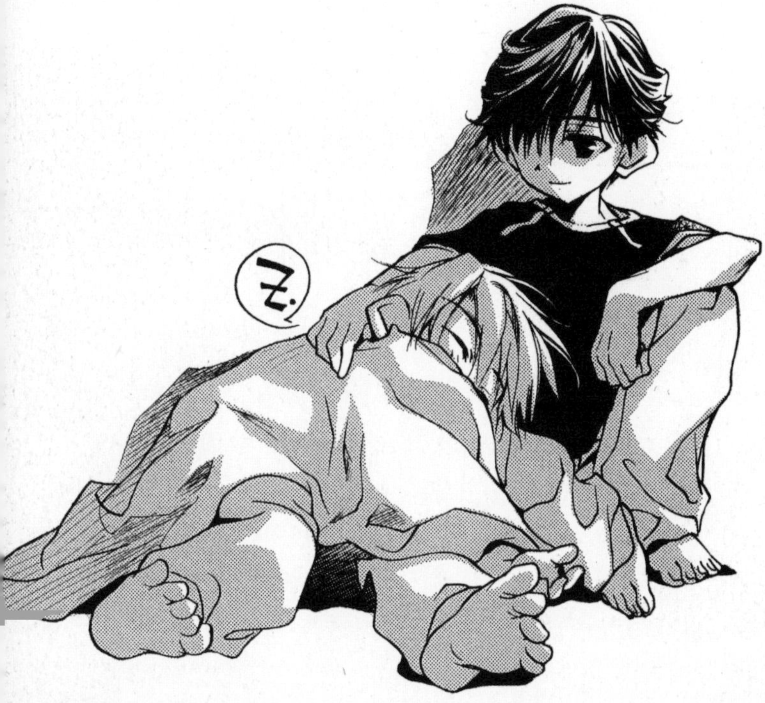
Z

IN THE NEXT VOLUME OF

LAGOON ENGINE

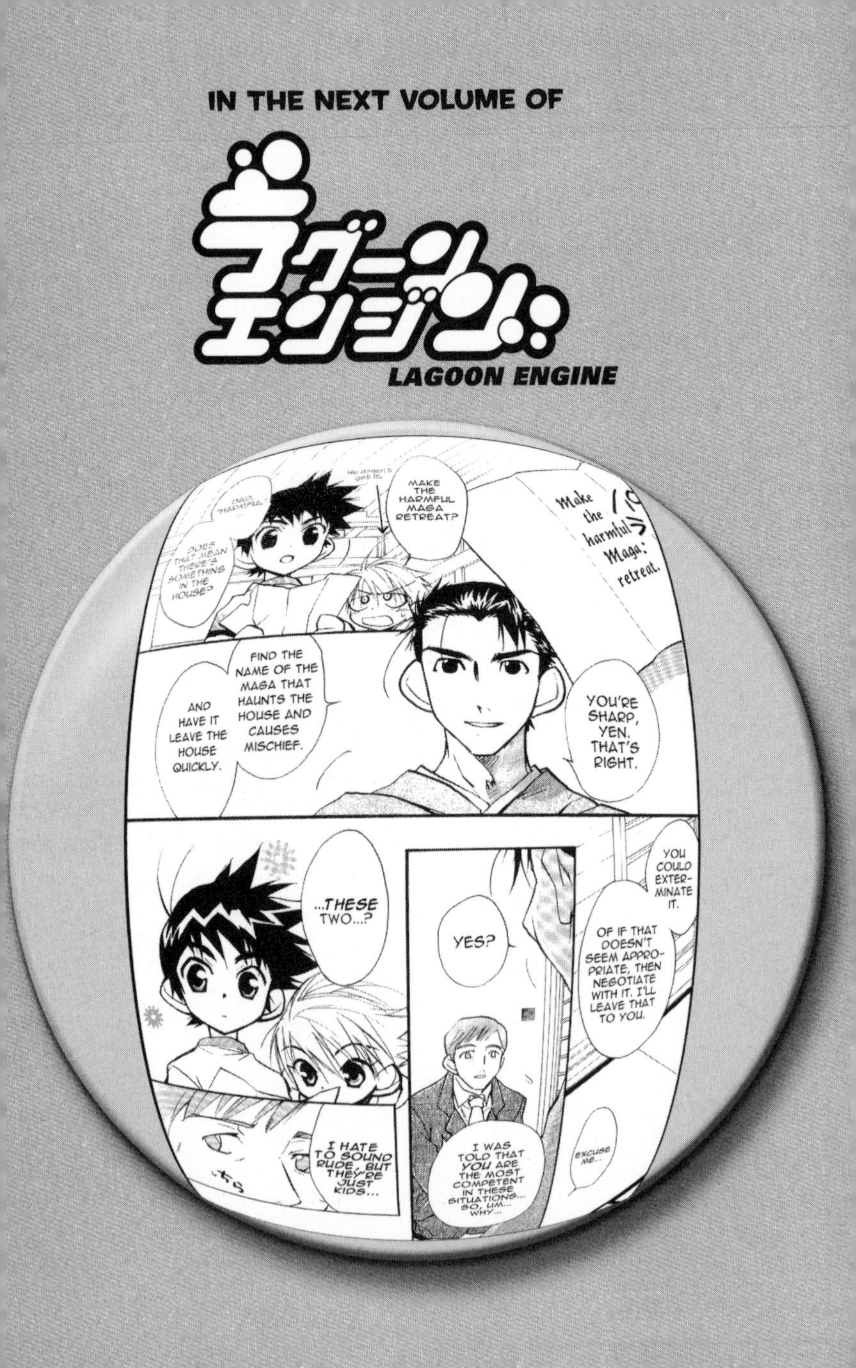
Make the harmful Maga: retreat.
MAKE THE HARMFUL MAGA RETREAT?
He doesn't get it.
DAD, "HARMFUL"...
DOES THAT MEAN THERE'S SOMETHING IN THE HOUSE?
YOU'RE SHARP, YEN. THAT'S RIGHT.
FIND THE NAME OF THE MAGA THAT HAUNTS THE HOUSE AND CAUSES MISCHIEF.
AND HAVE IT LEAVE THE HOUSE QUICKLY.
YOU COULD EXTERMINATE IT.
OF IF THAT DOESN'T SEEM APPROPRIATE, THEN NEGOTIATE WITH IT. I'LL LEAVE THAT TO YOU.
YES?
EXCUSE ME...
I WAS TOLD THAT YOU ARE THE MOST COMPETENT IN THESE SITUATIONS... SO, UM... WHY...
...THESE TWO...?
I HATE TO SOUND RUDE, BUT THEY'RE JUST KIDS...

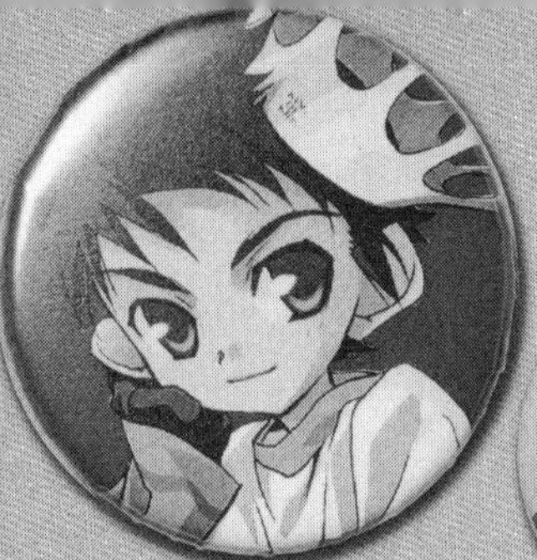
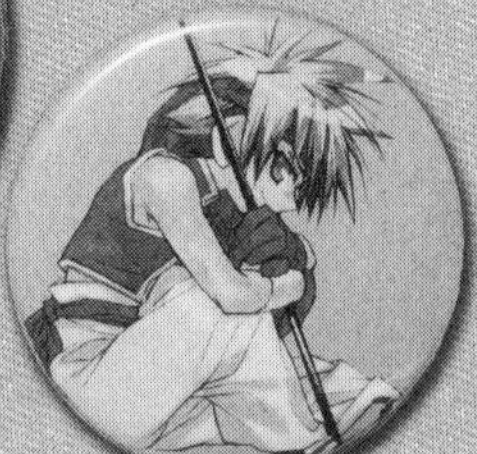
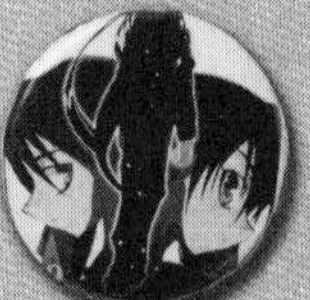
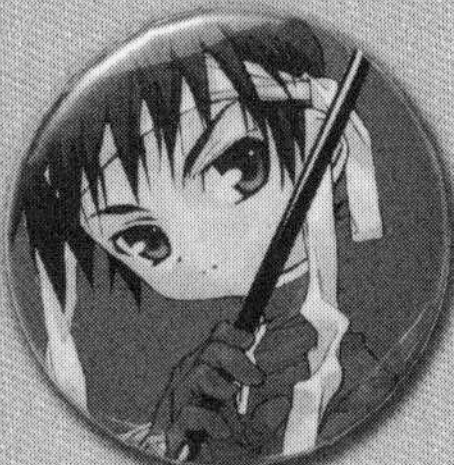

WHO'S GUARDING THE MANOR? THAT'S THE QUESTION YEN AND JIN MUST ANSWER WHEN THEY CONFRONT THE GHOSTLY MAGA THAT'S HAUNTING A CREEPY MANSION! CAN JIN MASTER HIS SPECIAL ATTACK IN TIME TO SLAY THE SPOOKY SPECTER?

VOLUME 3
AVAILABLE SEPTEMBER 2005

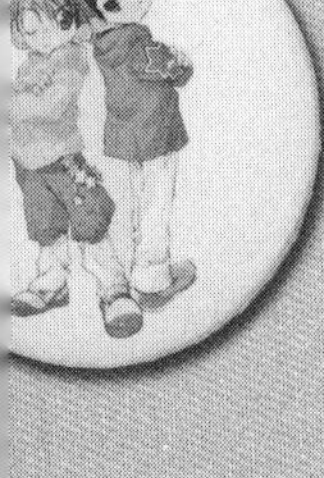
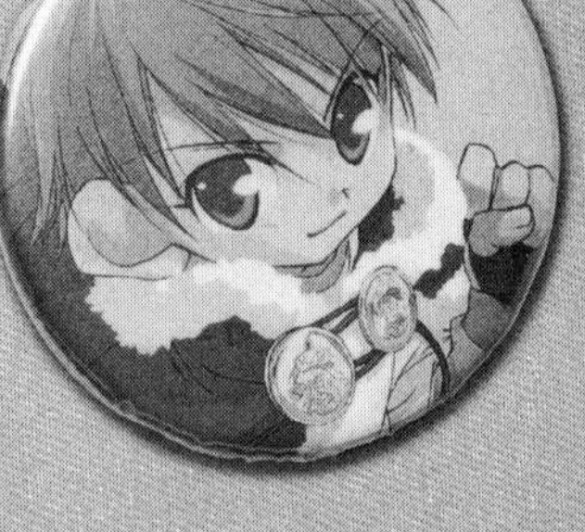

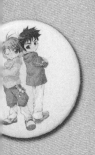

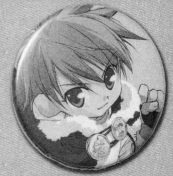

TOKYOPOP SHOP

BLAZIN' BARRELS

Sting may look harmless and naïve, but he's really an excellent fighter and a wannabe bounty hunter in the futuristic Wild West. When he comes across a notice that advertises a reward for the criminal outfit named Gold Romany, he decides that capturing the all-girl gang of bad guys is his ticket to fame and fortune!

MIN-SEO PARK HAS CREATED ONE WILD TUMBLEWEED TALE FILLED WITH ADVENTURE GALORE AND PLENTY OF SHOTGUN ACTION!

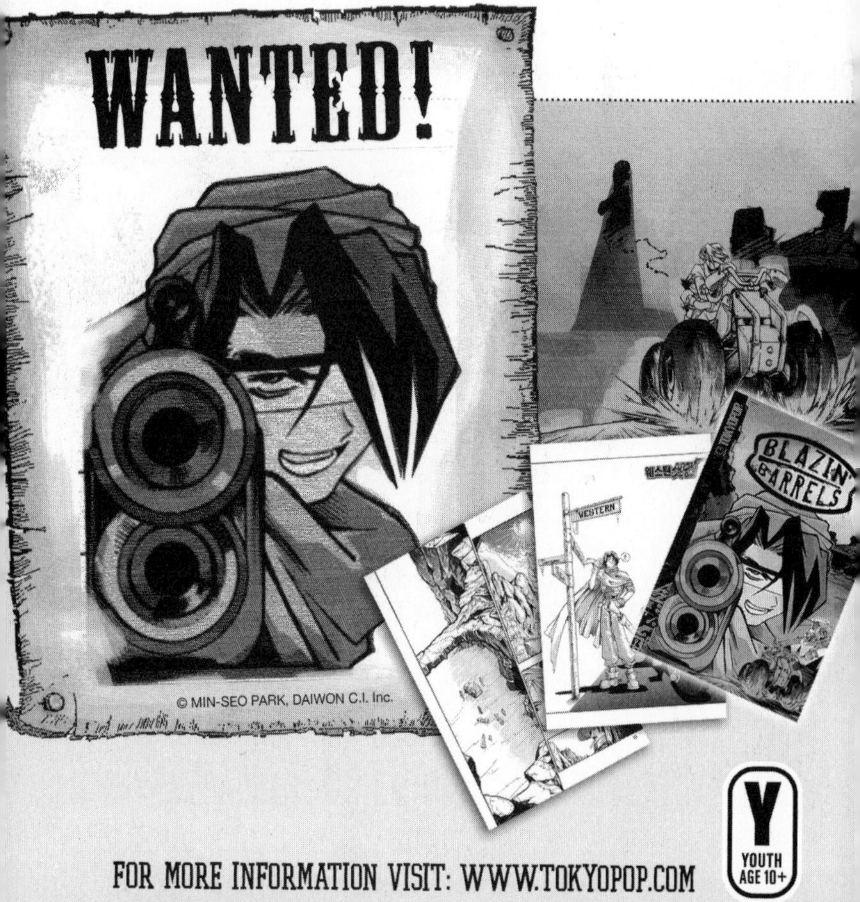
WANTED!
BLAZIN' BARRELS
WESTERN

FOR MORE INFORMATION VISIT: WWW.TOKYOPOP.COM

Y YOUTH AGE 10+

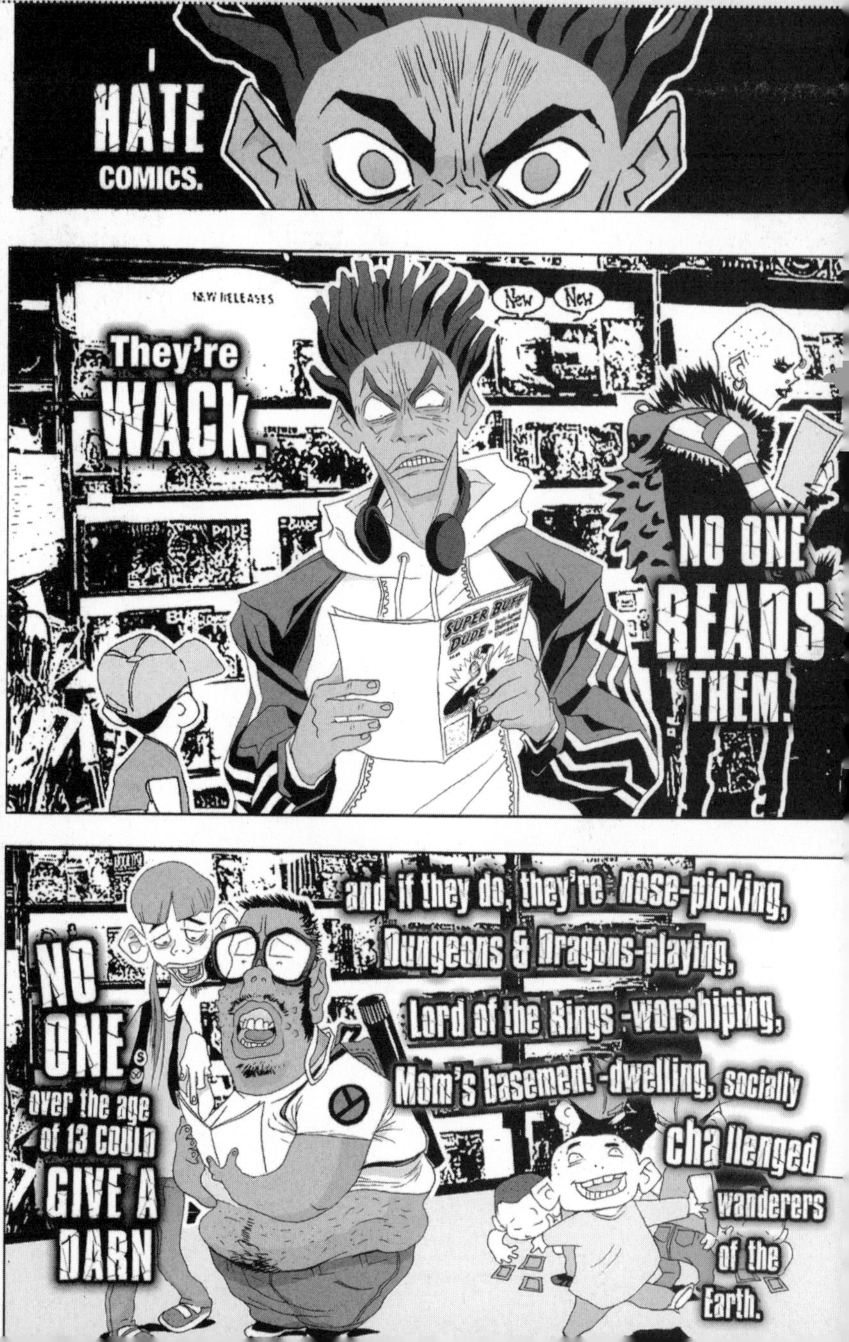
I HATE COMICS.
NEW RELEASES
New
New
They're WACK.
SUPER BUFF DUDE
DOPE
NO ONE READS THEM.
NO ONE over the age of 13 COULD GIVE A DARN
and if they do, they're nose-picking, Dungeons & Dragons-playing, Lord of the Rings -worshiping, Mom's basement -dwelling, socially challenged wanderers of the Earth.

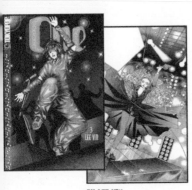

ONE

3
LEE VIN

BY LEE VIN

Like American Idol? Then you'll love *One*, an energetic manga that gives you a sneak peek into the pop music industry. Lee Vin, who also created *Crazy Love Story*, is an amazingly accomplished artist! The story centers on the boy band One, a powerhouse of good looks, hot moves, and raw talent. It also features Jenny You, a Britney-Avril hybrid who's shooting straight for the top. But fame always comes at a price—and their path to stardom is full of speed bumps and roadblocks. But no matter what happens, they keep on rockin'—and so does this manga!

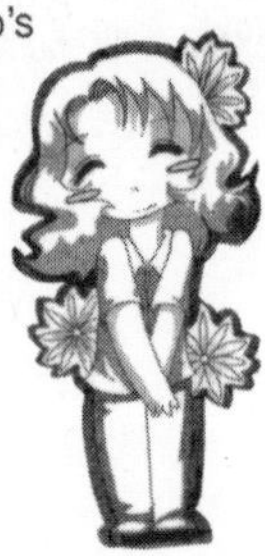

~Julie Taylor, Sr. Editor

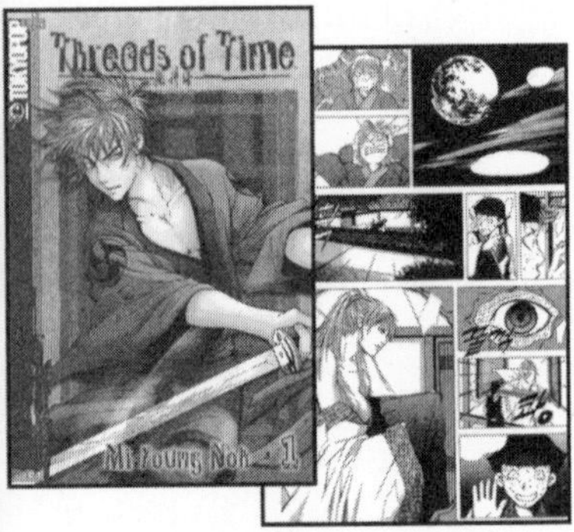

THREADS OF TIME

Threads of Time
Mi-Young Noh 1

BY MI-YOUNG NOH

The best thing about *Threads of Time* is its richly dramatic depiction of Korea's struggle to push back the Mongol Hordes in the 13th century. The plot focuses on a 20th century boy who ends up back in time. However, this science fiction conceit retreats to the background of this thrilling adventure in war-torn ancient Korea. Imagine a Korean general riding into battle with a battery of twelve men against two hundred Mongol warriors! Imagine back-stabbing politicians murdered in the clear of night. Imagine an entire village raped and slaughtered by Mongol hounds only to be avenged by a boy who just failed his high school science test.

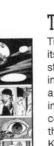

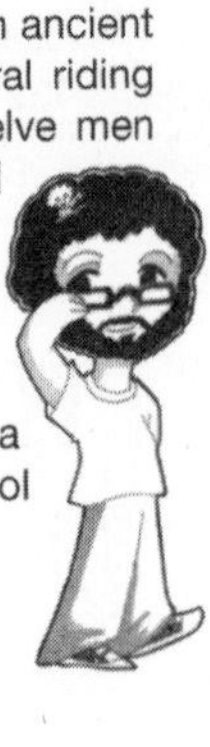

~Luis Reyes, Editor

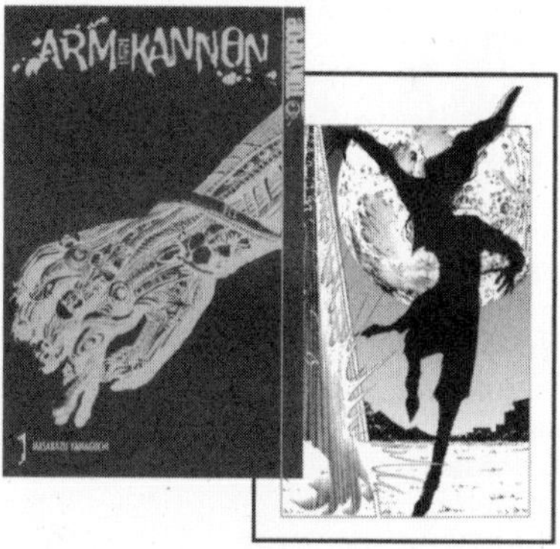
ARM KANNON

BY MASAKAZU YAMAGUCHI

ARM OF KANNON

Good and evil race to find the mysterious Arm of Kannon—an ancient Buddhist relic that has the power to bring about the end of humanity. The relic has been locked in a sacred temple for thousands of years. However, it is released and its demonic form soon takes over the will of a young boy, Mao, who must now flee from the evil forces that hunt the arm for control of its awesome power. This sexually charged action/horror story, traversing a vast landscape of demons, swordsmen, magicians, street gangs and government super-soldiers, will make the hairs on the back of your neck stand on edge.

~Rob Valois, Editor

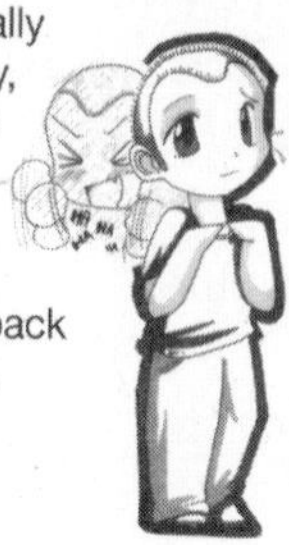

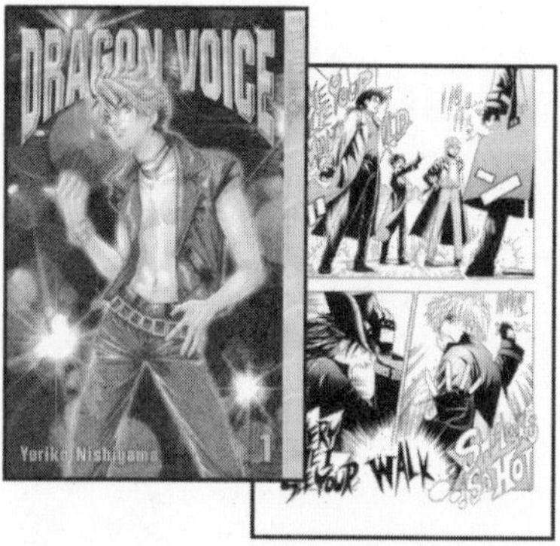
DRAGON VOICE
Yuriko Nishiyama
1
WALK

BY YURIKO NISHIYAMA

DRAGON VOICE

I have to admit that Yuriko Nishiyama's *Dragon Voice* was not at all what I was expecting. As more a fan of action/adventure stories like *Samurai Deeper Kyo*, the singing and dancing hijinks of a Japanese boy-band seemed hardly like my cup of tea. But upon proofreading Volume 3 for fellow editor Lillian Diaz-Przybyl, I found *Dragon Voice* to be one of my favorites! Rin and his fellow Beatmen dazzle their way past all obstacles—rival boy-band Privee, theme-park prima donnas, or TV production pitfalls—and do it with style! This book is one of the most fun reads I've had in a long time!

~Aaron Suhr, Sr. Editor

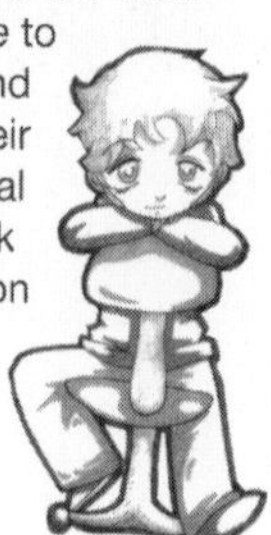

STOP!

This is the back of the book.
You wouldn't want to spoil a great ending!

This book is printed "manga-style," in the authentic Japanese right-to-left format. Since none of the artwork has been flipped or altered, readers get to experience the story just as the creator intended. You've been asking for it, so TOKYOPOP® delivered: authentic, hot-off-the-press, and far more fun!

DIRECTIONS

If this is your first time reading manga-style, here's a quick guide to help you understand how it works.

It's easy… just start in the top right panel and follow the numbers. Have fun, and look for more 100% authentic manga from TOKYOPOP®!